Stormy patriot

DATE DUE

NOV 14 '83			

Stormy Patriot

Stormy Patriot

THE LIFE OF
SAMUEL CHASE

James Haw
Francis F. Beirne
Rosamond R. Beirne
R. Samuel Jett

MARYLAND HISTORICAL SOCIETY

Baltimore

Library of Congress Catalog Card Number 80-83807
ISBN 0-938420-00-3

This book was set in Compugraphic Garamond text and display type by University Park Press. It was printed on 60-lb. offset, regular finish, and bound in Joanna Arrestox cloth by The John D. Lucas Printing Company. The editor was Ann Hofstra Grogg and the designer Susan Bishop.

Frontispiece: Samuel Chase, Engraved by J. B. Forrest from a drawing by J. B. Longacre after an original portrait by Jarvis.

Contents

Preface

WHILE WORKING with Paul Clarkson on a life of Luther Martin, I developed a keen interest in Samuel Chase. Martin was indebted to Chase for his appointment as attorney general of Maryland, and they were fast friends throughout their lives. Mr. Clarkson and I learned that Francis and Rosamond Randall Beirne were working on a life of Samuel Chase, and we exchanged ideas and information. Francis Beirne was the Baltimore *Sun*'s beloved Mr. Billopp, and both he and his wife had published many books and articles. Later we heard that the Beirnes had both died without publishing their life of Samuel Chase.

Through the kind efforts of Dr. Richard Randall of the Walters Art Gallery, the Beirnes' manuscript was lent to me. I later was given permission by the Beirnes' heirs, D. Randall Beirne and Mrs. Murray Dewart, to endeavor to have the manuscript published. I discussed publication with some publishers, but they felt that, due to the many studies of Chase's times that had appeared since the Beirnes had done their research, they could not take on the manuscript. After reviewing the matter with officials of the Maryland Historical Society, and particularly Dr. John Boles, I contacted James Haw. We concluded that additional research was necessary, and then a rewriting that would make as much use as possible of manuscript source material. By mutual agreement of all parties, the manuscript was placed in Dr. Haw's charge. It was understood that I would continue to contribute my research on Chase's life, with special emphasis on his judicial career, and act as critic for the revision.

Baltimore, Maryland   R. Samuel Jett

I WAS DELIGHTED to assume direction of the publication of a life of Samuel Chase. My earlier work on eighteenth-century Maryland had given me an interest in this fascinating and important figure, who had never before been the subject of a full-length biography. The Beirne manuscript furnished a solid starting point for the project. Mr. Jett and I have rechecked all of the Beirnes' sources and have added substantial additional primary and secondary source material. I have completely rewritten the manuscript, aided by Mr. Jett's helpful criticisms and advice, and have welded my own conclusions with the ideas of my joint authors to advance a reinterpretation of Samuel Chase. Credit for the merits of this book is shared by all the authors. Final responsibility for any errors of fact or interpretation is mine.

In undertaking this study, our primary aim has been neither to praise nor to criticize Samuel Chase but to explain him. Our effort to understand Chase has led us to try to see things through his eyes, remembering always that his perspective was not universally shared or necessarily accurate. We have tried to present Chase's point of view to the best of our ability and to explain the factors that determined his conduct.

Unfortunately, relatively few of Chase's personal papers have survived. One is forced at times to rely upon the public record, supplemented by the comments of Chase's contemporaries—often his political enemies. The problems posed by gaps in the sources make Chase especially subject to the differing interpretations that historians inevitably advance. While presenting the explanations that seem most tenable to us, we recognize that other interpretations can also be supported.

In a project with four authors, two working after the deaths of the others, it would be impossible to acknowledge by name all the persons and institutions to whom we are mutually indebted. The library staffs of the institutions at which our research was conducted deserve our thanks, with my special gratitude going to Ruth Harrod of the interlibrary loan department at Indiana-Purdue. The Maryland Historical Society and Dr. John Boles, now of Tulane University, encouraged the project and brought the authors together. Finally, part of my work on this project was supported by a grant from the Indiana University-Purdue University at Fort Wayne Research and Instructional Development Support Program.

Fort Wayne, Indiana   James Haw

Stormy Patriot

One

THE CHASE
HERITAGE

HE STORY of Samuel Chase is one of contrast and con-
tradiction, sorrow and celebration, admiration and
hatred, defeat and victory. He was an unabashed politician but a devout churchman, a relentless adversary
with a reputation for unrestrained invective but a loving, exemplary
family man. He inspired lifelong friendships, but made enemies
who persisted to his deathbed. He was chosen for enough offices of
distinction to fill more than one career, but was frustrated in some
of his deepest aspirations. His state and his country rewarded him
with gratitude and censure, praise and denunciation, resolutions of
thanks and resolutions of impeachment.

As a political leader, Samuel Chase upheld the leadership of an
elite, within the limits of responsibility, and championed the rights
of the common man, within the limits of an ordered society. A
staunch defender of republicanism as best suited to liberty, he denounced democracy as incompatible with liberty. No Marylander
did more than he to defend American rights against Britain in the
critical decade before 1776. When Maryland hesitated to accept independence, his untiring efforts led her to take that step. He
signed the Declaration of Independence on her behalf. A fiery
leader of crowds before independence, he helped write a conservative state constitution after independence—and insisted that it was

{ 1 }

not conservative enough. Soon, though, he was at odds with many of his conservative allies of 1776. In the late 1780s he seemed to attack the deferential political elitism he had helped establish. He opposed adoption of the United States Constitution, fearing that it would result in an aristocracy, but within a few years of its ratification he emerged as a violent Federalist thundering against the evils of rising democracy. Appointed to the United States Supreme Court by Washington, he suffered impeachment at the hands of Jefferson.

Because of the apparent contradictions in his career and character, Samuel Chase has been as much of a puzzle to historians as he was to many of his contemporaries. One of the latter, Alexander Contee Hanson, wrote of him:

> I am constrained by candour to declare, that vile as Chase has been held by most of the better kind of his fellow Citizens, he has been the mover of almost every thing, this State has to boast of. Strange inconsistent man! Without him, how very seldom would any thing good have passed the Legislature, and yet could he *always* have prevailed, how soon would he have defeated every thing good which has been done! . . . I have viewed him with admiration and with horror, with kindness and with detestation. In the main I always liked tho' never would I trust him for more than a single turn.[1]

AN ATTEMPT to understand this enigmatic man must begin with his origins and his family's place in the community. Samuel Chase's character was formed early in life. A strong-willed father left an indelible imprint upon the personality of his more famous son.

The Maryland Chases stemmed from the solid English middle class. Samuel Chase's grandfather, also named Samuel, of the parish of St. Giles in the Fields, was a prosperous bricklayer, a holder of houses and lands, and a freeman of London. Samuel Chase had five surviving children: Richard, Thomas, Samuel, Bridget, and Mary. The two eldest sons, Richard and Thomas, became clergymen of the Church of England, and the younger daughter, Mary, married a minister. All three ended up in Maryland.[2]

Thomas Chase, father of the future Maryland leader, was born in St. Giles in the Fields in 1703. He earned honors in Latin and Hebrew at Eton, then at eighteen matriculated to St. John's College, Cambridge. He soon transferred to Sidney College to study medicine, and graduated as a Bachelor of Physic. He taught Latin and Hebrew at Eton for a time, then in the late 1730s set sail for the island of St. Thomas in the West Indies to practice medicine. Chase remained there only briefly before returning to England to change callings once again. He was ordained a priest of the Church of England in February 1739 and immediately left for Maryland to become rector of Somerset Parish, Somerset County. The influence of his brother Richard, already a Maryland minister and a friend of Lord Baltimore, seems evident in Thomas Chase's preferment.[3]

In Somerset, Thomas Chase found not only his lifework but also a wife. Matilda Walker came from a prominent old family of the county. Her grandfather, Captain Thomas Walker, was a wealthy merchant and planter, a frequent local officeholder, and a patron of the Church of England. Thomas Walker, Jr., Matilda's father, inherited considerable property from the captain, including his 240-acre home plantation on the Wicomico River at the mouth of Dashiell's Creek.

Thomas Chase and Matilda Walker were married in 1740. Probably the newlyweds moved in with the bride's father, who was very advanced in years and died in 1744. At any rate, it was in the Walker house that on April 17, 1741, the Reverend Chase lost his wife and gained a son. Matilda Chase died in childbirth, her husband's medical training being of no avail. She left a strong little boy, named Samuel, to fight his way through an uncompromising world.[4]

Matilda Chase's death left father and son on their own, entirely dependent on the parson's salary for support. Young Samuel was given a substantial bequest in his maternal grandfather's will, payable if he survived to age twenty-one or to marriage, but he did not receive the money until 1770. The Walker plantation went to one of Thomas Walker's other daughters and her husband.[5] Perhaps the infant Samuel was left with them when, soon after the child's birth, Thomas Chase was called upon to undertake a diplomatic mission for the provincial government.

The likelihood of another war with France, in which the attitude of the Indians would be crucial, made it important for Maryland to settle a dispute over land ownership with the powerful Indian confederacy of the Six Nations. Accordingly Governor Samuel Ogle asked Chase to accompany Conrad Weiser, Pennsylvania's provincial interpreter, to the major Indian village of Shamokin on the Susquehanna. The two were to invite the Six Nations to come to Annapolis to negotiate a treaty. It is not clear why Chase was selected; perhaps he had gained experience in Indian relations by working among the Nanticoke tribe, who had a reservation in Somerset County. Chase's journey was the first in a series of contacts that finally produced a treaty three years later.[6]

The mission brought Chase to the attention of the provincial government and probably contributed to his further preferment. The death of the Reverend Benedict Bourdillon, rector of St. Paul's Parish, Baltimore County, created a vacancy that Governor Thomas Bladen offered to Chase. The offer came with one very large condition. Wishing to provide for Bourdillon's widow Jeanette, Bladen stipulated that Chase give bond to pay her twenty-six thousand pounds of tobacco within the next two years. Chase accepted, and in February 1744 he became rector of St. Paul's.[7]

The parish was a large one, measuring some twenty miles from east to west and twelve to eighteen miles north and south, and including the then tiny village of Baltimore Town. St. Paul's had about 860 taxable residents when Chase arrived, yielding an income of close to £100 sterling per annum. This sum was adequate for support but not for a gentleman's style of life. Baltimore Town's explosive growth beginning in the 1760s eventually made the parish a much more lucrative one. In the meantime, though, Thomas Chase was plagued with financial difficulties. There are indications that he regularly lived beyond his means in the 1740s and 1750s, a habit that his son Samuel inherited.[8]

Arriving in Baltimore, Chase and young Samuel at first took room and board with Mrs. Bourdillon. From her Thomas Chase also purchased her late husband's clerical garb and several books. When Chase did not pay for these items and also fell behind in his rent, the Widow Bourdillon was forced to bring suit to recover her debt. More serious was Chase's failure to meet the obligation of his bond. Jeanette Bourdillon sued him again, and Thomas Chase was clapped into jail under execution for debt. He spent a good part of late 1746 and early 1747 under lock and key.[9]

Baltimore County sheriff James Richards must have taken special satisfaction in carrying out the court's order to incarcerate Chase.

For some reason the two had become bitter enemies. On November 4, 1746, the very day Jeanette Bourdillon won judgment on Chase's bond, Thomas Chase wrote the governor complaining that Richards had "repeatedly cursed...the King for an Hanover Dog and a Turnep Man, and wished himself in the French or the Pretender's Army that he might drive that Hanover Dog home again." Chase demanded that Richards be removed as sheriff.

Investigation of Chase's charges led the governor and council to dismiss them as "groundless and malicious." Chase had gotten his information from one William Payne, who while roaring drunk had accused Richards of making the offending declarations. Later, when sober, he retracted his story but explained that Chase had violently insisted he swear to the original version. Payne and his wife added that Chase's colleague, Reverend Thomas Cradock, had also drunk the Pretender's health. When asked why he did not complain against Cradock as well, Chase replied, "Had It been that Rascall Richards I would have swore black enough against him, but you can't blame me to favour my poor Brother Cradock."[10] The incident illustrates the Reverend Thomas's pugnacity, which he passed on to his son, and also a streak of personal vindictiveness that was not in Samuel's character.

This incident was just the beginning. Richards, too, was capable of vituperation. In 1747 he published in the *Maryland Gazette* an article accusing Chase of plotting to destroy him. Chase responded by suing, unsuccessfully, printer Jonas Green for libel.[11] His imprisonment for debt by no means forgotten, Parson Chase in 1749 filed separate suits against both Richards and Mrs. Bourdillon for assault and battery and false imprisonment. Chase won both cases. He released the Widow Bourdillon from the nominal damages awarded against her but held Richards to a £25 sterling judgment. The sheriff appealed, and this tenacious feud dragged its way through the courts until 1753.[12]

By that time the contentious Parson Chase had found a new cause, the Catholic menace. In the eighteenth century, colonial Maryland's small Roman Catholic minority suffered under severe legal disabilities, though enforcement of the laws was often lax. A series of wars with Catholic France, together with the abortive attempt of the Stuart Pretender, "Bonnie Prince Charlie," to regain the throne of England in 1745–1746, kept alive ancient religious-political fears of Catholicism. Those fears were particularly strong in Maryland just before and during the French and Indian War. Thomas Chase, defender of his faith and sovereign, was a leader in fanning the flames.

Chase's name headed a petition to the Maryland assembly in 1753 warning of the alarming growth of "popery" in the province. Again in 1757 he complained to the legislature about illegal Catholic schools. Fearing that Maryland Catholics were just waiting for the right moment to rise in arms and aid the French, Reverend Chase "scrupled not to intimate from the Pulpit to his Congregation that the State or Situation of the Protestants in this Province was at that time very little different from that of the Protestants in Ireland at the Eve of the Irish Massacre." After a thorough investigation, however, Governor Horatio Sharpe could report to Lord Baltimore that Maryland's Catholics were if anything less of a problem for His Lordship's government than were her Protestants.[13]

Chase and his young son had enjoyed the presence in Baltimore of the parson's nephew Richard, an attorney and wealthy landowner. Richard Chase handled his uncle's legal affairs and apparently helped him financially as well. Richard died in 1757, leaving a large estate to his young son and daughter. As executors and guardians of the two orphan children he had designated Thomas Chase, the Reverend Hugh Dean, and Dr. John Stevenson. Chase and Dean either refused to serve as executors or failed legally to qualify, leaving the administration to Stevenson alone. But Thomas Chase did accept responsibility at least for his grandnephew, Jeremiah Townley Chase. Taking Jeremiah in his charge, Thomas impulsively moved into Richard Chase's home and took over much of the personal property of the estate without proper legal authority. The result was a complex dispute between Chase and Stevenson over Chase's alleged misappropriation of assets, his accounting for the estate property in his possession, and the means by which he was to be compensated for Jeremiah's living expenses and education. The legal wrangling briefly landed Thomas Chase in jail again in 1765, and the dispute was still in the courts a decade later.[14]

A happier result was that Samuel and Jeremiah developed a close relationship. Samuel assumed the role of Jeremiah's older brother. Thomas Chase gave both boys a proper gentleman's education in Latin and Greek, history and literature. He had retained an active interest in classical scholarship, demonstrated during the 1750s by his translation into English of the *Punicks* by Silius Italicus.[15] Though not college trained, the boys received a fair equivalent at home. Samuel and Jeremiah Townley Chase had parallel careers as attorneys, legislators, and judges; their success was testimony to Parson Chase's effectiveness as a teacher.

Of Thomas Chase's effectiveness as a minister little evidence survives. Methodist leader Francis Asbury, preaching in Baltimore in 1773, had a conversation with Chase and found him lamentably "ignorant of the deep things of God." Subsequently, however, Asbury commented favorably on one of Chase's sermons and noted that his preaching was well attended and much talked of in Baltimore, though he saw "but little fruit."[16] Whatever his impact on his parishioners, Reverend Chase instilled in his son a deep lifelong commitment to his church and to state support for religion.

Samuel Chase's only legacy from his father was his character. He inherited Thomas Chase's aggressiveness and impulsiveness, his tenacity in combat, his extravagance and carelessness in financial matters, and a strong loyalty to family. The parson's love of classical study and his religious commitment also became potent forces in his son's life. Perhaps, too, the absence of a mother in his years at home contributed to Samuel's roughhewn directness, his crude manners and lack of social polish.

More broadly, the Thomas Chase household's station in society shaped young Samuel in strong but subtle ways. If Samuel Chase's life revealed affinities for both small property holders and the gentry, it was in part because his origins gave him ties to both classes. As a clergyman's son of sound classical education, Samuel Chase was in a sense entitled to be considered a gentleman. Yet he lacked the wealth, especially in landed property, that was a prime requisite of a gentleman's social status in his day. Thomas Chase's quick descent upon his nephew Richard's estate indicated an aggressive pursuit of badly needed funds that his son even more conspicuously displayed. His own inferiority in property and status to the landed families of the Maryland gentry was long a major sore point for Samuel Chase. He longed to accumulate the landed wealth that would make him fully the equal of any gentleman in the province; and, failing to do so, he was quick to resent any slight from a gentleman that he could attribute to his lack of estate.[17] The sense of social inferiority thus generated heightened Chase's natural combativeness. His quest for the property that would bring status and remove that inner feeling of inferiority was a major theme of Samuel Chase's life at least until he reached late middle age. That quest began in 1759, when eighteen-year-old Samuel left home to study law in Annapolis.

Two

RISE OF AN

OUTSIDER

AMUEL CHASE's arrival in Annapolis brought him to the center of Maryland's political and social life. Beautifully situated on the Severn River, the bustling little capital of about one thousand residents was on the verge of its most prosperous era. Proprietary officers and wealthy planters built fine brick homes in the city during the decade before the Revolution. Meetings of the general assembly, court sessions, and horse races periodically brought in numerous visitors. Annapolis's economy boomed from 1763 to 1774, its expansion based to a striking degree on the luxury consumption of the wealthy families who frequented the city and furnished employment for a variety of tradesmen and artisans. These families also set the tone for a pleasure-loving society.[1] Here, too, was the center of a distinguished provincial bar. Annapolis was the right place for an ambitious law student who aspired to rise in society. Initially an outsider without connections, Chase over the next five years made his presence widely known if not universally welcomed.

The youth of eighteen who presented himself at the law offices of John Hammond and John Hall in 1759 was a strapping six-footer, large of frame, ruddy of complexion, and lean of purse. The cost of placing a student in an attorney's office at that time was generally $100 to $200 (£37 to £75 sterling),[2] and there would be personal living expenses as well. Chase must have had financial help from his father, but his funds were meager. He soon fell behind in paying his room and board to innkeeper Henry Gassaway, and he may have been forced to sell some of his personal property to meet expenses.[3] Necessity as well as ambition drove Samuel to hurry his studies while keeping a sharp eye out for opportunities for profit.

Chase's mentor in the law was John Hall. Hall's partner, John Hammond, was not practicing actively at the time. Hall was an able man, though less distinguished than such leaders of the Maryland bar as Daniel Dulany and Stephen Bordley. He was one of the busiest attorneys in the province, however, handling perhaps four hundred cases a year. Chase got along well with Hall and always retained a high regard for him despite their later political differences.

Chase's legal studies undoubtedly followed the usual pattern of the period. He spent long days poring over Hall's lawbooks and records of past cases, taking extensive notes for his own benefit. One of Chase's notebooks survives, a thick pad with notes on numerous points of law systematically arranged under alphabetical topic headings. Before long he was assisting his mentor by writing briefs, copying papers, and drawing up technical pleadings that had to follow precise forms in every detail. Attending court, he learned by watching the trials and rubbing elbows with the attorneys. By 1762 Chase was accompanying Hall on his rounds of the county courts, assisting his teacher and even accepting a few cases of his own that could be postponed until he was admitted to the bar.[4]

One very important feature of Chase's legal education was his involvement with the Mayor's Court of Annapolis, which enforced the city bylaws and heard small debt cases. It met four times a year, but normally proceeded to business only at the January session. Since cases before the Mayor's Court were few in number, minor in importance, and unremunerative, experienced lawyers avoided it. As of 1761 no attorneys were practicing before the court, and the office of prosecutor was vacant by the death of William Wilkins, an ordinary (tavern) keeper.

Chase and two other law students, John Brice, Jr. and William Paca, saw in the Mayor's Court an opportunity to gain some practical legal experience. On October 27, 1761, the three were admitted as attorneys of the court. The vacant prosecutor's office was offered first to Paca, then to Brice, and finally to Chase. The court's order of preference corresponded to the relative social standing of the three;

both Paca and Brice came from prominent families. After the first two declined the post, Chase accepted it. The prosecutorship paid very little; Chase received only about £40 in fees in five years. But he needed every penny, and he could still represent clients before the Mayor's Court in civil suits for debt.[5] Chase's appointment as prosecutor was more important than he probably realized at the time. The office gave him a familiarity with the workings of the city government that was instrumental in launching his political career.

Chase's legal studies did not prevent him from leading an active social life. Naturally gregarious, he enjoyed the company of other law students and young gentlemen of the town. William Paca, in particular, became a close friend. Scion of a wealthy Harford County family, graduate of the College of Philadelphia, and student of the renowned attorney Stephen Bordley, Paca possessed all the polish and social prestige that Chase lacked. The two nevertheless became intimate and remained so through life. Politically they were always of one mind. The talented Paca generally followed the lead of his more dynamic comrade.[6]

Undoubtedly it was Paca who introduced Chase to the Forensic Club, which Paca had helped to found in 1759. As a guest at one of the club's biweekly meetings in January 1760, Chase greatly enjoyed an evening of food and drink, mirthful good fellowship, and a debate on a topic of philosophical or political interest. He immediately asked to join but failed to get the required unanimous approval of the members. Perhaps humiliated by the rebuff but not daunted, Chase finally gained admission to the Forensic Club in 1761. He entered into its proceedings with gusto. Soon his fellow members found occasion to fine him sixpence "for impious language." Such fines were common in the club's meetings, levied in good humor, and not to be taken too seriously. But even at the none-too-decorous gatherings of the Forensic Club, Chase came to stand out for his coarse language and boisterous style of fun. In June 1762 he was expelled for "irregular and indecent" conduct and unkind comments about fellow members.[7] Chase continued to be attracted to clubs. When the Reverend Jonathan Boucher and others founded the prestigious Homony Club around 1771 for the sole purpose of promoting "innocent mirth and ingenious humor," Chase applied for membership but was refused. Instead he joined the similar but less prominent Independent Club.[8]

When not pursuing his studies or relaxing with his young comrades, Chase could be found courting a reputedly beautiful young girl who lived nearby. Ann (Nancy) Baldwin was about seventeen and Samuel had just turned twenty-one when the two were married by Reverend John Barclay of All Hallows Parish, Anne Arundel County, on May 2, 1762. The match was one of love, not convenience, for Samuel's bride enhanced neither his social standing nor his material prosperity. Nancy's father, Thomas Baldwin, an unsuccessful planter, had died the previous February in debtor's prison. His estate, consisting of only household furnishings plus one cow, was insolvent. Baldwin's widow Agnes had already opened an ordinary, or tavern, in Annapolis to support herself. Chase as prosecutor of the Mayor's Court was obliged to prosecute his mother-in-law for allegedly "Selling Rum to Servants" in 1765. Fortunately for the peace of the family, Agnes Baldwin was acquitted.

For several years the young couple experienced the joys and difficulties of married life on a shoestring. Their first child, Matilda, was born February 14, 1763. A son, Tommy, arrived in April 1764 but died the following year.[9] The growing family meant added responsibility for a young man just launching his career.

Thomas Chase undoubtedly continued to provide some financial assistance until his son's studies were completed, but once Samuel began to practice law he was on his own. Having satisfied his duty to his son, Reverend Chase felt free to pursue his own happiness. On July 19, 1763, Thomas Chase was married in Baltimore to Ann Birch, daughter of Thomas Birch, "Chirurgeon, and man midwife" of Warwick, England. The still vigorous sixty-year-old minister and his new bride produced three sons and two daughters in the next nine years before Ann Birch Chase died in 1772.[10] Samuel Chase thus acquired a new flock of half brothers and sisters whose ages corresponded to those of his own children.

While establishing his family, Samuel Chase was also launching his legal career. He was admitted to practice by the Frederick County Court in March 1763 and by other county courts later that year. At first he confined his practice to the lower courts while he gained experience; not until April 1765 did he take a case to the Provincial Court and gain admission to practice before it.

Maryland's county courts met quarterly—in March, June, August, and November. Different county courts held their sessions in different weeks of the month, so that an attorney could ride from one court to another, practicing in four counties each quarter. Chase's usual circuit included Baltimore County (or occasionally St. Mary's) for the first week of the month, Anne Arundel the second week, Frederick the third, and Prince George's the fourth. This was essentially the same circuit that John Hall traveled. Other frequent legal competitors and companions in Chase's early years included Edmund Key, Thomas Johnson, and Thomas Jenings.[11] The steady, deliberate Johnson became a close friend and political associate.

Lacking connections among the gentry, Chase received little of their business to help him get started. He handled only one large case in his first two years, a £130 suit for debt in which he represented the plaintiff, Benjamin Tasker. Such important cases continued to be rare for some time thereafter. Still the outsider seeking to break in, Chase was forced to scramble for business and make his own opportunities.

The avenue Chase found to increase his practice was unusual for his time and place. Necessarily relying on volume to make up for his lack of lucrative cases, Chase based his practice to a unique degree on the defense of debtors. Since quite a few debtors at that time did not bother to hire attorneys, Chase probably had to convince many of his prospective clients that they needed his services. True, Chase won few of his debt defense cases. But he could often secure postponements of the trial and stays of execution of the judgment, giving his client more time to pay and perhaps to avoid damages. Chase's clients discovered that he shared their tastes and manners. Perhaps, too, they sensed in him a genuine sympathy for the problems of the ordinary farmer or craftsman. While reaching out for personal advancement, this complex young attorney was also making contact with his natural political constituency.

With defenses of debtors most frequent among a variety of cases, Chase's practice expanded rapidly. He brought perhaps 170 cases to trial in the county courts in 1764, and at least 266 in the first three quarters of 1765. In the latter year his income for the first time exceeded the £150 sterling that might be considered minimal for a gentleman.[12]

Rising income did not mean an end to financial problems for Chase, though. Already he was heavily involved in land speculation, a common interest of those Marylanders who could afford to indulge in it. Chase could not yet afford to, but he was by nature a plunger. Impatient to accumulate landed wealth, he could not wait until he had surplus income to invest. Characteristically, he trusted to the future to provide the means of payment for his acquisitions. Chase's optimistic tendency to spend tomorrow's anticipated income today was a major reason for his inability to realize his dream of landed gentility. Ultimately it brought him to bankruptcy.

Chase began buying land early in 1762, a full year before his admission to the bar. Since he could not afford to pay cash, most of his early purchases were made through proclamation warrants, which gave the "first discoverer" the right to claim lands taken up by a previous claimant but not patented and paid for within the two-year legal time limit for completing the acquisition of wild lands from the Lord Proprietor. The holder of a proclamation warrant did not have to pay for his land until the tract was resurveyed and patented. In this way Chase could build his holdings while delaying payment until his income rose.

During the years 1762–1764 Chase acquired 2,036 acres of land, plus a half interest in an additional 5,446 acres bought in partnership with Thomas Johnson. His holdings, though undeveloped, already rivaled in size those of all but a few of the most prominent families, but the total cost considerably exceeded his income for the period. Chase was compelled to slow his pace somewhat in 1765, when he picked up nearly 1,200 acres more at a cost of just over £60 plus fees, while his income for the year reached £224 sterling.[13] Here, if all went well, was the foundation for Chase's establishment as a landed gentleman.

If Chase's ambitions were socially conservative, his temperament and his tactics often were not. The discrepancy was first demonstrated in 1764 when he turned to politics and quickly became a controversial figure in Annapolis.

The city of Annapolis was chartered as a municipal corporation by Queen Anne in 1708. Its government consisted of a ten-man Common Council elected by the voters when vacancies occurred, six aldermen who filled vacancies in their own body from among the members of the Common Council, a mayor chosen annually from the aldermen, and a recorder selected by the corporation. In the early 1760s the city government was solidly in the hands of Maryland's "court party," the political supporters of the proprietor. Proprietary officers and their connections also secured regular election to the capital's two seats in the lower house of the provincial legislature. Centered in Annapolis and exercising a strong influence over the city's tradesmen through their purchasing power, the proprietary officials were apparently secure in their domination of local politics.

For some years, however, there had been signs of discontent with the casually administered city government. Beginning in 1759, Annapolis grand juries adopted remonstrances complaining of such problems as inadequate maintenance of streets and harbor and the city administration's failure to publicize the bylaws. Even the town gatekeeper had trouble finding out what laws he was supposed to be enforcing.[14] The discontented needed only a leader to become politically potent.

Samuel Chase was very much aware of the complaints against the corporation. As prosecutor of the Mayor's Court, he knew from experience how hard it was to consult the city bylaws. Ever the activist, the energetic Chase could be expected to take direct steps to remedy the problem.

Tradition has it that a characteristically impulsive action touched off Chase's campaign against the court-dominated corporation. The story is that one day Chase and several companions were examining a portrait of Queen Anne in the State House. So exact was the picture that they were able to read the copy of the Annapolis charter she was holding. Concluding that the charter was not being observed, they "cleaned off the painting and buried a copy of the charter in a coffin at its foot. The word was passed, a crowd gathered, and amid much mirth, the supposedly lost charter rights were exhumed and rediscovered."[15]

An effective assault on the entrenched city fathers began in October 1764, when two vacancies on the Common Council were filled by election. Cordwainer Allen Quynn and ship's carpenter Samuel Middleton won without opposition.[16] Quynn soon began to display considerable political talent; he became an intimate friend and legislative ally of Samuel Chase. There is no direct evidence of Chase's part in this election, but subsequent events suggest that he was instrumental in mobilizing the shopkeepers and artisans of the city.

In November, Chase himself ran for one of Annapolis's seats in the lower house of the assembly. The other candidates were the two court party incumbents, Walter Dulany and George Steuart, both aldermen of Annapolis. Steuart was a judge of the provincial land office; Dulany's brother Daniel was deputy secretary of Maryland.

Chase, in addition to his popularity among the common people of Annapolis, had the support of Charles Carroll, Barrister, a wealthy leader of the country, or antiproprietary, party. Surprisingly, Chase was able also to make common cause with Walter Dulany. Perhaps Dulany sought to ensure his own reelection, or maybe he and Steuart had had some unrecorded private quarrel. At any rate, Chase and Dulany adopted the slogan "NO PLACE-MAN," signifying that Steuart as a proprietary officeholder should not sit in the assembly.

The election was unlike anything the city had ever experienced. Annapolis tradesman Charles Willson Peale recalled that "every engine was employed that each party could apply. The court dependents of office were threatened to be put out if they voted for Chase." Peale himself was sued by his court party creditors when he supported Chase. On the other side, "banners were displayed to designate the freedom of tradesmen, and parades of this nature were made through all the streets with friends of Chase at the head of them." Chase's remarkable ability to mobilize the "middling sort" for political action was first demonstrated in this election. When the polls closed, Dulany led with 132 votes; Chase was also elected with 88; and the defeated Steuart had only 59.[17] The court party's hold on Annapolis was slipping, and the assault of Chase and his friends had just begun.

By the end of 1764, Samuel Chase was a locally prominent figure in Annapolis. Popular with one faction and feared by the other, he could not be ignored by anyone. He was becoming an established lawyer, but his speculative plunges left his economic position uncertain. His land acquisitions revealed his determination to achieve wealth and status as quickly as possible; several social rebuffs showed that his full acceptance by the gentry would not be easily attained. The young Chase revealed a coarseness of manners and a headlong haste in pursuit of landed wealth that ill became a gentleman. His legal clientele and political constituency revealed that his natural affinities of personality lay more with the "middling sort" than the gentry. A complex, even contradictory man, this fledgling politician, but one to be reckoned with. Within a year he would be almost as well known throughout the province as he already was in the capital.

Three

"INCENDIARY" AND
ASSEMBLYMAN

AMUEL CHASE's entry into politics was well timed. Early in 1765 the British Parliament passed the Stamp Act, levying a tax on legal documents, newspapers, and a variety of other items in the colonies, which henceforth would have to be printed on stamped paper. In this law and the Sugar Act of 1764, Parliament sought for the first time to tax the colonies for revenue. Britain's legislation raised the issue of colonial rights and parliamentary authority in the British empire. Opposition to the Stamp Act was strong in the thirteen North American colonies. Chase achieved local prominence just in time to assume an important role in that opposition in Maryland, and he organized the tradesmen of Annapolis into a potent political force at just the right moment to make them an effective instrument in the contest.

In Maryland as elsewhere in America, there was great unity against the Stamp Act. Even some high proprietary officers condemned it. They were able to do so openly because Lord Baltimore saw the act as a violation of his charter rights. The 1632 charter promised the province immunity from taxation by England. The proprietor, ever jealous of his prerogatives, was therefore not likely to punish his officers for voicing opposition to the Stamp Act, though His Lordship's government was of course obliged to try to enforce the law.[1]

Marylanders did, however, disagree on the proper means of resistance to the Stamp Act. Some, like Daniel Dulany, wanted to stay within the law, supplementing petitions for repeal with only an economic boycott of British imports and a turn to home manufacturing. Others, including Samuel Chase, believed that the danger to colonial liberty also justified extralegal action to prevent the Stamp Act from being enforced. Massachusetts had set an example for the other colonies in that respect. Resisters in Boston knew that the new tax could not go into effect without stamped paper; without a stamp distributor to handle the paper, none would be available. In August 1765 a Boston mob forced their colony's stamp distributor to resign. So, when Annapolitans learned that Annapolis merchant Zachariah Hood had secured the distributorship for Maryland, they knew just what to do.

On August 26 a crowd assembled in Annapolis. Chase was probably a ringleader, since the mob was composed largely of the tradesmen who had gotten their training by parading for his election the previous November. The crowd fashioned an effigy of the stamp distributor, which they paraded through the town in a cart while a bell tolled mournfully. Hood's effigy was then flogged, placed in the pillory, hanged, and finally burned. Crowds elsewhere in the province soon staged similar proceedings.[2]

The Annapolis mob reassembled on September 2 and tore down a building Hood was repairing as a store or warehouse; undoubtedly the crowd assumed it would also be the stamp distributor's office. There is no evidence concerning Chase's part in this second venture at intimidation of the hapless Hood. The distributor, thoroughly frightened, fled to New York, where the local Sons of Liberty secured his resignation. With the stamp distributor gone, Governor Horatio Sharpe prudently arranged to have Maryland's supply of stamped paper kept on board a British warship to prevent its destruction. Chase and his friends had seen to it that the Stamp Act would not be enforced in Maryland.

Meanwhile, a general congress of the colonies had been called for New York in October to register a united protest against parliamentary taxation. Patriots like Chase knew that Maryland must be represented, but the provincial assembly was not scheduled to meet in time to select delegates. That problem was a leading topic of conversation among the lawyers who attended the September term of the

Provincial Court. Chase must have been among the attorneys who circulated a petition in Annapolis urging Governor Sharpe to convene the assembly quickly. Bowing to the united desire of the province and hoping to avoid further disorders, Sharpe agreed. The assembly met on September 23.[3]

Samuel Chase took his seat in the lower house for the first time at this extraordinary session. September was not a convenient time for the legislators to be away from their plantations and businesses; only the crisis could have brought them to Annapolis. Chase voted with the majority to take up no business other than the Stamp Act at this session. The assembly appointed three of its established leaders—Edward Tilghman, William Murdock, and Thomas Ringgold—to attend the Stamp Act Congress, and the governor's appointed councillors, who also constituted the upper house of the legislature, readily agreed. Chase as a freshman legislator could not have hoped to be chosen for this important mission, but he was appointed to a committee to draft resolutions stating "the Constitutional Rights and Privileges of the Freemen of this Province."

The committee drew up a declaration of rights similar to those advanced by other colonial legislatures in 1765, and the house unanimously adopted it. Marylanders, it said, enjoyed all the rights of Englishmen and could not be taxed without their consent. That consent could be registered only through their representatives in the Maryland assembly; taxation by any other body was "Unconstitutional and a Direct Violation of the Rights of the Freemen of this Province." Having taken this stand, the assembly adjourned until November to await the results of the Stamp Act Congress.[4]

The Stamp Act went into effect on November 1. Lacking stamped paper for legal documents, courts in the colonies ceased to function. Ports closed for want of legal clearance papers for ships, and newspapers, including the *Maryland Gazette,* stopped publication. The suspension of so much business showed the effectiveness of colonial resistance, but did it not also imply a tacit acceptance of the Stamp Act's legitimacy? If that law was in fact invalid, should not Americans ignore it completely by proceeding with business as usual using unstamped paper? Samuel Chase thought so, and a great many of his fellow colonists did too.

The first agency in Maryland to resume business in defiance of the Stamp Act was the Frederick County Court. Chase was present when the court decided to reopen, and he may have influenced its decision. At any rate, he did not hesitate to resume his legal practice in Frederick without stamped paper.[5] From late November 1765 through January 1766 a few other public offices reopened for business, and the *Maryland Gazette* reappeared. But most ports and courts remained closed.

In other colonies groups calling themselves Sons of Liberty were applying pressure for nullification of the Stamp Act. The Sons in New York wrote Baltimore merchant William Lux in February urging that a similar organization be formed in Maryland. Lux responded vigorously. Soon the Sons of Liberty were being organized in the Baltimore and Annapolis areas and in at least a few other counties. The Reverend Thomas Chase was a member of the Sons' committee in Baltimore Town; in Annapolis the organizers were Samuel Chase and William Paca.[6]

The Baltimore Sons of Liberty took the initiative by calling for all of Maryland's Sons to meet at Annapolis on February 28 to secure the reopening of the offices of the provincial government. To build support for this program in Annapolis, Chase and Paca called a public meeting. The gathering was very well attended, but Chase and Paca ran into opposition from some of the capital's leading citizens, who urged restraint in view of reports from England that American grievances would soon be redressed. To Chase's disappointment, the meeting reached no decison.[7]

This setback exerted a moderating influence when the Sons of Liberty assembled in the capital. The Baltimore Sons "were for opening the offices immediately," but the townsmen of Annapolis held back. After some discussion, the Sons of Liberty decided to demand that the proprietary officials reopen their offices by the end of March. Chase and other leaders transmitted the demand to the officers of government and requested written replies. The responses they received were evasive, but the Sons of Liberty meekly adjourned until March 31. When they reassembled and found that nothing had been done during March, they pressed their demands more strongly and this time succeeded. There had been no violence, and the Sons of Liberty, their objective achieved, resolved that law and order must be upheld.[8] A few days later Maryland received with rejoicing the news that the Stamp Act had been repealed.

In the Stamp Act resistance Samuel Chase first became widely known outside Annapolis as a political leader. He extended his contacts with other present and future leaders of the province. And his activities in Annapolis helped to stimulate a new consciousness that ordinary men could and should play an active role in politics. Aroused by the Stamp Act crisis to a greater awareness of the rights of Englishmen and the necessity of defending them, Chase and his supporters were simultaneously driving home their campaign against court party domination of Annapolis.

In February 1765 two more tradesmen had been elected to the Annapolis Common Council. The most significant event of the year in local politics, though, was the breakdown of the marriage of convenience between Chase and Walter Dulany. That gentleman was appointed naval officer (proprietary customs collector) of Patuxent in June. A member of the lower house of assembly who accepted appointive proprietary office forfeited his seat but could stand for reelection if he wished; consequently, when the assembly met in September 1765, the delegates ordered a new election for Annapolis in October. In this contest John Hall opposed Walter Dulany. Chase, consistent with the "NO PLACEMAN" slogan of 1764, abandoned Dulany and supported Hall. Dulany won, but some of Hall's supporters petitioned the lower house to void the election since Walter Dulany, now mayor of Annapolis, had sat as an election judge, and his brother Daniel, recorder of the city, had failed to certify the returns. (Daniel Dulany did not act because he believed it improper for him to officiate at his brother's election; the Dulanys, holding a plurality of offices, could be attacked either for acting or for failing to act at this election.) Chase voted with the majority of the assembly to void Walter Dulany's election. At that point Dulany gave up. John Hall was elected to the assembly without opposition in December. The country party now held both Annapolis seats, and Chase had incurred the lasting enmity of the powerful Dulany family.[9]

The climax came in March 1766, when the grand jury of the Mayor's Court asked Chase to draft another remonstrance against the administration of the city. Chase and his friends were exasperated when the court adjourned before the document could be presented. Interpreting the adjournment as a deliberate attempt to suppress criticism, Chase and the grand jurors published their remonstrance in the *Maryland Gazette,* thereby provoking a well-publicized showdown.

The remonstrance recited a variety of complaints: charter violations, overly severe and inadequately publicized bylaws, neglect of docks and streets, waste or misappropriation of funds, unnecessary delay in filling vacant offices, nonattendance of certain officials, and partiality in the administration of justice. The exchange that ensued leaves the impression that the city fathers had been casual, at times negligent, in their administration, but that some of the charges made in the remonstrance were exaggerated for political effect.

Mayor Walter Dulany and several aldermen answered the grand jury's charges in the next issue of the newspaper. Chase's name had not been affixed to the remonstrance, but the city fathers knew who to blame. With Chase continuing to write the grand jurors' side of the exchange, the newspaper argument became a personal altercation between the mayor and aldermen and Samuel Chase. Finally in the June 19 *Maryland Gazette* the mayor and aldermen threw off all restraint. They sarcastically referred to Chase's great *"public Merit"* and eminent social respectability. By indirection they labeled him *"a busy restless Incendiary—a Ringleader of Mobs—a foul-mouth'd and inflaming Son of Discord and Faction—a common Disturber of the public Tranquillity."* Chase, they added, was a "Demagogue, who seeks to render himself Important in the Eyes of his weak deluded votaries," who was willing "to sacrifice all Order and Authority to his factious Views and ambitious Schemes of Power."[10]

The most patient and peace-loving man might justifiably have been stirred to action by these studied insults, and Chase was neither. The aspersions cast upon his social respectability hit his psychologically most vulnerable spot. Chase's reply is the earliest and strongest extant sample of his talent for personal invective. It was such a violent assault on so many important gentlemen that printer Jonas Green refused to antagonize them and risk a libel suit by putting it in his paper. Chase was compelled to publish it in broadside form, apparently using a press outside the province.

Chase's reply clearly illustrated his defensive sense of social inferiority. The main theme of his broadside was the lack of merit and, in several cases, of social respectability, of his adversaries, and his consequent superiority to them. Denouncing the "Pride and Arrogance...natural to despicable Pimps, and Tools of Power emerged from Obscurity and basking in proprietary Sun shine," Chase told his opponents that they "must confess *them* to be your SUPERIORS, Men of Reputation and Merit, who are mentioned with Respect, while you are scorned with Contempt, pointed and hissed as Wretches." Chase's leadership against the Stamp Act proved his public merit, while the mayor and aldermen had supported it or remained silent.

Getting personal, Chase reminded the public that Mayor Walter Dulany had had a different opinion of his respectability when they allied for the 1764 election. The mayor's enmity, he charged, sprang from Chase's opposition to Dulany's reelection to the assembly in 1765. Chase claimed that alderman John Brice, chief judge of the Provincial Court, opposed him because Chase had alertly snapped up a tract of land that Brice had his greedy eye on.

Three other aldermen were of modest origins, like Chase, but they had risen to prominence through proprietary patronage. Chase reserved his choicest epithets for them. Land office judge George Steuart was labeled "a Man without *Merit, Integrity,* or *Abilities,*" with nothing to recommend him "but proprietary Influence, Court Favour and the Wealth and Interest of the Tools and Sycophants, who Infest this City.... *a Man in Universal Odium—crept into the Province from a Foreign Dunghill—raised by the Hand of Charity—* and by *Cringing,* and *Fawning,* and *Pimping,* and *Lying,* sneak'd into Proprietary Notice." Dr. Upton Scott, customs officer, examiner general, and clerk of the council, was assailed in similar terms. Did not Scott as a proprietary servant "feel a poignant Compunction for the Prostitution of your Freedom for dirty Gold?...Sir, with all your Wealth, you are a wretched *Dependant.*"

Chase's cruelest blow fell upon lower house clerk Michael Macnemara. Everyone in Annapolis knew that drink had ruined Macnemara, but Chase did not scruple to publicize in print "the unhappy Circumstances of your Children, reduced to Beggary, by your continued Round of *Vice, and Folly, Drunkenness, and Debauchery.* ...What pleasures, can *You* find in the Harlots Embraces, to induce you to fling from your Arms, your Infants in Distress, and weeping at the Feet of Charity?"

{ 23 }

Who really possessed greater respectability and merit, Chase asked: an independent lawyer acclaimed by the people for his public services, or unpopular creatures of the proprietor, however wealthy they might be? "My Purse is very small," he concluded, but "my Practice in the Courts...furnishes Me with such a genteel and independent Living, that...I can treat with Contempt the FAT PIMP, and give him sneer for sneer."[11] Despite his disparagement of the proprietary officers as dependents, there was a suggestion of envy in Chase's assault on them. He resented the fact that men of humble origins and (as he saw it) modest talents had achieved wealth and prominence through favor, while he struggled to make his own way. Chase was not attacking the existence of a social elite. But he believed that such an elite should be responsible to the people in politics and that admission to its ranks should depend on merit rather that patronage.

Samuel Chase indeed had a gift for invective, but it was directed only against political enemies. He claimed to have no personal ones.[12] He did not harbor enduring personal grudges; after a political battle was over, all was forgotten. Yesterday's bitterly denounced adversary might be befriended by Chase tomorrow.

Chase's broadside ended the newspaper battle of 1766. Having experienced his unrestrained assaults, his opponents did not care to renew the contest. But the struggle for control of the city government went on. Chase and Paca both won election to the Common Council during 1766. By October, Chase's party had a majority on the council, and John Hall was city recorder. The court party continued to hold the mayoralty and the aldermen. Chase and his allies were able to achieve some modest reforms and apparently were satisfied with that. After 1766 peace returned to local politics in the capital. Chase remained active in city politics and was chosen an alderman in 1773.[13]

The years 1765–1766 had been busy ones for Chase. His political experience and reputation had grown through his leadership in the streets against the Stamp Act, in the papers and at the polls against the Annapolis city government, and in the general assembly. The next five years were quieter. Chase continued to represent Annapolis (or after 1767 Anne Arundel County) in the assembly, but otherwise he was relatively inconspicuous in politics.

In the assembly, Chase's rise was rapid. The brief Stamp Act session of September 1765, Chase's first, had allowed the house leadership to test his ability to contribute to the work of an important committee. His performance must have been most satisfactory, for in the full session of November 1765 Chase served on twenty-one committees, including more than a third of the really important ones. His service was somewhat less heavy in the two 1766 sessions, but thereafter his rise was steady. In 1768 he chaired his first major committee, one dealing with the means of paying provincial judges' salaries. By 1770 he was a legislative workhorse and a first-line leader of the country party.[14]

Chase's heavy committee service was one reason for the extraordinary influence he came to wield in the lower house during the 1770s and 1780s. He was a very effective committeeman and drafter of bills and messages. His fellow delegates soon learned that he was willing to work long and hard behind the scenes at dull but necessary tasks of legislative housekeeping. Chase's committee service, together with his county court practice, gave him an increasing familiarity with the condition and needs of the province. He began to develop the vision that made him not just a workhorse but an initiator of legislative programs.

Chase always paid especially close attention to the interests of his own constituency. Here was a second foundation of his influence. Years later one of his political opponents candidly wrote that "Mr. Chase (altho' not my friend) can render you more important service [as a representative] than any other man you can find, amongst all the crimes he has been charged with, that of being unfaithfull to those who confided in him, cannot be alledged."[15]

Finally, Chase's power in the legislature rested on his talents as an orator, a publicist, and a mobilizer of the "middling sort." His eloquence could sway a large legislative body as well as a crowd in the street. Political opponents had to reckon with Chase's ability to bring his supporters among the public actively to his aid. It was a rare combination—fiery oratory, the talents of the mass agitator, and solid, diligent attention to the details of legislation—and it eventually brought Chase great power in Maryland.

As noted, Chase generally stood with the country party in the assembly. Several times he served on committees investigating the proprietor's right to the revenue from fines and forfeitures and from a port duty on tobacco. Country delegates wanted these funds applied to public purposes, not to Baltimore's own enrichment or the support of his officers. Little came of these efforts, but Chase was involved in the settlement of a decade-long dispute over the journal of accounts, the vehicle for paying the ordinary expenses of government, which had failed to pass because of a disagreement over payment of the clerk of the council. The court party contended that the clerk should continue to be paid in the journal from general revenues. The country majority in the lower house insisted that his salary should come from Lord Baltimore's ample personal income from the province. As the government's bills went unpaid year after year, the public creditors became angry. A group of them marched on Annapolis in December 1765 to demand action from the legislature. In 1766 agreement was reached on a compromise. The public creditors were paid, and the dispute over the clerk's salary was appealed to the king in council. Chase helped determine the lower house's stand on this issue in the 1765–1766 sessions, and he was appointed one of the twelve managers of the "Maryland Liberty Lottery" the delegates authorized to finance their side of the appeal.[16]

In one respect, though, Chase was out of step with the country party. There long had been discontent with the lack of church discipline in Maryland's established church, which made it impossible to remove or correct unfit ministers. In 1767–1768 several problems produced a strong demand for church reform. The most important centered around the Reverend Bennet Allen, an ambitious and unscrupulous proprietary favorite whose disregard for provincial law and the feelings of the people in pushing his insatiable claims for preferment aroused the province. The 1768 assembly passed a bill establishing a board headed by the governor to exercise effective disciplinary powers over the established clergy, but Governor Sharpe refused to sign it pending instructions from Lord Baltimore.[17] Chase was one of only two delegates to vote against this bill in the lower house. A constant friend of the established church, the clergyman's son may have considered the bill an undesirable means to a necessary end.

It is conceivable, too, that Chase opposed the board because of his friendship for Bennet Allen, a likely disciplinary target should it be established. Samuel Chase may have found something of a kindred spirit in the rollicking, irreverent, ambitious minister. In 1768 Allen ordered a gift for Chase, a sofa from England. Did the present indicate personal friendship only, or was Chase quietly supporting

Allen in the assembly? Chase did perform one service for Allen, introducing a petition for him in 1770.[18]

It is at least conceivable, too, that Chase hoped to win proprietary favor through Allen and later through Sharpe's successor as governor, Robert Eden. Some contemporaries believed that Chase aspired to proprietary office around 1770,[19] and it would not have been unusual for a country party leader to maneuver for preferment. But the evidence is simply too fragmentary to support any conclusion in Chase's case. His association with Eden and Allen may well have been purely social.

Whether he was a consistent antiproprietary leader or playing a more complex game, Chase confined his political activities largely to the provincial scene in the late sixties and early seventies. He did not play a prominent role in the opposition to the Townshend Acts. But then most Marylanders were slow to respond to this second major attempt at parliamentary taxation of the colonies in 1767. The Massachusetts Circular Letter, stating American rights and calling for united resistance, provoked no response in Maryland beyond a restatement of colonial rights by the lower house in 1768. This was so even though Britain had made an issue of the "seditious" Circular Letter, ordering all colonial legislatures to ignore it on pain of dissolution. When Governor Sharpe informed the assembly of these orders, Chase served on a committee that framed a spirited reply supporting the Circular Letter.[20] But the controversy led to no action outside the assembly.

Not until 1769 did Maryland follow other colonies in adopting an agreement for a partial nonimportation of British goods until the Townshend Acts were repealed. Chase played no recorded role in Maryland's adoption of nonimportation, which this time had so many loopholes that it proved ineffective. In one respect, though, the 1769 agreement went beyond the boycott of 1765. Local committees were established to enforce nonimportation upon the province's often reluctant merchants. Though Chase was not at first involved, he became a member of the Annapolis committee by 1770, the year of the Townshend Acts' partial repeal.

That same summer Chase was charged with violating the nonimportation agreement himself. Merchant Thomas Williams of Annapolis, whose firm had clashed with the local committee over its own violations, tried to discredit the committee by charging it with partiality in enforcing the boycott. Specifically, Chase was said to have landed in great secrecy two large packages of imported goods. The import, it developed, was actually Bennet Allen's gift sofa. Having been ordered in 1768, before nonimportation took effect, it was not a violation of the agreement.[21]

Chase's relative inactivity in politics outside the legislature from 1767 to 1772 can be attributed in part to the growing demands of his private affairs. His law practice continued to expand, requiring a large share of his time. In Anne Arundel County Court, for example, the number of cases he handled rose from 89 a year to 152 between 1764 and 1770. Even his legislative attendance became irregular when the county courts were in session. He also continued his land acquisitions, buying 1,446 acres in his own name and 2,037 acres in partnership with William Paca between 1766 and 1769. Several other tracts he sold at a nice profit. More important, Chase now began to develop some of his holdings, using the labor of indentured servants.[22] Here was another step in his projected rise to the status of landed gentleman.

Chase began also to widen the scope of his business activities. In 1766 he became involved in an unsuccessful tobacco trading venture with William Lux, his associate in the Sons of Liberty.[23] The project foreshadowed both Chase's strong interest in trading and his usual lack of success in that area.

Any added income would have been welcome, for the Chase household continued to grow. Sometime in the mid or late 1760s Chase's mother-in-law, Agnes Baldwin, and her two other daughters, Hester and Rebecca, moved in with Samuel and Ann. And the Chases continued to produce children regularly. Nancy and Fanny, born in 1768 and 1770, died in 1770 and 1771. At that point the Chases had lost their last three offspring in infancy; only the first child, Matilda, survived. Then their fortunes improved; Ann (Nancy), born in 1771, Sammy in 1773, and Tommy in 1774 all lived to fill the home with the sound of children.[24]

Except for the grief of three children's early death, the home was a happy one. Samuel Chase was the most devoted of fathers, while Ann Baldwin Chase's gentle serenity provided a steadying influence in the household. Many years later one of the Chase children recalled his mother's "mild virtue, her sweet disposition, and engaging manners to all," which had contributed so much to make the family "the most loving and happy on the face of the Earth."[25] In the home at least, Chase found during these years the peace and contentment so frequently denied him in his public career.

The growing household made larger quarters necessary. Searching for a suitable house, Chase learned in 1769 that a dwelling on the glebe land of St. Anne's Church, Annapolis, was available. The vestry of St. Anne's had given hatter William Reynolds a long-term lease on the property, and Reynolds in effect sublet it to Chase for as long as his rights continued or were renewed. The property adjoined Cathedral and West streets, and made the Chases next-door neighbors of John Hall and silversmith William Faris. Unfortunately, the Chases had been there only a few months when their new home was burglarized.[26]

Despite assuming a lease of indefinite duration, Samuel Chase intended his stay in the glebe land house to be temporary. Gentlemen like William Paca and James Brice were building fine brick homes in Annapolis at this period. Chase's ambition and nagging sense of social inferiority required that he follow suit: he must have one of the grandest mansions in the city. For £100 sterling he purchased lot 107 on Northeast Street at the corner of King George Street in May 1769.[27] Here the dream home would be built.

Chase's ambitious plan envisioned a house of two and a half stories, perhaps with wings, designed by an English master builder. Construction soon began, and with it a great strain on Chase's finances. He sold to William Paca his half of their joint land holdings, disposed of another 1,040 acres to other buyers, and borrowed money. Still he continued to sink money in other projects. Late in 1770 he bought "an obvious estate across the Severn from Annapolis" for £600 current money. By the middle of 1771 construction costs on Chase's house were nearing £3,000 current money. The building was not near completion, and Chase had exhausted his resources.

Fortunately there was a way out. Young Edward Lloyd IV, a Talbot County planter of one of Maryland's wealthiest families, wanted a home in Annapolis worthy of his high social standing. In July 1771 he purchased the half-finished house for £504:8:2 sterling and £2,491:17:7 current money. Chase thus recovered his full costs plus £250 sterling. For once he had acted prudently in a financial matter. Charles Carroll of Carrollton estimated that it would cost

Lloyd another £6,000 to finish the house; Chase could not have hoped to raise such a sum. As Carroll commented, "He has got rid of an encumbrance which must have ruined him at the long run: the money received of Lloyd will extricate him from all difficulties, he is now independent, and may if he pleases continue and become more serviceable to the Public."[28]

There were other signs of Chase's increasingly affluent, even extravagant, style of life. One small indication was a payment to his neighbor William Faris for gilding the head of his cane. In the early 1770s Chase commissioned his old supporter Charles Willson Peale, now a rising artist, to paint the family portraits. In Peale's portrait Chase—a sheet of paper before him, quill pen in hand, and lawbooks in the background—looks the thoughtful advocate, the man of importance. His brown wig and bottle-green coat with brass buttons set off the roughly handsome, ruddy countenance that led people to call him "Old Bacon Face."[29]

Still, Chase's inability to complete his mansion must have rankled in him. The dream of a fine home did not die. In 1780, during the Revolution, he unsuccessfully offered £3,000 sterling for the mansion of the last colonial governor, Robert Eden. A two-story brick house with two wings situated on five or six acres of land, "it was the best House in Annapolis."[30] It was Chase's unhappy fate long to pursue trappings of gentility that in the end always managed to elude him.

At thirty, Samuel Chase was established as a lawyer and legislator. He had clearly risen in the world, but his ambitions remained unfulfilled. Having become a prominent figure through his abilities as a leader of the "middling sort" in 1764–1766, he did not continue his out-of-doors political activities in subsequent years, even during the Townshend Acts controversy. He was rising to a position of leadership of the country party in the assembly but may not yet have been fully committed to the antiproprietary cause. If there was in fact any ambivalence in his political stand, a controversy that began in 1770 soon removed any doubt about where he stood.

Four

OFFICERS' FEES AND CLERGY SALARIES

MARYLAND's tobacco inspection act expired in 1770. A complex piece of legislation, the act included a table of fees that provincial government officers could charge for their services. It also fixed the salaries of ministers of the established church. Considering both officers' fees and clergy salaries to be too high, Chase and his country party colleagues in 1770 framed a bill to reduce them. The upper house, which included the principal officers whose incomes were jeopardized, refused to bend enough to satisfy the delegates. The two houses deadlocked as the old act expired.[1] Thus began a dispute that had important consequences for Maryland and Samuel Chase.

The act's expiration posed several serious problems. The tobacco inspection system was needed to maintain the quality and hence the price of the province's major export, and inspection receipts circulated as a form of currency. There was no disagreement over this part of the act. Maryland planters and merchants quickly established their own local inspection systems to replace the legal machinery, and for the moment tobacco prices remained strong. Some private inspection stations refused to certify tobacco belonging to government officials or Anglican ministers, thus applying economic pressure on the officers and clergy to make concessions on their fees and salaries.[2]

Interim regulation of officers' fees proved a more difficult matter. Citing the need for some fixed standard, Governor Robert Eden in November 1770 issued a proclamation that in effect authorized government officers to continue collecting fees at the former legal rates until a new law was adopted. The proclamation outraged Chase and the country party. Charging that establishing officers' fees by proclamation was taxation without representation, the lower house denounced the governor's action as oppressive and unconstitutional. The upper house's defense of high fees, they added, reflected "those *Schemes of Wealth and Power* which it is much to be apprehended are formed by *some* of the *great Officers* of this Government." Chase, who served on all the lower house committees that dealt with the inspection act and related issues, had a hand in framing these accusations.[3] Probably directed at Daniel Dulany, the charge that Lord Baltimore's principal officers were attacking public liberty in pursuit of "schemes of wealth and power" applied to Maryland politics a view of the British ministry that was widely shared in the colonies by 1770.

While the legislators argued over officers' fees, the question of clergy salaries was hotly disputed outside the assembly. The clergy contended that the inspection act's expiration actually entitled them to more money than the thirty pounds of tobacco per poll (taxable resident of a parish) that the act had prescribed. The Anglican establishment act of 1702 had granted the clergy forty pounds of tobacco per poll. Surely, the ministers claimed, the expiration of the tobacco inspection act meant that this earlier provision was once more in effect.

The country party considered the clergy's claim to the "forty per poll" outrageous, but they had difficulty finding a satisfactory response to it. The only possible legal objection to the clergy's argument was a theory that the act of 1702, though accepted for nearly seventy years, was technically invalid. The 1702 assembly had been summoned in the name of King William III, who, unbeknownst to Americans, had died before the establishment act was passed. His death, one could argue, dissolved the assembly and invalidated all its acts until new writs were issued in the name of the new sovereign.

Some country party spokesmen embraced this theory as early as 1770, and it steadily gained popularity. In March 1771 some country party lawyers offered to defend free of charge anyone who refused payment to an officer or clergyman.[4]

During 1771 and 1772 no fixed rule on clergy salaries prevailed in practice. Sheriffs, ministers, or individual taxpayers took the initiative in different parts of the province to give the clergy the equivalent in currency of forty, thirty, or thirty-two pounds of tobacco per poll, the last being a compromise figure almost adopted by the assembly in 1770. And some people apparently paid nothing at all.[5]

For Samuel Chase the issue presented a real dilemma. His position as a country party leader seemed to require opposition to the clergy's claims, but his own father's income was at stake. Thomas Chase stoutly asserted that he was entitled to the forty per poll, though he directed the sheriff to settle for the lesser sum of four shillings, the amount he would have received under the proposed compromise of 1770.[6] Samuel Chase realized also that denying the validity of the act of 1702 would call into question the legality of Anglican establishment itself. A strong supporter of the church, he had no desire to do that.

Chase's first recorded stand on clergy salaries was a legal opinion prepared for Talbot County minister John Barclay in April 1772. Chase stated that Barclay was entitled to collect the forty per poll under the act of 1702. Soon, though, whether for legal or political reasons, Chase had second thoughts and began to equivocate. A second opinion for Barclay in late May held that the sheriff was bound to collect the forty per poll despite the county court's failure to assess it—but only if the act of 1702 was valid, on which point Chase explicitly declined to rule.[7] Neither opinion was public knowledge at the time.

The question of clergy salaries came to a head in July 1772. Attorney General Thomas Jenings, acting on a complaint from Reverend David Love, filed suit against Anne Arundel County sheriff John Clapham for failing to collect the forty per poll. Love's action forced the issue and led the country party to close ranks behind the technical invalidity of the act as a defense against his claim. Arguments on that point immediately began in the newspaper.[8]

For Chase the immediate result was public embarrassment. Reverend Barclay must have shared Chase's legal opinions with other clergymen, for on August 6 the second opinion was published in the *Maryland Gazette* to bolster Love's position. Anxious citizens called on Chase to explain himself. Reversing field completely, he satisfied the crowd by telling them "that his Opinion was given, on Supposition that the Law of 1702 was in Force; but inasmuch as he believed that Law was not in Force; he could not be justly charged with contributing to the Support of the Cause of the Clergy." Then Chase's opponents embarrassed him further by publishing his first opinion, stating flatly that Barclay was entitled to the forty per poll, under the caption "Mr. C—e against Mr. C—e."[9]

If Chase had needed any further inducement to join his country party colleagues against the clergy, the obvious attempt to discredit him by publishing his opinions in reverse order supplied it. His friends Thomas Johnson and William Paca were defending Sheriff Clapham in the suit instigated by Love. Chase now joined them as defense counsel in two similar suits tried at the September term of the Cecil County Court. It is not clear how these three suits turned out, but all the verdicts were appealed to the Provincial Court, which never ruled on any of them.[10]

Chase, Paca, and Johnson were counsel for the plaintiff in one other suit involving the forty per poll, the well-publicized case of *Harrison v. Lee.* Charles County sheriff Richard Lee had arrested Joseph Hanson Harrison, a wealthy planter and country party assemblyman, for failure to pay the forty per poll. Harrison paid the tax to avoid jail, but then sued the sheriff for assault and battery and false imprisonment. At the trial in Feburary 1773, Lee cited the act of 1702 to justify his arrest of Harrison, but the county court refused to rule on the act's validity. Chase and his colleagues won their case, Lee's counsel entered a demurrer, and both sides agreed that final disposition of the suit would depend on the Provincial Court's ruling on the act of 1702.[11]

Chase's involvement in these suits identified him completely with the country party. Gone at last was his reluctance to support country initiatives where the established church was concerned. His tardy alignment against the forty per poll was personally painful; Chase had a heated argument with his father over the issue.[12] But Chase's stand was now firm, and the Reverend Jonathan Boucher, rector of St. Anne's Parish, Annapolis, instigated a controversy that made it irrevocable. An able, active, and contentious champion of the established church, Boucher believed he had found an opening to strike a telling blow against Chase and Paca, the most conspicuous opponents of the forty per poll.

Chase and Paca were both members of the St. Anne's Parish vestry. In November 1772 they had concurred in the vestry's decision to ask the county court to levy a special assessment on the residents of the parish for repairs to the church. In a signed letter to Chase and Paca appearing in the *Maryland Gazette* on December 31, 1772, Boucher feigned astonishment at their conduct. "By what authority," he asked, "do you act as *vestrymen?*" Chase and Paca, he suggested, had rejected the only legal foundation for the vestry's existence by denying the validity of the establishment act of 1702. If they honestly believed that law to be void, they could claim no right to act as vestrymen, and their recent levy constituted taxation without representation, *"taxation without the least pretense of law."* Boucher added that he himself believed the act of 1702 valid and the vestry's assessment request proper; "but *your tax* on the people cannot be justified on that foundation; because you deny the existence of any such law. The publick voice arraigns you of duplicity, of acting in direct opposition to the principles you avow." Given such inconsistent conduct, Boucher suggested, only "artifice and insincerity" could explain Chase and Paca's stand against the forty per poll.

Such a potentially damaging thrust could not be ignored. Chase and Paca responded, and their exchange with Boucher enlivened the paper for the next four months. Chase collaborated with Paca in two major replies to Boucher, then dropped the argument and left Paca to carry on the quarrel alone.[13] Having published his best defense, Chase had no desire to prolong the dispute. He did not want the attack on the forty per poll to widen into a general assault on the established church. Paca had no such qualms; the stronger expressions of anticlericalism in the exchange seem to have been his work.

Chase and Paca's replies to Boucher demonstrated that the parson had chosen his point of attack well. The legal existence of vestries and their right to tax could not be defended on the basis of statute law without reference to the act of 1702. Chase and Paca realized that they could escape from the debater's trap that Boucher had set for them only by invoking general principles of customary right and English common law. This line of reasoning came naturally to them, for Marylanders had long relied on natural and common law to claim all the rights of Englishmen and to support the idea that the legislative powers of the colonial assembly rested on the people's inherent "natural right to make their own laws" through their representatives.[14] Chase's own political thought relied heavily on the common law, precedent, and English tradition, with natural rights philosophy playing a lesser role.

It was not necessary, Chase and Paca contended, to base the powers of vestries on an act of assembly. "When a parish is established, the parishioners, by *common law,* founded upon publick utility, become a *body politic....*By *particular custom...*this authority of the whole body of the parishioners may be delegated to a *select number,* who are distinguished by the appellation of VESTRYMEN." The vestry thus was by common law representative of the people, and natural law confirmed that fact. "If a man has an independent authority originating in himself he may delegate it to another. The principle of natural right equally holds with respect to a society; and therefore the powers, which every assemblage of people possess as common and natural rights, they may transfer into the hands of a select body of men." As representatives of the people, the vestrymen unquestionably possessed the right to tax.

Chase and Paca embellished their arguments with personal attacks on Boucher. They charged that his motive in initiating the controversy was simply "Revenge, for thwarting the pretensions of the Clergy to the forty per poll." The two lawyers acknowledged that they had advised people not to pay the forty per poll, "and if you call this *inflaming* the people, we have done it, and shall continue to do it."[15] They struck a telling blow by reminding their readers of Boucher's recent leadership in trying to secure a resident Anglican bishop for the colonies. Another response to the problem of church discipline, this scheme had long been in the air in England and America. The idea of an American bishop aroused great opposition among colonial churchmen and dissenters alike. Chase and Paca feared the plan as much as anyone. Their newspaper letters raised the prospect of heavy new church taxes and oppressive ecclesiastical courts should a colonial bishop be appointed, tainting Boucher in the eyes of their readers as a supporter of ecclesiastical tyranny. Chase's loyalty was to the established church as it then existed in Maryland, not to the full-blown English form of church espoused by Boucher.

The radical implications of Chase and Paca's appeal from statute law to first principles deeply disturbed Boucher, who responded with an able argument that Maryland vestries were based on statute law alone. Assisted by an unnamed prominent lawyer (probably Daniel Dulany, Boucher's political patron), Boucher pointed out a number of flaws in Chase and Paca's application of common-law principles to the case of the vestries. Not the least of these objections was that established parishes and vestries had not existed in Maryland before 1691. "Where the origin of a custom can be traced, it destroys it," making common or customary law inapplicable.[16]

A debate judge might well have given Boucher the better of the exchange, but the readers of the *Maryland Gazette* were unlikely to assess both sides of the case impartially. Chase and Paca were defending the popular position. Boucher attracted some support, but in the eyes of most Marylanders his major point was academic. The legal existence of vestries was not in serious dispute outside the newspaper. Chase and Paca's resolute stand against a resident bishop and the forty per poll gave them the popular victory, as Boucher himself recognized by writing that he "was generally allowed to have the better of the argument, but they carried their point."[17]

Chase and Paca's dispute with Boucher shared the spotlight with a simultaneous exchange over the issue of officers' fees. Daniel Dulany began that newspaper controversy on January 7, 1773, with a pseudonymous defense of Governor Eden's fee proclamation. As the apparent adviser of that unpopular measure, Dulany found his influence with the governor declining. A persuasive defense of the proclamation, designed to help court party candidates in the coming May assembly elections, would go far toward restoring his lost prestige.[18]

Dulany's adversary in the newspapers was Charles Carroll of Carrollton, a disfranchised Catholic who had hitherto taken no public part in any political disputes. In his letters Carroll analyzed the fee controversy, and the Maryland politics in general, in the light of English Commonwealth ideology. Just as many Americans perceived in Britain's colonial policies after 1763 a conspiracy against liberty centered in a British ministry that used patronage to corrupt and destroy representative government, so Carroll saw behind the fee proclamation a plot of Lord Baltimore's "ministers," led by Dulany, to use provincial patronage to destroy liberty in Maryland. Carroll's widely popular argument merged the internal and external grievances of Marylanders into a common pattern of corruption and tyranny, and by so doing carried the province a long step closer to revolution.[19]

Chase was in close contact with the Carroll family during the controversy. On several occasions Chase, Paca, and Thomas Johnson dined with Carroll of Carrollton's father, talking politics and warmly praising the younger Carroll's efforts.[20] Toward the end of the controversy Chase, Johnson, and Paca contributed their own newspaper article on the issue of officers' fees. Written in response to a defense of the fee proclamation by John Hammond, the trio's letter appeared in the *Maryland Gazette* on September 9. Their arguments, while not new, were very well stated, making the letter an excellent piece of partisan argument.

Chase and his collaborators argued that executive proclamations were legitimate only if based upon existing law. Proclamations could not establish new legal standards, as the fee proclamation had done. Nor was Eden's fee proclamation necessary to limit officers' fees and prevent extortion, as the governor maintained. For under common law the power to determine fees in case of dispute properly lay with a jury. Chase, Paca, and Johnson objected that Eden, instead of reinforcing the common-law right of juries to decide the issue, had violated the principles of common law by his action. Nor could Eden justly claim to have acted for the public good.

> You highly extol the *amiable* motive of the proclamation to prevent extortion in the exaction of fees beyond the old table set up and established by it. You seem to have forgot, that the complaints of the people are pointed at the table itself. . . . What do the officers contend for? The old table of fees. What do the people object to as oppressive and unjust? The old table of fees. . . . What is the regulation established by the proclamation? The old table of fees. And what is the practice under it? A continuance of the abuses. What, then, was the *real object* and *intention* of the proclamation? Was it, the *publick good* or the *emolument* of the officers?

Chase and his friends charged that the proclamation threatened to undermine political liberty in the province. The people's representatives had refused to continue the old fee rates, and the people had signified their approval by reelecting those representatives twice since 1770. "What weight, then, have the people in the constitution...if *that* shall be enacted by *prerogative,* on the foundation of *necessity,* in the enaction of *which* they deliberately refuse to concur?"[21] Here indeed was a threat to liberty!

The newspaper controversy was received with avid public interest. By May, when the assembly elections were held, emotions were running high. The two newspaper battles and the hot electioneering brought the mutual hostility between Chase and Daniel Dulany to a new peak of intensity. It appears that they almost fought a duel shortly before the election. Charles Carroll of Annapolis wrote to his son Carroll of Carrollton that either Chase or Dulany "must have made Concessions or their Peaceable Return from the field of Battle is unaccountable."[22]

With public feeling inflamed against the fee proclamation and the forty per poll, the assembly election could only produce a triumph for the country party. A country slate including Chase and Johnson was elected unopposed in Anne Arundel County. In Annapolis, William Paca and political neophyte Matthias Hammond defeated the court party candidate, merchant Anthony Stewart, by such a wide margin that Stewart withdrew before the polls closed. Chase, who managed that campaign as well as his own, had predicted the result. He remarked exuberantly that "he could carry a broomstick against a courtier."[23]

Chase's hand was also evident in victory celebrations in Annapolis and Anne Arundel and Frederick counties that featured solemn funerals for the fee proclamation. He successfully urged the newly elected delegates of those constituencies to issue well-publicized addresses of thanks to Carroll of Carrollton for his defense of liberty against the proclamation. That Chase was indeed the driving force behind the country party's campaign effort is indicated by a letter he wrote to Captain Charles Ridgely, a prosperous entrepreneur who was emerging as the dominant politician in Baltimore County. Informing Ridgely of the actions taken in Annapolis, Anne Arundel, and Frederick, Chase urged, "I could wish to see Baltimore County join in Sentiment with Us, and if You approve, I hope You will exert your Influence....I think it absolutely necessary to let the Government see the Opinion of the people....Unanimity will obtain Redress. I beg You to consult the principal Gentlemen of your County. do what is right. act like Men."[24]

Chase's letter to Ridgely was an attempt to broaden a powerful coalition of country party leaders that had emerged during 1773: Samuel Chase, Charles Carroll of Carrollton, William Paca, Thomas Johnson, Charles Carroll, Barrister, Matthew Tilghman, and Robert Goldsborough. The fight over officers' fees and clergy salaries had brought together the core of the leadership that carried Maryland into the Revolution.[25] And Chase was now moving in some of the most prestigious political and social circles in Maryland.

Chase's group of country managers met their first practical challenge in the 1773 assembly sessions. Under their direction, the delegates succeeded in separating tobacco inspection from the issues of officers' fees and clergy salaries, and a new inspection act was passed. Tobacco prices had fallen greatly in late 1772, and reestablishment of official inspection was viewed as necessary for the restoration of prosperity.

With the various subjects linked by the 1747 inspection act now separated, agreement could be reached on clergy salaries as well. A new law set the ministers' compensation at thirty pounds of tobacco or four shillings currency per poll, the compromise that had almost succeeded in 1770. The two houses explicitly provided that the new act should not affect one way or the other the Provincial Court's decision on the validity of the establishment act of 1702. In the end, the final holdouts against the compromise were not the proprietary appointees in the upper house but a small group of insurgents within the country party. John Hall, Matthias Hammond, and Baltimore County's Captain Charles Ridgely and Thomas Cockey Deye were the most prominent of the irreconcilables.[26]

The insurgents actually were mounting a challenge to the Chase group's leadership of the country party. In the April 1774 legislative session, they succeeded in outvoting Chase's allies on the most important issues. The insurgents got the overwhelming endorsement of the delegates for an officers' fee bill that had no chance of acceptance in the upper house. Even Chase believed the fees it contained were too low.[27] The officers' fee issue remained unresolved until the Revolution abolished the proprietary government.

Chase and his allies had been too successful in their job of arousing active popular hostility to the officers of government. Vigorous defenders of colonial rights, they were also moderate men who did not want to overthrow the established political and social order. Now, owing ironically to the excitement generated by their own efforts, things were getting out of hand. Attorney General Thomas Jenings wrote to former governor Sharpe, "There is a schism among the patriots. Hall and young Hammond are as violent in their opposition to Chase, Johnson, and Paca, as the latter ever were to the measures of government." It was rumored that the latter three were ready to resign their assembly seats in frustration. Wits remarked that Matthias Hammond, the "broomstick" Chase had gotten elected in 1773, "has put the broom to the stick and fairly swept them all out of the House."[28]

Chase did not resign, nor was his influence in lasting decline. In 1774 the smoldering conflict with Britain burst into flame again, and Chase threw himself into the struggle with his usual vigor. But his efforts, along with those of Carroll of Carrollton, Paca, Johnson, and others, had changed Maryland's internal situation greatly in 1772 and 1773. The public controversies of those years aroused the province more than anything since the Stamp Act. Carroll clearly defined the nature of the internal threat to liberty in his letters against the fee proclamation, while Chase and Paca's replies to Boucher revealed their readiness to resort to first principles in defense of liberty. Chase won acceptance as a key figure in a socially elite circle of political leaders who sought to direct the province's course. But public opinion by late 1773 was so thoroughly aroused that the new country leadership found itself in danger of being left behind. The radical insurgency that emerged in the assembly was in a position effectively to challenge the Chase group in the critical years ahead.

Five

CONGRESS AND
CONVENTION

ROM 1770 through 1773 Maryland concentrated on her own internal disputes. The province displayed little interest in larger issues, even when Britain's Tea Act met with heated resistance in some other colonies. The assembly did respond in October 1773 to requests from other colonial legislatures that it appoint a committee of correspondence to aid intercolonial communications on British actions,[1] but this committee never functioned.

Chase, as a country party leader, was elected to the committee of correspondence. After 1774, as America's quarrel with Britain reached a showdown, he devoted more and more of his time to public affairs. By 1776 he had become perhaps the most important politician in Maryland and a very useful member of Congress as well.

In May 1774 news of the Boston Port Act, the first of the Intolerable Acts, again aroused Maryland to active resistance against Britain. Parliament's response to the Boston Tea Party, this act closed the port of Boston until that city paid for the tea it had destroyed. Everywhere in America the act rallied public sentiment to the support of Boston, which was seen as suffering in the common cause of colonial freedom.

As soon as word of the Boston Port Act arrived, Chase and his collaborators set to work to combat it. A public meeting in Annapolis on May 25 called for an immediate stoppage throughout the colonies of "all importations from, and exportations to, Great-Britain, till the said act be repealed." Chase, Charles Carroll, Thomas Johnson, and William Paca, together with John Hall and Matthias Hammond of the rival country party faction, were appointed a committee of correspondence to unite the rest of the province behind the proposed economic boycott of England.[2]

Chase and his fellow committeemen met with a strong response throughout Maryland. Baltimore patriots called for a provincial convention and a general American congress. Other counties generally endorsed the program of the two urban centers, but some wanted to postpone or forget about nonexportation.[3]

So rapid was Maryland's response that on June 25, one month after news of the Port Act arrived, delegates from every county met in provincial convention. Samuel Chase sat in the convention as a delegate for Annapolis and Anne Arundel County. Resolving that the Intolerable Acts "will lay a foundation for the utter destruction of *British* America," the delegates endorsed nonimportation, nonexportation, and a continental congress.[4] Their stand put Maryland for the moment in the vanguard of American resistance. The call for a congress was general and spontaneous across the thirteen colonies, but few other colonies so forthrightly advocated a complete cessation of trade at that time.

The convention selected Chase to represent his province in the forthcoming congress, along with Paca, Johnson, Matthew Tilghman, and Robert Goldsborough. As he set out for the First Continental Congress in Philadelphia, Chase was probably making his first trip beyond the borders of Maryland. He must have looked forward eagerly to meeting leaders of other colonies whose names he had often heard, and he may have wondered how he would measure up in their company.

Arriving in Philadelphia on Saturday, September 3, two days before Congress met, Chase attended a banquet held that evening for the early delegates. It was the first of many fine dinners they enjoyed over the next two months. Wealthy Philadelphians were most hospitable to their distinguished guests while Congress sat. John Adams wrote to his wife, "We go to Congress at nine, and there we stay, most earnestly engaged in debates upon the most abstruse mysteries of state, until three in the afternoon; then we adjourn, and go to dine with some of the nobles of Pennsylvania at four o'clock, and feast upon ten thousand delicacies, and sit drinking Madeira, Claret, and Burgundy, till six or seven, and then go home fatigued to death with business, company, and care." Chase, whose ample girth testified to his prowess with knife and fork, was in his element. On several occasions he shared bounteous tables with Adams and other delegates at the homes of men like John Dickinson and Thomas McKean.[5] Chase and Adams agreed on many issues in Congress as well, and a long-lasting association developed between them.

Other delegates, too, made a strong impression on Chase, and none more than the Virginia orators, Patrick Henry and Richard Henry Lee. Many years later Thomas Jefferson recalled a story that, after their initial exposure to Lee's and Henry's eloquence, Chase and Paca commented to each other, "We shall not be wanted here; those gentlemen from Virginia will be able to do every thing without us." But, Jefferson added, they soon saw that the two Virginians were better at oratory than day-to-day business.[6]

As soon as Congress assembled it became apparent that the delegates were deeply divided in opinion though determined to present an appearance of unity to the world. The more radical faction, led by Virginia and Massachusetts, wanted a total denial of Parliament's power over the colonies and a severance of trade with Britain. Conservatives, also committed to colonial rights but equally desirous of a reconciliation with England, urged a much more conciliatory stance.

Generally the radicals prevailed. Congress committed itself to a strong program of resistance by endorsing the Suffolk Resolves. The delegates narrowly rejected Joseph Galloway's Plan of Union, a proposal to preserve both American rights and imperial unity by creating a general American legislature with a royal president that, along with Parliament, would have to approve general legislation for the colonies as a whole. They adopted an Association for nonimportation beginning December 1, 1774, and nonexportation commencing in September 1775 if American rights were not yet secured. In a compromise statement of those rights, Congress denied Parliament's right to tax the colonies or regulate their internal affairs but "consented" to allow it to regulate their trade. Having also petitioned the king to redress their grievances, Congress resolved to meet again in May 1775 and then adjourned.

Samuel Chase was satisfied with all of those decisions except the postponement of nonexportation. His major contribution to the work of Congress dealt with trade questions. He served on a committee to report on the laws affecting the trade and manufactures of the colonies.[7] No record remains of the committee's proceedings beyond the bare fact that it submitted a report. But, absolutely convinced that the trade boycott Maryland had endorsed was the best way of securing American rights, Chase spoke out strongly in the debates on that subject.

Assuming, as did his fellow delegates, that the use of force was "out of the Question," Chase argued strenuously for both a total nonimportation and a total nonexportation of goods to England. He considered the latter more important than the former, for nonexportation would strike at Britain's "Merchants as well as Manufacturers, the Trade as well as the Revenue." Marshaling an array of statistics, Chase argued that the colonies accounted for a very large proportion of Britain's foreign trade. A total cutoff of the colonial trade, depriving Englishmen of income and the government of tax revenue, "must produce a national Bankruptcy, in a very short Space of Time."[8] On this issue Chase's position was decidedly radical. He was disappointed at Congress's postponement of nonexportation for another year.

When it came to the definition of Parliament's power over the colonies, though, Chase found himself among the more conservative delegates. The point in dispute in Congress was whether or not Parliament had a right to regulate colonial trade. Chase contended that it did and that Parliament could legislate generally for the colonies "in all Cases where the good of the whole Empire requires it."[9] He did not, of course, recognize any parliamentary power to tax the colonies or interfere in their internal affairs.

Chase could not, however, agree with the conservative delegates who backed Galloway's Plan of Union. He explained later that Galloway's proposed American legislature could be useful only in dealing with a few matters of general concern to both England and America: regulating trade for the empire and raising troops and taxes in the colonies. The former power he believed could safely be lodged in Parliament, and the colonial assemblies could be trusted to contribute the latter when England requested them in time of need. Therefore the Galloway Plan was unnecessary.[10]

Though not a leading figure in the First Continental Congress, Chase made his presence felt and gained the respect of his fellow delegates. He did not align completely with either the radical or the conservative faction. Radical in advocating strong measures of resistance to force England to concede American rights, he nevertheless desired only a return to the pre-1763 status quo as he understood it. England should confine its authority over the colonies to general supervision of the empire, including the regulation of trade but not taxation; the colonies should contribute tax money to England when needed, reserving implicitly the right to judge the need for themselves. Like most Americans in 1774, Chase wanted nothing more than equal rights and equal justice in the British empire, according to his understanding of traditional English liberties. Only if convinced that Britain would not allow colonial equality would he consider independence.

The adjournment of Congress on October 26 did not end the delegates' labors. They still had to explain Congress's policies to their various colonies, build support for those policies, and help create the machinery to enforce the economic boycott prescribed by the Association. Returning home, Chase found that he and his associates faced a formidable struggle to preserve both liberty and order in Maryland. During Chase's absence the burning of the *Peggy Stewart* had unleashed forces that threatened to plunge the province into chaos.

The *Peggy Stewart* arrived in Annapolis on October 14 carrying among its cargo a quantity of dutied tea. The ship's owner paid the parliamentary tax on the tea, thereby arousing the populace against him. The Annapolis committee called a mass meeting to decide what to do. The Barrister Carroll and most of the other committeemen advocated burning the tea, and a majority of the meeting supported them. But a radical minority, led by the Hammonds and Ridgelys, insisted on burning the ship as well and carried their point by threats of violence.[11] The *Peggy Stewart*'s destruction revealed the fragility of all authority in Maryland. Under strong challenge from an active radical faction, Chase and his collaborators faced the difficult task of uniting the province against England while restoring internal order, of restraining not just Tories but overzealous patriots as well.

The situation called for another provincial convention, which met in December 1774 with Chase again representing his home county. Steps were taken to enforce the Association and to prepare for whatever action the defense of liberty required. Resolving that Maryland would support any colony against which Britain might use force to impose its tyrannical measures, the delegates called for all able-bodied men to form militia companies and prepare for action if needed. Funds were to be raised by subscription to equip the militia. To promote internal unity, the convention urged that all political, religious, and personal quarrels be "forever buried in oblivion." Addressing themselves directly to the danger of disorder posed by the *Peggy Stewart* affair, the delegates resolved that the decisions of the county committees should be obeyed without interference from the public at large.[12]

Many counties had formed committees to enforce the Association even before the convention met. Thus the political machinery to raise and supply the militia already was in existence. Samuel Chase was a member of Anne Arundel and Annapolis's large committee of observation and the smaller committee of correspondence as well. Setting to work with his usual vigor, Chase became the most conspicuous member of the committee and the leading target of its Tory and "moderate" critics.

The Anne Arundel–Annapolis committee met on December 23 to make plans for the public subscription to arm the militia. The committee decided "that a memorandum be taken of the names of those (if any such) who are requested, and refuse to contribute." Their purpose became clear in January 1775 when a public meeting called by the committee resolved that noncontributors' names should be published in the *Maryland Gazette* as enemies to the American cause.[13] Publication would put social pressure upon nonsubscribers and quite possibly expose them to mob violence as well. Therefore the plan evoked howls of protest from the self-styled "moderates" against whom it was aimed.

"Moderates" held Chase responsible for the controversial resolution, and it would have been consistent with his single-minded advocacy of vigorous and united resistance. Proprietary official William Fitzhugh wrote an English friend that "Charles Carroll of

Carrollton (a Papist) and Samuel Chace a Factious and Desperate Lower [house member], are the Ringleaders of Mischief in this Province." Referring to the publication of nonsubscribers, Fitzhugh claimed that "Some talk of the *Moderate* Punishment of Tarring and feathering, but those two Mild—*Patriots*, *Humanely*, Prescribe, Jibbeting House-burning etc."[14]

Chase and Carroll did not actually advocate such extremes of violence; in fact, Chase had exhorted the public "to REFRAIN FROM PERSONAL OUTRAGE." But Annapolis Tories were not reassured. After the *Peggy Stewart* incident anything seemed possible, and Fitzhugh's extravagant charges reflected real fears. Complaining that it was inconsistent with true freedom to invite violence against honest political dissenters by naming them as enemies, Tory writers mounted a vigorous campaign against the committee's action. Their arguments were laced with attacks on an unnamed figure who was obviously Samuel Chase. This "turbulent man, of no consideration, unless with the needy and desperate like himself," this "son of distraction...whose very existence depends on public convulsion," was charged with the intention "of glutting private revenge with the sacrifice of a few individuals," presumably Chase's adversaries the Dulanys, who were among the nonsubscribers. In the face of spirited opposition Chase and the committee backed off. The plan to publish nonsubscribers was dropped.[15]

Chase also passed up an opportunity to strike at Jonathan Boucher about this time. Boucher had become "a marked man" by refusing repeatedly and publicly to support colonial resistance. He found himself hauled by a body of militia before the local committee, which that day included Chase and Paca. Boucher refused to admit the committee's authority but ventured an explanation of his conduct that those present accepted as satisfactory. Though he had already been prevented from preaching or writing in the newspapers for some time, he was released and incurred no further penalty.[16] Annapolis Tories found their situation uncomfortable, but they were in no immediate danger from Chase and his patriot colleagues.

Though they exaggerated his radicalism, "moderates" correctly perceived that Chase's ardent temperament would tolerate little opposition to the American cause. His attitude toward Tories became harsher as the battle lines became more clearly drawn. Already he could be stern in enforcing the resolves of Congress. Benjamin Galloway, a young Marylander of a wealthy and conservative family who had been studying law in London, found his return to Maryland delayed when Chase ruled that he could not bring his lawbooks with him on the ground that that would violate the nonimportation agreement. "What a scandalous thing it is," remarked Galloway, "that such a fellow should have it in his power to govern a whole Province."[17]

Young Galloway overstated Chase's power in Maryland, but clearly Chase was in the forefront of provincial resistance. In addition to his roles in Congress, convention, and local committees, he was very active in rallying the public to support their leaders. One Tory writer painted a graphic if prejudiced picture of Chase "haranguing, and urging the necessity of adopting every measure of the Association, and the other wild...views of the Congress." He worked especially hard to win over the Elk Ridge area, which had furnished a large part of the radical contingent that burned the *Peggy Stewart*.[18] Chase's efforts among the people made him the most nearly indispensable leader of his political faction. Men like Johnson, Paca, the Carrolls, and Tilghman could contribute as much as Chase in Congress and convention, but none could match Chase's influence among the "middling sort." That Maryland's established country party leaders were able to preserve their shaky grasp on the province in 1775 and 1776 and turn back the challenge of their political rivals can be attributed in part to Chase's ability to hold enough of the "middling sort" in line behind their program.

Chase's view of the crisis early in 1775 was expressed in a letter to New York's James Duane, whom Chase had met in Congress. His basic position had not changed since Congress adjourned. He still hoped for reconciliation with England and was willing to allow Parliament to regulate colonial trade, but he was determined to resist English violations of colonial rights by all necessary means. Chase believed that England could not afford to ride out the American commercial boycott. "Lord North is too well acquainted with his Weakness; he must be convinced that the Colonies, if they adhere to their association, must succeed." Chase predicted that England "must either give up the Right of Taxing America, or enforce obedience by the Sword." Influenced like so many other Americans by Commonwealth ideology, Chase saw little chance of the reconciliation he desired.

> When I reflect on the enormous Influence of the Crown, the System of Corruption introduced as the Art of Government, the Venality of the Electors (the radical Source of every other Evil), the open and repeated Violations, by Parliament, of the Constitution...I have not the least Dawn of Hope in the Justice, Humanity, Wisdom or Virtue of the British Nation. I consider them as one of the most abandoned and wicked People under the Sun....Our Dependance must be on God and ourselves.[19]

If vigorous resistance could not force Britain to concede colonial rights, Chase's commonly held view of a hopelessly corrupt England falling to tyranny would furnish a rationale for independence.

Chase's prediction of fighting to come was fulfilled at Lexington and Concord in April. Concerned that Maryland could not be effectively mobilized for war "while the present *forms* of Government subsist," Chase suggested that the convention should renounce the proprietary regime and seize power. Few other Maryland leaders were ready for such a bold step, however, and the transfer of power from the established to the revolutionary authorities proceeded on a *de facto* basis while the province's patriots continued to insist that the old government remained intact. Maryland still fought only for recognition of her rights within the empire. The provincial convention met again in May and unanimously reaffirmed its allegiance to George III. Chase and the other delegates to the first Congress were reelected to represent Maryland at the Second Continental Congress, with John Hall and Thomas Stone added to the delegation. The delegates were instructed that the convention desired reconciliation with England. They were not to support independence unless "indispensably necessary for the...preservation of our liberties."[20]

Prospects for reconciliation were undeniably poor, however, and in July 1775 the convention took steps to organize Maryland for sustained resistance while strengthening internal order. Chase served on a committee to devise a plan for putting the province in a defensible condition. Along with the other delegates, he signed the Association of the Freemen of Maryland, an agreement to support the contest against England while upholding law and order within the province. The Association was designed to serve as a test of loyalty to the patriot cause. All freemen would be asked to sign it, and the names of "nonassociators" who refused would be sent to a future convention. The July convention also regularized a provisional government for the province. New county committees of observation were to be elected, along with convention delegates to serve for a one-year term. Most important, a Council of Safety was created to govern the province between sessions of the convention. Samuel Chase was elected to the first Council of Safety.[21]

Chase's life by mid-1775 was almost wholly devoted to public service. Simultaneously a member of Congress, convention, and county committee, he could not be everywhere at once. Probably that is why he was not reelected to the Council of Safety, a full-time job in itself, in January 1776. After May 1775 Chase divided his time between Annapolis, Philadelphia, and occasional trouble spots elsewhere. In November 1775 he was at Frederick, presiding sternly over the local committee's interrogation of three captured British agents. It developed that they had been commissioned by Virginia's royal governor Lord Dunmore to collect a force at Detroit, then capture Pittsburgh and descend the Potomac to sever the southern colonies from the northern.[22]

While attending the Second Continental Congress, the Maryland delegates lodged with Mrs. Gunning Bedford. Chase took most of his meals at the City Tavern, where he and several other delegates "established a table for each day of the week, save Saturday, when there is a general dinner." Chase's usual dinner companions during the early months of the Congress were Peyton Randolph, George Washington, Richard Henry Lee, and Benjamin Harrison of Virginia; Caesar Rodney and George Read of Delaware; and John Alsop of New York.[23] Though Chase and Washington had met before, this daily contact deepened their friendship.

The delegates to Congress found that they had more than enough to do. There was a war to be fought; an army had to be organized, supplied, officered, and financed. Colonies sought advice and aid with their problems of government and defense. And always in one form or another there was the divisive issue of the proper means of resistance, the proper stance for America to take toward England, behind which now loomed the question of America's ultimate objective in this contest: reconciliation or independence.

{ 51 }

Chase, though not a leader in the Second Continental Congress, made a substantial contribution to its work. He served on more committees than any other Maryland delegate save perhaps Thomas Johnson. Several of those committees dealt with military problems in northern New York and Canada, giving Chase a knowledge and interest in that area that became important in 1776.[24]

Chase also took a vigorous part in the debates in Congress. He sided more and more frequently with the radical, proindependence faction led by the Adamses as the months went by and hopes of a settlement with Britain continued to fade. Chase's major theme in the debates was that American resistance must be bold and thoroughgoing if it was to succeed. His advocacy of strong measures was limited only by what he believed to be practical. There were some inconsistencies in his stand, but the frequently cryptic character of John Adams's notes of the debates may account for some of them.

Chase seemed inconsistent on the question of an American navy, a major subject of his attention in the debates. He realized the importance of naval power. When in October 1775 a motion was introduced recommending the arrest of persons like Virginia's Lord Dunmore who were dangerous to American safety, the practical Chase remarked that the resolution did not go "far enough" because it could not be executed without adequate naval force. Yet the next day he exploded, "It is the maddest Idea in the World, to think of building an American Fleet....We should mortgage the whole Continent." Like most other southern delegates, Chase doubted the practicality of building a navy strong enough to contest British control of the Chesapeake and safeguard the long, vulnerable southern coastline.[25] In December, however, when Congress decided to authorize construction of a navy, Chase was appointed to a committee to carry out the resolution for building armed ships. Though Chase was "entirely unacquainted with Ship Building," he joined with Samuel Purviance and David Stewart to supervise the construction at Baltimore of a warship for Congress.[26]

Another major subject of debate through late 1775 and early 1776 was trade. Should some exports to England be allowed as exceptions to the Association? Should America open her ports to foreign nations other than England, exporting her produce to buy military supplies, throwing off the restraints of England's mercantile system, and thus taking a long step toward independence?

Samuel Chase spoke frequently on these subjects. Above all he advocated a strict adherence to the Association. He repeated his conviction that a complete trade boycott was America's most effective weapon against England, whose wealth and strength depended on her trade. "We have given a deadly Blow to B[ritain] and Ireland, by our Non Export. Their People must murmur, must starve. The Nation must have become Bankrupt before this day if We had ceased Exports at first" instead of waiting until September 1775. Placing such an excessive faith in economic coercion, Chase fought against attempts to permit the export of some products to England. That, Chase argued, would undermine the Association and create dissension. People would be sure to complain if other colonies or producers were allowed to export.[27]

Chase's strong defense of the Association produced an altercation with the Reverend John Joachim Zubly, a delegate from Georgia and a strong conservative. Having opposed Zubly on several occasions, Chase reached the end of his patience when the reverend declared that the Association would "be the Ruin of the Cause." Chase retorted heatedly "that if the Revd. Gentlemans Positions are true and his Advice followed, We shall all be made Slaves." Why, he asked, had the Georgians come to Congress if they could not stomach firm measures? "Did they come here to ruin America. That Gentlemans Advice will bring Destruction upon all N. America."[28] Chase was justified in his suspicion of Zubly, who soon returned home and became an open Loyalist.

Chase's position on opening American trade to foreign nations, as reflected in Adams's notes, was more equivocal. In October 1775 Adams recorded Chase as arguing both that America could support the war effort without foreign trade and that it could not. He was inclined to favor opening American ports to the world, but delayed his final decision to await England's response to American grievances. Chase believed that "when you once offer your trade to foreign Nations, away with all Hopes of Reconciliation." But "let the Door of Reconciliation be once shutt, I would trade with foreign Powers and apply to them for Protection." In October, Chase had "not absolutely discarded every Glimpse of a Hope of Reconciliation," through he admitted that "Our Prospect is gloomy."[29] An advocate of strong resistance, Chase yet hesitated to take irrevocable actions that meant independence until he was certain that Congress's petitions to the Crown would not bring a redress of American grievances.

The end of October brought that certainty, at least in Chase's mind. Word arrived from England that the king had issued a proclamation declaring the Americans to be in a state of open rebellion. The news had a great effect on Congress. For Chase it was the last straw. Jocularly addressing the radical Rhode Island delegate Samuel Ward as "Brother Rebel," Chase announced that he was "now ready to join Us [New England radicals] heartily. We have got says He a sufficient Answer to our Petition; I want nothing more but am ready to declare Ourselves independent, send Ambassadors etc." Chase, according to Ward, said "much more which Prudence forbids me to commit to Paper."[30] Chase's assessment of the king's attitude was confirmed on November 9, when Congress learned that His Majesty had refused to receive the petitions of Congress.

Two old anecdotes, neither specifically dated, indicate that Chase advocated independence with his usual vehemence once he had made up his mind about it. One of these traditions has him exclaiming passionately in Congress, "By the God of heaven, he owed no allegiance to the king of Great Britain." According to the other, at an Annapolis dinner with Governor Eden and a group of Maryland patriot leaders, Eden confirmed that England had hired Hessian mercenaries to fight in America. Thereupon Chase is said to have exploded, "By God, I am for declaring ourselves independent."[31]

Chase's decision for independence brought him into close collaboration with John Adams. Adams had always liked Chase. He recognized a kindred spirit in the Marylander's "naturally quick and warm" temperament. On occasion the impatient Adams grew vexed with Chase in Congress's debates; once he called Chase "violent and boisterous," "tedious upon frivolous points." But Chase, "ever social and talkative," nevertheless held the prickly Adams's affection. Adams later recalled that his "constant topics" early in 1776 were independence, a confederation, and foreign alliances. Chase, he added, "when he did speak at all, was always powerful, and generally with us."[32]

Beginning in November 1775, Chase's position on almost every issue before Congress reflected his commitment to independence. First New Hampshire and then South Carolina asked Congress for advice respecting the establishment of new governments capable of maintaining internal order. Congress suggested early in November that both provinces establish such forms of government as their voters deemed proper for the duration of the contest with England. Chase served on the committee that considered South Carolina's request. He supported Congress's decision and, indeed, was "very ready for it."[33]

Others, however, viewed the resolutions with alarm as a long step toward independence. At John Dickinson's instigation, the Pennsylvania assembly instructed its congressional delegates to oppose any measure that might lead to independence or change Pennsylvania's old form of government. Chase, like other radicals, was disgusted with those instructions. "I heartily condemn them," he told John Adams. "I think them ill timed, timorous and weak. They were not drawn by Men fit to conquer the World and rule her when she's wildest. . . . But I may censure too vastly. I am young and Violent." When the Maryland convention met in December, Chase tried fruitlessly to convince his hesitant countrymen of "the Propriety, nay the Necessity" of replacing the proprietary regime with a new government. Chase was also premature in introducing a motion in Congress "for sending ambassadors to France with conditional instructions."[34] He was doing everything he could to push matters along toward a separation from England.

The events of the next few months made many delegates ready for bolder action. The war went on. Thomas Paine's *Common Sense,* with its electrifying denunciation of monarchy and call for independence, appeared in January 1776. Late in February, Congress learned that Parliament had passed an act suppressing colonial trade and authorizing the navy to seize and confiscate American ships. This American Prohibitory Act had an enormous impact in the colonies. To many it meant that Britain had put the colonies outside the pale of its protection, almost forcing them into independence by its own act.

Even before news of this act arrived, Chase had given notice of his intent to propose that Congress authorize privateering against England and order the navy to seize British ships. Congress was not at that time ready for such a radical step, but the American Prohibitory Act changed its mind. Privateering was authorized on March 19, and American ports were opened to the world on April 6. It was significant, too, that Virginia's George Wythe and Richard Henry Lee moved to amend the preamble to the resolution for privateering so as to blame Britain's tyrannical policies on the king, not on Parliament as in the past. A long debate ensued in which Chase supported the amendment and the other Maryland delegates opposed it.[35]

Another manifestation of Chase's desire to push forward toward independence came on February 21 when it was moved that Congress thank the Reverend Dr. William Smith for an oration in tribute to General Richard Montgomery, who had been killed at Quebec in December 1775. Chase was among the delegates who objected to the resolution because "the Dr. declared the Sentiments of the Congress to continue in a Dependency on G[reat] Britain which Doctrine this Congress cannot now approve." The resolution was withdrawn. The only discordant note in Chase's otherwise consistent radicalism was also struck in February, when he again opposed an immediate opening of foreign trade.[36]

Chase's advocacy of independence put him far ahead of his province. Sentiment for a separation from England was growing in Maryland as elsewhere, and by the spring of 1776 the convention and Council of Safety were fast losing popular support because of their conservatism. Still, most of the province's leaders clung desperately to the dwindling hope of reconciliation. Of Chase's close political associates, only Charles Carroll of Carrollton advocated independence by March 1776. In January the convention had reaffirmed its attachment to England, instructed the congressional delegates to pursue every possibility of a reconciliation that would secure American liberty, and forbidden the delegates from agreeing to independence, confederation, or foreign alliances without the convention's approval unless absolutely necessary to preserve liberty. The convention warned that Maryland would not be bound by a declaration of independence to which she did not consent.[37]

In March 1776 Chase and Carroll of Carrollton were the only proponents of independence in Maryland who had the influence to sway the province's other leaders toward a separation. There was thus plenty of work for them to do at home. But Chase had other plans for himself and Carroll: a mission to Canada to try to salvage deteriorating American prospects in that quarter. Congress agreed, and Chase's influence in Maryland was removed just when it was most needed. Without him and Carroll, the Council of Safety and convention continued to resist independence. Their increasingly unpopular conservatism threatened to undermine the uncertain degree of internal stability that remained in Maryland.

Six

CANADA AND

INDEPENDENCE

AMUEL CHASE was happy to be going to the province of Quebec.[1] His selection as one of the American commissioners to Canada was proof of Congress's confidence in him, for the mission was a very important one. Ever since 1774 Congress had been impressed with the desirability of persuading the Canadians to join in the struggle against Britain. Their accession would lend added strength to the cause and would contribute greatly to the defense of America. As long as the British held Canada, New York and New England lay exposed to invasion from the north, an invasion in which the Iroquois Indian tribes might well be persuaded to join. A friendly Canada would remove that grave threat.

The First Continental Congress, just before its adjournment, addressed a message to the inhabitants of Quebec inviting them to send delegates to the next Congress and join forces with the other colonies in defense of their mutual liberty. The Second Continental Congress in May 1775 attempted again to convince the Canadians that their interest was one with that of the other American colonies. By then, of course, fighting had begun. The colonial capture of forts Ticonderoga and Crown Point had opened the way for a military invasion of Canada, but on June 1 Congress rejected that idea on the grounds that American aims were strictly defensive. The more conservative delegates hesitated to take an offensive step that might cloud prospects of reconciliation with the mother country, and it could be argued as well that an invasion might alienate the Canadians.

By the end of the month, though, Congress became concerned at indications that Canada's British governor, Guy Carleton, was strengthening his weak military forces and trying to enlist the support of the Indians. On June 27 Congress ordered General Philip Schuyler to Ticonderoga with instructions to invade Canada if practicable and "if it will not be disagreeable to the Canadians."

Eventually, too late in the season, a two-pronged American thrust into Canada developed. General Richard Montgomery moved against Montreal by way of Lake Champlain and the Richelieu River, while Benedict Arnold advanced through the Maine wilderness toward Quebec. From the first the American offensive was plagued with tremendous problems. There was the inherent difficulty of operating in the wild north at the end of a long supply line, especially with the Canadian winter approaching. There were shortages of everything—from money, men, and supplies to military experience, energy, and discipline. Dissension broke out among the troops of different colonies, and short-term enlistments allowed units to melt away in the course of the campaign. Still, the capable Montgomery took Montreal in November, and most of Arnold's men survived a terrible march to emerge before Quebec. Joined by Montgomery and some of his troops, Arnold's little force laid siege to the city amid the deepening snows of the northern winter. A desperate American assault on Quebec failed on December 31; Montgomery was killed and Arnold wounded. Though short on supplies and suffering from smallpox, the Americans continued the fruitless siege.

An added disappointment was that few Canadians joined the colonial forces. The population of Canada was still overwhelmingly French Catholic, and the Americans' deserved reputation for anti-Catholicism hurt their cause. The Catholic clergy, led by their bishop, actively supported the British. Still, most of the French Canadian *habitants* were not unfriendly to the Americans, nor were they eager to fight for Britain. They simply saw little at stake for themselves in this quarrel of Englishmen. Prosperous and relieved of compulsory military service under British rule, they were waiting to give their allegiance to the winning side.[2] But the disposition of the Canadians was not well understood in Philadelphia.

Chase shared the general misconceptions about Canada, although he had served on several committees concerned with problems there. His acquaintance with the northern theater had convinced him that "the Success of the War will, in great Measure, depend on securing Canada to our Confederation." In January 1776 Chase suggested to John Adams that Congress send a mission to enlist Canadian support. "I would have a chosen Committee go to Canada as soon as the Lakes are frozen hard enough, let them call a Convention, explain the Views and designs of Congress, and persuade them to send Delegates there. . . . My Inclination to serve my Country would induce Me to offer my Services, if I did not esteem Myself unable to discharge the Trust."[3]

Nothing came of Chase's idea until February, when Congress's Committee of Secret Correspondence received an eyewitness account of the deteriorating American position in Canada. The witness testified that the people of Canada had generally favored the American side at first, but later had been swayed by the pro-British clergy and *seigneurs* and were now uncertain which side to take. Their change of attitude, he said, had been further encouraged by New York Tory newspapers, which charged that the Americans planned to suppress the Catholic Church. But he believed that support for the American side might be restored if Congress were to send some of its members to Canada to explain their cause and assure the Canadians of American friendship and good intentions toward them. If this was not done, he suggested, the Canadian campaign would be in danger of failing.

Congress immediately accepted the recommendation. The very next day, February 15, it appointed a three-man committee to go to Canada. Benjamin Franklin headed the commission. A talented diplomat with an engaging personality, Franklin was by far the best known and most respected American abroad. To many he symbolized the best traits of his country, making him the ideal person to win over the Canadians. Next on the list was Samuel Chase, an obvious choice since he had advocated the mission and was, as John Adams noted, "deeply impressed with a sense of the Importance of securing Canada, very active, eloquent, Spirited, and capable." For its third commissioner Congress went outside its own ranks and chose Charles Carroll of Carrollton. Chase had suggested the appointment, noting that Carroll was a wealthy Catholic who spoke French and was familiar with French manners and customs. Finally, Congress asked Carroll to persuade his cousin, Father John Carroll, to accompany the commissioners. A Catholic priest should be most useful, especially in influencing the Canadian clergy toward a more favorable view of America. Not relying on the commissioners alone, Congress decided also to reinforce the army in Canada and sent a new general to command it, John Thomas.[4]

Having acted so promptly to appoint the committee, Congress was very slow in agreeing upon the commissioners' instructions. Chase contributed somewhat to the delay be offering some additions to the instructions during their consideration on the floor,[5] but he was certainly justified in trying to perfect the mandate he was being given.

Finally, on March 20, the instructions were approved. The commissioners were to invite Canada again to join the colonial union on the same basis as the other thirteen provinces. They were to reiterate that American troops were in Canada only to frustrate British designs "against our common liberties" and to pledge that they would defend Canadian liberties as well as their own. The free exercise of the Catholic religion would be respected, provided Protestants were given equal political and religious freedom and exempted from church taxes in Canada. The commissioners were to "establish a free Press" to print matter useful to the cause. They were to settle disputes between the Continental soldiers and the Canadians, to reform abuses, to establish and enforce "regulations for preservation of peace and good order," and to sit and vote in military councils of war. The army was bound to obey their regulations, and they might suspend officers if necessary to enforce their decisions. They were to grant licenses for the Indian trade and to promote the circulation of Continental paper money in Canada. In short, they were authorized to act almost as proconsuls, representing the authority of Congress in the field.[6]

Armed with these instructions, the commissioners left Philadelphia on March 26. Initially they were full of optimism. Carroll of Carrollton had written earlier in the month that "it is the opinion here we shall get Quebec before the middle of April," in which event "I think it will not be very difficult to draw the Canadians into the union.''[7] How poorly did they yet understand the true state of affairs in Canada!

After a few days in New York the commissioners sailed up the Hudson River to Albany, inspecting the river forts along the way and finding most of them in a deplorable condition. Despite a storm that split the ship's mainsail and forced it to take shelter, the trip was a pleasant one. Franklin was the life of the party. He was ''a most engaging and entertaining companion of a sweet even and lively temper, full of facetious stories. . .always applied with judgment and introduced *a propos*,'' as well as wide knowledge and keen intelligence. ''In short,'' Carroll wrote, ''I am quite charmed with him.'' Chase's contribution to the comfort of the party was to act as cook, a responsibility for which he felt a lively personal interest. On one occasion when the group stopped to stretch their legs and admire a waterfall, Chase could not enjoy the diversion. He was ''very apprehensive of the leg of mutton being boiled too long, impatient to get on board.''[8]

Arriving at Albany on April 7, the commissioners were met by General Schuyler. They soon left for the general's mansion at Saratoga, accompanied by the whole Schuyler family and by General Thomas. There they stayed for a week, waiting for better weather and enjoying a hospitality that made them reluctant to leave. The aged Franklin especially needed the respite; he was beginning to fear that the journey might be beyond his strength. And the worst lay ahead. Ice obstructed navigation on the lakes. Early spring floods made the rivers run swiftly and impeded travel by land, and a fresh six-inch snowfall added to the difficulties.[9]

Beyond Saratoga travel grew slow and tedious, alternating between wagon, ferry, lake boat, and portages. The party ran into heavy ice floes on Lake George and were delayed by unfavorable winds on Lake Champlain. While waiting at Fort George, they met with a party of Indians returning from an Iroquois conference and learned that that powerful confederacy had decided to remain neutral for the time being. The commissioners reached St. John's in Canada on April 27 and Montreal two days later. Already they had learned their first lesson in the real state of Canadian affairs. The courier they sent to tell Benedict Arnold in Montreal of their approach was halted when a ferry keeper refused to accept his Continental paper money. The messenger proceeded only when a friend advanced hard cash. The same friend had to guarantee payment, again in specie, before carriages could be hired to bring the commissioners into the city. The Americans did not appear to be sure winners just then, and Canadians had had enough of their dubious paper and IOUs.

General Arnold arranged a formal entry into the city for the commissioners, evidently seeking to impress the Canadians with the importance of the mission and to restore American prestige. After the ceremony a formal reception and dinner were held for the commissioners.[10] For Arnold and his officers, though, the festive spirit of the occasion was clouded by a major disappointment: the commissioners had brought no hard money with them.

In fact, as Chase, Franklin, and Carroll soon discovered, gold and silver were more sorely needed than commissioners. "It is impossible to give you a just idea of the lowness of the Continental credit here, from the want of hard money, and the prejudice it is to our affairs," they reported to Congress. "Not the most trifling service can be procured without an assurance of instant pay in silver or gold." America's friends in Canada had advanced much in the way of money and supplies, but could or would do no more; some £14,000 was owed to them. The military had sometimes resorted to seizure of supplies and exaction of services without compensation, which had alienated the inhabitants. The failure of the commissioners to bring hard money had led the people of Montreal "to consider the Congress as bankrupt, and their cause as desperate. . . . The general apprehension that we shall be driven out of the Province as soon as the King's troops can arrive [from England], concurs with the frequent breaches of promise the inhabitants have experienced, in determining them to trust our people no further." Congress must send £20,000 in specie immediately, the commissioners urged; "otherwise it will be impossible to continue the war in this country."[11] But Congress had little money to send, and it was too late anyway.

A British fleet carrying ten thousand soldiers under General John Burgoyne was in the St. Lawrence River on its way to Quebec. When the vanguard of the expedition arrived on May 6, Carleton immediately ordered a sortie from the city. The ragtag American army was routed, abandoning its sick and much of its equipment and fleeing upriver toward Montreal. General Thomas assembled the survivors and received reinforcements around Sorel, at the mouth of the Richelieu River. The British, though, held the initiative, and their orders required an offensive toward Lake Champlain and the Hudson River.[12]

This reverse was highly discouraging to the commissioners. Carroll wrote that a principal part of their task—persuading the Canadians to join the resistance to England—was now impossible. War must decide the fate of Canada. Upon receipt of the bad news from Quebec, Franklin, whose health was getting worse, decided to return home. He left on May 11, accompanied by Father Carroll, who could make no progress with the Canadian clergy in the face of adamant opposition from the bishop of Quebec. Carroll of Carrollton and Chase believed they could accomplish little by staying, but since "in the present circumstances our departure would discourage our troops and friends in the country we have resolved to remain here."[13]

The entire burden of the commissioners' duties now fell on Chase and Carroll. "Every thing here is confusion for want of management and proper departments," Carroll wrote. In this chaotic and urgent situation the commissioners found themselves called upon to attend to everything at once. "We have no fixed abode," they told General Schuyler, "being obliged to... become Generals, Commissaries, Justices of the Peace; in short, to act in twenty different capacities." Chase wrote a friend that he served "in as many Capacities as Moliers Cook."

On May 15 the commissioners called a public meeting of the citizens of Montreal, which Chase addressed in an attempt to rally some public support. A few days later Chase and Carroll were off to Sorel to inspect the army there. They found it in a sad condition: "We cannot find words strong enough to describe our miserable situation; you will have a faint idea of it if you figure to yourself an Army broken and disheartened, half of it under inoculation [for smallpox], or under other diseases; soldiers without pay, without discipline, and altogether reduced to live from hand to mouth." "Our Affairs here are desperate," Chase unburdened himself to his friend in Congress, Richard Henry Lee. "For the Love of your Country cease the keen encounter of your Tongues, discard your Tongue Artillery and send Us some field [artillery] or We are undone."

From his firsthand experience both in Congress and at the front, Chase had concluded that the problems so evident in the conduct of the war could be traced to the highest level. "Congress are not a fit body to act as a Council of War," he told Lee. "They are too large, too slow and their Resolutions can never be kept secret. Pray divide your Business into different Departments a War office, a Treasury Board," and so forth.[14] Chase's recommendations anticipated by some years necessary reforms that were eventually adopted.

In the meantime reverses continued. Late in May a small British and Indian force captured an American garrison at the Cedars, thirty miles west of Montreal, and advanced within nine miles of the city. There was now no realistic possibility that Canada could be added to the American union. After attending one last council of war on May 30, which decided to try to hold the area between Montreal and Sorel while preparing plans for an orderly retreat southward, the commissioners left Canada. Anxious to get home and unhampered by the weather, Chase and Carroll made fast time. By June 9 they were in New York, where they told General Washington of the gloomy situation in Canada. At two o'clock in the morning on June 11 they reached Philadelphia.[15]

The American invasion of Canada failed because of initial delay, a lack of resources, inept use of what was available, and an overly optimistic view of the willingness of Canadians to join the resistance to England. No part of the blame can be laid at the door of the commissioners. Arriving in Canada just as the campaign began finally to unravel, they had no chance of succeeding in their mission. But they did their best. Samuel Chase and Charles Carroll of Carrollton conducted themselves with vigor and determination. Chase gained valuable experience in military affairs, which strengthened his conviction of the need for efficient organization and full mobilization of resources if the war effort was to succeed. He applied those insights through the rest of the war both in Congress and at the state level.

Though Chase's mission to Canada was important both to himself and to his country, his presence in Maryland and Philadelphia between late March and early June 1776 would also have been most valuable. For during Chase's absence the debate over independence had come to a head. Even in Canada that issue had been very much on Chase's mind. He wrote John Adams from St. John's on April 28 to urge that Congress give its full attention to the war effort and "not spend your precious Time on Debates about our Independancy. In my Judgment You have no alternative between Independancy and Slavery, and what American can hesitate in the Choice;

but don't harrangue about it, act as if we were [independent]. Make every preparation for War, take all prudent Measures to procure Success to our Arms, and the Consequence is obvious.''[16] Adams could not be kept from talking about independence, but otherwise the strategy Chase recommended was already being pursued. Advocates of independence were gaining strength and becoming increasingly impatient. Still, though, Maryland and several other colonies held back, threatening a breach of colonial unity if the others adopted independence before they were ready. Virtually the only first-ranking Maryland leaders who were committed to independence, Chase and Carroll of Carrollton were greatly needed at home.

Maryland's moderate patriot leaders did realize during the spring of 1776 that the time was fast approaching when they must make a final decision about independence. But, clinging desperately to the dimming hope of a reconciliation that would restore the past, they shrank from making the choice. Rising disorder within the province raised the specter of social revolution or anarchy if independence were adopted, increasing the reluctance of Chase's allies among the gentry to cut their stabilizing ties with England. On May 15 the convention unanimously reaffirmed its instructions to the congressional delegates to work for reconciliation and oppose independence.

Yet the Council of Safety and convention were coming under increasing criticism within the province for several reasons, including their conservatism. Their dilemma was that their stand against independence seemed to be increasing the possibility of the internal revolution they feared. Criticism mounted when in April the province's leaders refused to arrest Governor Eden following the revelation that he had been corresponding with the English government and was under orders to assist the coming campaign against the colonies. To placate their radical critics, the convention resolved in May that Eden should leave the province and suspended the old oaths of office and prayers for the king in the established church. Still they refused to admit that the proprietary government was at an end or to countenance independence.[17]

This was the situation in Maryland when on June 7 Richard Henry Lee introduced in Congress Virginia's resolutions that the colonies ''are, and of right ought to be, free and independent States,'' that a confederation should be devised and foreign alliances sought. After some discussion it appeared that six colonies—New York, Pennsylvania, New Jersey, Delaware, Maryland, and South Carolina—were not yet ready for the final step. On June 10 the resolutions were tabled until July 1 in the hope that these provinces would come around. But committees were appointed to prepare a declaration of independence, articles of confederation, and a plan of alliances in a clear indication that the majority would not wait much longer. Maryland's delegates wrote to the Council of Safety urging that the convention meet and the real wishes of the people be ascertained.[18] The final decision would now have to be made. Chase and Carroll's return to Philadelphia on June 11 could not have been more dramatically timed.

That same day Chase and Carroll reported to Congress on the state of affairs in Canada and submitted their recommendations. Undoubtedly, too, Chase had a chance to confer with his friend John Adams, who must have been very glad to have this staunch champion of independence return in time to sway a wavering Maryland. Chase also received news from Annapolis that made him more anxious than ever to get home: his wife was very ill. Hurriedly winding up his essential business in Congress, Chase left for Maryland early on June 14. Supposing that all the other colonies which had resisted independence were coming around, John Adams wrote after him, "Maryland now stands alone. I presume she will soon join company; if not, she must be left alone." Mr. Adams, he added, would always be happy to see Mr. Chase; "but Mr. Chase never was nor will be more welcome than if he should come next Monday or Tuesday fortnight, with the voice of Maryland in favor of independence."[19] Clearly much was expected of a busy man with a sick wife to care for, and time was short. The Maryland convention would meet in one week, on June 21.

From Maryland, Chase wrote John Adams that "a general dissatisfaction prevails here with our Convention." No one was better qualified to mold that dissatisfaction into an effective political force than Samuel Chase. He "appealed in *writing* to the people" in a circular letter calling upon them to instruct their convention delegates to support independence. The response was immediate and overwhelming. "County after county is instructing," Chase reported to Adams with satisfaction.[20] Undoubtedly Chase reinforced the impact of the instructions by exerting all his persuasiveness on the assembling convention delegates, and Carroll of Carrollton surely used his influence as well.

At length the province's hesitant political leaders were compelled to choose between independence and a break with the other colonies that probably meant subjection to England. Under pressure from an aroused segment of the populace who did not find the choice difficult, most of Maryland's leaders predictably chose the defense of liberty over continued allegiance to England. On June 28 the convention unanimously authorized its delegates to Congress to vote for independence. Chase exultantly dispatched the good news to his friends John Adams and Richard Henry Lee. "See the glorious effects of county instructions," he wrote. "Our people have fire if not smothered."[21]

Samuel Chase was not present when Congress, without a dissenting province, voted for independence on July 2 and adopted the Declaration of Independence on July 4. The work of the convention and Mrs. Chase's lingering illness kept him in Maryland; he returned to Philadelphia only on July 17. But Chase was anxious to associate his name in a lasting way with the decision for independence. On July 5 he wrote to John Adams, "I hope ere this time the decisive blow is struck....How shall I transmit to posterity that I gave my assent?" Adams replied, "As soon as an American seal is prepared, I conjecture the Declaration will be subscribed by all the members, which will give you the opportunity you wish for, of transmitting your name among the votaries of independence."[22]

And so it was done. On July 19 Congress ordered that the Declaration of Independence "be engrossed on parchment" and signed by all the delegates. The fine copy was ready on August 2. The members present signed it that day, and others added their signatures later.[23] Samuel Chase affixed his name to the historic document with a satisfaction born of achievement. No Marylander had done more than he to make the Declaration possible.

Chase realized clearly that the decision for independence marked not the end of his labors but the beginning of still greater tasks. On the very day that the Maryland convention voted for independence, his mind began to turn to the vital business of building a new nation that lay ahead. *"Now for a government,"* he wrote.[24]

Seven

"NOW FOR A GOVERNMENT"

AMUEL CHASE's view that independence required new governments reflected a national consensus. State conventions and the Continental Congress were universally recognized as temporary expedients, erected to tide the colonies over an emergency, and not settled governments. Now that the old colonial governments had been permanently renounced, state constitutions were needed to create a new political structure for the preservation of liberty, and a confederation to ensure American unity and treat with foreign nations. Chase played a significant role in framing both the Maryland constitution of 1776 and the Articles of Confederation.

Maryland's internal distractions added a note of urgency to the situation. Loyalists were armed and active, especially on the Eastern Shore. In some areas the convention's authority was ineffective. Ancient traditions of deference to the gentry were openly flouted. The patriots themselves were divided as the Hammonds and Ridgelys unfurled the banner of democracy to rally the discontented. The threat of anarchy or social upheaval seemed real enough that gentlemen like Charles Carroll of Carrollton were very apprehensive about the future of the state.[1]

Chase believed that a new government was needed to restore order as well as to safeguard the English liberties for which his revolution was being waged. He wanted to preserve the existing social order and ensure the political leadership of an elite of merit, but he had always believed that a ruling elite must in the end be responsible to a propertied electorate. Maryland's new republican government must be founded on the consent of the governed. Chase believed that a new convention should be elected to frame the state constitution. The existing convention agreed, and early in July it scheduled an election beginning August 1 for a new convention to meet August 14. Colonial property qualifications for voting were retained.[2]

Chase's faction faced a challenge from the Hammond-Ridgely group in the election. Strong in much of northern and western Maryland, the Hammond-Ridgely faction made a determined bid for the support of Chase's home county. Matthias and Rezin Hammond had established considerable influence among the Anne Arundel militia. Under their guidance, delegates chosen by the militia units proposed a new constitution for the consideration of the people. This plan made all branches of the state government subordinate to an annually elected bicameral legislature and also provided for annual election of all county officials. Poll taxes were to be abolished, and taxation in the future would be ''in proportion to every person's estate.''[3]

Chase and his associates considered the Anne Arundel militia constitution highly defective, but the Hammonds' reform proposals had considerable appeal. Rezin Hammond, the only local candidate of his faction, led the field in the Anne Arundel election with 513 votes. Brice Worthington, an unaligned candidate, had 506. The Barrister Carroll and Chase were also elected with 493 and 480 votes respectively. Thomas Johnson was defeated with only 151 votes, but he later won a seat from another county. The fact that Chase was in Congress in late July and early August, instead of campaigning at home, probably affected the result.

Trouble was narrowly avoided at the Anne Arundel election when militiamen who could not meet the property qualification attempted to vote. The problem was a common one, for the retention of suffrage restrictions was widely resented across the state. In four counties the property qualifications were ignored at the polls by popular demand, and in Kent County ''a number of people not qualified to vote'' prevented the election from being held at all.[4] When the convention met, Chase as chairman of the committee on elections was responsible for reviewing the credentials of the delegates. His committee ruled that new elections should be held in the counties where property qualifications were not observed. The convention agreed with near unanimity and also passed, with ten dissenting votes, Chase's motion to put the convention behind enforcement of the rule at a new election in Kent.[5] The Hammond-Ridgely faction was quick to capitalize upon what was obviously a major grievance by adding universal manhood suffrage for the native-born to their program.

Though they had run rather well in northern and western Maryland, the Hammond-Ridgely faction had no organization in the southern and eastern parts of the state. They would be a minority in the convention, but a strong enough minority to make their presence felt. Chase and his associates remained worried; Carroll of Carrollton at times seemed to be near panic. The latter foresaw "all the horrors of an ungovernable and revengeful Democracy" if the Hammonds succeeded.[6]

The convention had to perform the usual business of governing Maryland as well as writing a constitution, but Chase was eager to begin the latter task. Three days after the convention met he moved the appointment of a committee to draft a declaration of rights and a plan of government that would "best maintain peace and good order, and most effectually secure happiness and liberty to the people of this state." The composition of the drafting committee, which was elected by ballot, was a signal victory for Chase's faction. Convention president Matthew Tilghman headed the committee, on which Chase served along with Charles Carroll, Barrister, William Paca, Charles Carroll of Carrollton, George Plater, and Robert Goldsborough.[7]

Just when things seemed to be going so well for Chase's side, though, a major difficulty appeared. The Hammonds had not ceased politicking in Anne Arundel after the election. They had been circulating instructions ordering the county's convention delegates to work for their program. Those instructions, published in the *Maryland Gazette* on August 22, were signed by 885 freemen, so large a number that they had to be taken seriously. The instructions began by denouncing the "glaring injustice" of property qualifications for voting. Chase and the other county delegates were instructed to work for a constitution that would give the franchise to all native-born freemen who supported the Revolution and to all loyal foreign-born freemen who could meet modest residence and property qualifications. Reflecting the Hammonds' earlier proposals, the instructions also called for annual elections for the legislature, popular election of county officials and militia officers, the exclusion of executive influence from the legislature, and taxation in proportion to each man's property.[8]

The instructions put Chase in a most uncomfortable position. He believed in the ultimate sovereignty of the people and the consequent right of the majority to instruct their representatives. The majority of Chase's constituents had spoken, but he strongly disagreed with many of their desires. He could not support popular election of sheriffs and justices of the peace, and he believed that allowing men without property to vote would undermine public liberty and good government.[9] Chase's support for the political rights of the "middling sort" never extended to those who lacked the concrete stake in society that he believed was required to make a voter independent and responsible.

Chase, joined by Worthington and the Barrister Carroll, replied in the newspaper to the instructions. The three acknowledged that they were "bound by your instructions, though ever so contrary to our opinion. . . . We are reduced to this alternative, we must either endeavour to establish a government, without a proper security for liberty or property, or surrender the trust we have received from you." To avoid those disagreeable alternatives, the delegates called a public meeting at Annapolis on August 26 in the hope of getting the objectionable instructions reversed.[10]

The strategy failed. On August 27 Chase, the Barrister, and Worthington reluctantly resigned their convention seats rather than obey instructions they believed "incompatible with good government." A new election was ordered. Chase and Worthington were reelected and therefore considered themselves released from the instructions, but the Barrister Carroll lost his seat to John Hall.

In the meantime, Chase's and Carroll's resignations had removed them from the constitutional drafting committee. Thomas Johnson and Robert T. Hooe replaced them. This situation makes it difficult to assess Chase's role in drafting the constitution. Apparently the committee turned first to the declaration of rights, which they reported to the convention on August 27, the day Chase resigned. The draft constitution was laid before the convention on September 10. The logical inference is that most of the work on the constitution was done after Chase's resignation from the committee. In 1788, however, a newspaper writer asserted that both the declaration of rights and the constitution "as reported by the committee, were *principally* suggested, and draughted by" Chase.[11] This assertion is consistent with the fact that Chase by 1776 had become Maryland's principal legislative draftsman and initiator of political programs. Probably he had submitted a draft before his resignation, and perhaps he continued to work informally with the committee after he was no longer a member.

Right after the draft constitution was submitted to the convention, Chase, Paca, and Johnson were called to Philadelphia to help Congress deal with the emergency created by Washington's defeat on Long Island. The convention postponed consideration of the new government for two weeks to give them time to return, and a few days later it adjourned until the end of the month. Debate on the constitution and declaration of rights was thus delayed until October, allowing the delegates leisure to consider both documents. Chase took advantage of the interval to give copies of the two draft documents to John Dickinson in Philadelphia and to solicit his criticism. Dickinson suggested some changes, and Chase circulated the Pennsylvanian's recommendations among his convention friends. "I see the propriety of your Amendments," Chase told Dickinson, but he was still "afraid the popular Errors will prevail." Chase even tried to persuade Dickinson to come to Annapolis in the belief that his presence would lend weight to the fight against those "popular Errors."[12]

When the convention reassembled, the constitution and declaration of rights were debated and amended in committee of the whole, where most of the significant changes took place, and then reported to the floor of the convention for further discussion. Both documents were adopted in early November.

The declaration of rights that Chase had helped to draft was for the most part not controversial. It began by asserting that government originated with the people for the common good and that Maryland had the exclusive right to regulate its internal affairs, then proceeded to safeguard fundamental rights and liberties long cherished in the Anglo-American tradition, such as trial by jury,

{ 73 }

freedom of the press, and the right of petition. All officers of government were proclaimed to be trustees of the people. Plural officeholding was forbidden. The principles of separation of powers, rotation in executive office, and good-behavior tenure for judges to secure an independent judiciary were established. In one important respect the convention agreed with the Hammonds: poll taxes were abolished, and taxation in the future was to be in proportion to wealth.

The convention did make several changes in the declaration of rights, and Chase welcomed the most important of them. William Paca successfully moved to strengthen judicial independence by requiring a two-thirds vote of the full membership of the legislature, instead of the original majority of those present, to request the governor to remove a judge from the bench. Chase supported this amendment, little dreaming that another and greater fight for judicial independence lay many years in his future. The next day Somerset County's Gustavus Scott moved to amend the sections of the declaration guaranteeing religious freedom. The original provision stated that no one could be forced to support any church or ministry. Scott's proposal allowed a future legislature to adopt a general tax for the support of religion, with each taxpayer specifying the denomination that was to receive his money. Chase was delighted with this amendment, which was adopted by a majority of about two to one.[13] Throughout his life Chase believed religion so important that it deserved public support.

On one other matter Chase was overridden. At several points in its consideration of the declaration of rights and the constitution the convention had to decide whether or not to allow Quakers and others who objected to taking oaths to make affirmations instead. Chase did not place the same degree of confidence in affirmations as in oaths, especially in important matters. Twice he attempted unsuccessfully to strike from the declaration of rights clauses allowing the affirmation for witnesses in court. He did succeed in convincing the majority of the delegates not to let the clerk of the council take the oath of fidelity to the state on affirmation.[14]

Turning to the draft constitution, the delegates found themselves dealing with a very conservative document indeed. Chase and the drafting committee had produced a republican government, but one that greatly resembled the old proprietary structure safeguarded against the former abuses of influence and patronage. Resting upon an elitist Whig view of government, it sought to establish a system strong enough to contain the Revolution and preserve the political and social status quo. The plan was too conservative in some ways for the rank-and-file delegates of the Chase-Carroll faction. Carroll of Carrollton remarked apprehensively upon its introduction that the convention seemed hostile to it.[15]

The drafting committee proposed a legislature of three branches: a governor, a Senate, and a House of Delegates. The governor's part in legislation was not defined; he could not originate bills or propose amendments, and a veto power was not specified. The governor and his council would be chosen annually by joint ballot of the legislature. The House of Delegates, four from each county and two each from Annapolis and Baltimore Town, was to be elected by the voters for a three-year term. The fifteen-member Senate was to be chosen every seven years by an electoral college selected by the voters. Intended to embody the ideal of a natural aristocracy of wisdom and virtue as well as to protect property interests, the Senate was explicitly given complete freedom to exercise its own independent judgement on all matters coming before it. Governor, councillors, senators, and delegates were required to possess landed property, the exact amounts left blank for the convention to decide upon. Persons who had failed to sign the Association were barred from office. The colonial property qualifications for voters were retained without reduction. The governor and council were given extensive power to appoint administrative officers, including county sheriffs, assessors, and clerks.[16] This was an unusual amount of power to confide to the executive at a time when most Americans feared the encroachments of executive power.

During the convention's consideration of the constitution, Chase fought alongside the other drafting committee members to keep the basic features of the original draft intact. He was particularly disappointed when the convention reduced the terms of the senators from seven to five years and those of the delegates from three years to one. He argued to no avail that "five years was too short a period to make the Senate sufficiently independent, as a representation of the aristocratical part of government—to be a check on the democratical." A term longer than one year for the delegates, Chase and Paca reportedly stated, was necessary because the people could "judge of the benefit of laws enacted, only from experience." Given annual elections, the voters would be prone to remove from office "independent and worthy delegates" who supported initially unpopular legislation that would prove beneficial in the long run. Annual elections would discourage "gentlemen of delicate sentiments" from running for office, "as factious men, through prejudice, might make false representations, to inflame the minds of the people." There could be no danger to liberty in a longer term, Chase added, since the interests of the people and their delegates would be the same. Chase tried unsuccessfully to restore the three-year term for the lower house, then suggested two years, but the majority insisted on annual elections.[17]

The convention also broke with its leaders on the drafting committee by reducing property qualifications for voters and officeholders. The latter still had to be men of some means, but the convention allowed senators and delegates to qualify by owning real or personal property, not just land. For voters, the colonial fifty-acre freehold qualification was retained, but the alternative standard was reduced by more than one-half, from £40 sterling in property to £30 current money. Chase and his associates had to fight hard to prevent further reductions. The Hammonds tried twice to broaden the suffrage, coming closest to victory when a proposal to let all taxpayers vote failed by five votes.[18]

Other changes further eroded the strong conservative government that the framers had proposed. The governor was removed from the legislature, becoming simply an administrator in conjunction with his council. The executive retained extensive powers of appointment to office, but the convention decided that county sheriffs should be elected. Still opposed to the election of sheriffs, Chase tried to restore their appointment by the governor and council, but his proposal was overwhelmingly defeated. In a flurry of last-minute motions, Chase succeeded in strengthening the constitutional restrictions against appointment of legislators to offices of profit, in adding a provision that any voter might be requested to take an oath of loyalty to the state before voting, and in allowing justices of the peace, while forbidding field officers of the militia, to sit concurrently in the legislature or council. He sought unsuccessfully to restore the clause barring nonassociators from holding public office, which the convention had deleted.[19]

If Samuel Chase had gotten his way on every point, Maryland in 1776 would have established a conservative political system, with stricter property qualifications, longer terms of office, fewer elective officials, disabilities for those who had not indicated their support for the Revolution, and less tolerance for the affirmations of Quakers and Mennonites. Chase's goal in the American Revolution was to establish ordered liberty in a new, purified republican framework. From 1764 to 1776 he had sought to preserve traditional English liberties for colonists who were being denied equal rights and equal justice in the British empire, and to make a proprietary government dominated by an elite whose privileges rested in large part on patronage rather than achievement behave more responsibly toward its subjects. His viewpoint did not change in the constitutional convention of 1776. Government by a responsible elite of merit, answerable (except in the Senate, which was Carroll of Carrollton's brainchild) to the instructions of their constituents; a virtuous electorate of property holders; equal personal rights and equal justice for all under the rule of law; an independent judiciary: the draft constitution embodied the political philosophy that had guided Chase for a decade. Though his draft had been weakened in the convention, Chase was generally satisfied with the new constitution. He was relieved to see a satisfactory government created in Maryland, particularly since the other part of the new American political system with which he was concerned, the Articles of Confederation, was not progressing well at all.

Benjamin Franklin drew up the first plan for a confederation, which he laid before Congress in July 1775. The suggestion was as premature as independence at that time, and nothing came of it. Richard Henry Lee's motion of June 7, 1776, for independence, a confederation, and foreign alliances led to the appointment of a committee to prepare articles of confederation. The committee's draft, largely the work of John Dickinson, resembled Franklin's at many points. It was submitted to Congress on July 12, debated between the performance of other duties into August, laid aside until April 1777, discussed off and on through the year, and finally approved by Congress and sent to the states for ratification in November 1777.

The Articles of Confederation created a "firm League of friendship" among the states for their common defense and security. The central government would continue to be a one-house Congress, whose powers were better defined and limited in the final document than in Dickinson's draft. Congress's sphere of authority included foreign affairs, war and peace, and Indian relations; in neither the draft nor the finished version was it allowed to levy taxes or regulate commerce. Three controversial articles were responsible for Congress's long delay in approving a final draft. These articles dealt with the scheme for apportioning the expenses of the Confederation among the states, the method of voting in Congress, and control of western lands beyond the Appalachians. Bitter clashes of state interest and state advantage broke out over these three issues. Samuel Chase, chief spokesman for Maryland in Congress, was in the thick of the fray.

Chase in 1776 was anxious to complete the Articles. Beyond the intrinsic importance of a firm union, he believed that success in negotiating an alliance with France depended on formation of the Confederation. If so, long delay meant that "the opportunity may be lost of striking some great blow" in the war. All the disputes over the Articles could be settled, Chase told Richard Henry Lee at the end of July 1776, "if candour, justice, and the real interests of America were attended to. We do not all see the importance, nay the necessity, of a Confederacy. We shall remain weak, distracted, and divided in our councils; our strength will decrease; we shall be open to all the arts of the insidious Court of Britain, and no foreign Court will attend to our applications for assistance before we are confederated. What contract will a foreign State make with us, when we cannot agree among ourselves?"[20] The problem was that each state had its own notions of "candour, justice, and the real interests of America." Chase, too, fought for his state's interests in the debates on the three controversial articles.

The Dickinson draft provided that the expenses of the United States were to be borne by the states in proportion to their total populations. Total population included Negro slaves, and southern delegates were quick to protest the formula. Chase opened the slave state attack by moving that only white inhabitants be counted. Ideally, he said, taxation should be in proportion to wealth. But, since "the value of the property in every state could never be estimated justly and equally," white population was the next best alternative. Slaves, Chase argued, were property. Southerners invested their profits in slaves, just as northerners invested in live-stock; there was as much justification for counting one as the other. If sources of wealth as well as population were to be taken into account, why not include also New England's investments in trade and fisheries? Dickinson's method, he concluded, would "tax the Southern states according to their numbers and their wealth conjunctly, while the Northern would be taxed on numbers only."[21]

After considerable discussion Chase's amendment was defeated in a strictly sectional vote. The southern states remained indignant. One delegate wrote that "the bold and sonorous Chase (and some or all of his Colleagues) solemnly protest against the Taxation Article etc. and declare that they consider Maryland as having no further Concern in it, and that his Colony [sic] never will. . .agree to it." Eventually, in October 1777, the southerners succeeded in carrying an amendment to base state quotas on land values, leaving New England unhappy but settling the issue.[22]

A second point of controversy was the Dickinson draft's provision that each state should have one vote in Congress. Led by the Pennsylvanians, a number of delegates from the larger states asserted that each state should be represented in proportion to its population. Chase and the Maryland delegates voted against all motions for proportional representation. Chase feared that this issue would be the most divisive one raised in connection with the Articles. He reminded the delegates that division and civil war would likely result from a failure to confederate. To avoid this danger, Chase sought to act as a conciliator on the voting issue, which was less important to him than taxation. He proposed "that the smaller states should be secured in all questions concerning life and liberty" by an equal vote, while the large states should receive protection for their greater financial contribution to the Confederation by proportional voting on money issues. This proposal was not seriously considered. In the end each state retained its single vote in Congress, but as a concession to the large states the votes of nine states were required to decide certain important issues.[23]

Chase erred in supposing the vote issue was the most likely to divide. The bitterest controversy of all arose over ownership of the land beyond the Appalachian Mountains. This protracted dispute pitted the "landed" states, whose ancient colonial charters extended their territories into the then hazy western wilderness as far as the South Sea (the Pacific Ocean), against the "landless" states, which had precisely defined western boundaries. The landed states, Virginia foremost among them with a claim extending indefinitely west and northwest on both sides of the Ohio River, insisted on keeping title to their western claims. Landless states, notably Maryland, Pennsylvania, Delaware, and New Jersey, wanted the landed states to be cut off at the mountains, with Congress assuming control of the west for the common benefit of all the states. The problem was aggravated by the fact that western lands had long been objects of speculation by land companies in which members of Congress were involved. These companies would have their claims confirmed or nullified depending on whether Congress or the landed states controlled the west.

Dickinson's draft of the Articles of Confederation settled the issue in favor of Congress and the landless states. But early in the debates Thomas Jefferson offered an amendment that began to chip away at the language of the draft. Quickly Chase was on his feet to oppose the change. "No colony has a Right to go to the S[outh] Sea," he proclaimed. "They never had—they cant have. It would not be safe to the rest." The issue was so hotly contested that a revised draft of the Articles printed for the use of the delegates in August 1776 omitted the disputed sections entirely. When Congress again confronted the matter in October and November 1777, the landed states won. Maryland and Chase received little support for their attempts to give Congress the power to fix the limits of each state's claims. The final language of the Articles, suggested by Richard Henry Lee, was that "no State shall be deprived of territory for the benefit of the United States."[24]

Chase opposed the claims of the landed states to the west for several reasons. First, he saw the western lands as an important source of revenue for Congress. As early as April 1776 he had urged that Congress "immediately seize and appropriate all the Crown Lands . . . as a fund" to finance the war. He did not want this vast national treasure to be lost to the confederation. Second, personal self-interest made Chase eager for Congress to control the west. He was (or soon became) a member of the Wabash Land Company, formed in 1775, which claimed title by purchase from the Indians to two tracts of land north of the Ohio River in the vicinity of Vincennes. Among the Wabash Company's shareholders were Thomas Johnson, William Paca, Charles Carroll of Carrollton, and a number of

Baltimore merchants as well as Chase. These powerful Maryland politicians and businessmen stood to lose their land claims if Virginia controlled the west, for that state's convention had refused to recognize Indian land purchases made without Virginia's approval. Congress's decision not to interfere with Virginia's claims in the proposed Articles of Confederation was a serious setback for Chase and the other investors.

The Wabash Company and other similar groups did not give up, however. The Articles still had to be ratified by all thirteen states, providing continued opportunity for the land companies to salvage their interests. In November 1778 the Wabash Company held a joint meeting with the Illinois Company, a group centered in Pennsylvania that also stood to lose its western claims if Virginia controlled the area. The two companies merged their interests into the Illinois-Wabash Company, took in Robert Morris, Silas Deane, and several influential Frenchmen as members, and began to plan the settlement of their tracts. The new company constituted a powerful lobby that still looked to Congress to override Virginia and ratify its land purchases.[25]

The final factor in Chase's stand was the interest of his state. Maryland vigorously opposed Virginia's western claims because she feared domination by a gargantuan neighbor. "If they should not be incited by a superiority of wealth of strength to oppress by open force their less wealthy and less powerful neighbors," the Maryland legislature declared in 1778, "yet the depopulation, and consequently the impoverishment of those states, will necessarily follow." The lure of cheap land in Virginia, plus the low taxes that land sale revenues would make possible, would surely drain Maryland of much of its population. If the United States secured the west as a part of its territory after the war, Maryland argued, those lands would be won from England "by the blood and treasure of the thirteen states"; therefore the west "should be considered as common property." Western lands should be sold or granted by Congress to help pay the expenses of the war—excepting, of course, western lands already "granted to, surveyed for, or purchased by, individuals." Excepting, that is, the lands already claimed by Maryland speculators through their land company investments.[26]

Maryland's insistence on congressional control of the west had determined her stand on other issues before Congress while the Articles were being debated in 1776 and 1777. In September 1776

{ 81 }

Congress decided to enlist eighty-eight battalions of soldiers to serve in the Continental Army for the duration of the war. To encourage these long-term enlistments each soldier would receive a cash bounty and a promise of land, "to be purchased...from the general treasury" with the cost apportioned among the states in the usual manner.

At once Maryland objected, with Chase her leading spokesman as usual. The state's quota of enlistments was too high, being based on her slave as well as white population, but she would try to meet it nevertheless. What really hurt was the land bonus. Maryland had no land of her own to give her soldiers, and she refused to buy it from the landed states. Nor did she want those states to benefit at her expense by having former soldiers from Maryland settle their lands. Therefore Maryland decided that she would offer her soldiers an additional cash bounty instead of the land grant and would not be responsible for contributing to the general treasury to buy land for soldiers enlisted by other states.

Congress refused to accept Maryland's proposed alternative, and a lengthy dispute ensued. "I am amazed at the obstinacy of Congress," Chase told the Council of Safety. At length Congress agreed to allow the states to enlist men for three years with a cash bounty only, and Chase "by an obstinate perseverance" obtained in November 1776 a resolution that Congress's actions to that time should not affect the dispute over ownership of the west. But the question kept coming up, and Chase remained adamant. In July 1777 he declared his opposition to a proposed invasion of West Florida unless Congress first decided that the country, if conquered, would "belong to the United States generally."[27]

The completion of the Articles of Confederation in November 1777 with the landed states in control of the west was thus a major defeat for the interests of Chase and Maryland. But they continued to fight on, refusing to ratify the Articles unless their claims were recognized. Ten states had approved the Articles of Confederation by July 1778. New Jersey, Delaware, and Maryland held out, the Maryland House of Delegates having rejected ratification by a vote of forty-two to seven.

The accession of ten states to the Articles and the need to complete the Confederation caused Chase to change his mind at this point. He told a New Jersey congressman in July 1778 "that he imagined the Determination of Maryland would depend much upon that of New Jersey, and thought if our state [New Jersey] should accede, theirs would also—he therefore concluded to go immediately down and try what could be done." When the assembly met in October, Chase urged ratification. He was now willing to subordinate his own interests to completion of the union. But his new stand was highly unpopular. New Jersey ratified the Articles in November 1778 and Delaware in January 1779, but Maryland stood alone to prevent the completion of the Confederation for two more years.[28]

At length, in 1780 New York ceded her western land claims to Congress. In January 1781 Virginia ceded her claims north of the Ohio River, but only on condition that the area become new states and that "all private purchases of land from the Indians...be invalidated." At the same time, Maryland became very worried about her defenselessness against invasion by a British army then moving northward into Virginia. Applying to the French ambassador for naval assistance, Maryland was pointedly told that completion of the Confederation would greatly add to the security of the states. Under this pressure Maryland gave way and at last agreed to ratify, Chase voting with the majority. The land companies had not abandoned hope of securing their western claims, since at this point Congress would not agree to Virginia's demand that purchases from the Indians be voided. Not until 1783 did the Illinois-Wabash Company finally lose its struggle for a valuable chunk of the west. As late as 1797 Chase was still trying to get some compensation from Congress for his lost investment.[29]

Samuel Chase thus played an important early role in Maryland's long obstruction of the formation of a lasting union, but he changed his mind long before his state was ready to go along with him. Yet in the end Maryland's obstinacy served the infant country well. By contributing to the cession of the Old Northwest, it helped ensure that a national domain would be created, that the west would be erected into new states, and that no state would dominate the new nation.

Eight

A VIGOROUS
RESISTANCE

HOPE AMERICA will never submit to the tyrant of Britain," Chase wrote to General John Sullivan in December 1776. "I declare, as an individual, I would rather become a subject of France; but I am afraid all my countrymen are not of my stubborn temper. The sullen, unrelenting monarch of Britain should never lord it over me. I despise, I hate, and wish to destroy him and all such tyrants. I forbear to add. I feel my temper to rise." This mood—a fierce commitment to victory, a recognition that many others were less ardent than he, and a belief that his countrymen must be persuaded or forced to do what was necessary for the cause—underlay Chase's wartime activities. His resolve faltered once, in the darkest days of November 1776, but only briefly.[1]

Chase concerned himself with virtually every phase of the war effort. He sought to bolster the Continental Army and took an interest in its command arrangements. He was instrumental in seeing that Maryland's soldiers were raised and supplied. He devised legislation at the state level to deal with the economic problems of the war and to discover and suppress the disloyal. All of these activities reflected his conviction that victory required a full mobilization of resources and a vigorous prosecution of the war. Many of Chase's programs were controversial, and his growing disgust with those who obstructed the measures he considered so important involved him in further difficulties. By 1778 the Chase-Carroll faction in Maryland was unraveling, and Chase was once again in the storm center of political controversy.

A vigorous resistance required first that British overtures for conciliation be rejected. The first of those overtures came from the British military commanders in America, Admiral Lord Richard Howe and General William Howe, who had also been appointed peace commissioners. The Howes were authorized to offer pardons for the rebels and an end to parliamentary taxation of the colonies in exchange for American submission. There was no chance of these terms being accepted, but the Howes nevertheless took the task of conciliation seriously. In February 1777 they encouraged the American general Charles Lee, who had been captured by the British in December 1776, to write to Congress proposing a conference "upon matters of the last importance to himself, and his opinion to America." Congress, suspecting that the British intended only to deceive and divide America by hints of peace, replied that they would hear Lee only on matters related to his personal situation.

During the discussion of Lee's letter, Chase spoke against any conference with the British. He was sure that England did not seriously want peace on terms short of American surrender, but he feared the effect that the feigned peace overtures might have on the public. Accordingly he moved that General Lee's letter be published "in order to satisfy our constituents who have heard that it contains propositions of peace."[2] Congress did not adopt Chase's suggestion, so he acted on his own to warn Marylanders against the British proposals.

Enlisting the help of Baltimore newspaper publisher William Goddard, whose ardent temperament matched his own, Chase published in Goddard's *Maryland Journal and Baltimore Advertiser* a letter signed "Tom Tell-Truth" that purported to praise the Howes' peace offer. The terms of that offer, said the letter, "manifest the magnanimity, generosity, humanity, and virtue of the British nation....My soul overflows with gratitude to the patriotic virtuous King, the august incorruptible Parliament, and wise disinterested Ministry of Britain....I disbelieve and forget... that the monarch of Britain is a sullen and inexorable tyrant, the Parliament venal and corrupt, and the Ministry abandoned and bloody." The writer professed to rejoice at the obvious prospect of peace.

Chase's "Tom Tell-Truth" letter was, of course, heavily sarcastic. Just in case any reader did not get the message, Chase wrote another letter signed "Caveto," which appeared on the opposite page of the paper. "Caveto" warned that "many and various Strategems have been already practised by the insidious and wicked Court of Britain and her artful Agents, to deceive and divide the open, generous, unsuspecting Americans." The rumor that Britain had offered Congress honorable peace terms was just another trick. "Be not deceived my Countrymen. Expect nothing but Fraud, Force, Rapine, Murder and Desolation from the Hands of the Tyrant of Britain.... Neglect not one moment to collect your forces, to drive the enemies of peace, liberty and virtue from your country."[3]

Chase's letters attracted plenty of attention, but not entirely of the sort he had intended. There was in Baltimore an organization of radical patriots called the Whig Club whose announced purpose was to expose secret enemies of the Revolution. The Whig Club's patriotism was of a humorless and literal-minded variety, and its members read Chase's "Tom Tell-Truth" letter as a serious call for submission to England's peace terms. Concluding that the author of the letter must be brought to justice, the Whig Club called upon Goddard to disclose his identity. The editor refused, even when he was dragged forcibly before a meeting of the club. Consequently the Whig Club told Goddard that he was banished from Baltimore, according to their usual prescription for Tories.

Goddard set out posthaste for Annapolis to appeal to the legislature for protection. Chase took the lead in supporting his collaborator. The Committee of Grievances and Courts of Justice, on which Chase served, reported a resolution condemning the Whig Club's action as "a manifest violation of the Constitution" and the declaration of rights.

There the matter might have ended but for the desire of the principals to seek public vindication. The Whig Club issued a handbill rather apologetically defending its conduct, and Goddard replied with a pamphlet entitled *The Prowess of the Whig Club* that heaped pointed ridicule on his adversaries. When the members of the Whig Club read the pamphlet, they again ordered Goddard to leave town. Back to Annapolis went the printer, and this time the House of Delegates sent its sergeant at arms to bring the club's leaders to the capital to answer for their conduct at the bar of the House. The unhappy Whigs were received sternly. Chase drafted an apology that the chairman of the club was made to read. The House then resolved that the Whig Club's proceedings tended to the "destruction of all regular government" and asked Governor Thomas Johnson to issue a proclamation ordering all vigilante organizations to disperse.[4] In the end Chase had used the misadventure not only to call attention to the unacceptability of British overtures but also to establish by public demonstration the authority of the new state government.

One more British peace effort was made early in 1778. The American victory at Saratoga and the subsequent negotiations for the French alliance alarmed the English into making concessions. Word of the French alliance had not yet reached America when in April 1778 General Howe began distributing handbills that contained an act of Parliament renouncing taxation of the colonies, suspending all of its offensive colonial legislation made since 1763, and appointing commissioners to negotiate with America. Congress believed the handbill to be another trick and resolved not to negotiate unless England first withdrew its forces from America or acknowledged the independence of the United States. "The manifest Intention," Chase informed Maryland governor Thomas Johnson, "is to amuse us with a Prospect of Peace and to relax our Preparations. I hope my Countrymen will have too much good sense to be deceived." Again he advised publishing the British proposal "with some Remarks to expose its Design and remove the baneful Effects it may have on the credulous and weak among the People....It ought not to be attempted to be suppressed."[5] Instead of negotiating, Chase urged, Americans should redouble their efforts. "The Hour to try the Firmness and prudence of Man is near at Hand."[6]

The sense of crisis soon gave way to joy. On May 2 Congress received the text of the alliance with France, which had been concluded in February 1778. "America has now taken her rank among the Nations," Chase told Johnson, "and has it in her power to secure her Liberty and Independence. Let us be grateful to God for this singular unmerited mark of his favour and protection." Yet Chase was not lulled into a false sense of security by the good news. He again emphasized his constant theme of the war years: America must "continue to exert every means in our power to support the war. This can only be effectually done by speedy and liberal loans of money to the Continent and a respectable Army."[7]

With one exception—the dispute over western land bounties for long-term enlistments in 1776—Chase did everything in his power to see that Maryland helped to supply the United States with "a respectable Army." Through 1776 and 1777 he acted as self-appointed chief liaison officer between Congress and the state government. From Chase in Congress to the authorities at Annapolis went a steady stream of letters containing war news, advice on what supplies were needed and how to get them, and even, on occasion, suggestions for deployment of the military forces at the state's command. To Chase from Annapolis went another stream of requests for personal and congressional action. Where could the state purchase knapsacks, haversacks, canteens, and blankets for its troops, and at what price? Could Chase supply badly needed shoes? All the state's congressional delegates were called on for such services, but Maryland relied most upon Chase. Often he advanced his own money to meet emergency demands for supplies or recruiting funds, being reimbursed later by Congress or the state. Constantly he urged upon the state authorities the necessity of "the most vigorous exertions" to support the cause.[8] Once more Chase proved his willingness to work long and hard attending to prosaic details. This was not the least of his services to his state and country.

In Congress, too, Chase generally advocated a stronger and more efficient central government. In December 1776 he told General John Sullivan that "if we expect to succeed in the present war, we must change our mode of conduct." The states should not be allowed to nominate Continental Army officers because "local attachments" produced "injudicious" choices. Furthermore, "the business of the Congress must be placed in different hands. Distinct and Precise Departments ought to be established, and a gentleman of the military must be of the Board of War." In 1778, when Washington urged the necessity of granting pensions of half pay for life to Continental Army officers in order to combat discontent and resignations stemming from lack of compensation, Chase offered a resolution in Congress authorizing the plan. Opposition to the scheme developed, based largely on traditional fears of a standing army and a professional officer class, but in the end Congress voted

{ 88 }

half pay for seven years after the war to officers who served until the war's end.[9]

Realizing that correct policy judgments required accurate information, Chase asked the generals he had met to keep him posted. To Horatio Gates, Philip Schuyler, John Sullivan, and Benedict Arnold went requests for confidential information on the military situation, the "condition of our Army," and the officers' personal views, along with the assurance that "no more will be disclosed than you desire."[10]

Chase's keen interest in the success of the army and the personal connections he developed among its officers also involved him in some of the quarrels over rank, promotion, and the merits of officers that inevitably accompanied the war. Chase was most deeply involved in the squabbles that arose in Canada and northern New York, the theater with which he was best acquainted in 1776.

Chase's stand in army politics was unusually complex. He was a supporter of Schuyler, Gates, and Washington, who were on opposing sides in several of the leading congressional conflicts. First, writing from Canada in May 1776, Chase and Carroll of Carrollton sided with Schuyler in recommending the recall of General David Wooster of Connecticut. Returning to Congress, they extended their indictment of Wooster to a general attack on the conduct of the New England troops in the Canadian army. "By their account," remarked one New England congressman, "never [have] men behaved so badly." Finally, according to Benjamin Rush, John Adams became exasperated enough to lash out angrily against his friend. Chase, said Adams, was stirring up "jealousies and quarrels between the troops from the New England and Southern States." For this "improper and wicked conduct" Chase should beg the forgiveness of Congress. "He [should] afterwards retire with shame, and spend the remainder of his life in sackcloth and ashes, deploring the mischief he had done to his country." Congress eventually voted to exonerate Wooster of any improper conduct, a verdict that galled Chase and Schuyler.[11]

Soon afterward Chase supported Congress's selection of General Horatio Gates to command the Canadian army. In June 1776 he urged Gates to accept the appointment. "Laurels are still to be reaped in Canada," he wrote. "You will have a respectable army and every measure we can suggest is taking to supply them." Chase also stressed to Gates that his success or failure in Canada would depend largely on his ability to cooperate with Schuyler, who commanded in northern New York. Chase hoped that his two friends would get along well, but when Gates's army retreated into Schuyler's department, the two clashed over the command relationship between them. Congress decided that they should share joint command of the Canadian army, but Gates was not happy with the arrangement. He did not have the independent command he expected, and instead of the laurels Chase had promised the military situation portended disaster. In July 1776 Gates wrote to Samuel Adams to complain that Chase had misled him. "Tell him if he and I meet, he must expect to be called to a serious account upon this matter," Gates wrote. "I know he is my sincere friend.... I am not angry; I am only vexed with him." In reply Chase asked Gates to detail specifically how he had "been *deceived* and *disappointed* by your removal from New York to the command in Canada." Apparently Gates's response was conciliatory; he and Chase remained friends.[12]

By later 1776 a strong faction in Congress had become dissatisfied with Philip Schuyler, whose abilities were not as great as Chase believed. Though Schuyler enjoyed a temporary triumph when Congress vindicated his conduct and gave him supreme command in the north, he again came under attack after the British under General Burgoyne captured Fort Ticonderoga in July 1777. When a motion was made to replace Schuyler with Gates, Chase sprang to Schuyler's defense. Ticonderoga, he argued, was lost because of a lack of soldiers to defend it, not because of poor generalship. Removing Schuyler would "disgrace officers without just foundation" and also reflect badly on Congress, which had just put him in command. But Chase lost. Schuyler was recalled and Gates put in charge of the campaign that resulted in Burgoyne's surrender at Saratoga.[13] Chase's belief that Gates could win laurels in the northern theater, unlikely though it seemed for a time, was vindicated in the end.

The other major military campaign of 1777 saw Howe capture Philadelphia after defeating Washington at Brandywine Creek. Congressman Thomas Burke of North Carolina, who witnessed the battle, blamed the defeat on General John Sullivan, who commanded the American right. A friend and correspondent of Chase in 1776, Sullivan had not long before incurred Chase's anger by launching an unsuccessful raid on Staten Island in which a number of Maryland soldiers were captured. The New Hampshire general already faced a court of inquiry for that incident. Hence Chase was ready to believe the worst of Sullivan's leadership at Brandywine, even though Washington and other officers testified that he was not to blame.

In the congressional outcry following Brandywine, "the Maryland officers in his [Sullivan's] Division, the Delegates of that State, the great Burk...and the connexion of Schuyler...cast such Reflections upon his want of capacity...that a Majority...effected the Resolve to recall Sullivan till his Conduct should be enquired into as per former orders." But Washington believed he needed Sullivan and implored Congress to reconsider. When a motion was introduced in Congress to allow Washington to suspend Sullivan's recall, Chase countered with an amendment requesting Washington to remove the Maryland and Delaware troops from Sullivan's command and put them under another general. As a New Hampshire delegate was quick to note, this request "would have been in effect throwing out Sullivan, for the soldiers of other Divisions would be unwilling to serve under a Man discarded by the Marylanders." Only Maryland and Delaware voted for Chase's amendment, and the motion allowing Washington to keep Sullivan in command was adopted.[14]

Washington himself was also criticized for the Brandywine defeat. The subsequent fall of Philadelphia and another American defeat at Germantown increased dissatisfaction with the commander-in-chief, especially since his critics could soon contrast Washington's reverses with Gates's decisive victory at Saratoga. This situation gave birth to the Conway Cabal, a movement of sorts to remove Washington in favor of Gates. During this period Chase strongly supported Washington. But upon the collapse of the cabal he was one of the few congressmen to vote against accepting the resignation of General Thomas Conway, one of the principal malcontents.[15] This vote was not as inconsistent as it seems on the surface, given Chase's friendship for Gates as well as Washington and Schuyler.

Chase's efforts to mobilize the country's resources extended to economic as well as military measures. One of the major problems of the war years was steep inflation caused by shortages of some goods and the overissue of paper money. In February 1777 Chase was appointed to a committee of Congress to "devise ways and means of supporting the credit of the continental currency, and supplying the treasury with money." At the same time Congress was debating a remedy for inflation suggested by a meeting of commissioners from the New England states: strict governmental regulation of prices. Chase favored this plan as "a necessary resolution. It is true it failed formerly in Philadelphia," Chase acknowledged, but he blamed that failure on the numerous Tories of the city. "It succeeded in Maryland," he claimed. "The mines of Peru would not support a war at the present high prices of the necessaries of life." Opponents of the scheme replied correctly that price-fixing laws could not remedy an inflation that proceeded from economic causes deeper than Tory sabotage. In the end the resolution was referred to the states for their consideration.[16]

Through 1778 Chase continued to serve on a variety of congressional committees. He was also concerned that Congress until 1777 had carried on its work in secrecy. In February of that year Chase moved that "all the proceedings of Congress be entered on the Journal," that the vote of each member be recorded on any question when requested by any state, and that the journal of Congress be published, "except such parts which a majority shall order to be kept secret." Chase's motion was postponed, but the action he desired was taken in August.[17]

It should not be inferred that Congress was always engaged in purposeful activity. During 1778, especially, the delegates spent many hours quibbling over minor points and engaging in pointless oratory. On one occasion Henry Laurens wearily recorded that a large part of the morning had been occupied with "an Oration by S. C. Esquire on the improvement of time with the life and characters of Elizabeth and Mary Qu[een] of Scots, the comparative beauty of black Eyes and blue Eyes."[18] None of which, presumably, advanced the cause of American liberty one whit.

A valuable but secondary figure in Congress, Chase after independence became the political prime mover in Maryland. He sought to organize the state as well as the union for vigorous prosecution of the war. His forum was the House of Delegates, in which he represented Annapolis. Chase's election to that body early in 1777 scarcely represented an overwhelming mandate. On election day no one showed up at the polls in Annapolis. The assembly resolved that the election should be held again, resulting in the selection of Chase and John Brice by the three voters who came.[19] Though an extreme case, the Annapolis election reflected the popular mood in Maryland at the beginning of 1777. Many people appear to have received their new constitution without enthusiasm, and apathy was widespread.[20] Even if the disorder of 1775 and 1776 could be brought under control—and slowly it was—mobilizing Maryland for an all-out war effort would not be easy.

Chase's faction controlled the new state government. Thomas Johnson was elected Maryland's first governor, with Chase a distant second in the balloting.[21] Paca, Matthew Tilghman, Robert Goldsborough, and Charles Carroll, Barrister, sat in the Senate along with Carroll of Carrollton and other prominent gentlemen. Chase was the only first-ranking member of his faction left in the House of Delegates. Many familiar faces there were in the lower chamber, but Chase was not impressed with the changes the Revolution had wrought in it. According to an Annapolis Loyalist, Chase remarked disgustedly (and with considerable exaggeration) that "Six *Gentlemenlike* Persons could not be found" in the first House of Delegates.[22]

For most of the decade after 1777 Chase dominated the lower house. The elevation of other leaders to higher office helped him do so, but more important were his energy and the fact that he knew precisely what he wanted to accomplish. When the second session of the new state legislature opened in June 1777, Senator Daniel of St. Thomas Jenifer wrote, "Yesterday S[amuel] C[hase] opened his Budget of Business in a Committee of the whole House, and Carved out enough to take up the time of Six Months." One high priority item of Chase's, a legal tender act, had already been adopted at the previous session. Chase's other "great objects," according to Jenifer, were a bill to suppress Tories, confiscation of the proprietary estates, legislation for drafting the militia, an act to restrain engrossing of supplies and provisions, and state support for religion.[23] The last proposal Chase did not seriously press at the time. Opposition to it was overwhelming, and he concluded that taxes for religion were best postponed until the end of the war eased the tax burden.

Since the Senate generally followed the colonial upper house's custom of allowing most legislation to originate in the lower house, the initiative lay with Chase. So it went for the next ten years. The majority of the important and controversial proposals before the Maryland legislature were Chase's. More than any other politician he set the state's agenda; other leaders reacted to his ideas. Several of Chase's 1777 goals were very controversial. The fight over them began to open a breach between Chase and the delegates on one hand and Carroll of Carrollton and the Senate on the other.

The first of Chase's major bills to be adopted, the tender act, was an attempt to support the credit of wartime paper currency. Congress in January 1777 had asked the states to make Continental money a legal tender. Chase supported this resolution, and he believed that Maryland's paper currency should be made legal tender as well. "The intention," he later wrote, "was to give credit to the money, to render it of universal use, and to force *tory* creditors to contribute their aid to the war" by making them accept paper currency. Chase believed that the refusal of open and secret Loyalists to accept the paper was an important cause of its depreciation. He also found it outrageous that the disloyal or selfish could refuse paper money while patriots voluntarily accepted it and suffered the financial loss involved in taking a depreciating currency. A tender act with teeth in it, he believed, would remedy these defects and contribute greatly to the war effort.[24]

The tender act met very little initial opposition. It passed the House of Delegates on a voice vote, and only Carroll of Carrollton opposed it in the Senate. The act as adopted made Continental and state paper money a legal tender for all purchases and all debts, including loans made in sterling before the war and by contract repayable in sterling only. A creditor who refused to take it in payment for goods and services, or who demanded extra currency to allow for depreciation, faced a fine proportionate to the sum involved.[25]

Carroll of Carrollton's objections to the act centered on the clause allowing the discharge of previous sterling debts in depreciating paper currency. This he considered a glaring injustice, a breach of contracts that allowed debtors to defraud their creditors with impunity. The Carrolls were among the largest moneylenders in Maryland and stood to lose substantial sums on their outstanding sterling loans. "These are times in wh[ich] men do not stick at trifles," Carroll wrote; "they mean to cancel debts under a pretence of keeping up the value of the currency—if the bill would answer the purpose it should have my hearty concurrence, altho' it bears so hard on me." But Carroll did not think the bill would be effective in achieving its stated ends. He told his father that some of his fellow senators privately admitted the bill's injustice but voted for it anyway. Senator Jenifer added that "the Violence of the times" influenced the Senate's acquiescence. It has been argued that Maryland's conservative gentry accepted a scaling down of debts in order to win popular support for the conservative new government.[26]

Carroll of Carrollton's indignation over this "most infamous action" did not at first extend to the bill's author. He believed that Chase had acted as he honestly thought best but had fallen prey to "an error in judgment, and to an impetuosity of temper" that sometimes made him act with insufficient thought to the consequences. Once the bill passed Carroll resigned himself to making the best of it.[27]

Not so for Carroll's aged father. Charles Carroll of Annapolis told his son that the tender act "will Surpass in Iniquity all the Acts of the British Parliament against America. . . . It cannot be consistent with Justice to Bestow the Property of Creditors on Debtors and I shall look on every Man who Assents to Such a Law as Infamous, and I would as soon Associate with Highway men and Pickpockets as with them. . . . Not One of them shall ever hereafter Darken my doors."[28]

In June, Carroll of Annapolis wrote a long letter to Chase illustrating the "Villainy and fraud countenanced by the Law." Angered by a rumor that Chase had "said the Law was a Bitter pill to their Honours, but that they must swallow it"—a statement which proved to him that Chase had promoted "a law which you knew to be unjust"—the elder Carroll invited Chase to point out where his objections were ill founded. If Chase could not, concluded Carroll, "can you reflect on this with a tranquil Conscience?"[29]

Chase took offense at the tone as well as the content of Carroll's letter. Carroll of Annapolis had not addressed him "with the Temper and good Manners, I have a Right to expect (notwithstanding our Disparity of fortune)." Clearly Chase's sense of social inferiority remained strong. Since Carroll had not treated him "with Respect, and as a Gentleman," Chase would not reply beyond saying that he no longer cared what Carroll of Annapolis thought of him. The elder Carroll continued to address scathing letters to Chase despite Carroll of Carrollton's pleas that he desist. Finally Chase refused to receive his letters in order to avoid further argument.[30] Neither Chase nor Carroll of Carrollton wanted to let old Carroll's adamant outrage come between them. Charles Carroll of Annapolis finally gave up his attack on Chase and began instead to send fruitless petitions for a repeal of the law to the legislature.

In the meantime Carroll of Carrollton, affected by his father's attitude, his financial losses, and other emerging differences with Chase, had also begun privately to question Chase's integrity. He was angry with Chase for opposing repeal of the tender act after experience had proven it ineffective in preventing depreciation of the currency. Carroll believed that Chase was taking advantage of the law to pay his own debts in depreciated currency, but Chase maintained that he had actually been hurt by the tender act. In 1781 he said that he had received from his debtors more than twice as much as he paid his creditors under the law. "I have sunk by the tender law, and the depreciation, two... well improved plantations, worth £2500 specie, some thousands of acres of land, and a sum of money in debts," Chase stated.[31]

The tender act thus began to open a breach between Chase and Carroll. This one difference would not have destroyed their collaboration, but in 1777 the two also clashed over Chase's program for the suppression of internal enemies of the Revolution. In Chase's view the machinations of Tories were a major obstacle to a vigorous and successful war effort. Even if they did not actively support the British, the disloyalty and defeatism of the disaffected undermined the cause. Chase in his zeal for victory had little tolerance for those who were not wholeheartedly committed to America. Many of the measures he advocated were common in revolutionary America, but the total package was severe.

The first legislature in March 1777 joined battle over Chase's bill "to punish certain crimes and misdemeanors, and to prevent the growth of toryism." As passed by the House of Delegates, the bill provided penalties for a variety of offenses, from treason, sedition, and corresponding with the enemy to discouraging enlistments, acknowledging any dependence on England, trying to depreciate the currency, and spreading false news injurious to the cause. Of great importance in Chase's eyes was a test oath that could be administered to anyone suspected of disloyalty in order "to discover, if possible, our internal and secret enemies."

The Senate objected strongly to many parts of the bill. Carroll of Carrollton remarked that it would "create a great deal of rancour and ill blood in the State'' and endanger freedom of speech and of the press by its loosely drawn language. The test oath, in the opinion of the Senate majority, was ''not only improper, but contrary to the spirit of our declaration of rights;...no government has a right to dive into the secret thoughts of subjects conforming their conduct to the known laws of the state.'' Accordingly the Senate proposed a number of amendments, striking out the test oath and several other sections of the bill and defining other offenses more narrowly. After a lengthy exchange of messages the two houses agreed on a compromise version that prescribed a loyalty oath only for officeholders and lawyers, and for voters upon request. Carroll, Tilghman, and two other senators still opposed the bill.[32]

Chase remained convinced that a more effective test act was needed. In the June 1777 session the House of Delegates again passed such a bill, but the Senate rejected it. The delegates then ordered it printed for the consideration of their constituents.[33] Samuel Chase was taking his case to the people. Writing under the name of ''Rationalis'' in the *Maryland Gazette,* he urged public support for the test act.

The strong, independent Senate that Chase had helped to create in 1776 was proving an obstacle to his program, and Chase now began to argue that it, too, was bound by the instructions of the voters. When the two houses differed on any question, Chase told his readers,

> it remains *solely* with you to determine in favour of the one or the other. Both branches originate from you, and from you alone derive all their authority.... The senate are the *mediate,* and the house of delegates the immediate representatives of the people. They are both equally bound to speak your opinion, and to carry your will, when known, into execution. Each branch of your legislature is, and ought to be, perfectly free and independent of each other; both ought to be subject to, and dependent on you.

Chase thus abandoned the constitutional view of the Senate as a body of natural aristocrats exercising their own independent judgment. He applied to that body the idea that representatives were trustees or agents of their constituents, bound to obey their instructions, in which he had demonstrated his deep belief by resigning from the constitutional convention in 1776. Chase's revised view of the Senate's responsibility to the people remained consistent for the rest of his legislative career.

Having established the theoretical groundwork, Chase sought to convince his readers of the necessity of the test oath. He believed it was necessary to deal with two varieties of Tories. "The first artfully take care to...conform their *public* conduct" to the law while "with their poisonous doctrines they taint and corrupt the principles of our people." The second were the "neutrals" who took no stand. "The man who by his neutrality deserts the cause, is a traitor to his country," Chase asserted. As an illustration of the harm a neutral could do, Chase attacked (without naming him) Daniel Dulany, who had taken "the *appearance* of a neutrality, injurious to his native country, and infamous to himself." Chase was "satisfied that the inhabitants of this state would have been generally united, from the beginning, but from the fatal example of [this] one man."[34]

Chase's appeal to the people evoked no perceptible response, but in the next session the legislature passed a test act. The House of Delegates overrode Chase's wishes in one respect, providing that all adult males, not just those who fell under suspicion, be required to take an oath of loyalty to the state by March 1778. Refugee nonassociators who had fled the state since 1775 had until September 1779 to return and take the oath or incur the heavy penalties prescribed in the act, which included disfranchisement and payment of triple taxes for life.[35]

The conflict over the test act widened the breach between Chase and Carroll. The latter continued to oppose the act, admitting the "necessity of doing something to make all ranks [of] People take a more active part" in their country's struggle but doubting that the test oath would do the trick. "I have little reliance on such extorted oaths," Carroll told his father; "by all, who are really disaffected they will be deemed as imposed by violence and consequently not binding."[36] During the dispute over this question Chase and Carroll of Carrollton began for the first time seriously to question each other's motives. The Carrolls came to believe that Chase's main object was personal revenge against Daniel Dulany. In August 1777, after the appearance of the "Rationalis" article, Carroll sent Chase a note charging that "to hang or banish" Dulany, Chase "would even wound the Constitution, and endanger the Safety of the

State.'' The accusation was unjust. Whether wise or unwise, Chase's relentless pursuit of Tories and neutrals, including Dulany, stemmed from his zeal for an all-out prosecution of the War for Independence, not from personal hatred. If the cause would benefit, Chase would reverse his policy. In April 1778, just before official word of the French alliance arrived, he recommended to Governor Johnson a general pardon for all Loyalists, even those who had fought for the king, if they would renounce England and take the oath of allegiance. "I believe it would thin their Ranks, and detach their friends,'' he explained. "We know our People, [m]any of them, are desirous of quitting them.''[37]

Chase for his part became increasingly impatient with what he regarded as Carroll's obstruction of measures vital to the safety of the country. Carroll's opposition to the test act made him in Chase's eyes "the advocate of the disaffected, tories, and refugees.'' Chase later recalled that Carroll's "Conduct on the Test Act created a Coolness, and a Suspension of our Former Intercourse,'' which the developing clash over the tender act reinforced.[38] A powerful political alliance was beginning to break apart.

By the end of 1777 a substantial number of Chase's programs had been passed, including laws governing the militia and preventing engrossing as well as the test and tender acts. But the test act had encountered strong resistance, some military measures were unsatisfactory to Chase, and he was growing impatient with the opposition to his program. The climax came in the October 1777 session when Chase introduced a bill to confiscate the proprietary estates and make all quitrents payable to the state. Chase attached great importance to the bill as a means of shoring up the government and helping finance the war. To his dismay, John Hall backed an amendment to the bill to abolish the quitrents. Hall argued that Chase's bill would "put the whole expence of supporting and maintaining all the Officers of Government'' upon landowners, which "would be very unequal and therefore unjust.'' With the support of the Hammond-Ridgely faction and a number of other delegates, Hall's amendment was adopted.[39]

This galling defeat, very damaging in his eyes to the needs of the state, so disgusted Samuel Chase that he immediately resigned his seat in the legislature. In an open letter to Mayor Paca and his Annapolis constituents, Chase explained that he could be of no use to the state as long as a certain "baneful influence" was strong enough "to prevent the adopting effectual measures for the raising our quota of troops, or supporting our new government, with firmness, dignity and honour." "Chase is too impetuous," remarked Carroll of Carrollton, "and gives his adversaries by this a great advantage over him." One advantage those enemies did not gain: the delegates reconsidered and rejected the confiscation bill, leaving the quitrent question also unsettled.[40]

For a year and a half, until July 1779, Chase was not a member of the legislature. Though he readily admitted that "the house are wanting in Men of Abilities and business," he refused to run for his old seat unless Hall and John Brice declined to stand for reelection. Chase "often and publickly declared that I never would serve with him [Hall], and resigned for that cause alone, because I am still convinced from our diversity of Sentiments on political Questions I could render no essential service to my Country by being in the house with him, and because I am so desireous of being on good terms with Mr. Hall that I wish to remove all grounds of disagreement." Chase still respected his old law teacher as an individual, and in fact tried unsuccessfully to get Hall appointed chief justice of Maryland—an appointment that would have had the added advantage of removing him from the assembly. Later in the year a friend offered to mediate between Chase and Hall in order to achieve a reconciliation. Chase accepted with alacrity. Perhaps the mediation succeeded, for Hall still sat in the assembly when Chase returned to the House in 1779.

In the meantime Chase enjoyed some respite from his political labors, though he continued to serve in Congress until late 1778. He claimed to be "fixed as fate . . . to live in peace and quiet" and even toyed with the idea of leaving Maryland. Only partially successful in his legislative goals and under public attack from political foes who were beginning to claim that his bills served his own personal ends, Chase had suffered some loss of influence in Maryland. By 1778 he was able to take his legislative reverses philosophically, though he strongly resented the assaults on his integrity. While recognizing the sovereignty of the people, Chase never romanticized them. "Our people are the same with those of all other Countries," he told a friend. "They have neither more or less Virtue. The Conduct of the populace and of popular Assemblies is much oftener dictated by passion and prejudice than by Wisdom. Whim, humour or Caprice frequently influence their determinations. To this may be added that Republicks are seldom grateful. With these Sentiments why do you think I love Noise and Politicks?''[41] But love it he did. Politics, religion, the law, and his family were Samuel Chase's life.

Nine

BUSINESS AND POLITICS: THE FLOUR SCANDAL

HE 1770s brought repeated tragedy to the Chase family. Ann Birch Chase, second wife of the Reverend Thomas, died in 1772. "The same fatal furious Fever" that took her life also claimed the parson's eight-year-old son Tommy.[1] A widower for the second time, the elderly clergyman was left to raise his other four children alone.

With the Revolution came hard times for Thomas Chase. The Anglican establishment fell with the proprietary government, and clergymen no longer enjoyed tax support. Parson Chase was forced to turn schoolmaster to augment his income. Though he was a former Son of Liberty, Thomas Chase found it difficult to support independence. John Adams noted in 1777 that the reverend, "they say, is not so zealous a Whig as his son." Anglican clergymen owed allegiance to the king as head of the church as well as political sovereign; some hesitated to accept independence for that reason. But following the passage of the test act, Thomas Chase took the oath of allegiance to the new state in February 1778.[2]

The Reverend Thomas Chase died on April 4, 1779, at the age of seventy-six. By the parson's will his eldest son inherited a large responsibility and little else. The entire estate, including seven slaves, books, papers, and household goods, was put in Samuel Chase's hands for the use of his young half brothers and sisters, who came to live with Samuel in Annapolis. The newcomers fit in nicely with Samuel's own brood of four; of the parson's children, Ann was nearly fifteen, Elizabeth eleven, George Russel Birch nine, and Richard going on seven. For himself Samuel Chase received from his father's estate only a magnifying glass "as a small memorial of me."[3] A man of modest means, the reverend was obliged to provide first for the upbringing of his minor children. Samuel understood, and he accepted without hesitation the responsibility thrust upon him.

That responsibility was all the greater since by then Chase had probably lost his own wife Nancy. There is no record of the date of Ann Baldwin Chase's death, but indications are that she passed away some time between late 1776 and the winter of 1779. Ann's maiden sister Rebecca Baldwin ("Aunt Becky") remained in the household, helping care for the eight children who in 1779 ranged in age from sixteen to five. As of 1782 the Chase household in Annapolis included also six slaves (three adults and three children) and two free males over eighteen. That the Chases lived in style is indicated not only by the numbers of their domestic help but also by their possession of 268 ounces of plate. The total assessed value of Chase's Annapolis homestead came to £1134:13:4.[4]

While Chase lived well as always, the Revolution was creating financial difficulties for him. The disruption and temporary closure of the courts, coupled with Chase's heavy political duties, played havoc with his law practice. Between 1777 and 1781 Chase sold a number of tracts of land to raise money. He sustained losses on many of these transactions by accepting payment in depreciating paper currency under the tender act. "By the war I have sunk one third of all my property; a considerable sum I expended in the public service," Chase wrote in 1781.[5]

The need to mend his finances again forced Chase to look for new sources of income. His penchant for speculative ventures was well suited to the business atmosphere of the War for Independence. Chase's political position made him aware of state and congressional needs for supplies of all sorts. He had the connections to get state supply contracts if he could go into business for himself. As he saw it, he would be helping the war effort by supplying needed goods, while also advancing his own fortunes. Many prominent merchants of the day, such as Philadelphia's Robert Morris, closely intertwined business and politics with no thought of wrongdoing. Some contemporaries found such dealings improper, but Chase did not.

Chase's first business venture of the war was a partnership in a saltworks established by William Whetcroft in 1777. There was a serious shortage of salt in Maryland at that time, so the project appeared promising. Looking for investors, Whetcroft approached Chase's friend Allen Quynn, who agreed to become a partner on condition that Chase also be offered a share. Quynn acted as Chase's agent in overseeing their mutual interests. After considerable money had been invested, Quynn visited the saltworks and reported that it was not succeeding. In 1778 Whetcroft agreed to buy Chase's and Quynn's shares for £442:10 each, to be paid over the next ten years. A complex web of debts among the three, resulting from this and other sources, landed them in court in 1793.[6]

In May or June 1778 Chase launched his biggest business venture of the war years, a partnership for foreign trade with John and Thomas Dorsey of Baltimore under the name of John Dorsey and Company. John Dorsey was an experienced tobacco merchant. His cousin Thomas was the Continental Army's agent for purchasing provisions in Baltimore County.[7] The Dorseys supplied business expertise and undertook the day-to-day management of the new partnership. Chase's political knowledge and influence helped the firm establish a close relationship with the state government.

John Dorsey and Company did substantial business with the state of Maryland during the latter years of the war. The firm sold the state cloth, rum, and other goods for the use of the army and maintained a ropewalk that produced cordage for Maryland's naval vessels. The company purchased tobacco from the state for sale in the West Indies, from whence European goods and sugar were imported. On at least one occasion John Dorsey and Company entered into a contract to ship state-owned flour to Havana, with the profits of the voyage to be split evenly. The firm sent truce vessels to British-held New York, again in a partnership with the state that permitted the company to trade on its own account as well. The records of the governor and council indicate that John Dorsey and Company's business with the state was heaviest in late 1779 and 1780. During the first quarter of 1780 the state paid the company nearly £114,000 on account for goods purchased.[8]

Chase and his partners also engaged in privateering against British shipping, a risky but potentially rewarding business. Between 1779 and 1782 letters of marque were issued to thirteen ships owned by John Dorsey and Company. Guns and ammunition for the vessels were purchased from the state, which apparently had surplus naval equipment at the time. The hazards of the company's wartime ventures were brought home to Chase when the 319-ton ship *Matilda* was captured by a British frigate. After the war Chase tried to enlist the help of Benjamin Franklin in seeking compensation for the seizure.[9]

Chase later stated that the partnership of John Dorsey and Company was dissolved around December 1, 1780, but the records of the council indicate that the firm did business under that name into 1782. By then Chase and the Dorseys had formed a second company, Dorsey, Wheeler and Company, with Luke Wheeler as an added partner. Despite their government connections, neither firm prospered, at least not for long. Both were out of business by 1784, leaving the partners with large debts to pay.[10]

No contemporary, not even Chase's political enemies, questioned the propriety of the dealings between the two trading companies and the state of Maryland. One other venture of John Dorsey and Company, however, damaged Chase's career in 1778, produced his final break with Charles Carroll of Carrollton, and haunted him for the rest of his life. It was charged that Chase had disclosed to his partners a secret resolution of Congress in order to speculate in wheat and flour to the detriment of the public good. The incident was so important to Chase's reputation that it deserves to be explored in some detail.

In the summer of 1778 a shortage of wheat and flour developed in New England. The arrival in New England waters of a French fleet under the Count d'Estaing, coupled with the usual needs of the army, created an exceptionally large demand for provisions. Congress learned of the problem at the end of July and referred it to a committee for study. On August 24, pursuant to the committee's report, Congress directed the commissary general to purchase twenty thousand barrels of flour in Pennsylvania, Maryland, Delaware, and Virginia for shipment to New England.

Commissary General Jeremiah Wadsworth, arriving in Baltimore around the first of September to begin the purchases, found that the flour mills in the area were all engaged by private interests. Wadsworth complained to Congress that the resolution of August 24, which he said should have been a secret, was known in Baltimore before his arrival. Wadsworth's letter was referred to a committee, which recommended on October 2 that Congress should authorize the seizure of wheat and flour from anyone who appeared to have engrossed an extraordinary amount of those commodities. In the meantime, whether because of heavy public and private demand or because of currency depreciation and crop damage by insects, the price of wheat in Baltimore had risen substantially.

The principal buyer of wheat and flour in Baltimore in August and September 1778 was John Dorsey and Company. In early August, Chase advised his partners to begin buying those commodities in large amounts. The Dorseys were able to contract for seven thousand bushels of wheat at 15s. per bushel, and four hundred barrels of flour at prices of 40s. to £4. On October 24, after Congress authorized the seizure of wheat and flour, John Dorsey sold his purchase contracts to Deputy Commissary Ephraim Blaine at 22s. 6d. for the wheat and £3:2:6 to £5:10 for the flour.

The question was what interpretation should be placed upon these facts. Wadsworth, Henry Laurens, Congressman Henry Marchant of Rhode Island, and others concluded that Chase had used inside information he obtained as a congressman to speculate in flour at the expense of the public. By late fall it was widely reported that Chase had betrayed his trust by disclosing a secret resolution of Congress to his partners; that he had contrived to prolong the congressional committee's consideration of Wadsworth's letter in order to allow the Dorseys to complete their purchases; that Samuel Chase was a monopolizer and engrosser of necessary provisions, one of the lowest of sharpers in the Revolution's catalog of profiteers.

In Congress, Marchant confronted the Maryland delegates with the charge that one of them had disclosed the supposedly secret resolution of August 24. Chase sat silent while the other delegates present denied that they were responsible. In October and November, Alexander Hamilton, relying on information supplied by Wadsworth and Laurens, attacked Chase in three articles signed "Publius" in the *New York Journal*. Chase, said Hamilton, deserved

> to be immortalized in infamy....You have shown that America can already boast at least one public character as abandoned as any the history of past or present times can produce....The love of money and the love of power are the predominating ingredients of your mind—*cunning* the characteristic of your understanding. *This,* has hitherto carried you successfully through life....*It* has now proceeded one step too far, and precipitated you into measures, from the consequences of which, you will not easily extricate yourself; your avarice will be fatal to your ambition.[11]

Chase's transgression appeared all the more glaring to his critics because he had taken the lead in advocating Maryland's first law against forestalling and engrossing, passed in June 1777. The law attempted to restrain speculation by prohibiting the purchase of certain important commodities for resale. The act did not apply to wheat and flour, so that speculation in those items was not illegal in the summer of 1778, but Chase's critics considered his dealings inconsistent as well as unethical. And in November 1778 the legislature responded to Congress's call for the seizure of grain from engrossers with a new act authorizing the seizures and ordering engrossers of grain bound over for trial. The act recited that "the wicked arts of speculators, forestallers, and engrossers, who infest every part of the country, and are industriously purchasing up grain and flour at the most exorbitant prices, render it impracticable to obtain timely and sufficient supplies for the operations of the army and navy, unless the most vigorous measures are...adopted."[12]

Chase's response to the accusations was relatively subdued for a man of his fiery temperament. When in November 1778 the congressional delegates reported to the Maryland legislature on the state of Continental affairs, Chase offered to answer "*any questions,* any member should propose" relating to the reports circulating against him. No questions were asked. After seeing the "Publius" letters, Chase wrote the printer of the paper "that the publication was a false and malicious libel." He asked the identity of "Publius," which the printer refused to divulge. Apparently Chase never learned that Hamilton wrote the letters. On several other occasions Chase denied the charges against him in general terms, and in July 1779, following his reelection to the House of Delegates, he explained his side of the story in a speech to the citizens of Annapolis.[13]

Not until 1781, though, did Chase confront his accusers and put his defense in print. According to Chase, only the fact that he advised his partners to buy wheat and flour in August and September 1778 was true. Congress had not ordered the resolution of August 24 to be kept secret, and he had not disclosed it in any case. That he had delayed Congress's deliberations to allow his partners to complete their purchases was totally false.

The truth, Chase said, was that his decision to purchase grain was based not on confidential information but on "facts publicly known to every merchant in America." The wheat and flour shortage in New England was common knowledge in Philadelphia. It was likewise known that Count d'Estaing's fleet had taken a number of British prizes and was likely to capture more. Chase therefore advised his partners to buy wheat and flour to be sold to the French in exchange for prize vessels. "This scheme was not of my invention," Chase said; "not only private persons, but congress, wished to purchase prizes of the count...and the proposal to pay in flour was advantageous to this state, and most acceptable to the count, whose fleet would require two thirds as much flour as the American army." Chase had intended only a legitimate business deal; his purchases had had nothing to do with Congress's decision to buy grain for the army, nor had he intended to engross flour to drive up its price. The charges against him rested upon the "mere fact" of his transactions at the same time the army was purchasing grain.[14] On this last point at least, the facts sustain Chase. The evidence against him was purely circumstantial, however suspicious the circumstances were. No direct proof of Chase's breach of congressional trust or of his intention to engross was ever produced.

Nevertheless many contemporaries found the circumstantial evidence sufficient to convict Chase. On November 13, 1778, he lost the seat in Congress he had held since 1774. The legislature failed to reelect him "on the current report of his being a speculator." Chase never sat in Congress again. He was reelected in November 1781 and again in 1783 and 1784, but he did not accept or attend. After 1778 Chase became purely a state-level politician. From November

1778 to July 1779 he held no public office for the first time since 1764.

Among those who believed the reports of Chase's flour speculation was Charles Carroll of Carrollton. Already estranged from Chase, he did not ask his former friend for an explanation. Instead, when a Senate committee drew up instructions for the new congressmen in 1778, Carroll inserted a clause aimed at Chase: "Reports have circulated, much to the disadvantage of some of the delegates; they have been accused of combining with the monopolizers and engrossers of the necessaries of life, and sharing in iniquitous gain. The resolves of Congress...to check those pernicious practices, will lose much of their efficacy and force, while members of their own body, under the suspicion of the same guilt, are suffered to retain their seats in that assembly." The House of Delegates, where Chase still had many friends, struck out this section of the instructions. But in July 1779 the legislature overwhelmingly approved a law prohibiting the state's congressional delegates from engaging in trade for two years.[15]

Carroll's proposed instruction deeply offended Chase. Why had not Carroll asked him for an explanation before attacking him publicly? Surely Carroll owed Chase that much. "The malice of enemies may be forgiven," Chase later wrote, "but it requires some time to forget the ungenerous perfidious conduct of false friends." By December 1778 Chase and Carroll had cut off "all private intercourse" with each other.[16] Their political faction remained intact as a voting bloc on most issues, continuing to oppose the agrarian localists of the Hammond-Ridgely faction. But the conflict between Chase and Carroll was the more dramatic, though not the more fundamental, division in the legislature during the war years. On the limited range of issues over which Chase and Carroll clashed, their faction was sundered into sharply opposed camps.

Their next confrontation came in March 1779, when Chase remarked there were Tories, perhaps even a traitor, in the Senate. Called before the upper house to testify, Chase singled out five senators. He charged that Matthew Tilghman and Charles Carroll, Barrister in December 1776 and Daniel of St. Thomas Jenifer early in 1778 had favored negotiations with England. Samuel Wilson, despairing of victory in the war early in 1778, had suggested trying to make the best possible terms with England and was in Chase's view "a tory and a traitor." Thomas Jenings had been neutral in the war until lately.

The Senate, unimpressed by Chase's charges, postponed consideration of the matter until the next session. It then appeared that Chase's information was inaccurate as to Carroll and Tilghman and partially so as to Jenifer. Samuel Wilson had made the statements attributed to him, but the senators unanimously exonerated him of toryism. Jenifer believed that Chase had "made a poor figure" at the hearing, adding that Chase had "lost much ground, indeed in the opinion of all thinking men sunk even below contempt." What influence Chase still had, said Jenifer, he had retained "by keeping open house."[17]

Clearly Chase's definition of toryism was a broad one. Ardent and impulsive, Chase felt that anyone who faltered in support of the patriot cause was as good as an enemy. Despite the Senate's verdict, he continued to believe that the state's failure to support the war with proper vigor could be attributed to "Tories" in the legislature. In 1781 he wrote that, after the French alliance, "some who had openly, and others secretly opposed our independence, and many who had only acquiesced in the measures of America, commenced...flaming patriots....They *pretended* love of country, and resentment to Great Britain...when their *real* view was to obtain trust, office and power under the government." Could members of the House of Delegates who had "voted against every measure proposed...to raise men, or money, since the war" be patriots?[18] Chase considered the fainthearted, the reluctant revolutionaries, and late converts to the cause to be unworthy of public trust. Some of those people were his former political allies. Here was another source of dissension between Chase and some gentlemen of the old country party.

Even Charles Carroll of Carrollton, Chase came to believe, had "changed his political conduct, and published principles destructive of the freedom and independence of America." Both "in and out of congress he betrayed an unmanly fear of our success in the war." By opposing the test act Carroll "became the advocate of the disaffected, tories, and refugees."[19] Chase's suspicion of Carroll's "Tory" leanings was increased in 1779 when the two clashed over Chase's proposal for the confiscation of British property in Maryland.

After Chase's bill to confiscate the proprietary estates failed in 1777, the issue of confiscation did not come up again for two years. Chase was out of the legislature, and the test act gave absentee non-associators until September 1779 to return and take the oath of loyalty. Until that deadline passed, it would be difficult to define precisely which Maryland property owners were still British subjects. In the fall session of 1779, with the deadline past and Chase back in the lower house, the issue resurfaced. A committee chaired by Chase reported that a large new congressional requisition for funds could not be met without confiscating the property of all British subjects in the state.

The proposal was not novel; Congress had recommended confiscation in November 1777, other states were adopting it, and Chase's committee argued that it was justified under the rules of war. A confiscation bill passed the House of Delegates unanimously, but the Senate rejected it. The Senate majority was "not convinced of the justice of the bill, less of its policy, and least of all its necessity." The delegates resolved unanimously that the Senate had "prevented this House from complying with the Requisition of Congress" and called upon the voters to decide the issue by making their wishes known. Again Chase appealed to the sovereign people in an attempt to break the resistance of the Senate.[20]

This time the Senate and its supporters fought back. Carroll of Carrollton and other newspaper writers defended the Senate's independence and assailed the confiscation proposal. Carroll suggested that the purchasers of British property under Chase's bill would have been mostly speculators, since the property was to be sold quickly. He believed the property would have brought only a fraction of its value and the state would have benefited little. Another writer suggested that speculators might have framed the bill for their own benefit. Assuming correctly that these insinuations were directed at him, Chase took further offense.[21] After the flour scandal of 1778, his enemies imputed his every controversial move to motives of personal gain. Despite the increasingly pointed assaults on his character, however, Chase's influence in the House of Delegates was greater after 1779 than before.

Chase's appeal to the people did not move the Senate. Again in the March 1780 session it rejected a confiscation bill, though the proposal was now advanced in a different context. Congress, faced with the collapse of Continental paper currency, had just adopted a major financial reform. It asked the states to take the old Continental money out of circulation at a devalued rate of forty to one. A smaller quantity of new Continental currency was to be issued, and the states were asked to provide funds to support the value of the new bills. Chase now proposed to seize and sell British property for that purpose.[22]

After the confiscation bill failed again, the House of Delegates advanced another proposal for implementing Congress's currency reform. Chase and Kent County delegate Peregrine Leatherbury were chiefly responsible for writing into the bill several clauses to which the Senate objected. The most controversial was a pledge to redeem the state's paper money and loan office certificates at full face value, while accepting the devaluation of Continental money. Both currencies were circulating at about the same rate of depreciation, yet the delegates proposed to treat them quite differently. The Senate rejected this bill as well, complaining that the state should not assume the huge financial burden of redeeming its depreciated currency at par when the only beneficiaries would be speculators "who may have been so fortunate and long-sighted as to have got this kind of money at the depreciated value, for continental money, or otherwise." As usual the Senate had Chase in mind. "I have been informed that certain persons have been busily engaged in buying up our State certificates," wrote Carroll of Carrollton. Carroll added that Chase now ruled the House of Delegates "without controul: I believe a majority do not see into his schemes and views. The acts of that branch...respecting money-matters seem calculated to answer his particular contracts and interests." In May 1780 Carroll told his father that Chase was "the most prostitute scoundrel, who ever existed."[23]

Though Chase denied ever having purchased state currency, it appears that he did try to acquire Maryland paper money while the currency reform bill was under consideration. Frederick County sheriff Christopher Edelen reported that Chase's friend Thomas Dorsey told him "he had received a letter from a friend of his, desiring him to get a sum of [state] convention money." Dorsey gave Edelen about $4,000 in Continental money, which he was to exchange for state currency. Soon afterward, though, it became known in Frederick that the assembly proposed to devalue Continental and prop up state paper. Public disapproval of Dorsey's transactions caused Edelen to call off the deal and return Dorsey's Continental currency. Chase's response to Edelen's charge was unconvincing. He declared in 1781 that, while he had never purchased convention money, he saw nothing morally or politically wrong with such transactions. Tacitly admitting the accuracy of Edelen's account, Chase wrote that it contained "not one word of a purchase of convention money, and a proposal to *exchange* is called. . .a *speculation*."[24]

Chase's effort to support the face value of Maryland currency failed. In the October 1780 session the legislature passed an act devaluing and calling in both state and Continental money at forty to one. Chase was disgusted at this turn of events. He termed the devaluation of state currency "an unnecessary and wanton violation" of the state's "plighted faith; dictated by passion, party, and faction. . . . At once all confidence in our government was pulled up by the roots." This act, Chase claimed rather simplistically, was responsible for the depreciation of the state's later currency issues.[25] He did not object to the repeal of the 1777 tender act, which accompanied the currency reform.

Chase's goal of confiscating British property fared better in the end. Confiscation was adopted in January 1781 when the state failed in an attempt to recover its stock in the Bank of England. The colonial government had purchased the stock to furnish solid backing for its paper currency and by 1775 owned some £29,000 worth. In 1779, when the 1766 currency issue was due to be retired, the legislature called upon its London trustees to sell the stock and remit the proceeds. Their repeated refusal to do so finally moved the Senate to accept confiscation of British property, excepting debts due to Englishmen and the property of "neutral" Loyalists who had remained in Maryland, on the principle of retaliation.[26]

Incessant attacks on Chase's character and motives continued to accompany the legislature's deliberations, and finally Chase's friends began to strike back. In November 1780 Delegate James Hindman of Talbot County "was called to the Bar [of the House] for speaking freely of the public Character of Mr. Chase and other Members in a Tavern." The House voted to censure Hindman, and he was excluded from the assembly for nearly two weeks when he refused to make an apology in the form the delegates demanded.[27]

Thus far Chase himself had responded to the charges against him only with general denials, his Annapolis speech explaining his side of the flour scandal, and his letter to the New York printer denying the allegations of "Publius." Carroll considered his failure to defend himself more aggressively to be further proof of his guilt. "To the assembly I was always ready and desirous to render an account of my public trust," Chase explained in 1781; "general slanders, and the authors of them, I ever did and shall despise, having learned that the best way to overcome calumny is steadily to persevere in such conduct as my mind and judgment approved, and to neglect and contemn any consequences which might happen." Therefore "I was silent, and would not gratify my enemies so far as even to complain."[28]

In May 1781 Chase finally changed his policy. A new Senate was to be elected in September, and Chase decided to take the offensive in order to persuade the voters and the electoral college to remove from the upper house "men, who have violated our public faith, and fomented quarrels and divisions." Chase published four articles signed "Censor" in the *Maryland Gazette* in May and June. The first two attacked the Senate for forcing the devaluation of Maryland currency, undermining in Chase's view any chance of financial stability. The third argued that "the true source of all the discord" between the two houses was the treatment of "our British enemies, and our refugees, and tories. The house of delegates urged a test to discriminate our enemies, and penalties on the absentees, and a confiscation of their property. The senate and their advocates, aided by all the disaffected, non-jurors and tories, were for moderate measures."

The fourth "Censor" article claimed that Tory machinations were especially outrageous in the treatment accorded a certain faithful public servant. "He devoted his youth, gave up his profession, and greatly injured his private fortune, for the public service. He bestowed his time and labour and sacrificed his domestic felicity to his public station." And what was his reward? Chase proceeded to enumerate the "infamous slanders" heaped upon him by "calumniators and villains" who "dare not attempt to support them."[29]

Upon reading the first three "Censor" letters, Carroll of Carrollton remarked that Chase "has exposed Himself to be severely

Handled and I hope some One will undertake it." The final article provoked Carroll to answer Chase himself. Chase replied, and at last the public was given a full exposition of the positions of both men on all their differences since 1777, centering on the flour scandal.[30]

Having aired their differences, Chase and Carroll were ready to let the matter rest, but General John Cadwalader was not. A prominent Pennsylvanian who had married into the wealthy Lloyd family of Maryland's Eastern Shore, Cadwalader won election to the legislature in 1780. He quickly emerged as an ally of Carroll's and one of Chase's most unrestrained detractors. In 1780 Cadwalader wrote Carroll that Chase's design was "to amass a fortune, from the robbery of private persons as well as the public—he has no feeling—nor does he seem to be held in that contempt that a gentleman would be, in the best company—He seems to be a licenced person, who is suffered to roam at large."[31]

Late in 1781, after the newspaper exchange between Chase and Carroll, Cadwalader rose in the House of Delegates to charge that that body had been strangely reluctant to investigate the charges against Chase. Cadwalader complained that Chase had just been reelected to Congress when, if the allegations against him were true, he should instead have been banished from the state. On January 11, 1782, Cadwalader introduced a resolution for Chase's recall from Congress, citing his alleged breach of trust in the flour scandal. The House ordered that any charge Cadwalader wished to make be laid before it in writing, and Cadwalader complied.[32]

Cadwalader's formal charge of breach of congressional trust against Chase led to a hearing in the House of Delegates on January 15 and 16. A number of witnesses were examined, but none could support Cadwalader's charges with more than vague hearsay and circumstantial evidence. The delegates resolved by a vote of thirty-six to two "that the charge aforesaid, in the opinion of this house, is not true, and that Mr. Chase was not guilty of a breach of his duty, as a member of congress, by revealing a secret resolve of that assembly." Only Cadwalader and his kinsman James Lloyd voted against the resolution.[33] On the basis of the evidence given at the hearing the delegates decided correctly; not guilty or at least not proven was the only reasonable verdict. At last Chase stood vindicated in the flour scandal insofar as a rather hasty public inquiry could repair the damage already done to his reputation.

Shortly before the hearing Chase lashed back at Cadwalader in the first of two articles signed "Censor" in the *Maryland Gazette*. "You have given no quarter, and shall have none," Chase warned savagely. Assailing both Cadwalader's character and his stands on many issues in the assembly, Chase charged that Cadwalader was in league with the Tories. One of Cadwalader's charges against him Chase defiantly confirmed: he did believe "that our present government is not competent to the war"; he had declared that of necessity "he would not take the constitution as his rule in the formation of laws, *during the war*"; and he did believe that "a military government is necessary to maintain our liberties" in time of actual invasion of the state.[34] Cadwalader in reply repeated all the instances in which Chase had supposedly used his political position for his own gain and detailed his case for Chase's guilt in the flour scandal.[35]

In the meantime, shortly after the lower house hearing, "a mutual Friend" arranged a surprise meeting between Chase and Carroll of Carrollton in the hope of reconciling the two. Chase and Carroll exchanged letters for the next month, ultimately agreeing (in Chase's words) "that there is an immense Interval between Enmity and Friendship. We both express a Wish to avoid the first, and neither desire the latter."[36]

The personal truce between Chase and Carroll could succeed because for three years after 1782 they were in general agreement on the major issues confronting the state. Chase was not alone in believing the government inadequate to the challenges it faced. In Maryland as in Congress, the last years of the War for Independence brought a move to strengthen government and to rationalize its administrative functions for greater effectiveness. While Congress was creating executive departments and installing Robert Morris as superintendent of finance, the Chase and Carroll factions in Maryland worked together to create the office of intendant of the revenue.

The intendancy was Chase's idea. Adopted with exceptionally broad support in the legislature in January 1782, Chase's plan created an officer with sweeping power over the state's financial affairs. The intendant of the revenue was to manage the state's funds, decide which of its bills should be paid if all could not be met, oversee the collection of taxes and the sale of confiscated British property, and prepare a rough budget for the legislature. He was expected to bring order and system to Maryland's fiscal affairs. The office was created for a period of one year, but was annually renewed with some modification until 1786. Daniel of St. Thomas Jenifer was named intendant in the original bill and continued to serve until the post was abolished.[37]

Until 1782 Jenifer had been one of Chase's critics, but his appointment as intendant began a rapprochement between the two. Not only did Chase and Jenifer share a common interest in Maryland's fiscal stability, but Jenifer's power over confiscated property and Chase's growing interest in it also brought them together.

There is no evidence beyond the allegations of his enemies that Chase proposed confiscation with his own benefit in mind, but once the measure was adopted Chase plunged eagerly into the purchase of confiscated property. It was an irresistible opportunity to acquire choice lands and business investments. Many other prominent politicians and gentlemen were investing in British property, but Chase was one of the largest purchasers. Again, as in his first land acquisitions in 1762–1764, Chase plunged ahead, counting on future gains to provide the means of payment. His law practice was reviving, and income from the property he bought should help pay for it, but Chase still purchased beyond the limits of prudence.

Chase bought most of his confiscated property in 1781 and 1782, when sales were heaviest. By the end of 1785 he had purchased more than £6,000 worth of property in his own name, including lots in Annapolis and Baltimore and household goods and books from the home of Lloyd Dulany. In addition, Chase held a one-fourth interest in the £625 purchase of Chase, Martin, Ridgely, and Chase. He had a one-eighth share in Charles Ridgely and Company, which made purchases totaling over £47,000, and the same interest in Samuel Norwood and Company, which invested nearly £8,000.

Charles Ridgely and Company and Samuel Norwood and Company were identical in membership. Their purchases put Chase in the iron-making business. Between them the two companies acquired the property of the Nottingham Iron Works—land, furnaces, forges, mills, slaves, and equipment.[38] Captain Ridgely, an experienced iron maker, had the knowledge to run the new acquisition. Thus Chase became a business partner of one of the leaders of his political opposition, an arrangement that was not without political ramifications.

Like most transactions in confiscated property, Chase's purchases were made on credit, the terms varying with the purposes for which the assembly had appropriated the proceeds. Three commissioners conducted the sales, which were generally at public auction, under the supervision of the intendant of the revenue. In 1781 and 1782 bidding was often spirited, resulting in high sale prices. That was where Chase's and Ridgely's connections came in handy. Besides their power in the legislature, Chase was building a helpful relationship with Jenifer, and Chase's partner Thomas Dorsey was clerk to the commissioners for the sale of confiscated British property. These contacts on occasion enabled Chase to arrange private sales of property he was interested in, bypassing public auctions and holding the price down. In 1782 Chase wrote Ridgely, ''I think with you it would be best to delay the Sale of the lands, We want. I do propose to have the Sale referred till after the Assembly meets, and then to obtain a power for the Commissioners to sell it at private sale, for not less than the assessment.''[39]

There was also another way to reduce the cost of British property. As of 1781 the state accepted Maryland paper money in payment for confiscated property only at the prevailing rate of depreciation. If the assembly could be persuaded to order the currency accepted at face value, the purchasers' real debts could be considerably reduced. Resolutions to that effect were introduced in the assembly as early as December 1781. The first attempts were defeated, but in 1783 limited success was achieved. As Maryland paper money became an object of speculation among purchasers of confiscated property, it began to go out of circulation. Chase voted for the resolutions to accept currency at par for British property, but there is no direct evidence of his further involvement in currency speculation.[40] The financial strain imposed by his purchases of confiscated property was an ever-present factor in Samuel Chase's plans during the 1780s. That burden, coupled with the collapse of his mercantile partnership with the Dorseys, had put him in a ''rather embarrassed'' financial position by 1783.[41]

After 1778 Samuel Chase had begun to mix business and politics. It was not an uncommon combination in his day, but it left him open to charges of corruption and manipulation by his political enemies. There is no doubt that Chase did use his political position to further his personal business interests. He manipulated sales of confiscated property, and he attempted to purchase state currency in Frederick in 1780. Beyond those episodes, though, the evidence consists mostly of the allegations of Chase's adversaries and his own replies, and it is difficult to arrive at the truth. If Chase was not entirely innocent of the accusations hurled at him, it is equally clear that some of his opponents would use any pretext to discredit him. Charges of corruption against Chase must therefore be viewed with some skepticism.

One apparent example of a distorted accusation thrown at Chase occurred in 1783. The governor and council agreed with Dorsey, Wheeler and Company to export a cargo of grain and flour to British-occupied New York under a flag of truce. A stated portion of the sale proceeds of the cargo was to be used to buy clothing for Maryland soldiers being held prisoner in New York. On the way north, the ship was seized by a Rhode Island vessel and taken as a prize to Newport on the theory that it was illegally trading with the enemy. The Maryland executive promptly sent a strong protest to Rhode Island's governor informing him of the legitimacy of the voyage. Nevertheless Chase was accused then and later in the Maryland papers of using a sham truce device to mask a profitable trade with the enemy.[42]

Perhaps James McHenry's later comment on Chase's real and alleged use of his political position for his own gain is as just an estimate as any: "If some of his conduct procured him enemies, whatever might have been exceptionable in it was greatly exaggerated at the moment by the zeal of patriotism which makes no allowance for human situations, and afterwards by persons who seem to me to have been always more intent upon removing obstructions to their own advancement than in...doing justice to the merits of competitors."[43]

Ten

LONDON INTERLUDE: THE BANK STOCK CASE

EGARDLESS of the ebb and flow of Chase's political fortunes, his reputation as a lawyer continued to grow. By the later 1770s, if not before, he was taking on eager young law students of his own. Most sought him out, but that was not always the case. Mindful of his own past and naturally generous, Chase was willing to extend a helping hand to a poor boy who displayed a bent for the law. He proved an excellent judge of raw legal talent.

Chase's most famous discovery was a youth named William Pinkney. Early in 1783 Chase was invited to attend a meeting of a young men's debating club in Baltimore. Pinkney made a presentation at the meeting, and Chase was greatly impressed with him. Talking with Pinkney afterward and finding that he was without means, Chase not only encouraged him to take up the study of law but also offered him "the benefit of his library, his instruction, and his table." Pinkney began to study in Chase's office that same year, and in 1786 he was admitted to the bar. A distinguished career as a lawyer, politician, and diplomat lay ahead of him. Among Chase's other students were Hugh Henry Brackenridge, an author and later a Pennsylvania supreme court justice, and Kensey Johns, who became chief justice of Delaware.[1]

As his students became more numerous, Chase at some time before 1796 drew up a detailed course of study for them. Chase's curriculum reveals that his view of a proper legal education was a broad one, embracing history, politics, geography, rhetoric, logic, and philosophy as well as the law. Chase explained that a lawyer needed "classical attainments [to] enlarge the ideas, refine the understanding, and embellish the style." While acquiring this broad background, the student would also be acquainting himself with the law of nature and with its practical embodiment "in the Laws of Imperial Rome." The student next took up the laws of the United States and of Maryland, tracing the legal principles of his country to their origins. Special pleading and other technical skills rounded out the course, along with practical observation of the law in action through attendance at court. Upon completion of this rigorous program, Chase's law students would have the skills of the generalist that every successful American lawyer had to be: "a skilful attorney, sollicitor, and proctor; an able special pleader; an expert draftsman; a ready conveyancer; a learned counsellor; and a Judicious speaker." The entire course took five years to complete. It is interesting that Chase carefully divided his course of study into morning and afternoon reading. The more difficult and technical volumes were scheduled for the morning, the less demanding for later in the day. This arrangement seems to have reflected Chase's own work habits.[2]

There were times when Chase's law students had to get along on their own with little or no help from their mentor, though cousin Jeremiah Townley Chase may have been available to consult with them. One of those occasions arose in 1783, when Chase was called upon to undertake a foreign mission for the state that, as it turned out, required all of his legal skill. Samuel Chase was going to London to recover Maryland's stock in the Bank of England.

The bank stock, as noted, had been purchased with tax funds by the proprietary government to support the value of its paper money. The new state government had failed in its efforts to draw upon the stock during the War for Independence, a failure that helped produce the confiscation of British property. The conclusion of peace with England seemed to remove the major obstacle to recovery of the stock, and the legislature in its April 1783 session passed an act appointing an agent to receive the bank stock from the colonial government's London trustees and sell it for the benefit of the state. Accumulated dividends having been reinvested in additional stock, Maryland's holdings now totaled £43,000 face value and considerably more in market value, for the shares sold at well above par.[3] Such a sum would go far toward paying Maryland's sizable war debt.

As the assembly had undoubtedly anticipated, Governor William Paca and his council (which included Jeremiah Townley Chase) appointed Samuel Chase as the state's agent. Chase accepted, partly from a sense of public duty and partly because the mission offered him a chance to rebuild his own finances. If successful, he was to receive a generous commission of 4 percent of the amount recovered, which would come to well over £2,000 sterling. There was a substantial risk involved, however, for the legislature provided that the agent would receive nothing, not even his expenses, in the event of failure. But Chase, ever sanguine about his future prospects, was more than willing to take that chance. He had wanted to visit Europe after the war anyway.[4] To go with the fair hope of extricating both himself and his state from financial embarrassment was an opportunity not to be neglected.

Chase set sail for England in August 1783, accompanied by William Quynn, son of his close friend Allen Quynn. This young man was a medical student who wished to complete his studies in Edinburgh. Chase's mission provided the perfect opportunity for the youth to be seen safely across the ocean, at the same time giving Chase a familiar companion on the crossing.

Chase and Quynn landed at Dover after a pleasant voyage of twenty-six days. Then, proceeding at a leisurely pace, they stopped to see Dover Castle and the sights of Canterbury on the way to London. Arriving there on September 7, they attended an evening of plays at the Haymarket Theatre before Quynn went on his way to Scotland, leaving Chase to begin negotiations with the bank stock trustees. However pleasant the long trip may have been, its rigors had their effect on Chase. He fell ill for a time soon after he reached London.[5]

Despite his illness, Chase promptly wrote to Maryland's trustees demanding that they transfer the bank stock to him. The trustees—Sylvanus Grove, Osgood Hanbury, and James Russell, all prominent London merchants with ties to the old proprietary government of Maryland—were in no hurry to comply. Chase waited for months while they talked to one another and consulted their attorneys. The new year brought the death of Hanbury on January 4, leaving full control of the stock with the remaining trustees. Only in February 1784 could Chase begin serious negotiations with them, and the talks proved frustrating in the extreme.

By February, Sylvanus Grove was willing to transfer the bank stock to Chase; the real obstacle was James Russell. Elderly and crotchety, Russell had suffered greatly as a result of the American Revolution. Maryland had confiscated property of Russell's that he estimated to be worth at least £15,000 sterling. The greatest of Russell's losses was his one-third interest in the Nottingham Iron Works in Baltimore County. Russell was undoubtedly aware that Chase not only had led the fight for confiscation but also had been one of the purchasers of the Nottingham property, and that knowledge surely did not improve his disposition toward the Maryland agent. Russell contended that his property had been confiscated not under the general provisions of a law applying to all British subjects but specifically in retaliation for his earlier refusal to surrender the bank stock during the war. The wording of the Maryland confiscation act lent at least superficial credence to his claim. Chase's explanations of the act could not convince Russell to the contrary. Russell demanded compensation for his losses from the bank stock before he would transfer the remainder to Chase. He also wanted assurances that he would be allowed to collect prewar debts owed to him in Maryland, as the peace treaty of 1783 guaranteed. Apparently those debts represented most of Russell's remaining assets.

Russell's obstinacy put Chase in a most difficult position. The quickest solution would have been to accede to Russell's demand for compensation, thus securing most of the stock and returning home with rather more than half a loaf. But Chase had been explicitly directed by the governor and council not to compromise. He was authorized, though, to accept part of the stock if the state's claim to the remainder was preserved. That is what he now sought to do. Chase's negotiations with Russell in the late winter of 1784 revolved around the possibility of leaving £12,000 of stock in trust pending a resolution of Russell's claim, while releasing the remainder to Chase immediately. Several times an understanding seemed within grasp, but always Russell's suspicion that his interests would not be sufficiently protected prevented Chase from concluding a firm agreement. Limited in action by his instructions and frustrated by Russell's inflexibility, Chase nevertheless persisted in his increasingly discouraging task.

The annoying delays that Chase encountered gave him plenty of time to see the sights of London, to renew old acquaintances and make new ones. At least Chase was not all alone in a strange city. London contained a number of former Marylanders, many of whom Chase had known before the Revolution. In fact, he found lodging in the household of William Deards, who had been a business agent for the Carrolls in the days when Chase and Carroll of Carrollton were on close terms. In his letters home Chase commented appreciatively on the kindness of Mr. and Mrs. Deards toward him. From another former Marylander, Edmund Jenings, Chase borrowed £200 sterling to meet the mounting expenses of a trip that was taking much longer than anticipated.[6]

Chase received many callers at the Deards residence, among them former governor Horatio Sharpe. There was some awkwardness at first between the two old political adversaries, but Chase and Sharpe had never allowed their differences to stand in the way of friendship. The "old time cordiality" soon revived as Sharpe inquired eagerly about old friends in Maryland. Homesick Loyalist refugees came too. One of them was Major Walter Dulany, son of Chase's one-time antagonist, who had served in the British army during the war. Dulany wanted to consult Chase about the advisability of returning the Maryland. Chase urged Dulany to go back.[7] Unrelenting in his suppression of Tories during the War for Independence, Chase did not hold personal grudges after a political battle was over. Loyalist refugees like Dulany were no longer dangerous enemies. Now they were simply unfortunate human beings, depressed in spirit and often in fortune as well. Another Dulany relative whom Chase befriended was forced to admit (despite his inability to forgive Chase for past injuries) that Chase had "a native generosity of spirit."[8] That spirit now reached out, even to the Dulanys, to heal the wounds of civil war.

It appears likely, too, that Chase came into contact with Henry Harford, the young heir to the proprietorship of Maryland. Harford intended to seek compensation from the state for his confiscated estates, and Chase probably agreed to help him. His motive in this case may have been the hope of personal reward rather than concern for Harford; at any rate, some in Maryland had expected Chase and Harford to reach a mutually advantageous understanding even before the former set out for England.[9]

Samuel Chase had relatives as well as old acquaintances in England. Now for the first time he met his English cousins. One of them, the son of his uncle Samuel, wanted to go to America to seek his fortune. Chase helped the young man on his way with a letter of introduction to the Dorseys in Baltimore. "You will also speak to him," Chase urged his cousin Jeremiah Townley Chase in Annapolis. "I doubt not of your Civility to our Relation tho poor....My Daughter will be kind to him. If he should want four or five Guineas let him have them."[10]

Especially gratifying to Chase was the opportunity to rub elbows with some of England's most accomplished lawyers and politicians. He met William Pitt, Charles James Fox, and Lord Buchan, made friends with the rising young lawyer Thomas Erskine, and spent a memorable week as the guest of Edmund Burke at Beaconsfield. Once at the theater he saw the royal family, describing their appearance and dress in observant detail in a journal kept for his family that has since disappeared. The simple republican from Maryland clearly enjoyed seeing the pomp and magnificence of royalty. In fact, he was quite taken with England in general, reportedly speaking of the Old Country "in Raptures" upon his return to America.[11]

The only unpleasant part of Chase's stay in London, aside from the frustration of his mission, was his separation from home and family. Already, only a month after his arrival, Chase wrote that he was "wretched at my absence from all I love in this World." To add to his anxiety, Chase learned that his thirteen-year-old half brother, George Russel Birch Chase, intended to leave home and go to sea. "Tell him to learn Navigation, and Geography, and then he may begin his adventure," Chase wrote home; otherwise "I will never notice him again."[12] Perhaps Chase did not intend this threat to be taken at face value; certainly he would have found it very hard to carry out.

Thoughts of his beloved family were never far from Chase's mind. The ladies at home had not neglected the opportunity to send their shopping lists with him to London. Dutifully Chase searched the stores to fulfill their desires. His purchases were sent back across the Atlantic, along with a typical Chase extravagance: "One Chariott Compleat," no doubt of the latest design and finest quality.[13]

The dangers of an Atlantic crossing being what they were, Chase also had to face "the possibility that it may not please God to permit me to return to you." Moved by that somber but realistic thought, Chase late in his stay addressed a letter to his children containing his "last advice" should he not get home. He urged them to get a good education, "always remembering that time is precious and once lost can never be recalled, that life is short, and improperly applied is a neglect of duty to your God, your country, family and friends." Daughter Nancy should apply herself to reading, needlework, "domestic knowledge," dancing, and music, modeling herself after "Aunt Becky" Baldwin and "Mrs. Chase." The boys, Sammy and Tommy, were exhorted to pursue the usual male education of classical studies, history, geography, philosophy, rhetoric, and mathematics, along with French, dancing, and fencing. Chase hoped that his sons would follow their father's footsteps in the law but recommended "the business of a merchant" if they lacked the ability or inclination for legal studies.

"I advise you never to accept an office under government, or a seat in the legislature or council," Chase continued, "unless you are fully convinced that your services are really necessary to promote the good of your country. Never seek to acquire power or property from a public station." Was Chase thinking of the pitfalls into which he himself had fallen in the last few years? Finally, "the first object you are to learn and never forsake is your duty to God and man without which anything else is useless. The duties of religion and morality are never to be dispensed with....Follies I may excuse, but certain vices I will never pardon, such as impiety, gaming and drinking, and as you desire my affection avoid all low company of both sexes."[14] Here was the parson's son speaking, revealing a religious commitment as strong now as in his youth.

The "Mrs. Chase" to whom Samuel referred in his advice to Nancy was probably Mrs. Jeremiah Townley Chase, who seems to have been thus imperfectly identified in some earlier correspondence. But it may also have been the new second wife that Chase had just taken in London. Samuel Chase was married on March 3,

1784, to Hannah Kitty Giles, daughter of Samuel Giles, a physician of Kentbury, Berks. The bride was twenty-five, a woman of good family, sound education, and a forceful personality. Only the bare fact of their marriage is known; there is no reliable evidence of how they met, and the surviving record is entirely silent concerning their life together in London.[15] The children at home in Maryland must have looked forward nervously to meeting a new mother whom they had never seen. And Aunt Becky can be excused if she was apprehensive at the prospect of surrendering the management of the household—and perhaps the security of her place in it—to this unknown Englishwoman.

A few weeks after the wedding, Samuel Chase encountered yet another obstacle to his recovery of the bank stock. Late in March he learned that Russell had filed suit in the Court of Chancery against Chase, Grove, and the Bank of England. Russell wanted the court to grant him compensation from the bank stock for his losses in Maryland and to enjoin transfer of the stock in the meantime.[16]

Chase continued to negotiate with Russell, but with an increasing sense of futility. Retaining English counsel, he responded to Russell's suit by initiating a countersuit of his own. The complexity of the case grew as some of Russell's partners in the Nottingham Iron Works intervened with the claim that they, too, were entitled to compensation out of the bank stock funds.[17] Chase's mission had turned into a nightmare of litigation, and Maryland's unhappy agent had no assurance that his state would reimburse him for the mounting expenses he was incurring on its behalf.

The Court of Chancery took its first action on the case in June, when it ordered the bank stock turned over to its accountant general. That officer would hold the stock in trust until the issue was decided. Chase was content with this decision; at least Russell no longer had direct control over the bank stock, which was all to the good. Promptly Chase asked the court to release to him all the stock above the value of the claims made against it. To his dismay, the Lord Chancellor raised a new objection: Did the *state* of Maryland really have any right at all to bank stock once owned by the *colony* of Maryland, an entity that no longer existed? The implications of the chancellor's question were alarming. If the state was not a legal successor to the colony, the stock would revert to the English Crown ''as the property of a defunct corporation.'' The court thought that His Majesty's attorney general should have a chance to enter the case before proceedings went any further.[18]

Chase's attempts at out-of-court maneuvering over the next few weeks proved as fruitless as his previous efforts. Seeing no chance of speedy progress, he instructed his English counsel to conduct a holding action while he returned home to consult the authorities at Annapolis. Chase left England in mid-August 1784, bringing his only trip to Europe to an unsatisfying conclusion.

Chase's decision to return to Maryland proved to be a wise one. He could have accomplished nothing by remaining in London. The case dragged on interminably, becoming even more complicated as yet other parties intervened. Chase, in conjunction with Maryland's executive board and occasionally the assembly, continued to direct the state's strategy throughout the protracted controversy. Finally in 1797 the Lord Chancellor ventured an opinion that the bank stock belonged to the king, who could, of course, honor such claims against it as he wished. But the chancellor declined to execute his opinion, leaving the whole matter still in litigation.

By that time it had become clear that the issue was more a political than a legal one. The bank stock case had become entangled with the larger question of the payment of prerevolutionary debts owed by Americans to Englishmen and the resolution of American claims against England. The settlement of mutual claims between the two nations was a matter for diplomacy. United States minister to England Rufus King took up Maryland's cause. Chase's protégé William Pinkney, now an American representative on the joint claims commission in London, contributed his efforts as well. It was fitting that Pinkney had the satisfaction of repaying his benefactor Samuel Chase by achieving a final settlement of the bank stock case in 1804. Maryland got most of the stock, with the rest going to pay several English claimants, and inevitably, the lawyers. The stock had continued to increase in value as the Bank of England prospered and dividends were reinvested, and in the end Maryland realized around £140,000 from its sale. Samuel Chase received in 1804 a commission amounting to nearly £6,500. There remained a question as to whether certain expenses of the case should be assumed by the state or deducted from a small additional commission payment which Chase had yet to receive. That question resulted in a lawsuit by Chase against the state, which he finally won in December 1810. Thus the bank stock case and its aftermath occupied some of Chase's time and attention for all but a few months of the rest of his life.

Final success, however, was nowhere in sight as Chase set sail for home in August 1784. Had it been in his nature, Chase would have been justified in entertaining some apprehensions about his own future on the long voyage. There would be no commission in the foreseeable future to help him pay for his investments in confiscated property and rebuild his shrunken estate. The expenses of the trip merely compounded his financial problems. To be sure, he had found a bride in London, and Hannah Kitty could be expected to bring him a happiness far more valuable than money. But what kind of future could he give her and the large family in Annapolis if his fortunes did not soon improve? Samuel Chase probably put such thoughts firmly out of his mind, trusting as always that tomorrow would provide the means of meeting tomorrow's bills.

Eleven

THE PAPER MONEY
MOVEMENT

AMUEL CHASE returned from England to a country vibrant with activity as Americans sought to overcome the problems and exploit the possibilities of independence. In Maryland a number of plans were being advanced to promote the future development of the state. Chase joined enthusiastically in the spirit of improvement and became a leader in several projects. Improving the navigation of the Potomac, promoting education, restoring tax support for religion, and putting the state's finances in order were among the major objectives of Chase and his political allies at the November 1784 legislative session.

The major project for economic growth and development that concerned Chase was the navigation of the Potomac. The chief promoter of this venture was George Washington, who had long been impressed with the potentialities of the river as a trade route connecting the seaboard with the Ohio Valley. If the Potomac could be opened to navigation from the Great Falls near present-day Georgetown westward to Fort Cumberland and a good road built from there to the head of navigation on the Ohio system, the river might become a major artery of western commerce.

In December 1784 Washington and a Virginia delegation arrived in Annapolis to lobby for the scheme. The Virginians were armed with a study which estimated that the necessary work of dredging the Potomac's channel and building a canal around the Great Falls could be done in two years at the moderate cost of $92,000. The Maryland legislature appointed Chase to a committee to confer with the Virginians. The result was a plan for a company funded by both states as well as private investors to do the work in the expectation of profiting from tolls on river traffic. Chase helped draft an authorization bill for the Maryland assembly, and Virginia soon adopted a similar measure. The Potomac Company began operations in 1785 with Washington as president. Chase bought a share of stock in the company for £100 sterling. He was not involved in its management, but Washington did rely on him to procure modifications of its authority from the Maryland legislature in 1785. Unfortunately for all concerned, the project proved vastly more difficult than expected. The Potomac Company's hopes were not realized during Chase's lifetime, although its limited successes did aid the commercial growth of the upper Potomac Valley.[1] Chase's substantial investment in the scheme only added to his financial embarrassment.

The Potomac project made it more important than ever that Virginia and Maryland settle questions of jurisdiction and navigation on Chesapeake Bay and the Potomac and Pocomoke rivers. As early as 1777 Chase had been appointed to a Maryland commission to deal with these matters, but nothing was accomplished. Virginia revived the issue in 1784, and both states appointed commissioners to discuss the situation. Chase, Daniel of St. Thomas Jenifer, and Thomas Stone met with Virginia's George Mason and Alexander Henderson at Alexandria in March 1785, adjourned to Mount Vernon at Washington's invitation, and reached agreement in sessions reportedly marked by a "most amicable spirit." Fishing rights, trade regulations and tolls, piracy, buoys and lighthouses, and the like were provided for.[2]

The Mount Vernon conference had consequences more important than anyone realized at the time. The commissioners, pleased with their success, recommended that the two states meet annually in the future. At Maryland's November 1785 assembly session, a committee chaired by Chase proposed an agenda for further commercial cooperation between Maryland and Virginia and suggested that Pennsylvania and Delaware be invited to the next meeting as well. Virginia replied by proposing a convention of all the states to discuss questions of commercial regulation. The result was the Annapolis convention of 1786, which in turn issued the call for the 1787 convention that wrote the United States Constitution.[3]

Chase believed that the future of the republic required attention to its mental and moral as well as material development. Education would promote all three. At the November 1784 legislative session, Chase helped frame laws calling for two state-supported schools, Washington College at Chestertown on the Eastern Shore and St. John's at Annapolis. The former already existed as a private college; the latter could get started by absorbing an existing institution, King William's School. Together the two colleges were to be known as the University of Maryland. Chase and his fellow legislators expected the colleges to promote "the principles of religious and civil liberty, private and public virtue, and those liberal arts and sciences, which are at once the greatest ornament of a free republic, and the surest basis of its stability and glory." Deeply interested in education, as his letters to his children testify, Chase served on the boards of visitors of both colleges.[4]

Chase believed strongly that the well-being of the community depended also on religion. Ever since 1776 he had wanted to provide state support for religion as the constitution allowed, but unfavorable reaction in 1777 had compelled him to postpone his plans until the war ended. The idea remained alive among leaders of the once-established Church of England (now the Episcopal Church) such as the Reverend William Smith of Chestertown, distinguished former provost of the College of Philadelphia. Smith's friend and former pupil, Governor William Paca, recommended a general tax for the support of all Christian denominations to the assembly in May 1783. The proposal remained controversial, though, and nothing was done at that time.

The spirit of civic improvement manifest in the November 1784 session seemed encouraging to Chase, and he was determined to wait no longer to introduce his plan. Late in the session he brought in a bill for the support of the Christian religion. His proposal gave tax support to the church of each taxpayer's choice and exempted non-Christians entirely from the tax.[5]

The bill faced considerable opposition, and Chase found it necessary to proceed with caution. The House of Delegates endorsed a resolution favoring state support for religion in the abstract by a vote of twenty-seven to twenty-one, but a more specific resolution supporting Chase's concept of an equal tax on all for the support of all Christian ministers passed by only twenty-six to twenty-four.

Unwilling to risk a final vote on the bill itself in such an evenly divided house, Chase decided to have the bill referred to the next session and published for public discussion. The strategy backfired. Public opposition was strong, a collapsing economy during 1785 made any new tax unacceptable, and the House of Delegates resoundingly defeated the bill in November 1785.[6]

Despite the postponement of Chase's religious bill, the 1784 assembly had demonstrated its readiness to spend money for public improvements. Chase and his associates' confidence in Maryland's ability to finance these projects stemmed in part from the fact that they had also adopted a plan to pay the state's debt and put its fiscal affairs on a sound basis. Chase did not originate the consolidating act of 1784, but he played an important role in its shaping and passage.

The legislature had first turned its attention to the state debt in November 1783, while Chase was in England. The major result of its deliberations was a plan suggested by General Court judge Alexander Contee Hanson, who proposed that the state pay its creditors quickly by demanding speedy payment from its debtors, chief among whom were the purchasers of confiscated British property.[7]

Chase was as anxious as anyone to restore Maryland's fiscal stability, but he believed the state's accounts could not be closed as quickly as Hanson proposed. Certainly Chase himself could not pay for his investments in confiscated property within a very few years. Chase's personal interests influenced his thinking as a member of the committee that framed the consolidating act of 1784. The act as passed set aside most bonds for confiscated property, plus certain other revenues, as a fund for payment of the state debt by January 1, 1790. In the meantime, interest paid by the state's debtors was supposed to furnish the means of paying interest to its creditors. Chase and most other legislators agreed that these provisions put Maryland on a sound financial basis, and Chase had secured an acceptable length of time to pay his debts to the state. An added bonus was a provision making all of Maryland's depreciated currency and certificates receivable at face value in payment for confiscated property.[8]

Hanson, Charles Carroll of Carrollton, and a few others disowned the consolidating act as overgenerous to the state's debtors. Carroll revived the familiar charge that Chase and other speculators had molded the law to serve their own interest.[9] But, generally speaking, the old Chase-Carroll rift was hard to detect in the votes of the 1784 session. Their factions worked together on the major legislation of the session. Opposition came only from Captain Charles Ridgely's faction of agrarian localists, mostly from northern and western Maryland, who opposed almost any plan for government spending that might mean higher taxes for their small-farmer constituents.[10] Little did Chase suspect that within a year changing circumstances would reverse the alignments of 1784 and bring him into alliance with Ridgely for one of the great political battles of his life, the paper money controversy of 1785–1787.

Chase's realignment with Ridgely against Carroll was the result of a severe economic depression that affected all of America from about 1784 through 1788. Signs of trouble began to appear in Maryland in 1784: a shortage of money, growing difficulty in collecting debts, swollen merchants' inventories and slow sales, several business failures, and declining tobacco prices. Still the year was a good one for many Marylanders, at least on paper, and the legislature showed few signs of concern at its November 1784 session. The collapse came in 1785. Mercantile houses failed, farm prices dropped sharply, and everywhere men found it hard to pay their debts.[11] The state's mood changed considerably in 1785. By the end of the year, the optimistic spirit of building for the future evident in 1784 had largely given way to a preoccupation with immediate survival.

Samuel Chase as a substantial debtor saw his own prospects blighted by the depression. He sold or mortgaged thousands of acres of land in the mid-1780s. His business partnership with the Dorseys and Luke Wheeler collapsed in late 1784, leaving all the partners in debt.[12] While seeking to serve his state, Chase had to maneuver desperately to meet his own obligations and save the investments that represented perhaps his last chance to establish the secure landed fortune of a true gentleman.

One pressing concern was the expense of the bank stock case. During the 1784 session the legislature formally approved Chase's conduct as agent and authorized him to continue the suits against Russell.[13] That was gratifying, but it did not help Chase financially. The agent estimated that his trip to England had cost him £500 sterling. He acknowledged that that loss was legally his responsibility, but he thought the unexpected difficulties he had encountered justified him in seeking compensation. He also insisted that the state must assume the cost of the suit in chancery, which he could not continue at his own expense. Chase's friends in the House of Delegates agreed to give him £500, but the Senate refused to approve any compensation at all.[14]

Failing in the legislature, Chase warned Governor Paca that he would have to drop the suit unless the state paid for it. In April 1785 Paca and Intendant of the Revenue Jenifer agreed to advance Chase £500 sterling in order to save the suit. The advance was legally irregular, but the assembly at its next session agreed to pay the legal expenses of the bank stock case on condition that the £500 advance to Chase be applied to that purpose.[15] That helped, but it still left Chase saddled with the full cost of his trip to England.

Chase's new ally Jenifer tried to help him in other ways as well during 1785. In February the intendant retained Chase and Thomas Stone to advise the state in legal questions concerning confiscated property. It appeared to be a mutually advantageous arrangement; the state got sound counsel, and Chase and Stone received one hundred guineas each.[16]

The sum was generous, but it did not begin to satisfy Chase's need for money. In March he tried to borrow from Captain Ridgely to meet his payments on their company's confiscated property purchases. "I cannot engage to take my Share unless You can furnish Me with £1,200," Chase wrote. "I wish to continue a Partner, and will procure the Balance. . . but if You will not positively engage to lend me the 1200£, I must. . .relinquish any purchase, and also be liable to a Suit." Ridgely was unable to pay his own debts and could not help. Still Chase persisted, even warning Ridgely in April that "I have offered the Intendant to relinquish my Part, and I believe, you may get a Partner less able to serve the Company." The threat did not succeed. In September, Chase's name appeared along with three other partners in Charles Ridgely and Company on a list of delinquent state debtors who were subject to suit. Jenifer, however, endorsed the list with the notation that Chase and two of his partners "need not I think be sued."[17]

Despite his financial plight, Chase plunged ahead with another large purchase of British property. In August 1785 Chase and John Churchman agreed with Jenifer to buy all the ungranted proprietary reserve lands in Baltimore and Harford counties, up to twenty thousand acres, at 3s. 9d. per acre.[18] The price was good and the lands were a tempting acquisition, but even for a plunger like Chase the deal seems incredible.

The intendant's official acts of partiality toward Chase during 1785 did not escape attention. Carroll of Carrollton, Edward Lloyd, John Hall, and other powerful politicians turned against Jenifer for this and other reasons. Late in the year Jenifer's critics in the assembly brought in a report attacking his conduct and recommending the abolition of his office. Faced with the prospect of losing a well-placed ally, Chase "exerted his utmost abilities and Influence to prevent a Censure" of Jenifer in the House of Delegates. But he could not prevent the Senate from refusing to renew the intendancy for another year. Jenifer remained in office as an agent charged with winding up the affairs of his old position, but Chase lost a degree of the protection that Jenifer had previously given to his interests.[19]

Foundering financially in the depression year of 1785, Samuel Chase was in the same predicament as many other debtors both great and small. Overextended speculators shared a common problem with small farmers who found themselves unable to pay debts and taxes. The remedy they all advocated was an emission of state paper money. Chase was the generally recognized leader of their campaign for relief. His personal plight was largely responsible for his metamorphosis once again into the seemingly radical champion of the "middling sort." But his sympathy for the problems of small property holders was genuine, and he sincerely believed that paper money would benefit the state as a whole.

Chase and his allies made a strong case for an emission of currency. Stagnating trade, unemployment, low prices for farm produce, unpaid debts and taxes, property sold under execution for debt at a fraction of its true value—all these conditions were caused in part by a shortage of currency. Increasing the money supply to an adequate level would stimulate trade, help raise prices, make money available for loans, and give the distressed sorely needed help in paying debts and taxes.[20] Paper money had served the colony of Maryland well; surely it would succeed again.

By the fall of 1785 a majority of Marylanders probably favored paper money. But an influential minority of creditors, wealthy planters, and merchants, led by senators Charles Carroll of Carrollton and Edward Lloyd, were prepared to put up a strong fight against the plan. Having suffered from the severe depreciation of paper money during the War for Independence when the tender act compelled its acceptance, these men believed another emission would produce the same results. Striking back at Chase where he was most vulnerable, his opponents charged incessantly that paper money "was calculated only to enable speculators, and public and private debtors (some of them involved more than they are worth)" to pay their obligations in depreciated currency, defrauding the state and private creditors in the process.[21]

The paper money fight began when the legislature assembled for its November 1785 session. Chase chaired the committee that prepared a plan for a state currency emission. The money was to be issued on loan to citizens who could put up lands worth twice the amount of the loan as collateral. Chase realized that his bill had little or no chance of passing the Senate, where Carroll and Lloyd led a strong body of like-minded gentlemen of means. Chase's strategy apparently was to put a specific paper money plan on the record for public consideration. A new Senate was to be elected in 1786. If the popular demand for an emission was strong enough, the composition of the upper chamber might be changed sufficiently to secure adoption of paper money at the next session.

Thinking along those lines, Chase voted with the opponents of his own bill in the House of Delegates to table the issue until the next session. But that motion failed by a vote of thirty-four to twenty-five, and the delegates went on to pass the bill thirty-eight to twenty-two. Chase and most of his usual supporters joined with the Ridgely faction to provide the margin of victory.[22]

As Chase had anticipated, the Senate unanimously rejected the bill. The 1786 election would be the key to victory or defeat. It would not be easy to reverse a unanimously hostile Senate, but at least circumstances seemed favorable to the effort. Seventeen eighty-six was the worst year of the depression. Unrest grew as a mob in Charles County prevented the county court from hearing debt cases in June. Other parts of the state seemed to be on the verge of disorder, and local courts did little if any business during the summer. Support for paper money and debt relief grew, and some opponents of Chase's plan began to contemplate making concessions to quiet the state's disorders.[23]

Chase himself led the fight for a favorable new upper house by running for Annapolis's seat in the electoral college that chose the senators. Probably Chase hoped also to be chosen a senator himself.

He was about to move from Annapolis to Baltimore, which would cast doubt on his ability to meet the residence requirements for the House of Delegates.

The Senate election presented Chase with his toughest political challenge in his old constituency in years. His political opponents believed that he was vulnerable in 1786. His advocacy of paper money could be attributed with considerable justice to self-interest, reviving all the old charges of corruption against him. Chase's stand for state support of religion in 1784–1785 had proven unpopular, and his relationship with Jenifer as intendant of the revenue was still controversial. Moreover, Chase had induced the legislature to consider Henry Harford's petition for compensation for his proprietary estates in December 1785, only to have Harford's claim overwhelmingly rejected.[24] And he had taken another unpopular position by advocating state payment of the so-called "black list" debts.

The "black list" referred to Maryland debtors of English creditors who had taken advantage of a 1780 act of assembly to discharge their debts by paying depreciated state or Continental paper money into the state treasury, where it was accepted at face value. Supporters of that act had reasoned that Marylanders who were forced to accept state currency at par under the tender act should be allowed to pay their foreign debts in the same way. Surely English creditors should fare no better than native patriots! Under this act, some fifty Marylanders had discharged debts of about £145,000 with currency worth only £3,600 in current passing value. Among the "black list" debtors were Chase's partners the Ridgelys and Dorseys.[25]

The peace treaty of 1783 upset this arrangement by providing that English creditors should be allowed to collect prewar debts in full. Ever since 1783 Chase had urged publicly that the state had an obligation to pay the "black list" debts. He and Ridgely argued that the state had assured the "black list" debtors that their debts were legally discharged. If further payment now had to be made, the state was in all justice responsible.[26] There was some logic to Chase's argument, but critics naturally charged that he was trying to protect the interests of his friends at the taxpayers' expense.

Chase's interest in the bank stock also influenced his stand on the British debt issue. "I have authentic but confidential Information that the Bank Stock will not be recovered, so long as there is any Impediment thrown in the Way of the recovery of British Debts by any One of the States," he informed the council in 1786. For that reason as well as from his desire to heal the wounds of war, Chase had sponsored laws to restore full political rights to wartime non-jurors and had helped a few men like the Reverend Henry Addison recover their confiscated property. But Chase's proposal for public payment of the "black list" debts was so unpopular that he never introduced it in the legislature.[27]

A politician who had taken so many controversial positions, who was in financial trouble, and who was moving out of his district should be vulnerable to attack, even if he was the formidable Samuel Chase. The man who stepped forward to make the attack shortly before the 1786 Senate election was young James Carroll, nephew and heir of the late Charles Carroll, Barrister. Under the signature of "A Citizen," the politically ambitious Carroll assailed Chase in a series of letters to the Annapolis newspaper.

The "Citizen" claimed that Chase's legislative agenda included paper money, state payment of the "black list" debts, and revival of the intendancy of the revenue. He was confident that the voters opposed Chase on at least the two latter issues. Carroll warned that Chase sought to exclude Carroll of Carrollton and Lloyd from the Senate and to secure an upper house favorable to his plans. It was improper for Chase as a member of the House of Delegates to help choose the Senate, he charged. James Carroll urged the voters to turn out on election day to defeat Chase's schemes.[28]

Provoked again to public combat, Chase replied with a vindication of his positions on the issues and a pointed personal attack on his adversary. Alluding frankly to his personal problems, Chase appealed to the voters to stand by their old and faithful servant.

> The public and private character of *your delegate* is well known to you; and his long and faithful services, for above twenty years, cannot be forgot. Necessity, not choice, compels him to remove from among you. For your *public* confidence, and *private* esteem. . .he is under obligations to you, but for upright, laborious, and disinterested services. . .as your representative, you are under obligations to him. The *political relation* between you and him is soon to be dissolved from the situation of his private affairs, greatly injured from his attention to the public characters he has sustained from his youth, without any reward.

Chase believed that his old constituents still supported him, but an unaccustomed note of worry could be detected in his appeal to the voters.[29]

Chase's apprehensions proved justified. John Brice defeated him for the Annapolis elector's position. Shortly thereafter Chase won an electoral seat from his other old constituency, Anne Arundel County, but the thin and contradictory excuses he offered for his loss in Annapolis showed that the setback was mortifying to him. Spurred on by Chase's embarrassment, James Carroll crowed with considerable exaggeration that Chase had "become a mere cypher" through loss of popularity.[30]

Chase's presence in the electoral college did him little good. Two-thirds of the incumbent senators, including Carroll of Carrollton and Lloyd, were reelected. Chase himself fell one vote short of election to the Senate. The upper chamber remained solidly in the hands of Chase's opponents.[31]

Despite his move to Baltimore, Chase was returned to the House of Delegates from Anne Arundel County. He stood third among the county's four successful candidates, 180 votes behind the leading vote getter. James Carroll filed a petition challenging Chase's eligibility when the legislature met in November 1786, but the delegates, needing their leader's direction, dismissed it.[32] The stage was set for a showdown on paper money.

Chase served on three lower house committees, all chaired by William Paca, which produced legislation for paper money and debt relief. The paper money bill provided for the gradual issue on loan of up to £350,000 of currency. The bills would not be legal tender, nor could they be used to pay for confiscated property. By these two provisions Chase hoped to answer some of the principal criticisms of his opponents. Debt relief legislation included a bankruptcy bill and a plan allowing debtors to pay their obligations in real or personal property at a "true" value set by impartial assessors.[33]

Debate on the paper money bill was hot in the House of Delegates. At one point Chase "said He would *stake* his *Reputation* to [i.e., against] a *Farthing* on the propriety" of the bill. Delegate Thomas Jenings retorted that "He thought it an *equal Bet*," since Chase's reputation was worth no more than that small coin.[34] Chase's supporters narrowly defeated an amendment to the bill reducing the amount of currency to be issued and guarding against depreciation—an amendment that might have given the bill a chance of adoption in the Senate. In the end the lower house passed the paper money, debt relief, and bankruptcy bills by sizable margins. The Senate unanimously rejected all three.[35]

Twice before, in 1777 and 1779–1780, Chase had tried to overcome Senate opposition to his programs by appealing directly to the people. That tactic now offered his only remaining hope of success. In January 1787 the House of Delegates ordered the rejected bills printed, appointed Chase chairman of a committee to prepare an address to their constituents, and adjourned for two months to mobilize public support.[36]

Chase's appeal brought the greatest political struggle of the Confederation period in Maryland to a climax. Debate on the merits of paper money was intense as both sides sought to gain maximum support. The appeal raised a serious constitutional question as well: Was the Senate bound to follow instructions from a majority of its constituents? That question posed a fundamental issue concerning the nature of republicanism in Maryland. William Paca and Alexander Contee Hanson were the principals in the newspaper debate on the constitutional question, but Chase wrote the most striking argument for his side.

Chase agreed that the two branches of the legislature were meant to be *"checks* upon each other; and thence the evident necessity that *each* body should be entirely and absolutely free and independent *of the other."* But, he argued, if republicanism meant anything, it meant that both houses were bound to follow the instructions of a majority of the voters.

All *lawful* authority originates from the people, and their power is like the light of the sun, native, original, inherent and unlimited by human authority. Power in the rulers or governors of the people is like the reflected light of the moon, and is only borrowed, delegated and limited by the grant of the people. The right of the people to participate in the legislature is the foundation of all free government, and where that right is not enjoyed, the people are not free. ...Both branches of the legislature derive *all* their power from the people...and there is no difference between them but *only* in the *duration of their commission....* From the nature of a government by *representation*, the *deputies* must be subject to the will of their *principals,* or this manifest absurdity... must follow, that a *few* men would be *greater* than the *whole* community, and might act in opposition to the *declared* sense of *all their constituents.*[37]

The Senate's supporters disagreed. Hanson argued that instructions by way of advice or information were acceptable, but binding instructions were incompatible with republicanism, which was government by representatives of the people, not by direct popular action between elections.[38] The Senate, explicitly left free by the constitution to form its own judgment on legislation, was in its own view a natural aristocracy of wisdom and virtue established to check the turbulence, faction, and proneness to error of the more democratic branch. To subject senators to instruction by the people was to destroy their independence and subvert their proper constitutional role.

To these arguments Chase replied passionately that the Senate's doctrines, "if submitted to, will subvert and destroy our free government, and establish an *aristocratic* tyranny in its stead." Was there no danger of aristocracy from the likes of Carroll of Carrollton? "The influence of Mr. Carroll in this government, from his vast riches, is very great and extensive indeed; and his fortune, most rapidly accumulating, will, in a few years, render him most formidable; and increase the number of his debtors and dependants to such a degree, as may endanger the liberties of Maryland."[39]

The charge of aristocracy that Chase and others raised in the paper money debate was more than a political ploy. Long an advocate of the binding force of instructions, Chase thought he saw the will of the majority being denied by a self-interested elite of wealth and power. It was not the political leadership of a socioeconomic elite *per se* to which Chase objected, but rather what he perceived as the Maryland elite's unresponsiveness to the electorate and abuse of power in the paper money contest. Concern for the good of the state as he saw it and sympathy for the plight of the "middling sort" as well as self-interest explain Chase's conduct in 1786–1787. Believing that the danger to ordered liberty now came from above, he emerged again, as in 1764–1765, the fiery champion of the common man against the abuse of governmental authority.

What might have happened had a clear majority of Marylanders instructed the Senate to adopt paper money is a matter for conjecture. To Chase's dismay, his adversaries for once proved more successful at arousing vocal public support than he. The majority of those who spoke up in 1787, so far as can be ascertained, expressed opposition to Chase's paper money bill.

This surprising turn of events probably did not represent a sudden reversal of opinion on the desirability of paper money in the abstract. But many people found much to criticize in the specifics of Chase's plan. Probably, too, Chase's opponents succeeded in portraying the bill as a selfish scheme of speculators and large public debtors, "intended," as one writer put it, "to serve private, rather than public usefulness."[40] Chase's own reputation suffered from the acceptance of this claim.

When the legislature met again in April, the paper money bill was not even discussed. The Senate's opposition made any attempt to revive the plan useless. Nor could agreement be reached on any plan for debt relief. The only fruit of Chase and Ridgely's efforts was a bankruptcy act, which would be in effect for only a little more than a year.

While the bankruptcy bill was still under consideration, Samuel Chase petitioned the legislature to "be discharged from all his debts...upon surrendering up all his property for the use of his creditors."[41] No final action was taken on the petition, probably because the delegates thought the bankruptcy act made special consideration of Chase's case unnecessary. The failure of the paper money movement meant financial collapse for Samuel Chase. His lifelong dream of accumulating the landed estate of the true gentleman ended in a nightmare of unpayable bills and unreachable hopes. Both economically and politically, Chase's fortunes in 1787 stood at a low ebb. More defeats lay ahead.

Twelve

ANTIFEDERALIST

AMUEL CHASE's public statement that necessity prompted his move to Baltimore was accurate as far as it went, but it did not tell the full story. It was true that Baltimore offered better prospects to a lawyer seeking to mend his fortunes than the capital. Postwar Annapolis, its economic position weakened by the War for Independence and the rise of Baltimore, did not regain its prosperity of the 1760s. It stagnated in the 1780s, while Baltimore continued the spectacular growth that made it the boomtown of revolutionary America. Baltimore's population more than doubled between 1775 and 1790, reaching 13,500 in the latter year. Chase was convinced that he could "make much more Money by his profession in that place ...and living as he does with so large a Family to support, it is absolutely necessary he should...get a great Deal." During the 1780s, while liquidating many of his other landholdings, Chase had acquired property in Baltimore, a clear indication of his growing interest in that city's potential.[1]

An additional stimulus for the move came from Colonel John Eager Howard, one of Baltimore's leading citizens and civic promoters. In February 1786 Howard offered to give Chase "one square of ten lots of my land, near the square laid out and intended for the public buildings," in order to encourage him to come to Baltimore. Chase accepted the offer, soon building a comfortable three-and-a-half story brick townhouse on the tract at Lexington and Eutaw streets.

Howard's generosity has usually been attributed to friendship for Chase, but in fact Howard had more interested motives. In 1786 he and other Baltimore promoters were trying to get the state capital moved to their city. Chase had blocked the move in the assembly, and Annapolis residents presented him with an address of thanks for his efforts. Howard hoped—and others suspected—that the capital would soon follow Chase to Baltimore. Howard's offer to Chase included the promise of "another square of ten lots...if the seat of government should be removed [to Baltimore], and the public buildings shall be erected on my land."[2]

Chase's return to his boyhood hometown proved a happy move in the long run. For the immediate future, though, troubles continued to plague him. Howard's hopes of securing the capital through Chase's influence were not realized, for as it developed Chase had only one major political battle ahead of him before he retired permanently from the legislature. In that battle, the contest over ratification of the United States Constitution, residence in Baltimore was a hindrance to him.

Chase had no part in the writing of the Constitution. When the Maryland legislature selected its delegates to the Philadelphia convention in April and May 1787, he was nominated but withdrew his name from consideration. Ten other men also declined to serve, including Charles Carroll of Carrollton, Thomas Johnson, and William Paca. One observer believed that state politics was responsible for this extraordinary series of refusals. Chase's opponents, he believed, were afraid to leave the state lest Chase renew the paper money fight in their absence.[3] Maryland's internal disputes may have influenced Chase's decision as well, but it seems more likely that his personal financial plight made it impossible for him to go to Philadelphia.

Chase did believe that the Articles of Confederation needed some revision to strengthen the central government. He had supported the impost of 1781, a proposed amendment to the Articles that would have given Congress the power to collect import duties as a source of revenue independent of the states.[4] But his reaction to the new Constitution written at Philadelphia in 1787 was negative from the start. In Chase's view the convention had exceeded its authority by proposing an entirely new government to replace the

Confederation. That new government, national rather than truly federal in principle,[5] virtually unlimited in its powers, must inevitably swallow up the hitherto sovereign states. It seemed to Chase that the executive and Congress outlined in the Constitution would be too distant from the average voter to represent the "people at large." Aristocratic domination of this powerful new government appeared inevitable, and after the paper money fight Chase was in no mood to trust implicitly the public virtue and responsibility of a ruling elite. Such a Constitution could not protect the rights and interests of the "middling sort," and it would at the same time destroy the states' power to do so. Chase concluded that even the addition of a bill of rights would be inadequate. Only structural alteration of the proposed national government by amendment of the Constitution before its adoption could safeguard liberty and make the plan acceptable.[6] As it stood, the Constitution appeared to Chase to upset the delicate balance between order and liberty, and to leave liberty in grave danger.

It seems logical to assume that Chase's reaction to the Constitution was influenced also by his close friend and protégé Luther Martin. An exceptionally able lawyer who thanks in part to Chase's influence served as Maryland's attorney general, Martin was the only Marylander to play a significant role at the Philadelphia convention. In a sense he may have represented Chase there. Martin, too, viewed the Constitution as dangerous to state sovereignty and popular liberty. He saw it as the product of an alliance in the convention between large-state delegates, who wanted a national government that their states could dominate, and a group of overt and covert monarchists pursuing centralization of power. Chase must have received a thorough account of the proceedings at Philadelphia from Martin, and the latter's negative impressions of the convention reinforced Chase's alarm upon reading the document itself.[7]

Despite his strong feelings on the matter, Chase was in no position to assume active public leadership of the campaign against ratification of the Constitution in Maryland. He was running for a seat in the House of Delegates in the fall elections of 1787. His new constituency of Baltimore Town, like America's other commercial cities, was strongly in favor of the Constitution. Chase's adversaries sought to make his presumed opposition to ratification their major issue. Consequently Chase was forced to soften his public stand as a matter of practical political survival.

Chase's first public statement on ratification came at a meeting at Fell's Point in late September. Responding to questions from those present, he said he had not yet made up his mind on the Constitution, but he cautioned against being too quick to change Maryland's established government. This noncommital response must have proven unsatisfactory to the voters, for very shortly thereafter Chase found it necessary to clarify his position. Repeating that he was still undecided on ratification, Chase stated that he believed the Confederation government should "be greatly altered" to increase the powers of Congress. But the Constitution would "*alter,* and in some Instances, *abolish* our [state] Bill of Rights and Form of Government." The legislature, he argued, could properly agree to the federal Constitution only by following Maryland's prescribed procedure for constitutional amendments. Still, promising as always to obey the instructions of his constituents, Chase pledged to support the calling of a state convention to consider ratification of the Constitution "as early in the Spring as may be."[8]

Equivocal though his stand was, Chase's promise to support a speedy ratification convention satisfied the voters of Baltimore. He led the field in the city election, polling 612 of 830 votes cast, and his ally David McMechen took the city's other assembly seat with 593 votes. Disgruntled Federalists (as supporters of the Constitution were beginning to call themselves) grumbled that Chase had prevailed through the aid of constables and tavern keepers, who spared "neither wine nor rum" to collect "into taverns, in obscure quarters of the town, a few nights before the election, those persons whose situation in life renders them easy dupes to a florid harangue, to whom he must promise anything."[9] Such charges were becoming routine in Baltimore's carefully organized and hotly contested politics.

Immediately after the election, Baltimore Federalists began circulating a petition to the assembly calling for a convention and unconditional ratification of the Constitution. Chase warned his constituents against signing the petition in a letter to the *Maryland Journal* under the signature of "Caution." People should not commit themselves to a blanket endorsement of the new government, he urged, until they had had time to hear the arguments on both sides and to consider the question carefully. "When men urge you to determine in *haste,* on so momentous a subject, it is not *unreasonable* to inquire their motives; and . . . to suspect that they are improper," Chase concluded.[10] This parting shot at the Federalists was the only bold note in an essay that was otherwise as cautious as Chase's preelection statements. Federalists like Daniel Carroll and James Madison believed that Baltimore Town's enthusiasm for the Constitution would continue to prevent Chase from taking a strong stand against it.[11] Though his opposition was widely known, Chase apparently did no campaigning against ratification among the people for the next five months.

With Chase handicapped by his constituency and his personal problems, Luther Martin became the principal spokesman for Maryland Antifederalism. William Paca, Captain Charles Ridgely, and some of Chase's other associates in the paper money fight were also active in the Antifederal campaign. The rhetoric of the paper money contest carried over into the ratification struggle. Prominent among the public arguments of Maryland Antifederalists was the fear, held by Chase as well, that the new government represented a bid for unrestrained power by the rich and well born. "Aristocracy . . . is therein concealed in the most artful writ plan that ever was formed to entrap a free people."[12] Chase and his Antifederal colleagues considered themselves champions of popular liberty, which they associated with powerful state legislatures and a limited if strengthened central government.

Federalist writers, while extolling the Constitution, had a different explanation for the motives of its Maryland opponents. Accurately identifying Antifederalism with the principal supporters of paper money, they made the familiar charge that narrow self-interest lay at the root of their adversaries' position. Chase was, as usual, their principal target. One writer charged that Chase's opposition stemmed "both from ambition, because he cannot expect to be so powerful in the general government as he is in the state and because [of] his shattered circumstances." Federalist Alexander Contee Hanson noted an "extreme reluctance to surrender power" on the part of "those, whose ambition, or private interest, would have all things subservient to the omnipotence of assembly."[13] Certainly Chase's political talents were well suited to the arena of the House of Delegates, and he could not hope to be as influential if considerable power was transferred to the national level. It was plausible, too, to contend that the Constitution's provisions against state issues of paper money and laws impairing the obligations of contracts would forever deny the forms of legislative debt relief that Chase had fought for in 1785–1786, and thus further narrow his chances of financial recovery. The Federalist charges were convincing to many voters.

While the debate over the Constitution continued, the assembly met in November 1787. Chase supported the call for a ratifying convention, as he had promised, but he also made a speech in the House of Delegates opposing the Constitution. The legislature scheduled convention elections for early April 1788, and the convention itself for April 21.[14]

The electoral contest for convention seats was an unequal one. The Constitution enjoyed the support of most of Maryland's political leaders and had broad popular backing in most parts of the state. The Antifederalists could count on only a hard core of the men who had followed Chase and Ridgely in previous legislative battles. Chase's faction was in disarray, greatly weakened and partially discredited by the paper money fight. Chase himself, potentially the most effective Antifederal campaigner, was handicapped by personal bankruptcy, past allegations of self-interested manipulation, and his residence in Baltimore. Given those circumstances the outcome was never really in doubt. More than a month before the election, Federalists in other states were anticipating a sure victory in Maryland.[15]

Though Samuel Chase may have had a hand in Antifederalist strategy behind the scenes, he took no public part in the campaign until shortly before the election. Then he suddenly stepped to the fore in his old district, Anne Arundel County. There the Federalist ticket of Charles Carroll of Carrollton, James Carroll, Brice Worthington, and John Hall had been anticipating a victory without opposition. Four days before the election, however, Antifederalists Samuel and Jeremiah Townley Chase, John Francis Mercer (a delegate to the Philadelphia convention), and Benjamin Harrison suddenly declared their candidacy. Samuel Chase's appearance on the slate was surprising, since he was not a resident of the county and was therefore ineligible to represent it. According to one account, Chase's name was put forward "without his Knowledge or Intention" when former governor William Smallwood, whom the other candidates had originally wanted to round out the slate, could not be reached in time to secure his consent before the election.

Whether or not he originally intended to run himself, Chase had already begun to speak against unconditional ratification in Anne Arundel.

The Antifederalists' surprise campaign was very effective. "S. Chase went into one part of the County and harangued, Mercer and J. Chase did the same in another part," Federalist Daniel Carroll reported. "The two latter had signed and dispersed a hand Bill" warning of the dangers of the Constitution. The handbill emphasized the Constitution's lack of a bill of rights, its failure to prohibit a standing army in peacetime, the president's emergency power to control state militia without consent of the legislature, and the federal government's broad powers of direct taxation. These objections made a strong impression on many voters. Carroll noted that "a wildness appeared in many which showed they were really frightened by what they had just heard." The Federalists, caught by surprise, could not counteract this last-minute blitz, and Chase and his running mates were elected by about fifty votes.[16]

The skillfully conducted campaign in Anne Arundel was one of only three Antifederalist victories in Maryland. The Ridgelys carried Baltimore County in a disputed election, and neighboring Harford as usual went along even though three of the Antifederalist candidates there—Luther Martin, William Paca, and William Pinkney—were ineligible as nonresidents. Antifederal candidates were badly defeated in Washington and Montgomery counties. In the other thirteen counties, so far as the record reveals, no Antifederalists sought election to the convention.[17] The well-organized Federalists, having carried sixty-four of the seventy-six convention seats, did not bother to challenge the credentials of Chase and the three nonresident Harford delegates.

Chase had hoped the Constitution could be amended before its adoption "to declare and secure the...essential rights of the people." To safeguard liberty, he believed, "a declaration of rights alone will be of no essential service. Some of the powers must be abridged, or public liberty will be endangered, and, in time, destroyed." Given the obvious determination of Federalists across the country to put their system into operation without alteration, Chase feared that the necessary amendments would not be made after ratification if they could not be forced on the Federalists beforehand.[18] Now, though, it appeared that little if anything could be accomplished in Maryland.

Antifederalist strategy in Maryland was to try to persuade the convention to endorse amendments to the Constitution, preferably as a condition of ratification but at least as recommendations accompanying it. As Maryland Federalists realized, Chase and his collaborators hoped to secure from the convention at least some indication that Maryland had reservations about the Constitution in order to influence the neighboring state of Virginia, where ratification was very much in doubt.

When the Maryland convention met, six of the nine states needed to put the Constitution into effect among themselves had ratified, and New Hampshire had adjourned its convention without a decision. Maryland and South Carolina would act before Virginia's convention met on June 2. Virginia was vital to the success of the Constitution; a union without her, and in that event probably without New York as well, could not endure. The battle in Virginia was too close to call. If both Maryland and South Carolina ratified, the resulting momentum could sway the delicate balance in Virginia. If one or both at least indicated a desire for amendments, Virginia Antifederalists would be strengthened. Hence both sides in Maryland went to the convention with one eye always upon the effect their actions might have across the Potomac.[19]

The convention assembled on Monday, April 21. Six of the twelve Antifederal delegates, including Samuel Chase, Martin, and Paca, did not arrive until Thursday. That was a tactical error, for it left the Federalists free to establish the procedural rules of the convention without objection.

The Federalists, well organized and skillfully led in the convention by Judge Alexander Contee Hanson, had held a caucus before the first session. They agreed that, since the Constitution had already been fully discussed and the people of Maryland had made their decision to adopt it, speeches in favor of the new government should be dispensed with and the Constitution ratified as quickly as possible. Consequently the convention adopted a procedural rule that the Constitution be discussed and voted on as a whole.[20] That would be the fastest method, and it would prevent expert debaters like Chase and Martin from achieving a surprise rejection of some particular clause of the document.

Nothing else of importance was done before Chase and Martin arrived on Thursday morning. Discussion of the Constitution then began, and Chase opened the debate with a long and notable speech. The best evidence of what he said is a manuscript statement of his objections to the Constitution, which may well have been prepared for this occasion.

Chase began with the familiar Antifederalist argument that the constitutional convention had been called explicitly to revise the Articles of Confederation. The delegates had no authority from their states to form an entirely new government. Nevertheless, "the separate sovereignty and independence of each State, and their union by a confederate league is destroyed and they are melted down and consolidated into one *national* government. . . . It swallows up the State governments and states legislatures. It alters our [state] Constitution and annuls our Bill of Rights in many of its most essential parts."

Which was preferable for America, a consolidated national government or a decentralized league of sovereign states? Chase favored the latter. Perhaps the most important Antifederalist argument was that a republic was best suited to a geographically small state. Chase was restating what had until 1787 been an orthodoxy of eighteenth-century political theory when he told the convention that "a national or general government however constructed over so extensive a country as America must end in despotism."

Getting down to particulars, Chase charged that both houses of the proposed Congress were too small. The legislators would be vulnerable to executive or external corruption. More seriously, so few men could not "possibly represent the *opinions,* wishes and interests" of the "many different classes or orders of people" in the United States. Again Chase voiced his conviction that "a representative should be the image of those he represents. He should know their sentiments and their wants and desires. . . . He should be governed by their interests with which his own should be inseparably connected." Under the Constitution, Chase argued, "only the *gentry,* the rich and well born will be elected" to the handful of seats allotted to each state.[21] These representatives would not know or sympathize with the middle and lower classes. Consequently the supposed representation of the people provided by the Constitution would be a fraud. An aristocracy would dominate the nation.

Along with representation, Chase put particular stress on the national government's sweeping authority to tax. Control of taxation, the root of governmental power, would allow it to preempt the states' sources of revenue, leaving them impotent for lack of funds and concentrating power at the center. Chase had many other objections as well. There were no real limits to the power of the national government. The president should be popularly elected, less powerful, and limited in length of service. The national judiciary should have jurisdiction only over "cases arising on treaties." Sketching his own idea of a proper national government, Chase indicated he could support the three branches established by the Constitution provided the Congress was truly representative and the executive and judiciary more strictly limited. But he would give the national government only a few specific powers beyond those possessed by the Confederation Congress and would allow it to tax only if states failed to furnish their assigned quotas of funds. *"There is no injury for which our present laws do not provide a remedy,"* Chase summed up. The few "defects in our form of government . . . may at any time be amended . . . . We might be happy under our present state government, if we knew our own good, and would be contented."[22]

Chase spoke for two and a half hours. He had not covered all of the points outlined in his notes, but he was exhausted. So he sat down, announcing that he would continue his speech the next day. No one else asked for the floor, and a long silence ensued. Luther Martin, who might have been expected to occupy the rest of the day with his own eloquent opposition to the Constitution, was silenced by a painful sore throat.[23] The Federalists adhered to their preconvention decision not to debate the issue at all. The convention soon adjourned for dinner.

The adjournment gave Chase and the little band of Antifederalists, reinforced now by the arrival of William Paca, a chance to reassess their strategy. Clearly Chase's best effort had accomplished nothing. The Federalist majority already had their minds made up and awaited only the chance to vote. The Antifederalists apparently decided to let Paca try to achieve the less ambitious objective he advocated: the adoption of suggested amendments accompanying unconditional ratification.

When the convention reassembled, Paca rose and stated that he wanted to introduce some amendments to the Constitution to accompany ratification "as standing instructions to our representatives in congress." He added that he might vote for the Constitution if he was given reason to expect its future alteration. He asked for an adjournment until the next morning to prepare his amendments. Paca's ploy succeeded in breaching the majority's hitherto monolithic unity. Thomas Johnson, always the conciliator, remarked that Paca "ought to be indulged," and the convention adjourned.

Paca's clever ploy and Johnson's response threatened to produce a prolonged discussion of amendments that would greatly delay ratification. It also raised the possibility of suggested amendments that might hearten Virginia Antifederalists. By the next morning, though, Hanson and the Federalist managers had regained control of the situation. When Paca rose to present his amendments, he was ruled out of order. There was some further discussion of the Constitution; Chase may have finished his speech. Then on Saturday the convention proceeded to ratify the Constitution by a vote of sixty-three to eleven. Paca voted with the majority to demonstrate his good faith.

Following ratification, Paca succeeded in obtaining the appointment of a committee to consider his amendments. Chase and Paca were among the four Antifederalists named with nine Federalists to the committee, which at first agreed to recommend thirteen amendments to accompany ratification. These limited the national government to those powers expressly given by the Constitution, circumscribed the scope of the federal judiciary, and guaranteed basic rights. Fifteen other Antifederalist proposals were rejected, and the Federalists on the committee declared they would report the first thirteen amendments to the convention only if the Antifederalists agreed not to bring up the others. The Federalists also insisted on adoption of an address to the people stating that the amendments were not endorsed by the convention but were simply the suggestions of individual members. Samuel Chase objected vehemently to both conditions. After some further argument the committee broke up without making a formal report. Squelching a final attempt to bring amendments to the floor of the convention, the Federalist majority completed their triumph by voting to adjourn.

The wrangling over amendments left Chase's group with the feeling that they had been badly treated at the convention. They decided to make one more attempt to take their case to the people.

Chase and the other Antifederalist delegates published a pamphlet giving their version of the convention proceedings and explaining the necessity of the amendments they supported.[24] But the public did not respond.

Still Chase continued to fight on. "I believe a very great majority of the people of this state are in favor of amendments," he insisted, "but they are depressed and inactive. They have lost all their former spirit and seem ready to submit to any master." Yet Chase had to mobilize his followers for the fall assembly elections, which were particularly important since the next legislature would choose Maryland's first United States senators and establish the rules for selection of the state's six congressmen. "An attempt will be made to elect none but *Federalists*...to our house of delegates," Chase told a friend. He noted that "violent opposition" to the Federalists was being organized in Baltimore. "I am called on for this," Chase concluded.[25]

Chase and David McMechen faced a hard struggle to retain their assembly seats in strongly Federalist Baltimore. Their opponents were doctors James McHenry and John Coulter, who had represented the city in the ratification convention. As was now customary in Baltimore, both sides were highly organized. Public rallies, active solicitation of voters, and a barrage of highly publicized charges, denials, and countercharges, some of them outrageous, characterized the campaign. Partisans of the rival candidates seemed constantly on the verge of coming to blows, and scuffles broke out with alarming regularity. With unconscious humor, one writer characterized this election as the most "improper and disorderly" ever held in Maryland except for Baltimore's last one.[26]

Chase was kept busy from July to October wooing the voters, attacking his opponents, and defending himself against their assaults. The most telling issue the doctors used against Chase was his Antifederalism, a factor that made the difference in the election. Chase announced that he still favored amendments to the Constitution, but he tried to neutralize the issue by pledging that, since the new government had been ratified, he would support it as a good citizen should. He promised "to carry it into execution with vigour and expedition." His Federalist opponents replied that sending Chase to the legislature to put the Constitution into effect would be like entrusting one's house keys to a burglar. They capitalized on a typically extreme, emotional outburst of Chase's to the effect that, had he known the American Revolution would end in "such a government as this...he would have been the *greatest Tory in all America*," a piece of hyperbole that Chase quickly regretted. Even Chase's own physical safety was endangered on the night of September 15, when a group of Federalist sympathizers attacked persons leaving one of his rallies. The rowdies then proceeded to Chase's home and smashed his windows.[27]

The constant tension and recurrent violence that marked the campaign boded ill for the election itself. In late September, Chase and McMechen sent a letter to their opponents proposing that they agree to a list of rules to "preserve peace, decency, and order" at the polls. When McHenry and Coulter equivocated, Chase published his proposal for whatever political advantage it might have.[28]

The election was as chaotic as Chase had feared it would be. McHenry and Coulter won by about 130 votes amid charges of violence and harassment by both sides. Chase and McMechen petitioned the House of Delegates to declare the election void, but after hearing testimony on the petition, the assembly simply dropped the matter.[29]

Chase's electoral defeat in Baltimore in 1788 was the last in a long string of reverses he had endured over the past four years. The sum total of those reverses had brought him to the lowest point of his career. The year 1788 ended one major phase of Samuel Chase's life; never again would he hold legislative office. Bankrupt and out of power, Chase set about picking up the pieces of a shattered career and providing financial security for his family.

Thirteen

A CAREER REBORN: FROM BAR TO BENCH

AMUEL CHASE's spirits in 1789 were understandably depressed. Bankruptcy and political defeat, as well as his fears for the future of the nation under the new Constitution, brought him closer to despondency than at any time in his life. His remark that "in this State We are prepared to submit to any government. The Hearts of our people are broke, they are born down to the Earth with their Debts," reveals his own mood, not that of Maryland. "His spirits are much broken," wrote a friend of Chase's, "and all things considered I am not surprized at it. Like an old wounded weather-beaten soldier, he wishes for repose."[1]

Chase's spirits revived with his personal fortunes after 1789, but the experience left him a changed man. Painful as it was, Chase had to face the fact that some of his youthful ambitions would not be realized. The dream of landed gentility had been exploded. Chastened by the collapse of his speculations, Chase was no longer the plunger and manipulator. His personal goal after 1788 was a safe position of honor and dignity that would provide economic security for himself and his family in his declining years.

{ 157 }

Chase's new realism in financial matters after 1788 reflected not only his recent reverses but also the knowledge that he was no longer young. Forty-seven years old in 1788, Samuel Chase felt every year of his age. His eyes required the aid of spectacles, or soon would. More seriously, gout and sciatica had begun to impair his health by 1786. The steady progress of these infirmities forced an ever-greater curtailment of his activities. Chase's physical ills account for the gruff and crusty manner that characterized his later years. Still, his native good humor and sociability continued to charm those who took the trouble to penetrate his imposing, not to say formidable, exterior. An anonymous newspaper writer drew a vivid portrait of Chase in 1792:

> A face full, florid, and, by the multitude, denominated hand-some—A countenance bold, assuming, and oppressive—An eye which affects to scrutinize the inmost recesses of the soul, but, when met with assurance, is cast down, or averted—Stature towering, body cumbrous, and limbs ungainly swinging—His body, nevertheless, imposing awe—The whole exterior expressive of ardent passion, and of a mind in which there is much to dazzle, much to be deplored, something to be despised, and not a little to be respected.[2]

Chase's first step toward economic recovery was to satisfy his creditors. He had not taken advantage of the general bankruptcy act of 1787, perhaps because his affairs were too tangled to permit a simple solution. The most complex problem arose from Chase's old partnerships with John and Thomas Dorsey and Luke Wheeler. The firms owed £42,000, and had less than £5,000 in company assets. Thomas Dorsey, the only partner with substantial personal assets, assumed the major burden of the difference. After paying or giving security for some £30,000 of the debt, Dorsey was insolvent. The other partners, also insolvent, contributed lesser sums. Seeking release from the two companies' obligations, Chase proposed to transfer to Thomas Dorsey his interest in Charles Ridgely and Company's purchase of the Nottingham Iron Works and White Marsh Furnace, in exchange for a release from further liability for the two Dorsey companies' debts. Dorsey agreed, and in November 1789 the legislature passed a special act ratifying the arrangement.[3] That removed Chase's largest single worry.

The legislature also helped by agreeing to cancel some of Chase's purchases of confiscated British property. His remaining landholdings were conveyed or mortgaged to private creditors. Finally, to secure a £478 debt to merchants Uriah Forrest and Benjamin Stoddert of Georgetown, Chase mortgaged to them his four household slaves, his carriage, and all his household goods—furniture, silver plate, books, tablecloths, even the bedsheets and pillowcases. Still he owed an additional £2,000 in unsecured debts, offset only by £1,200 in good debts owed to him. Of necessity he instituted legal proceedings against his debtors, even while defending himself from the suits of his creditors.[4] Gradually Chase's financial position stabilized, aided by a £350 advance from the legislature for his continued efforts in the English bank stock suit, by a gift of land from the faithful William Paca, and by the proceeds of his active legal practice. By the early 1790s Chase was able to make a modest and prudent investment in Baltimore lots.[5] At last the family's immediate future seemed reasonably secure.

The composition of the large household in Baltimore was changing as the older children grew up and began to leave home. Chase's eldest daughter Matilda married Elk Ridge attorney Henry Ridgely, who was later to become a General Court judge, in 1787. In the following year the young couple made Samuel Chase a grandfather for the first time. George Russel Birch Chase, Samuel's adventurous young half brother who had almost run away to sea in 1783, was also gone. He had secured an ensign's commission in the army. Serving under General Arthur St. Clair in the Northwest Territory, he was killed when Indians led by the Miami chief Little Turtle surprised and defeated St. Clair near Fort Wayne in November 1791. The family's only consolation was the knowledge that George died bravely while leading a charge, encouraging his men to continue the advance as he fell. Richard, the Reverend Thomas's other son by his second marriage, died of yellow fever in Philadelphia in the mid-1790s. Samuel, Jr. and Thomas were in and out of the household as they attended St. John's College, but both returned to Baltimore after completing their studies. Chase's grown daughter Ann remained home, as did his adult half sisters Ann and Elizabeth. The latter was built to the same generous proportions as Samuel. She also shared Chase's intelligence and lack of social grace, and a little of his gruff good humor, but some of the neighbors found her the least attractive member of the family.[6]

The Chase household did not lack children, however. In 1784 and 1785 Hannah Kitty Chase had borne her husband two daughters, Eliza and Mary. The long-range security of his wife and youngest children was of particular concern to Chase as he struggled to rebuild his fortunes. In 1793 he prevailed upon Colonel John Eager Howard to make a new deed to the Chase home in Baltimore. The property was now conveyed in trust to William Paca, to be held for the use of Samuel and Hannah Kitty during their lives and for Eliza and Mary after their parents' death. Understandable though it was, this action contributed to strife in the family for many years to come. After Chase's death Hannah Kitty, Eliza, and Mary quarreled over the property.[7]

More immediately, the arrangement added to existing tensions within the family. The children of Chase's first marriage had never really accepted their strong-willed, sometimes imperious[8] stepmother. Rightly or wrongly, they eventually came to believe that she sought control of the family's property for herself and her own daughters. Some years later Thomas Chase wrote that his father's "strange infatuation" had given Hannah Kitty an "unaccountable ascendancy" over him. It is difficult to picture Samuel Chase being dominated by anyone, but his declining health may have led him to lean more and more on his wife for management of the family's affairs. The older children still loved their father deeply and tried to suppress their discontent for his sake, but the home situation was not entirely a happy one.[9]

While mending his personal fortunes, Chase remained active in civic affairs. He continued to play an important role in his church, often representing St. Paul's Parish at Episcopal diocesan conventions. Since the 1780s Chase had collaborated with such Episcopal leaders as the Reverend William Smith in preparing legislation to secure the church's rights and property. In the 1790s he worked for several years with Bishop Thomas Claggett and others in writing and lobbying for a bill to incorporate the parish vestries.[10] The act finally passed the legislature in 1798. So skillfully was it drawn that Episcopal parishes in the Maryland Diocese are largely governed by it to the present day.

Samuel Chase was one of the first Marylanders to become involved in the organized antislavery movement. In 1789 the Maryland Society for Promoting the Abolition of Slavery and the Relief of Free Negroes and Others unlawfully held in Bondage was founded in Baltimore. Drawing its membership largely from Quakers and Methodists, the society opposed slavery in every form on Christian principles. It was the fourth antislavery society founded in the United States, reflecting a rising sentiment against slavery since the Revolution. Chase as a slaveholder was barred from membership by the society's constitution, but he and Luther Martin served for a time as honorary counsellors to the group. The title was apparently more than honorific, for the Baltimore Society was so active in helping slaves sue for their freedom that it incurred the anger of worried slaveholders. In 1791 the House of Delegates censured the society's conduct in one case, passed resolutions designed to curb its suits for freedom, and came very close to condemning the society altogether. In addition to its success in freeing a number of slaves, the society circulated antislavery petitions, worked for laws to make the peculiar institution more humane, and encouraged manumissions. Chase freed one of his own slaves with some provision for her support. Societies such as Baltimore's and the interstate organization they founded in 1794 were overshadowed in the nineteenth century by other and larger antislavery groups, but these early societies "established the broad outlines of the organized antislavery movement."[11]

Chase's appointment as honorary counsellor to the society may have been related to his success in winning freedom for a slave woman in a notable suit then making its way through the courts. The case of *Mary Butler v. Adam Craig* was decided by the Maryland General Court in 1787 and affirmed by the Court of Appeals in 1791. Butler, a mulatto slave, claimed her freedom on the ground that she was descended from a free white woman. Her great-grandmother, known as Irish Nell, had married a Negro slave in the seventeenth century. Under the Maryland colonial law then in effect but soon afterward repealed, a white woman who married a slave was bound to serve the slave's master until her husband's death and all children of the marriage were to be slaves. Irish Nell's descendants had been held in slavery under that law for more than a century. Mary Butler's parents had earlier sued for their freedom on different grounds than the ones she now raised, but had lost their case in the colonial Court of Appeals in 1770.

As counsel for Butler, Chase first had to persuade the Court of Appeals that the 1770 decision by a court of last resort did not bar his client from bringing her suit. Succeeding in that, he then had to overcome the argument that proof of Irish Nell's marriage established her descendants' slavery under the law then in force. Chase began by denouncing that law as "unjust and cruel; unjust to the mother because she is guilty of no crime, and most unjust and cruel to the offspring, who are wholly innocent." Irish Nell, he argued, was an English subject, entitled to the rights of Englishmen. She could not be punished unless convicted of some crime, and by common law was entitled to trial by jury. "As the act points out *no mode of conviction,*" he summed up, "I contend that there must be a trial according to the common law. . . . The law makes the marriage a crime. The marriage is a fact, and every fact created a crime, must be proved before a Jury." Since Irish Nell had never been convicted by a jury of the crime of marrying a slave, no penalty could be inflicted on her or her descendants. The seventeenth-century assembly surely intended no such thing, but the Court of Appeals accepted Chase's ingenious appeal to higher legal principles and set his client free.[12]

Chase's legal practice also included service to the state. On several occasions in the early 1790s, he was employed as special counsel to assist his friend, Attorney General Luther Martin, in important suits. He was also appointed by the legislature in 1794 to a commission to prepare a new testamentary code for the state.[13] There were, however, courts before which Chase could not practice because he was the judge. In 1788 Chase embarked upon a new second career in the judiciary that led him to new achievements and, predictably, new controversies.

In the spring of 1788 the legislature created a five-member criminal court for Baltimore County, the Court of Oyer and Terminer and Gaol Delivery, to provide swifter justice and deal with a rising crime rate in the growing town. Governor William Smallwood, a long-time political ally of Chase's, promptly appointed Chase to head the new court. At its first session Chase and his colleagues convicted forty-three persons, mostly felons and "some of them atrocious daring Villains." An uneasy Chase asked the governor for "twenty Stand of the public Arms...to prevent their Escape, which it is feared they will attempt, from labour on the public Roads."[14]

The criminal court also was given functions that overlapped the authority of the commissioners of Baltimore Town, another of the four governing bodies that shared jurisdiction over the as yet unincorporated city. The judges had jurisdiction over the town constables and night watch, street lighting, and road maintenance. Though Chase praised his colleagues and took pride in the court's work, he found its broad duties burdensome, especially since the judges received only a small daily attendance fee in compensation for their work. Early in 1790 he resigned, telling Governor John Eager Howard that he could no longer serve "in justice to my Family, who depend altogether on the profits of my profession, for their Support."

Chase added that recent troubles had made further service disagreeable to him. Already he had become embroiled in the controversy that characterized his entire career on the bench. He complained that it was impossible to enforce the law upon certain leading citizens of Baltimore, some of whom "openly traduce and vilify my Judicial Character." Chase stated that a licentious press, libeling with impunity the characters of private citizens, was a major problem in Baltimore. "The liberty of the press to enquire into the Measures of Government, and the public Conduct of its Officers (or even their private Characters) ought not to be restrained; but the publishing and exposing the follies (or even Vices) of *private* Citizens is truly the Licentiousness of the press, and ought to be punished." The distinction between liberty and licentiousness of the press, first raised in 1790, became a major theme in Chase's thinking. Founded upon English legal tradition and endorsed by Blackstone, that distinction was current among American lawyers of the period.[15]

Chase's resignation from the criminal court did not end his responsibility for local government. In June 1790 he was chosen by the commissioners of Baltimore Town to fill a vacancy on that body. The commissioners made appointments to minor local offices, kept up the market, set the standards of weights and measures, and performed a variety of similar functions. Chase's attendance at the commissioners' meetings was irregular, but he served on the body until 1798. By then the incorporation of Baltimore in 1796, which Chase actively supported, had established a mayor and council to govern the city. The commissioners retained only the power to conduct elections for representatives to the House of Delegates.[16]

Samuel Chase's most prominent action as commissioner was his conduct as an election judge in 1792. Federalists John O'Donnell and David McMechen won Baltimore's assembly seats, but the latter had a margin of only about ten votes over the third most popular candidate, Thomas Coulson. Coulson's supporters believed that some of McMechen's votes were "not...fairly Obtained." Chase as election judge was said to have "Acted in the most Arbitrary and Outrageous manner" in upholding his friend McMechen's narrow victory. When the polls closed, "a powerfull party of the Mechanics...provided a chair and were determined to hustle him into it and carry him to the Dock and there leave him to find his way out the best Way he could, they were however prevented by some prudent persons." The incident does not necessarily establish that Chase had become a partisan of the emerging Federalist party by 1792, but he was certainly moving in that direction.[17]

Chase's conversion from Antifederalist to Federalist was a gradual one. His attitude toward the new national government changed between 1788 and 1796 from opposition to apprehensive acquiescence in the people's verdict to reconciliation to enthusiastic support. Changing circumstances—personal, local, national, and international—were responsible for his shifting position.

After 1788 Chase gave up the fight against the Constitution and abided publicly by his pledge to support the new government. Still he remained worried about the Constitution. "I retain my Republican principles, though our Governments and the principles of the people, are changed, and are monarchical," he confided to his old Antifederalist friend Richard Henry Lee in July 1789. "I have the same Affection, and Attachment, as ever, to my Native Country, and her Rights; but for once, in all my life, I despair of the Republic." This was the statement of a passionate man in a fit of despondency. It should be read in the light of Chase's general depression at the time.

Preoccupied with his personal problems and his law practice in 1789, Chase claimed to be "little informed of what passes.... I see no News Papers, and I do not mix with the World." His letters to Lee, however, reveal that Chase remained abreast of current events. He generally approved of the Judiciary Act of 1789, which established the federal judiciary, finding it "ably drawn" but with "some defects." He would have preferred fewer restrictions on equity jurisdiction, a separate court of chancery, and changes in the provisions regarding juries. He criticized Washington's practice of nominating only one person to the Senate for each administrative office to be filled, finding it too reminiscent of the English idea "that all acts of Society should flow from the King alone—all Refusals from his Ministers." He feared that the salaries of Congress were set so low that only "the *wealthy*, or *adventurers*" could afford to serve.[18]

While finding plenty to criticize in the first moves of the new government, Chase rejoiced in the election of George Washington as president. Having the respected national hero at the head of the government was reassuring, even if Chase did not agree with all of Washington's early policies. Congress's approval in September 1789 of the constitutional amendments that became the Bill of Rights also helped reconcile Chase to the national government. He had originally expected "no essential alteration" from Congress's consideration of amendments. "I fear that no Check will be placed on the Exercise of any of the powers granted," Chase told Lee.[19] He was not mistaken, for the first ten amendments did little to restrict the powers of the national government. But the Bill of Rights did safeguard personal and civil liberty and the traditional guarantees of fair legal process, thus removing some of Chase's original objections to the Constitution. It certainly made the document more acceptable in his eyes.

While frankly expressing his fears about the new government to Lee, Chase cautioned his correspondent to keep his opinions confidential. "If I notice any thing to you it is without the least Intention of giving offence to anyone."[20] For the moment the defeated old warrior had had enough of controversy. His doubts about the federal structure must be kept private also because Chase was thinking of seeking appointment to office under the Constitition. He saw no inconsistency in doing so. Like it or not, the Constitution was an established fact. He had accepted the people's decision to adopt it, and its sweeping powers would be safer in his hands than in some others.

In September 1789 Chase wrote to Washington to solicit appointment to the United States Supreme Court. Again he pledged "that I will support the present government, agreeably to my late solemn engagement." Four days later Chase's friend Matthew Ridley wrote to John Jay asking the latter to use his influence on Chase's behalf. Ridley added that Chase would accept appointment as attorney general if he could not serve on the Supreme Court. Both Chase and Ridley frankly admitted that personal needs prompted Chase to seek the security of the federal bench. "He has a large Family," Ridley explained, "has met with many hard Rubs, and I believe at this Time feels heavily the weight of his Family from the difficulty of making such a provision for them as he might heretofore have reasonably expected. . . . He gets rather too much advanced in Life for the drudgery of the Law."[21]

The application was unsuccessful. Jay told Ridley that his request had come too late, adding that Washington's "personal knowledge of distinguished Characters throughout the States" made him independent of advice on high appointments anyway.[22] Chase and Washington may have been old friends and collaborators, but Chase's recent outspoken Antifederalism disqualified him for national office.

Before long, though, shifts occurred in Maryland politics that began to bring Chase and some of his former adversaries closer together. For Maryland the major political issue of 1790 was the location of the national capital. Baltimore wanted the capital badly, but Congress chose a Potomac River site. Maryland's senators and the majority of her congressmen voted for the Potomac location. Feeling betrayed, Baltimore, Annapolis, and northern Chesapeake interests launched a "Chesapeake" party ticket for the 1790 elections that swept out of Congress the "Potomac" party based in southern and western Maryland. Chase helped organize the Chesapeake slate, collaborating not only with his former Antifederalist colleagues William Pinkney and John Francis Mercer but also with Federalists like Robert and Samuel Smith, Alexander Contee Hanson, Philip B. Key, James McHenry, and Otho Holland Williams. The Chesapeake party fell apart after the 1790 election, and it contained both future Federalists and future Republicans. But the 1790 campaign did ease Chase's slow transition from Antifederalist to Federalist, and it marked his political rehabilitation in his home state. Especially significant was Chase's first rapprochement with McHenry, a close friend of Washington who had a powerful voice in appointments to federal office in Maryland. McHenry had already been instrumental in securing William Paca's appointment as federal district judge for Maryland in an astute move to reconcile the state's Antifederalists.[23] Thus by the end of 1790 the Federalist-Antifederalist lines of 1788 in Maryland were dissolving, and Chase was again becoming respectable in the eyes of some of his old opponents.

The extent of Chase's rehabilitation with the state's leaders became clear in September 1791, when he was elected to the state Senate. He received twenty-nine votes from the thirty-nine electors present. Chase was honored to be chosen at last for the post he had sought so eagerly five years earlier, but he quickly resigned in order to accept a position he now wanted more. In August, Governor Howard and his council appointed Chase chief judge of the General Court. Chase hesitated briefly before accepting, telling the governor that he needed to arrange his personal and legal affairs, but there was little doubt that he would take the position. As Luther Martin noted, the chief judgeship was "a tolerable Provision for him in the decline of Health and Life."[24]

Here was the post of honor and security that Chase had been seeking to provide for his family in his declining years. The only drawback was that the chief judge's salary of £600 was generally admitted to be inadequate. That may well have been the real reason for Chase's hesitation about accepting the appointment. Perhaps he received some private assurances on that point, however, for not long after his acceptance the legislature came up with a roundabout way of augmenting his salary that bore the seeds of future trouble.

In 1790 the legislature had passed an act aimed at upgrading the professional competence of the county courts by grouping them into five judicial districts, with a legally trained chief justice and two associate justices for each district. A similar attempt was made to upgrade the Baltimore County criminal court by requiring that its chief justice be a man of legal knowledge and experience and providing an attractive salary for the post, but the bill died in the

Senate. In the fall session of 1791, when that bill was reintroduced, everyone understood that the chief justiceship of the Baltimore County criminal court, with its proposed salary of £200, would go to Samuel Chase to supplement his income as chief judge of the General Court.

A strong and vocal opposition to the proposal quickly developed in Baltimore County, led by city delegate Samuel Smith. The critics pointed out that the £200 salary of the chief justice of the criminal court would be borne by the taxpayers of the county. This "indirect mode" of supplementing the income of the chief judge of the General Court was seen as unfair. The whole state, not just one county, should provide the judge with an adequate salary. Smith believed the arrangement unconstitutional, since plural officeholding was explicitly forbidden. And would not the right of appeal be undermined in cases appealed from Judge Chase of Baltimore County to Judge Chase of the General Court?

Despite these objections the legislature passed the bill. In December 1791 Chase accepted his second appointment as chief justice of the Baltimore County Court of Oyer and Terminer. Resentment of the arrangement remained alive in Baltimore and reemerged in 1794. Nor was Chase entirely satisfied with his income, even though he could continue to practice law on a limited basis before courts other than his own. In 1793 he asked the legislature for an increase in his General Court salary.[25]

The General Court was the "one chief trial court" of Maryland. It heard appeals from the county courts in both civil and criminal cases and also had original jurisdiction in suits between residents of different counties. The General Court's decisions could be appealed to the Court of Appeals, which stood at the apex of the state judicial system, but the General Court was considered the more important of the two. It was regarded as the chief court of Maryland. The General Court met twice a year at both Annapolis on the Western Shore and Easton on the Eastern Shore, thus requiring the judges to travel. Chase's colleagues on the court were judges Robert Goldsborough and Jeremiah Townley Chase.[26]

The General Court's business consisted mostly of routine cases involving debts, land titles and occupancy, estates, and other ordinary civil and criminal matters. The nature of the court's business provided very few opportunities for landmark decisions. In one case, though, Chase expressed an opinion that a 1791 act of assembly "was in opposition to the [state] declaration of rights, and therefore void." His colleagues overruled him, but the case was an early illustration of Chase's belief that the courts possessed the power to strike down unconstitutional laws.[27]

Chase's service on the Baltimore County criminal court was more significant in shaping his political position. Revolution in France was giving rise to a series of events in the world, the nation, and Baltimore that caused him enthusiastically to embrace the Federalist persuasion. Chase's judicial duties in Baltimore provided his point of direct contact with these events.

Americans at first hailed the outbreak of the French Revolution with joy, but the rise of the Jacobins and the Reign of Terror resulted in a deep division of opinion. Polarization increased in 1793, when France went to war with England. Federalists supported Britain as the defender of ordered liberty; Republicans sympathized with France as the champion of democracy and the rights of man. Washington's proclamation of neutrality in the war was nevertheless generally approved, in Baltimore as elsewhere in America,[28] though Republicans disliked the president's call for impartiality. During 1793 Federalists, alarmed at the spread of radical French ideas in America, were horrified by French ambassador Edmond Genêt's attempts to enlist Americans in aiding his country and by his appeals for popular support against Washington's enforcement of neutral conduct.

Late in the year, however, American opinion turned strongly against Britain. The British suddenly began seizing large numbers of American ships engaged in the French West Indies trade. Congress rejected a Republican plan for commercial retaliation against England but in March 1794 adopted a thirty-day embargo on foreign trade, which was later extended for another month. The administration sent John Jay to England in an attempt to avoid war by negotiating a settlement.

Chase's hometown followed these developments with keen interest. The newspapers were filled with reports from France and England. A commercial center with a large stake in the West Indies trade, Baltimore suffered from English seizures and gave priority to protecting her commerce. The city strongly supported the embargo. Feeling against England ran high, and pro-French sentiment increased. From the Baltimore newspapers it appears that the towns-people generally favored preparations for military defense against England. Some people wanted war, while others hoped that Jay could achieve a settlement. Volunteer militia companies formed and drilled. One enthusiastically pro-French unit called itself the Baltimore Sans Culottes.[29]

Samuel Chase viewed the spread of French revolutionary doctrines in his town and nation with great alarm. Since the 1780s he had consistently leaned toward England. His regard for English institutions, especially in the legal realm, was high. The English tradition, he believed, furnished the basis for a properly ordered liberty. French radicalism, on the other hand, seemed to him to threaten the principle of social order on which the stability of the still fragile American experiment in republicanism largely rested. He was indignant over the conduct of Ambassador Genêt and alarmed by the degree of support the Frenchman initially received in America.[30]

Chase saw the spread of French ideas in America as a threat not only to ordered liberty but also to religion, which he believed vital to republican virtue. French writings, and especially Thomas Paine's *Age of Reason,* were arousing great debate in Baltimore by 1794. A loyal and active churchman, Chase reacted strongly against French "atheism." His parish, St. Paul's, was a citadel of high-church Episcopalianism. The rector, Reverend Joseph G. J. Bend, and the most prominent members of the congregation were staunchly Federalist, pro-British, and vocally opposed to French irreligion.[31] For religious as well as political reasons, Chase became convinced that the effects of the French Revolution in America threatened decisively to upset the balance between order and liberty and to destroy both. Responsible as chief justice of the Baltimore County criminal court for the preservation of order in Baltimore, he confronted the threat of disorder head on during the tumultuous year of 1794.

Chase's first opportunity to strengthen the hand of order came in March 1794, when the Court of Oyer and Terminer heard the case of two Baltimore printers charged with publishing just the sort of libel against a private citizen that Chase had denounced four years earlier. In his charge to the jury, Chase undertook to educate the public with a long address on the "distinction between the freedom and licentiousness of the press." His interpretation of the law would have led to the defendants' conviction, but the jury disre-

garded it and returned a verdict of acquittal.[32] The defeat strengthened Chase's fear that disorder in Baltimore was getting out of
hand.

In May his fears received graphic confirmation. The embargo was
then in effect,[33] and many ships lay idle in Baltimore Harbor. Passersby noticed that a ship captain named Ramsdell was flying the flag
upside down on his vessel at Fell's Point. Ramsdell was apparently
drunk, and he refused to right his colors. His disrespect to the
American flag infuriated the residents of Fell's Point, a poor neighborhood, dependent on shipping, that was becoming Baltimore's
Republican stronghold. It was rumored that Ramsdell was "in the
service of England." Soon a mob assembled, and Ramsdell and
another unfortunate man were tarred and feathered.

Chase immediately convened the Court of Oyer and Terminer to
investigate the riot. The result was the arrest of Captain David Stodder and six other presumed ringleaders of the mob. When the suspects were brought before the court, Chase ordered them to give
bond for their appearance at the court's next regular session and for
their good behavior in the meantime. Stodder and the others refused, to the cheers of the numerous spectators. Stodder later told
Chase he would rather "go to gaol, as it appeared...there were
near two thousand people in Baltimore Town, who said I ought not
to enter into a recognizance for what I had done." Chase ordered
the prisoners jailed, but the sheriff reported that he could not do it
because of the crowd, and that no one would serve on a posse to help
him. "Summon me, sir," Chase stoutly replied, "I will be the
posse comitatus, I will take him to jail."

In the meantime threats were flying through the crowd. Some
said the jail would be destroyed and the rioters rescued; others
threatened to pull down Chase's house and even assault the judge
himself. Some leading citizens who were in the courtroom advised
Chase to let the prisoners go for his own safety. "God forbid,"
Chase answered, "that my countrymen should ever be guilty of so
daring an outrage; but, sir, with the blessing of God, I will do my
duty...the life of one man is of little consequence compared to the
prostration of the laws of the land; with the blessing of God, I will
do my duty, be the consequences what they may."

To alleviate the tension, Chase then adjourned the court to allow
the defendants to reconsider giving bond. The situation was alarming; many citizens obviously opposed the execution of the law, and

{ 171 }

the rest—except for his fellow justices and a few others—seemed to Chase to be indifferent. Chase was informed that "the privates of the volunteer companies would not turn out to prevent the rioters being rescued" from custody. He issued a handbill detailing the threats he had heard, reaffirming his determination "to do my duty at every risque," and asking the citizens of Baltimore to consider "whether you ought to suffer an outrage to your laws . . . so destructive of all order, and so subversive of your government." Chase feared he would have to ask the governor for help in enforcing the law, but in the end some responsible gentlemen persuaded Stodder and his accomplices to give the required security.[34] Chase had won the first round.

Particularly worrisome to Chase was the fact that some of those involved in the riot were officers who should have been trying to keep order. Stodder was a militia captain. Robert Townsend, a captain of the night watch, had "carried the colours" at the head of the mob. The Court of Oyer and Terminer promptly broke Townsend of his rank, but when the night watch assembled the next evening Townsend and a group of his Fell's Point supporters argued that he had been "put in by the Citizens of Fell's Point" and should not be demoted.[35] The notion of direct popular rule reflected in this incident, stimulated by French revolutionary ideas, implied to Chase an overturn of duly constituted authority that threatened the foundations of republican order. The disorders in Baltimore were magnified in his eyes by the outbreak of the Whiskey Rebellion in Pennsylvania.

As if things were not bad enough, June 1794 brought the founding of the Republican Society of Baltimore, one of a number of similar political clubs that were springing up across the nation. Fearing that Federalist policies endangered liberty again as England had in the 1760s, Republicans responded by reviving the popular political organizations of the American revolutionary period. The Baltimore society's stated purpose was "to study the laws and constitution of their own and other countries—to watch the operations of government and scrutinize the principles and conduct of men in power. . . . to beget a knowledge of our rights" and thereby help a vigilant people preserve their liberty.[36]

Innocuous as the societies were, Federalists tended to see them as dangerous combinations "associated with pro-French opinions and democractic excess." The French influence was indeed strong in the societies. The members of the Republican Society of Baltimore drank toasts to the French Republic and addressed one another as "Citizen." Chase was probably aware, too, that at least one of those arrested for leading the Fell's Point riot was very active in the society.[37]

To Chase's dismay, the Republican Society quickly became politically powerful in Baltimore. Both of the city delegates to the legislature elected in the fall of 1794 were officers of the society. The Republican Society, supported by the people of Fell's Point, was instrumental in blocking the incorporation of Baltimore, for which Chase was working, until 1796. Chase undoubtedly read with approval the Federalist newspaper satirist who wrote "opposing" incorporation "that almost every law heretofore passed at Annapolis, either abridges natural liberty, which I do not understand, or lays restraints upon the rights of man, of which I am equally ignorant. . . . No, no, my dear fellow citizens! Continue to respect the laws of tar and feathers, club laws, and committee laws, as the only laws by which freeman ought to be governed!"[38]

The climax of Chase's struggle with disorder in Baltimore came at the August 1794 session of the Court of Oyer and Terminer. Chase opened the session by rebuking the sheriff for summoning a very poor grand jury, which included a supporter of the Fell's Point riot. His apprehension was justified. Instead of indicting the rioters, the grand jury seized the opportunity to strike back at Chase and pursue an old Baltimore grievance. The jurors returned presentments against Samuel Chase "for abuse of power in daring to Censure the Sheriff for not summoning a Jury to his approbation," against the governor for appointing Chase to two offices of profit in violation of the state constitution, and against Chase for accepting the unconstitutional appointments. The grand jurors cited those matters as grievances on the theory that they had "by natural law, a right to complain of all grievances."

Chase responded by informing the grand jury that they had no power to present offenses committed outside the county or to present grievances. Inquiry into grievances was a function of the House of Delegates, to whom complaints should be directed. "If my acceptance of the office is an offence," Chase stated, "I shall readily submit to the Decision of the Law." But the grand jury had no right to judge questions of constitutionality "and presume to censure the Conduct of your *Superiors.*" In Chase's view, the grand jury's erroneous and exaggerated view of natural rights, stimulated no doubt by pernicious French doctrines, was another example of the threat to social and political order in America. If the grand jury could present the governor for a grievance, it could also present the president, Congress, or the legislature. "Do not such principles tend to set up the inferior departments of government (as in the present case Grand Juries...) above the superior departments...? Do not such principles tend to overturn all government?"[39]

Chase's opponents took his advice to bring their grievances before the legislature. At the fall session, Delegate Walter Dorsey of St. Mary's County introduced resolutions stating that Chase's plural officeholding violated the constitution and formally requesting the governor to remove him as chief judge of the General Court. Given a chance to argue his side of the case before the House, Chase defended the constitutionality of his appointments. In any case, he reminded the delegates, judges could be constitutionally removed "*only* for *misbehaviour* on *conviction in a court of law.*" By a narrow margin of thirty-two to twenty-nine, the House declined to put the question on the resolution asserting the unconstitutionality of Chase's appointments. The request for his removal was defeated forty-one to twenty.[40]

There was another way to remove Chase from one of his offices, however. The legislature proceeded to pass a bill abolishing the Baltimore County Court of Oyer and Terminer and replacing it with separate criminal courts for the city and county. Another bill was introduced to curtail the jurisdiction of the General Court.[41] Thus by the end of 1794 Chase found his salary reduced by the abolition of one of his offices. He and, through him, the state judiciary were under assault. His position in state government was not a comfortable one.

Chase had never given up his wish for federal office, and the events of 1794 strengthened both his desire for a federal appointment and his chances of success. Even before 1794 he was working assiduously to enlist support for his preferment. In 1793 he obtained the backing of Commissioner of the Revenue Tench Coxe, who promised to promote Chase's interests. Confident of Coxe's aid, Chase in July 1794 applied unsuccessfully to President Washington for the vacant collectorship of the port of Baltimore, the most lucrative federal plum in Maryland.[42]

The key to Chase's eventual success was James McHenry, Washington's chief adviser on Maryland appointments. McHenry was favorably impressed with Chase's defense of order in Baltimore in 1794 and was increasingly willing to forget their past differences. Chase, reconciled to the Constitution by the Bill of Rights, by Washington's presidency, by the failure of his prophecies of disaster to come true, by his own need for a secure position and a good income, and by the necessity of a strong government to defend republican order in the 1790s, had in 1794 demonstrated his conversion to Federalism. He and McHenry began a regular correspondence. By November 1794 Chase felt close enough to McHenry to solicit his support for William Pinkney's brother Ninian, who wanted to be appointed clerk of the Senate.[43]

McHenry considered himself and Chase "on neither good nor bad terms, neither friends nor enemies." By the middle of 1795, though, he was ready to write Washington recommending Chase for the next vacancy on the Supreme Court. "Among the inducements I feel for presenting his name," McHenry wrote, "...is his general conduct since the adoption of our government and the sense I entertain of the part he bore in the revolutionary efforts of a long and trying crisis. You know that his services and abilities were of much use to the cause...sometimes by the measures he proposed or had influence to get adopted, and sometimes by the steady opposition he gave to the intrigues raised against yourself." Chase's reputed misdeeds, McHenry thought, had been "greatly exaggerated" and were still trumpeted only by "a few men who seem determined to pursue him to old age with a rancour, which...no political quarrel can excuse." He added that Charles Carroll of Carrollton and "most persons in the State of influence and discernment" seemed to feel the same way. Finally, Chase had "professional knowledge" plus "a very valuable stock of political science and information" and had performed his judicial duties in Maryland with great integrity. William Vans Murray seconded McHenry's lobbying efforts on Chase's behalf.[44]

Though he was grateful for Chase's services during the War for Independence, Washington still had his doubts. Late in 1795 he considered Chase for the office of attorney general, but decided against him. Admitting Chase's ability, the president noted that he was "violently opposed in his own State, by a party, and...has been, accused of some impurity in his conduct."[45]

By the beginning of 1796 Washington had overcome his misgivings. On January 20 he wrote McHenry asking him to see if Chase would accept a seat on the Supreme Court made available by the resignation of Justice John Blair of Virginia. In the same letter he asked McHenry to become secretary of war. McHenry accepted and reported that Chase would also. "You have made an old veteran very proud and happy," he told Washington of Chase.

The Senate confirmed Chase's nomination the day after Washington submitted it. But many Federalists doubted its wisdom. William Plumer thought that the appointment did "not increase the respectability and dignity of the Judiciary." Oliver Wolcott confided to a friend that he had "but an unworthy opinion of" Chase, and Supreme Court Justice James Iredell was "not impressed with a very favorable opinion of his moral character, whatever his professional abilities may be."[46] His checkered past still hanging over him, Chase was not fully accepted by his own party as he set out for Philadelphia to assume his duties as associate justice of the United States Supreme Court.

Fourteen

ASSOCIATE JUSTICE

N 1796 Samuel Chase became part of an infant federal judiciary struggling to define in practice its constitutional role. The Constitution provided for a Supreme Court and such inferior courts as Congress chose to establish, and it outlined the boundaries of the federal judiciary's jurisdiction. But the fundamental law could not specify the details of judicial procedure, structure, and function. It did not explicitly give the judiciary the power to declare acts of Congress and the executive unconstitutional, but most of the founders believed that this keystone of the Supreme Court's influence as guardian of the Constitution was necessarily implied. During the 1790s it was left to Congress and the Court itself to fill in the specifics of the judiciary's constitutional mandate. The federal courts had to establish their place in the American system of government, to make their own precedents and establish their procedures. The justices of the formative decade before 1800 therefore played a very important role in giving life to the Constitution. None made a greater contribution to the work of the high court than Samuel Chase.[1]

The federal judiciary at the time of Chase's appointment was organized under the Judiciary Act of 1789 as amended in 1793. There were six Supreme Court justices, three federal circuit courts, and thirteen district courts. The Supreme Court met twice a year in Philadelphia. The circuit courts, which held two sessions a year in each district in the circuit, were each composed of one Supreme Court justice and a judge of the relevant district court. The Supreme Court justices therefore had to ride circuit. They took the three circuits—

Eastern, Middle, and Southern—in rotation, each justice normally being assigned to one term of one circuit court per year.[2]

The rigors of riding circuit in an age of bad roads and poor to indifferent accommodations took a physical toll on the justices, who also disliked being away from their families for a substantial part of the year. The illness of some justices and the nonjudicial duties assigned to others—such as the diplomatic missions of chief justices John Jay and Oliver Ellsworth—often caused the circuit courts to fall behind in their dockets, a source of criticism throughout the country.[3] Chase's growing physical infirmity made it especially difficult for him to cope with the burdens of circuit duty.

These physical demands were attached to an appointment that prominent attorneys and politicians in the 1790s generally considered neither a great honor, nor a post of great influence, nor a particularly good living. The high court tried no cases at all from 1789 to 1792. By 1801 it had heard only sixty-three, "averaging less than one of real significance each year." For all these reasons it was not easy to persuade outstanding lawyers to serve on the Court. Justice John Rutledge had resigned to become chief justice of South Carolina; John Jay gave up the chief justiceship of the United States to become governor of New York. By 1801 ten men had resigned or refused appointments to the Supreme Court.[4] A lawyer of Chase's ability and Federalist persuasion who wanted to serve was a find not to be lightly overlooked.

Chase's appointment as associate justice came immediately before the February 1796 term of the Supreme Court. Worried that the Court might not have a quorum without him, Washington impressed on Chase the importance of hurrying to Philadelphia. Chase set out immediately, postponing personal and family business until after the session. His haste is revealed by the fact that he had to ask one of his colleagues to meet the April circuit court at New York for him so that he could tend to his personal affairs.[5]

The new justice was immediately included in the social life of the capital. During this term he was the guest of honor at a dinner given by Senator William Bingham and his wife. The accomplished hostess served a fine banquet prepared by a French chef. Chase, "having searched in vain for some familiar dish," bluntly announced to his hostess that he could eat nothing on the table. Mrs. Bingham was not at all disconcerted; she inquired what Chase would like and sent a servant for the roast beef he requested. The judge devoured this repast with gusto, ignoring the fine French wines on the table and drinking brown stout instead. Having finished, he is said to have remarked with great satisfaction to his long-suffering hostess, "There, Madam, I have made a sensible, and an excellent dinner, but no thanks to your French cook!"[6] Chase's social graces obviously had not improved since his youth, and he was now too old to change the habits of a lifetime.

Meanwhile Chase renewed his acquaintance with the new chief justice, Oliver Ellsworth of Connecticut, and with Justice James Wilson of Pennsylvania. He had served with both in the Continental Congress. He also met his other colleagues, justices William Cushing of Massachusetts, James Iredell of North Carolina, and William Paterson of New Jersey, and the Court settled down to business. Chase's first term on the Supreme Court gave rise to two of his most important decisions. One came in the case of *Ware v. Hylton,* in which Chase issued his first Supreme Court opinion.

During the War for Independence, Virginia, like Maryland and other states, had passed an act authorizing debtors of British creditors to discharge their obligations by paying paper money into the state loan office. Daniel Hylton had taken advantage of that law. Later the Treaty of Paris of 1783, which ended the war, had provided that British creditors should meet with no obstacles in collecting prewar debts in full from Americans. Ware, as administrator of the estate of Hylton's British creditor, claimed that he was entitled to collect under the treaty; Hylton replied that his payment into the Virginia loan office extinguished the debt and the treaty could not revive it. The circuit court had ruled for Hylton, and Ware was appealing its decision. The case was very important, for upon the Supreme Court's ruling depended the fate of many other prewar British creditors and American debtors. At stake was an estimated $2 million or more in debts in Virginia alone. In addition, since party sentiment in America was running high over the British-French conflict in Europe, "political excitement over the case was intense."[7]

Chase at first wanted to abstain from the decision. He had been counsel for American debtors in an earlier suit in Maryland that involved the same issue and had taken a strong public stand on the British debt question in the 1780s. His colleagues, though, advised him not to withdraw. The advice was fortunate, for Chase's lengthy opinion in *Ware v. Hylton* has been described as "something of a *tour de force.*" In the 1790s the justices often read their opinions *seriatim,* beginning with the least senior member of the Court. Chase therefore spoke first, and his "close and exhaustive analysis and...trenchant presentation of the issues" left his concurring brethren with nothing new of substance to add.[8]

Chase began by arguing that Virginia during the War for Independence was a sovereign state. Her legislature was "invested with the supreme and sovereign power of the state," limited only by the state constitution. As a sovereign and independent state, Virginia had the right to confiscate enemy property, including private debts. Hylton's payment under Virginia law therefore was "a bar to the plaintiff's action" unless the peace treaty removed the obstacle. Chase held that the Confederation Congress had the power to annul a previous state act by treaty. The Treaty of Paris was obligatory on the states under the Articles of Confederation. The Constitution, by making treaties the supreme law of the land, removed any doubt on the point. "A treaty cannot be the supreme law of the land...if any act of a state legislature can stand in its way." State laws like Virginia's were therefore "null and void," and the courts were obliged so to declare them. Adding a personal note reminiscent of his stand on British debts in Maryland in the 1780s, Chase suggested that Virginia indemnify debtors like Hylton who had depended on the state's faith and been injured by the treaty.[9] Chase's opinion on the supremacy of national treaties over state law has stood the test of time.

Daniel Hylton was a busy man in 1796. He was also a principal in the other significant case of the term, *Hylton v. United States,* in which the Supreme Court was called upon for the first time to consider the constitutionality of an act of Congress. In 1794 Congress had imposed a tax of eight dollars on carriages. Hylton refused to pay the levy, contending that it was a direct tax within the meaning of the Constitution and therefore violated the provision that all such taxes must be apportioned among the states in proportion to population. The government replied that the tax was constitutionally a duty, impost or excise, which need only be uniform throughout the United States. The circuit court for the district of Virginia being divided on the issue, the government and the defendant agreed upon a fictitious statement of facts to bring the case before the Supreme Court for the sole purpose of testing the constitutionality of the tax.

The case attracted great interest, not only because of the issue involved but also because Alexander Hamilton appeared along with Attorney General Charles Lee as counsel for the United States. Justice Iredell noted that the hearing, at which Hamilton spoke with "astonishing ability," was "attended by the most crowded audience I ever saw" at a Supreme Court session, "both Houses of Congress being almost deserted on the occasion."[10]

The four justices who participated in the decision ruled unanimously for the government. Chase again gave his opinion first. He commented that, if the Supreme Court had the power to declare an unconstitutional act of Congress void, he would exercise that power only "in a very clear case." If the issue was doubtful, the Court should accept the opinion of Congress that its act was constitutional. It was unnecessary in this case, however, to determine whether or not the Supreme Court possessed the power to strike down an act of Congress; the tax on carriages was a duty and therefore constitutional. "The Constitution evidently contemplated no taxes as direct taxes, but only such as Congress could lay in proportion to the *census*" without "great inequality and injustice." Chase easily showed that it would be unreasonable and unequal to apportion a tax on carriages among the states according to population.

Beyond the implication that the Supreme Court could strike down unconstitutional acts of Congress as well as of state legislatures, what made Chase's opinion significant was a pithy definition of direct taxation: "I am inclined to think, but of this I do not give a judicial opinion, that the direct taxes contemplated by the constitution, are only two, to wit, a capitation or poll tax, simply, without regard to property, profession or any other circumstance; and a tax on land." In spite of its informality, Chase's *obiter dictum* was accepted l the Court for a century. Its reversal in the income tax cases of 1895 necessitated the Sixteenth Amendment to the Constitution.[11]

In the fall term of 1796 the Supreme Court faced another explosive case that raised the question of the effect of the peace treaty on confiscated British property. *Hunter v. Fairfax's Devisee* directly or indirectly involved title to some thirty thousand acres of land in Virginia. Hunter's counsel died shortly before the Court met, and Hunter requested a continuance. The Court overruled the opposition's vehement objections and granted the delay on the grounds that new counsel should have adequate time to study and prepare such an important case. "It is a matter . . . of great moment," Chase commented, "and ought to be deliberately and finally settled." The Court's postponement of the issue was fortunate for the nation. When finally issued in 1816, after Chase's death, the Court's ruling produced a confrontation between Virginia and the federal judiciary. Had that conflict come in 1796, when the nation was bitterly divided over other issues and the Supreme Court's place in the American system of government not yet firmly established, it could have been damaging.[12]

In the meantime, Chase was getting used to the arduous business of riding circuit. His first assignments to the Eastern and Southern circuits required a great deal of advance planning, for they took Chase into unfamiliar territory. Before his first trip to the South in 1797 Chase wrote Justice Iredell in North Carolina to inquire about travel arrangements. His letters reveal the problems that Chase had to deal with as he planned his official rounds. How long would it take to reach Savannah by water? Were there reliable stage lines between the major cities in the Carolinas with connections to Virginia, or should he bring along his own carriage on the boat? If the latter, could good horses be bought at a reasonable price? Could Iredell give him directions on the roads? What were the names of the federal court officers on the Southern Circuit?[13]

Chase on circuit traveled by stage whenever possible to avoid the trouble and expense of driving his own carriage. This arrangement may have been more satisfactory for him, but his great bulk could pose problems for his fellow passengers in a crowded public conveyance. One traveler encountered Chase late in 1797:

On leaving Baltimore the last person to enter the stage was a huge man with a stentorian voice. Behold justice incarnate! He was Chase, one of the most prominent judges of Maryland, and the greatest cart-horse I ever knew! He planted himself in front of me on top of me, and I had to turn sideways and thrust my elbow in his back. The man having evidently had the lion's share everywhere . . . took exception to my posture. I replied spiritedly that I was in my right place and he should confine himself to his. . . . "Never mind, never mind" was his reply. However he did not change his posture, and it may have been through antipathy to his profession that I called his attention to my discomfort. Finally he complied with my request, but woe to my pleas before the Supreme Court![14]

The traveler might have been more understanding had he realized that Chase's gout limited his mobility.

Chase's declining health hindered his circuit duties. Early in 1799 he was sick for ten weeks. "For some Days I was very ill. I was so very weak, that I could not walk across my Room without assistance.... my Cough is still bad and the Spitting continues. My Lungs are so very weak, that I cannot bear any but very gentle Exercise." Convinced that "a Relapse would be fatal," Chase missed most of his assigned tour of the Eastern Circuit. Another six weeks of rest restored his health, and he set out for New Hampshire to meet the latter sessions of the circuit, though he was apprehensive that "the fatigue will bring on some [illegible] of my Complaints."[15]

Chase on circuit stood out among his colleagues for his attempt to follow standardized common-law principles of construction and procedure in the federal courts. Having as yet no uniform rules of federal procedure in the 1790s, the federal district and circuit courts generally followed the practice of the state courts in the state where they sat. This practice became the rule, but Chase was never comfortable with it. In the April term of 1797 he and District Judge Joseph Clay promulgated codes of procedural rules for cases at common law and equity in the circuit court for Georgia. These rules have been called "the boldest attempt made by any [federal] court during this early period to supplement the generalities of the statutes, and to settle details that we suspect were still at large." For pleadings, too, Chase consistently insisted on using common-law forms.[16]

In the Supreme Court, as well, Chase was conspicuous for his belief in following the common law rather than state practice. The case of *Brown v. Van Braam*, an action to recover the value of protested bills of exchange, hinged upon points of procedure and construction. The Court decided the case on the basis of the laws and judicial construction of Rhode Island, where it had originated. But Chase, while concurring in the judgment, pointedly stated that he based his opinion "on common-law principles, and not...the laws and practice of the state." During the trial he commented, "If, indeed, the practice of the several states were, in every case, to be adopted, we should be involved in an endless labyrinth of false constructions, and idle forms.''[17] Chase's desire for regular federal rules of procedure and construction put him ahead of his time.

Chase's advocacy of the common law extended only to procedure and construction. He also differed from his colleagues in asserting that the federal courts could not entertain criminal prosecutions at common law. Chase announced this surprising conclusion in the case of *United States v. Worrall,* heard in the circuit court for Pennsylvania in April term 1798. The defendant was charged with attempting to bribe Commissioner of the Revenue Tench Coxe in order to get a contract for building a lighthouse at Cape Hatteras. Robert Worrall had been convicted in federal district court, but on appeal his attorney, Alexander J. Dallas, pointed out that neither the Constitution nor any federal statute made it a crime to bribe a commissioner of the revenue. District Attorney William Rawle sought to correct this legislative oversight by arguing that the offense could be indicted at common law. Chase interrupted to inform Rawle that such an "indictment cannot be maintained in this court." He then launched into an opinion endorsing Dallas's argument that the federal government's powers were derived only from the Constitution and constitutional acts of Congress. The courts could not "punish a man for any act, before it is declared by a law of the United States to be criminal." As for the common law, "If, indeed, the United States can be supposed. . . to have a common law, it must, I presume, be that of England; and yet, it is impossible to trace when, or how, the system was adopted or introduced." The colonies had indeed adopted "so much of the common law, as was applicable to their local situation," but there was a great difference from colony to colony. "What is the common law to which we are referred? Is it the common law entire as it exists in England; or modified as it exists in some of the states; and of the various modifications, which are we to select?" No authority, Chase concluded, could be produced for the United States, as opposed to the states, having adopted a common law at all.

Chase's colleague on the court, District Judge Richard Peters, strongly disagreed with his position. Since the court was divided and the parties could not agree on an appeal to the Supreme Court, Chase and Peters held a short consultation. They then affirmed

Worrall's conviction but mitigated his sentence. Perhaps Peters reminded Chase that all the precedents were against him. Indictments at common law were generally entertained in federal courts, and had been since 1793. Chase on this point found himself in company with the Jeffersonians against the position of most Federalists. His position was eventually accepted by the Supreme Court in 1812.[18]

Later in 1798 Chase laid down in a Supreme Court opinion a definition of *ex post facto* laws under the Constitution that is still accepted today. The case of *Calder v. Bull* involved inheritance of property under a contested will. A Connecticut state court had originally invalidated the will and awarded the property in question to the Calders. The state legislature, however, passed a special act setting aside the court's decree and granting a new hearing, at which the will was upheld and the Bulls received the property. The Calders appealed, claiming that the legislature's act was an *ex post facto* law prohibited by the United States Constitution.

The Calders lost their case. The four justices who participated in the decision all agreed that *ex post facto* laws under the Constitution referred only to criminal cases and penalties, not to all retrospective legislation. The prohibition, Chase explained, was intended to eliminate abuses, such as bills of attainder, that *ex post facto* criminal laws had given rise to in England. It did not "secure the citizen in his private rights of either property or contracts." Then came Chase's lasting definition of *ex post facto* laws:

> 1st. Every law that makes an action done before the passing of the law, and which was innocent when done, criminal; . . . 2d. Every law that aggravates a crime, or makes it greater than it was, when committed. 3d. Every law that . . . inflicts a greater punishment, than the law annexed to the crime, when committed. 4th. Every law that alters the legal rules of evidence, and receives less, or different testimony, than the law required at the time of . . . the offence, in order to convict the offender.

The decision met with considerable criticism. Many people had looked upon the prohibition of *ex post facto* laws as a protection against legislative interference with property rights. Chase seemed to anticipate that objection in his opinion, for he stated another principle designed to curb legislative infringements on person and property. The nature of the social contract and "certain vital principles in our free republican governments," he asserted, would "overrule an apparent and flagrant abuse of legislative power" even in the absence of an express constitutional prohibition.

> The people of the United States erected their constitution . . . to establish justice, to promote the general welfare, to secure the blessings of liberty, and to protect their persons and property from violence. The purposes for which men enter into society . . . are the foundation of the legislative power, [and] they will decide what are the proper objects of it. . . . An act of the legislature (for I cannot call it a law) contrary to the great first principles of the social compact, cannot be a rightful exercise of legislative authority.

Here Chase, like some other Federalist judges, sought to incorporate into the Constitution a doctrine of vested rights that would allow the courts to protect fundamental personal and property rights by an appeal to first principles. Though it was contested and its sweeping potential for judicial restriction of legislative acts was never realized, this doctrine remained alive. In the 1870s "it served to some extent to incorporate into Constitutional law the doctrine of *laissez faire* as a protection against objectionable legislation." By the 1890s the due-process clause was being interpreted to guarantee the vested rights that Chase had first propounded a century earlier. His doctrine has been called "the germ of the modern doctrine of due process of law as 'reasonable law.' "[19]

Chase's reputation as one of the most important justices of the early Supreme Court rests primarily on his opinions of the years 1796–1800. With the appointment of John Marshall as chief justice in 1801, the practice of *seriatim* opinions ceased. Marshall announced almost all the decisions of the Court himself, making it difficult to assess the extent of Chase's influence in shaping the decisions of the Marshall court. Chase's opinions before 1800, coupled with his surviving grand jury charges, are nevertheless sufficient to provide a good picture of the political and constitutional philosophy that shaped his thinking during his Supreme Court career. The same philosophy can be seen to underlie his entire life in politics.

Justice Chase based his political thought on a peculiar version of social contract theory. He considered the state of nature to be entirely imaginary, finding it inconceivable "that any number of men ever existed...without some...chief" whom they obeyed. At any rate, there could be no liberty and no rights of man in a state of nature. "It seems to me, that *personal Liberty*, and *rights* can only be acquired by becoming a member of a Community, which gives the protection of the *whole* to every *individual*." Men therefore form goverments "to obtain security to their *persons*, and *property* from violence....From hence I conclude that *Liberty*, and *rights* (and also *property*) must spring out of *Civil Society*, and must be for ever subject to the modification of particular governments. I hold the position *clear*, and *safe*, that all the *rights of man* can be derived only from the conventions of society; and may, with propriety, be called *social rights*."[20]

Having in effect denied the conventional version of natural rights altogether, Chase nevertheless asserted that personal and property rights constituted an inherent limitation on the powers of government. The limitation—Chase's concept of a "higher law"—arose from the sovereignty of the people and the purposes of the social contract. (Chase never distinguished between the social and political contracts.) For Chase, the sovereign people were the highest source of authority; "there can be no limitation on the power of the people of the United States" in their capacity as constituent power. The people establish the form of government and grant to government "the supreme and sovereign power of the state" to make all laws not contrary to the constitution.[21] The ends of the sovereign people in establishing civil society—to secure their rights of liberty and property—become part of the terms or "great first principles of the social compact," and as such limit the power of government.[22] Here is a paradox in Chase's thought: the rights of the people are "social rights" arising out of the social contract; yet, as conditions of the contract, they have an independent existence that allows them to serve the same function as higher "natural rights" in circumscribing the actions of the state.

Chase believed with John Locke that the rights and liberty of the people could be secured under different forms of government.

The History of mankind...informs us, "that a *monarchy* may be *free*; and that a *Republic* may be a *tyranny*." The true test of Liberty is in the *practical* enjoyment of protection to the *person*, and the *property* of the Citizen, from all injury. Where the *same* Laws govern the *whole* Society, without any distinction. . . ; *where* Justice is *impartially* and *speedily* administered, and the poorest man. . .may obtain redress against the most wealthy and powerful. . . ; and where the person, and property of every man are secure from insult or injury; in that Country *the people are free.*

From this definition it followed that an independent judiciary was indispensable to the preservation of liberty.

The fundamental precondition for liberty, then, was the rule and restraint of law. Good laws and their enforcement, Chase believed, required *"good morals."* Hence "there can be no *liberty* without *morality;* and. . .no *morality* without *Religion.* The distinction between *Liberty* and *licentiousness;* between *virtue* and *vice,* and between *Religion* and *infidelity,* should be inviolably preserved in all Societies." In a republic, liberty rested also upon "the *Republican* virtues of *probity,* and *industry; frugality,* and *temperance."*

Chase's definition of equality—*"equal liberty,* and *equal rights"*—was precise and limited: equal civil liberty, equal protection of the laws, and equal security in person and property. Defined in this manner, the concept of equality had Chase's firm support. But he bitterly opposed the attempt of the political opposition to extend the idea of equality beyond those limits. He denounced as fanciful and pernicious what he saw as the popular theory that men in a state of society were "entitled to exercise" all the rights they allegedly "possessed in a *State of Nature."*

In particular, Chase denied that the extension of political rights to all citizens had anything to do with liberty or equality. "From the year 1776 I have been a decided and avowed advocate for a *Representative,* or *Republican* form of Government, as since established. . . . It is my sincere wish that *freemen* should be governed by their Representatives, fairly and freely elected, by *that class of Citizens.* . .who have *property* in, a common interest with, and an attachment to the Community." Universal manhood suffrage, far from extending rights and liberty, would destroy both, for "the great Body of the people" were easily deceived; "the bulk of mankind are governed by their passions, and not by reason." The fear that democracy, stimulated by the doctrines of the French Revolution, would destroy American liberty lay at the heart of Chase's Federalism.

On the other hand, the national and state constitutions, if not tampered with, were "more favourable to *Civil* and *religious* liberty, than any other...in the whole world."[23] Preserving the national Constitution inviolate, Chase had become convinced, was the special charge of the federal judiciary. His Supreme Court opinions of the 1790s had taken care not to rule on the question of whether or not the Court could declare an act of Congress unconstitutional. Only in 1800 did he indicate in a Supreme Court decision that he agreed with "the general sentiment" of bar and bench that the high court did possess this power. By that time, however, he had gone much further in a grand jury charge: "The Judicial power... are the only *proper* and *competent* authority to decide whether any law made by Congress or any of the State Legislatures, is contrary to or in Violation of the *federal* Constitution." Chase made the same point in two 1800 circuit court cases.[24] In stating that the determination of constitutionality belonged *only* to the judicial branch, Chase went beyond the views of many of his contemporaries.

The reasoning behind Chase's assertion of the federal courts' exclusive right to determine questions of constitutionality was expressed in an opinion given during the 1800 sedition trial of James Callender in the circuit court for Virginia. That right, he argued, was "expressly granted to the judicial power of the United States, and is recognized by Congress by a perpetual statute." The Constitution was explicitly made the supreme law of the land, and by the Constitution the federal judiciary's jurisdiction extended to all cases arising under the Constitution and federal laws. "Among the cases which may arise under the Constitution, are all the restrictions on the authority of Congress, and of the state legislatures." The Constitution being the supreme law, and the judges being required both by that document and by the Judiciary Act of 1789 to take an oath to uphold the Constitution, it was clear that the judges must "regulate their decisions" according to the supreme law. Therefore the determination of the constitutionality of laws belonged to the judicial branch.

Chase's belief in the Court's power to determine the constitutionality of laws was coupled with advocacy of judicial restraint. He had stated in *Hylton v. United States* that he would strike down an act of Congress only in a very clear case. If there was doubt, the courts should accept the judgment of the legislators. Chase reiterated this position more strongly in the Callender case. In his grand jury charges he explained that the people's representatives could not intentionally violate the Constitution and infringe the people's rights, since they must be bound by the same laws as their constituents. The courts would be called upon to act only in case of an inadvertent violation through Congress's error. In addition, Congress was the proper "judge of the *Justice* of its laws"; the judiciary could consider only their constitutionality.[25] The latter assertion would appear to clash with Chase's notion of an enforceable "higher law" stemming from the social contract.

Justice Chase, contrary to the reputation of his party, was also a strict constructionist. One of his clearest statements of that point of view came in *United States v. Worrall:* all powers of the national government are derived from the Constitution, "so that the departments of the government can never assume any power, that is not expressly granted by that instrument, nor exercise a power in any other manner than is there prescribed." Chase reaffirmed the point in his opinion in *Calder v. Bull:* "All the powers delegated by the people of the United States to the federal government are defined, and no *constructive* powers can be exercised by it." In contrast to the expressly defined and limited powers of the national government, Chase believed that the states possessed all authority given them by the state constitutions and "not expressly taken away by the constitution of the United States."[26] In this respect there was a continuity of sentiment between Chase the Antifederalist and Chase the High Federalist. But High Federalist he was by 1796 despite his idiosyncrasies, and his activities both on and off the bench during the presidency of John Adams left no doubt about it.

Fifteen

THE POLITICAL
JUSTICE: THE
SEDITION CASES

THE FEDERAL judiciary in the twentieth century carefully follows a long tradition of noninvolvement in partisan politics. The judges preserve their reputation for judicial impartiality by staying out of electoral contests and refraining from public comment on controversial issues that might come before the courts. In the 1790s that tradition was not yet established. Solidly Federalist, the justices of the Supreme Court and the district courts openly supported their party's position. Their partisanship was especially apparent in their charges to grand juries. Used as vehicles for educating the public in good citizenship and the law, the grand jury charges of the Federalist judges often became political speeches. The executive branch also contributed to the impression of the judiciary as "an annex to the Federalist party" by appointing two successive chief justices, John Jay and Oliver Ellsworth, to undertake diplomatic missions. The opposition party was naturally indignant at what it viewed as the abuse of judicial power.[1]

One danger in this situation was that the judiciary's partisanship could call into question the fairness of the judges on the bench, particularly if they were enforcing a law which itself was seen as a partisan instrument. That is what happened between 1798 and 1800, when political conflict reached a dangerous peak of intensity. No justice was more controversial during those years than Samuel Chase. Republicans came to see him as the epitome of the biased political judge. Chase had all the qualities of an outstanding judge except a judicial temperament. His impulsiveness and ardent disposition, coupled with his habit of speaking his mind in the strongest terms, would have made it difficult for him to appear detached from politics in any case. The established practice of his day gave him no reason for trying to do so. His perception that the republic was in grave danger gave him every reason to act and speak forcefully.

John Jay's treaty with England, barely ratified by the Senate in 1795, had smoothed over the conflicts of 1794 with the British. But the treaty antagonized France, which began to look upon the United States as an enemy. Hoping to reverse American policy, French ambassador Pierre Adet worked openly for a Republican victory in the presidential election of 1796, in which Thomas Jefferson opposed Federalist John Adams. In the newspapers Adet attacked Washington's foreign policy, which he blamed for deteriorating Franco-American relations, and revealed the strong measures France was taking in retaliation.

Chase's indignation at Adet's interference in American politics reflected the anger of his party. He considered the ambassador's publications "such a breach of truth and good manners, and such an inter-meddling in our Government as wound the feelings and ruins the Dignity of our People." Returning to a favorite theme, Chase turned his wrath on the publishers of the articles as well. "I think the Printer ought to be indicted for a false and base *Libel* on our Government. A free Press is the Support of Liberty and a Republican Government, but a licentious press is the bane of freedom, and the peril of Society, and will do more to destroy real liberty than any other Instrument in the Hands of knaves and fools." In fact Adet's electioneering had little effect. John Adams won the presidency, as Chase had predicted he would.[2]

President Adams had to deal with a rising crisis with France. The French began seizing American ships and refused to receive the new American ambassador. When Adams sent a special mission to negotiate with France, agents of the French government demanded an apology, a bribe, and a loan as the price of discussions. Public revelation of this XYZ Affair in 1798 swung American opinion against France and opened the way for strong action. Overriding continued Republican opposition, Congress accelerated defensive measures already under way, levied new taxes to pay for those measures, and authorized American ships to wage an undeclared naval war with France. Full-scale war seemed likely, and the more extreme Federalists would have welcomed it. War, they believed, would not only align the United States with England against France but also expose the real loyalties of pro-French Republicans and facilitate the suppression of internal "sedition."

Chase was convinced that war was coming. In a grand jury charge he summarized the *"injuries and insults"* the United States had received from France and exhorted his listeners to support the government and prepare to "meet...the events of War." Though he opposed a standing army in principle, he believed "a respectable military establishment is absolutely necessary at this time; and probably for some years to come." He rejoiced in a report—false, as it turned out—that an offensive and defensive alliance with England had been concluded. Even after a moderating attitude on the part of France prompted Adams to send a new diplomatic mission to that country in 1799, Chase had "very little (if any) hope of any sincere and permanent conciliation."[3]

Chase's analysis of the French problem received a restrained but clear exposition in a Supreme Court decision of August term 1800. The case involved a salvage claim on an American ship captured by a French privateer and then retaken by an American vessel. It raised the question of what laws of war were applicable to the captures and invited the Court to define the nature of the conflict with France. Chase concurred with a unanimous Court that France was legally an enemy of the United States in a limited war. That Congress had not formally declared a general war, Chase commented,

> only proves the circumspection and prudence of the legislature. Considering our national prepossessions in favor of the French republic, congress had an arduous task to perform, even in preparing for necessary defence and just retaliation. As the temper of the people rose, however, in resentment of accumulated wrongs, the...measures of the government became more and more energetic...; though hitherto the popular feeling may not have been ripe for a solemn

declaration of war; and an active and powerful opposition in our public councils, has postponed, if not prevented, that decisive event, which many thought would have best suited the interest, as well as the honor, of the United States. The progress of our contest with France, indeed, resembles much the progress of our revolutionary contest; in which, watching the current of public sentiment, the patriots of the day proceeded, step by step, from...petitions... to...independence.[4]

That Chase could write of war with France as an event to be anticipated as late as August 1800 reveals the depth of his antipathy to that country.

The full dimensions of the "very critical and alarming situation" of the country in 1798–1800, Chase commented, resulted from the fact that while *"Dangers* approach our *infant* Republic from *abroad*...Divisions threaten it from *within*."* Those divisions, every Federalist knew, arose from the "French party," the Republicans, whose loyalty was actually suspect in the fevered atmosphere of 1798. To deal with an internal opposition that was viewed as dangerous to the stability of the young republic, Congress in 1798 passed the Alien and Sedition Acts.

The Sedition Act was a Federalist attempt to suppress the licentiousness of the press of which Chase had long complained. Virtually all Federalists agreed by 1798 that the Republican newspapers' intemperate attacks on the administration had to be stopped to ensure the survival of republican order, which they identified with continued Federalist control of the government. The first two sedition prosecutions in 1798 had been commenced at common law. But that method promised to be unsatisfactory, partly because of Chase's own declaration in *United States v. Worrall* that the United States had no common law. Congress therefore passed the Sedition Act, which made it a crime to conspire to oppose the laws or the government; to incite any riot or unlawful combination; or to "write, print, utter, or publish...any false, scandalous, and malicious writing" against the government, the president, or Congress "with intent to defame...or to bring them...into contempt or disrepute; or to excite against them...the hatred of the... people...or to stir up sedition."[5]

To Republican protests that the Sedition Act was an unconstitutional violation of freedom of expression, Federalists answered that freedom of the press in the English tradition meant freedom only from prior restraint, or censorship before publication. In fact, Federalists claimed, the act liberalized the common-law doctrine of seditious libel in three respects. It allowed juries to judge law as well as fact in prosecutions; it required proof of a malicious intent for conviction; and it made the truth of the allegedly libelous statements a defense against conviction. Aware as he was of English precedents, Chase approved this interpretation. In fact, however, the supposed liberalizations offered little aid to defendants under the Sedition Act. The author's seditious intent was generally inferred from his statements, and the truth of political opinions or rhetoric was impossible to prove in court.[6] Republicans, fearing that the supposedly monarchist and pro-British Federalists had betrayed the principles of the American Revolution, were driven to even stronger opposition, manifested in the Virginia and Kentucky Resolutions.

At least fourteen prosecutions were launched under the Sedition Act, and three more at common law. Some, notably the case of Luther Baldwin, went to ridiculous lengths. When President Adams passed through Newark, New Jersey, in 1798, he was received with a celebration that included an artillery salute as he departed. One Republican watching from a tavern remarked, "There goes the President and they are firing at his a—," to which the drunken Baldwin replied "that he did not care if they fired thro' his a—." Baldwin and his confederate were convicted of sedition. The Federalist judges of the federal courts all interpreted and enforced the law in much the same way. Their charges reminded grand juries of their duty to enforce the act, and no challenge to its constitutionality was permitted. Justice Chase, however, came to stand out for special zeal in enforcing the act.[7]

Chase's first trials under the Sedition Act came at the June 1799 session of the United States Circuit Court for Massachusetts. These cases stemmed from the erection by Republican citizens in Dedham the previous October of a liberty pole bearing, among other captions, the slogan "Downfall to the Tyrants of America." Federalists looked fearfully upon liberty poles as "emblems of sedition," and this incident was not to be overlooked since Dedham was the home of Federalist leader Fisher Ames. Two principals in the Dedham protest were arrested for sedition: Benjamin Fairbanks, a leading citizen of the town, and David Brown, a semiliterate but effective itinerant orator and publicist whose allegedly seditious speeches and writings had presumably instigated the incident.

When the cases came to trial, both defendants changed their original pleas to guilty. Fairbanks told the court that he had been misled, had not realized the seriousness of his offense, and was now thoroughly reformed. None other than Fisher Ames supported these declarations. Impressed by Fairbanks's repentance and Ames's intercession, Chase pronounced the most lenient sentence any judge imposed under the Sedition Act: a five-dollar fine and six hours in jail. Chase remarked that the sentence showed the government was not vindictive "but mild, dispassionate and considerate; and exercised its authority with humane and liberal views."

Entirely different was the treatment accorded Brown. Fairbanks may have been an honest man momentarily led astray, but in Chase's mind Brown was an inveterate purveyor of sedition. Despite Brown's plea of guilty, Chase insisted on examining the prosecution witnesses in order to illustrate "the degree of his guilt." Brown also expressed sorrow for his offense, but he refused Chase's request to name those who had aided him. Stressing Brown's "disorganizing doctrines and impudent falsehoods, and the very alarming and dangerous excesses to which he attempted to incite the uninformed part of the community," Chase fined him $450 and sentenced him to a year and a half in jail. This was the harshest sentence meted out under the Sedition Act.[8]

Chase's career as suppressor of sedition almost ended at that point. Early in January 1800, while he and a group of travelers were crossing the frozen Patapsco River on foot, Chase fell through the ice into the frigid water. Young Sammy, who was accompanying his father, quickly ran up, grabbed Chase's coat near the neck to help keep him afloat, and also fell into the river. Chase's great bulk, increased by his heavy fur coat, made it difficult for his companions to rescue him. It took Sammy and two other men about five minutes to pull him out. "I was perfectly collected, but quite exhausted, I relied only on the protection of my God, and he saved Me," Chase later wrote to his wife. He was placed on a baggage sledge, taken to the nearest house, "rubbed dry and put into bed between Blankets." After a day of rest Chase reported, "I cannot discover that I have taken Cold, and I think I am as well as if the accident had not happened."[9]

Chase's escape from an icy death preserved him for the most important circuit court tour of his career. From April through June 1800 he roamed the Middle Circuit stamping out sedition wherever he could. The pyrotechnics began at Philadelphia, where the first important case to come before Chase and District Judge Richard Peters was that of Thomas Cooper.

An English-born radical, Cooper had come to the United States in 1794 seeking greater freedom of expression and recovery from financial reverses. He was a man of many talents—a lawyer, manufacturer, chemist, doctor, philosopher, and reformer. As temporary editor of a small country newspaper, the Sunbury and Northumberland *Gazette,* he strongly criticized the Adams administration. His newspaper writings, collected and published in 1799 as *Political Essays,* made him a prominent figure in the Republican camp. His writings, together with the help Cooper gave Republican editor William Duane in defying the Senate's attempt to punish Duane for breach of privilege, made Cooper an object of Federalist animosity. A charge of seditious libel was lodged against Cooper, based on a November 1799 handbill criticizing Adams's conduct as president. Cooper's trial in April 1800, falling during the presidential election campaign, attracted national attention.[10]

Cooper first sought to delay the proceedings by asking for subpoenas addressed to President Adams, the secretary of state, and a number of congressmen. Chase refused to subpoena the president on the ground that Adams could not be compelled to testify as to whether or not Cooper was correct in charging him with maladministration. The other subpoenas were granted, but after a delay of a few days Chase refused Cooper's request for a further postponement to assemble more witnesses and collect documents to show that his statements were true. Chase stated that Cooper should have had proof of the truth of his writings at hand before publishing. That Chase was justified in cutting off Cooper's attempts to delay the proceedings is indicated by the fact that Cooper called none of the witnesses he had subpoenaed.

The trial itself was brief. The prosecution called only one witness, a justice of the peace who testified that Cooper had acknowledged authorship of the offending handbill. Cooper, acting as his own counsel, read at length from public documents to demonstrate that Adams's policies were as he had described them in the handbill.

Though Chase doubted the admissibility of some of this evidence, he indulgently allowed Cooper to proceed as he wished. Resting his case on the truth of his publication and lack of malicious intent, Cooper made an impressive defense of his right honestly to criticize the conduct of government. District Attorney William Rawle replied that Cooper's attempts to demonstrate the truth of his attacks on the president were further proof of his malignancy.[11]

Chase's charge to the jury was more an argument for the prosecution than a statement of the legal issues. "If a man attempts to destroy the confidence of the people in their officers. . .he effectively saps the foundation of government," he stated. "A republican government can only be destroyed in two ways; the introduction of luxury, or the licentiousness of the press. This latter is the more slow, but most sure and certain, means of bringing about the destruction of government."

As to Cooper's defense of truth, Chase told the jury that he "must prove every charge he has made to be true; he must prove it to the marrow. If he asserts three things, and. . .proves but two, he fails in his defence." Going through Cooper's statements about Adams in the handbill, Chase attacked them point by point. On one point Chase flatly stated that Cooper "has published an untruth, knowing it to be an untruth." The judge asserted also that Cooper's malicious intent was self-evident, not only from the publication itself but also from his "outrageous" avowal of authorship to an officer of the law, and from his admission in court that he intended "to censure the conduct of the President, which his conduct, as he thought, deserved." "Take this publication in all its parts," Chase concluded, "and it is the boldest attempt I have known to poison the minds of the people. . . . This publication is evidently intended to mislead the ignorant, and inflame their minds against the President, and to influence their votes on the next election." Chase added that the jurors must make up their own minds on all these matters, but his charge left them no choice but to convict Cooper unless they decided to ignore Chase altogether. The verdict of guilty was soon forthcoming.[12]

Before passing sentence, Chase asked if Cooper had anything to say. The latter mentioned that his financial circumstances were quite modest. Chase did not want to impose an overly burdensome penalty, but he suspected that Cooper's fine might be paid by his party. "If I could believe you were supported by a party inimical to the government, and that *they* were to pay the fine, not you," Chase stated, "I would go to the utmost extent of the power of the court." Cooper stoutly asserted his independence of party, and Judge Peters agreed that this should not be a consideration. The court sentenced Cooper to six months in jail and a fine of $400.[13]

Despite the bias of Chase's charge to the jury, Cooper's trial was probably one of the fairest under the Sedition Act. Cooper believed Chase's conduct improper and said so in print, and his accusation received some support from the Republican press. But in this case the main opposition criticism was directed at the Sedition Act itself. Later, in establishing the grounds for Chase's impeachment, the Republicans did not include his conduct in the Cooper trial.[14]

Chase and Peters faced another politically sensitive case at the same session, the treason trial of John Fries. This case arose from resistance in eastern Pennsylvania to the property taxes levied to finance defensive preparations in the crisis with France. Citizens in three counties offered resistance to the tax assessors. When federal officers arrested several of the resisters, auctioneer Fries led a group of armed men who rescued the prisoners from the jail at Bethlehem. Troops sent to suppress Fries's Rebellion found everything tranquil, but Fries was arrested for treason on the theory that his armed defiance of federal officers amounted to levying war against the United States.

Fries had been convicted before Justice James Iredell and Judge Peters in the United States Circuit Court for Pennsylvania in April 1799. But evidence of prior bias against Fries on the part of a juror had persuaded the court to grant him a new trial. Consequently the case came before Chase late in April 1800.

Chase's reaction to Fries's Rebellion and the earlier Whiskey Rebellion had been strong. He believed that these incidents endangered the very foundations of American government and rejoiced that the uprisings had been "speedily quelled by the Vigilance and Energy of our Government." Chase argued that every American had bound himself to abide by the acts of the majority expressed through their representatives, "however repugnant to his own views of *propriety*, or even Justice. *Private* opinion must give way to *public* Judgement, or there must be an end of Government." If a law was unconstitutional, burdensome, or oppressive, the Constitution itself provided channels for redress through petition, elections, the legislative process, and the courts. No other mode of redress could "be adopted *without a violation of the Constitution, and the Laws*.... If a Law burthensome, or even *oppressive*...is to be opposed by *force,* there can be no Government in this Country.... because if the *open* resistance of a *small part* of the Community is the *effectual* means to obtain a *repeal* of a Law, it will be the height of folly to expect afterwards to see any Law executed."[15]

Whatever his feelings, Chase as a judge had to ensure a fair trial for John Fries. The other consideration that influenced his preparations for the trial was a desire to expedite the proceedings. The circuit court had an exceptionally crowded docket at this session, including 107 civil suits—many of them already long delayed—as well as a list of criminal cases swollen by a number of other indictments arising from Fries's Rebellion. In the interest of speedy justice, Chase was determined to proceed as quickly as possible.[16]

Chase anticipated that Fries's counsel, William Lewis and Alexander J. Dallas, would make the same defense at the second trial as they had at the first. Since there was no doubt about the facts of what Fries had done, the defense could only contend that his actions did not amount to treason. Fries was guilty, they claimed, of the lesser offense of riot. Chase knew that this argument had been fully considered and rejected at the first trial. He knew that Justice William Paterson in 1795 had also given an opinion that supported the definition of treason under which Fries was indicted. These two decisions were in accord with English rulings; Chase agreed with them; and he considered himself bound by the weight of precedent. Since the point was settled, and since the court must give its opinion on the issue in the course of the trial anyway, why not rule on it at the beginning and spare the defense the trouble of "wasting very precious time in addressing to the court a useless argument on a point which that court held itself precluded from deciding in their favour?" Knowing from the start that this argument would fail, the defense would then be able to adopt a more promising strategy if it could.

It was one of those characteristically impetuous actions that Chase often regretted later. He drew up a written opinion on the law of treason and showed it to Peters, who agreed with its substance. At the beginning of the trial, Chase presented copies of the opinion to counsel on both sides in the interest, he said, of saving time.[17]

However correct Chase's ruling may have been, its delivery at the start of the trial was highly irregular procedure. The shocked defense attorneys immediately realized that their whole case had been destroyed. Chase, they believed, had decided the case before hearing it. Without reading the paper Lewis thrust it from him, saying, "I will never permit my hand to be tainted with a prejudged opinion." Chase added to the defense's consternation by informing them that they could not introduce certain English precedents that he considered irrelevant. According to Lewis, Chase also said that arguments on questions of law must be addressed to the court, not the jury, but others present believed that Lewis misunderstood the judge on that point.

There were no further proceedings in the case that day, but word got around that Lewis and Dallas intended to withdraw as Fries's counsel in light of Chase's opinion. The report made Peters very uneasy. He did not like Chase to begin with, later recalling that "I never sat with him without pain, as he was forever getting into some intemperate and unnecessary squabble." This particular indiscretion of Chase seemed serious to Peters. That evening he and District Attorney Rawle managed to persuade Chase that the defense attorneys were probably in earnest about withdrawing. Chase expressed regret that his opinion had provoked such a strong reaction "and said, that he did not mean that anything which he had done should preclude the counsel from making a defence in the usual manner." Chase agreed to withdraw his written opinion and proceed as if it had never existed.[18]

The damage, however, was done. Lewis and Dallas's decision to withdraw was based in part on the perception that Chase's irregular conduct could be turned to the advantage of their client. They must have known even before the trial began that the odds were very much against them, and Chase's opinion made conviction certain. But if they refused to act in protest against Chase's conduct, and if Fries rejected other counsel, the circumstances of the trial would give Fries a good chance of a presidental pardon. After some hesitation a fearful Fries agreed to pursue this strategy.

When the trial resumed, Lewis and Dallas insisted on withdrawing despite the assurances of Chase and Peters that they could conduct the defense as they wished, restrained only by their regard for their professional reputations. Unable to shake their resolution, Chase remarked, "You can't bring the court into difficulties, gentlemen; you do not know me if you think so." When Fries refused other counsel, Chase said, "Then by the blessing of God, the court will be your counsel, and will do you as much justice as those who were your counsel."[19]

Chase was as good as his word. Through the rest of the trial he took special care to advise Fries of his rights and explain how he could proceed, but the latter could make little attempt to conduct a defense.[20] Fries was convicted and sentenced to death, but the defense strategy succeeded. Believing that Fries was more deluded than dangerous, President Adams pardoned him.

From Philadelphia, Chase's circuit duties took him to Annapolis. No trials of major importance awaited him there, but Chase left his mark in the case of a postmaster convicted of having tampered with the mail. Chase sentenced the man to be publicly whipped. This old penalty having fallen into disuse, no whipping post was available. Chase ordered the offender tied to a column on the State House portico, where the sentence was carried out. It was the last public whipping to occur in Maryland.[21]

While Chase was at Annapolis, Luther Martin passed on to him a copy of a pamphlet entitled *The Prospect before Us*, in which Martin had underlined a number of passages. The pamphlet, a campaign paper for the 1800 presidential election, was the work of a Virginia Republican named James Thompson Callender. This Scottish-born radical was one of the most scurrilous political writers of the day. The pamphlet's tone may be gathered from Callender's statement that "the reign of Mr. Adams has been one continued tempest of malignant passions. . . . The grand object of his administration has been to exasperate the rage of contending parties, to calumniate and destroy every man who differs with his opinions." There followed a review of Adams's policies in a similar vein. Martin maintained that he gave the pamphlet to Chase to amuse him on the way to Richmond, the next stop on Chase's circuit, and to use as he wished. But Martin considered the pamphlet seditious,[22] and he could have had no doubt that Chase would share his opinion and act upon it.

Chase was thoroughly aroused by the pamphlet. He considered it "a libel so profligate and atrocious, that it excited disgust and in-dignation in every breast not wholly depraved." Before leaving An-napolis he remarked publicly that he would take the pamphlet to Richmond and submit it to the grand jury for prosecution. Chase continued in a jocular manner "that before he left Richmond, he would teach the people to distinguish between the liberty and the licentiousness of the press." That would be no easy task, for Vir-ginia was the center of opposition to the Sedition Act. But that fact only made Chase all the more determined to enforce the law. He went on to say that he would bring Callender to justice if Virginia was "not too depraved to furnish a jury of good and respectable men." Chase compounded these indiscreet words when, on the stage to Richmond, a passenger remarked that Callender had once been arrested under a Virginia vagrancy law. "It is a pity you have not hanged the rascal," Chase commented.[23]

Chase got his wish. On May 24 the Richmond grand jury indicted Callender on twenty charges of seditious libel stemming from *The Prospect before Us*. Political feelings over the case ran high in Vir-ginia as Republicans rallied to Callender's defense. Jefferson, who had often helped Callender financially and had seen part of *The Prospect before Us* prior to its publication, was among those who desired that he be well defended. Three distinguished lawyers vol-unteered to defend Callender: Philip Norborne Nicholas, Vir-ginia's attorney general; George Hay, Governor James Monroe's son-in-law and a later attorney general; and William Wirt, clerk of the House of Delegates and a future attorney general of the United States. Hay and Nicholas stated that their motive in undertaking Callender's defense was to demonstrate the unconstitutionality of the Sedition Act, on which point they proposed to base their case.[24] Thus a judge determined to show that federal law could be enforced even where it was most unpopular encountered counsel determined to put the law itself on trial. The trial was bound to be stormy.

The defense first tried to get a continuance until the fall term of the circuit court to give them time to summon distant witnesses, as-semble their evidence, and study the law of sedition. Hay added that under Virginia practice, cases were not tried at the same session as the indictment. Unimpressed, Chase refused to continue the case, but he did offer to postpone the trial for as much as six weeks.

That the defense ignored this offer lends credence to the suspicion that they wanted a continuance mainly in order to try the case before a different judge.[25]

Repeated arguments between the court and Callender's counsel on points of law and procedure punctuated the trial. Again and again Chase told the defense lawyers that their interpretations of the law were mistaken, and he suggested that they knew it. One of Hay's contentions he labeled a "wild notion." The conflict began with the motions for continuance and went on through the selection of the jury. Chase clashed with Nicholas and Hay over how prospective jurors should be examined and what questions might be put to them. One juror, John Basset, informed the court after being sworn that he had seen excerpts from *The Prospect before Us* and considered them seditious if correct. But Chase ruled that that alone was not sufficient to disqualify him.[26]

Conflict resumed when the defense presented its case. Callender's counsel began by calling John Taylor of Caroline. Chase immediately asked "what they intended to prove by this witness." The defense counsel in fact did not know exactly what Taylor would say. They expected his testimony to support Callender's statement that President Adams was a professed aristocrat, thus establishing the truth of part of one of the twenty charges against their client. Chase required that the questions the defense intended to ask Taylor be put in writing so that he could determine whether or not Taylor's testimony was admissible. Studying the written questions, Chase ruled that Taylor could not testify because his evidence would not refute the whole charge.

This ruling produced another argument on points of law and another statement by Chase that "you have all along mistaken the law, and press your mistakes on the court." However disconcerting this ruling may have been to the defense, it was well founded. Chase's rulings demonstrated his familiarity with both long-established and recent rules of pleading and evidence in libel cases. In regard to Taylor, Chase in the end erred if at all on the side of lenity. He offered to permit Taylor to testify, even though it was "certainly irregular," if the district attorney would agree. The latter would not. Chase then offered to let the defense attorneys put their objections on the record as the basis for a writ of error and an appeal to the Supreme Court on the point. That would have been the proper procedure for the defense to follow, but for the second time they passed up an opportunity Chase handed them.[27]

Apparently the defense was anxious to get on to its main contention. Taylor was the only witness for Callender who was present. The defense had no evidence to offer on the other nineteen charges of libel. Wirt now began to argue that the jury, as the judge of law as well as fact, could find the Sedition Act unconstitutional and refuse to enforce it. Chase interrupted to inform him that the argument was inadmissible. Anticipating that the point would be raised, Chase had prepared an opinion on it, which he proceeded to read. He argued cogently that the power to determine questions of constitutionality belonged to the federal judiciary alone. The jury had the power only "to determine what *the law is* in the case before them; and not to decide whether a statute of the United States...is a *law or not*.... If this power be once admitted, petit jurors will be superior to the national legislature, and its laws will be subject to their control." Inevitably one jury would uphold a federal statute, another would find it unconstitutional. There would be no uniformity in the law, and the union would be disrupted. Chase told the defense attorneys that he would entertain arguments to the contrary, but they must be addressed to the court and not the jury.[28]

The confrontation between judge and counsel reached a climax as Wirt, Nicholas, and Hay pressed their arguments. Repeatedly Chase interrupted them as they returned again and again to arguments that the court had rejected. Chase considered their conduct "disrespectful, irritating, and highly incorrect." The defense's persistence, Chase later admitted, "produced some irritation in a temper naturally quick and warm," but he maintained outward good humor as he parried the arguments of Wirt and Hay with sarcastic wittiness. "Since...the jury have a right to consider the law, and since the constitution is law," Wirt urged, "the conclusion is certainly syllogistic, that the jury have a right to consider the Constitution." "A *non sequitur,* sir," replied Chase, bowing toward Wirt as he spoke. At one point Chase told Wirt to sit down. But Wirt persisted, "I am going on sir, to —." Chase again interrupted, "No sir, you are not going on; I am going on." Hay received the same treatment.[29]

Chase's sallies provoked considerable mirth among the spectators in the courtroom at the expense of Hay and Wirt. Those two gentlemen considered Chase's conduct personally insulting to them. At length Hay sat down and refused to proceed, believing that he had been "subjected to more humiliation than any man vindicating another in a court of justice was bound on any principle to encounter." Chase urged him to go on and make any argument he pleased, promising not to interrupt any more. But the defense, their every argument destroyed by Chase, had nothing more to say. Callender was convicted and sentenced to nine months in jail and a $200 fine.[30] President Jefferson eventually pardoned him.

Indignation over Chase's conduct of the trial ran high in the Republican press. A pattern was emerging from Chase's circuit court trials in 1800. The outcry against Chase was directed less against the convictions of the defendants—for the verdicts would have been the same with any Federalist judge presiding—than against Chase's obvious desire to secure convictions and his conduct of the trials. "I think had G. Washington been on the Bench...Callender would under the existing Law have been condemned," reflected one judicious observer. "Yet all would have acquessed [sic] in the Judgment. But Judge Chase came on...so sovereignly and cowed the Attorneys so indignifyidly...that He sowred even the British and Scotts party in this City [Richmond]." Callender wrote to St. George Tucker in November 1800 suggesting that Chase be impeached. First advanced by Callender, that idea steadily gained currency in Republican circles.[31]

If Chase's critics needed more ammunition to use against him, he supplied it at the next stop on the circuit, Newcastle, Delaware. The grand jury there returned no indictments and asked to be discharged. Chase appeared surprised. He refused to release the jurors, remarking that he had been told there was a seditious newspaper in Newcastle. He started to name the printer, but thought better of it and checked himself. Chase believed it was his duty to call to the attention of the grand jury any federal crime it might have overlooked. He therefore asked District Attorney George Read to get a file of the paper in question, look over its contents, and report back the next morning. After the court adjourned, Chase's colleague on the bench, District Judge Gunning Bedford, remarked that Chase's action would be unpopular, since the Sedition Act was opposed in Delaware. "My dear Bedford," Chase replied, "no matter where we are...we must do our duty."

After a cursory examination of the file, Read reported that he had found nothing seditious, with the possible exception of an article attacking Chase himself. "Take no notice of that," Chase replied; "my shoulders are broad, and they are able to bear it." He then dismissed the grand jury, and there the matter ended. Chase afterward grumbled jokingly to a group of friends "that it was hard he could not get a single man indicted in Delaware, while he could in every other place."[32]

Chase's zeal in enforcing the Sedition Act sprang from his political philosophy and his belief that the republic was in danger, strengthened by a stern and uncompromising sense of duty. The law had to be enforced, and he meant to see that it was. Probably, too, his personal regard for John Adams heightened his indignation at Republican attacks on his old friend. Adams returned Chase's esteem, but the president to his regret had to pass up his one opportunity to serve Chase in a tangible way. In July 1800 Chase's son Thomas sought appointment as federal marshal for Maryland. Adams at first seemed inclined to appoint young Chase out of regard for his father, but in the end he gave the job to a rival applicant who had the support of Secretary of the Navy Benjamin Stoddert, another Marylander to whom Adams owed much. "It was a great disappointment and mortification to me to lose the only opportunity I shall ever have of testifying to the world the high opinion I have of the merits of a great magistrate," Adams wrote to John Marshall.[33]

Despite this disappointment Chase actively supported Adams in the presidential election of 1800. Federalist prospects were not good. Not only were measures such as the Alien and Sedition Acts unpopular but the Federalist party itself was deeply divided. Adams's decision in 1799 to make another attempt to negotiate with France had alienated the Hamiltonian wing of the party. The Hamiltonians maneuvered to give the presidency to Adams's running mate, Charles Cotesworth Pinckney, by getting some Federalist electors to drop Adams from their ballots.

In Maryland, influential Federalists like James McHenry, dismissed as secretary of war in the wake of the party rift, and Charles Carroll of Carrollton supported the intrigue for Pinckney. Samuel and Jeremiah Townley Chase were conspicuous leaders in the Adams camp. McHenry sourly attributed the Chases' stand in this intraparty squabble to their belief that Adams would win and to Jeremiah's desire for a federal judgeship. In reality the Chases urged the election of both candidates on the Federalist ticket, though their speeches extolled Adams and said little of Pinckney.[34] Their first priority was to defeat Jefferson and keep the Republicans out of power.

Samuel Chase campaigned for Adams at election canvasses in Elk Ridge and Annapolis. Canvasses consisted of stump speeches by candidates for office or their advocates and took place at horse races, major church meetings, or wherever else a large crowd was expected. At Elk Ridge, Chase's former ally John Francis Mercer spoke for four hours in support of Jefferson. Chase interrupted him frequently, then took the stump for a two-hour rebuttal "in which he endeavored to shew that the sole objects of Mr. Adams have been to ensure *justice* and promote tranquillity." Earlier in the campaign Chase had denounced Jefferson as an atheist.[35]

Republicans were quick to point out that Chase's electioneering made him late for the August session of the Supreme Court, which began shortly before the Elk Ridge canvass. With Chief Justice Oliver Ellsworth in France trying to negotiate peace and Justice William Cushing sick, Chase's absence left the court without a quorum. "The suspension of the business of the highest court," clucked the nation's leading Republican paper, ". . .to allow a *Chief Justice* to add NINE THOUSAND DOLLARS a year to his salary, and to permit *Chase* to make electioneering harangues. . .is a mere bagatelle. . . .What a becoming spectacle to see *Chase* mounted on a stump, with a face like a full moon, vociferating in favour of the present President, and the Supreme Court adjourning from day to day, and the business of the nation hung up, until Chase shall have disgorged himself!! *O tempora! O mores!*"[36]

The two parties evenly split Maryland's electoral votes, but nationwide the Republicans captured the presidency and both houses of Congress. Again Chase feared for the future of his country. He may have wondered, too, how the Federalist judiciary in general, and the "hanging judge"[37] Samuel Chase in particular, would fare under the new Republican administration.

Sixteen

IMPEACHMENT

S IF TO SYMBOLIZE the overturn that the election of 1800 had brought about in the nation's politics, the federal government at the beginning of 1801 took up new quarters in the permanent capital city of Washington. Emerging slowly from the wilderness near the established towns of Georgetown, Maryland, and Alexandria, Virginia, the new capital was a shock to those accustomed to the comforts of Philadelphia. Stumps still dotted Washington's wide boulevards, which stood hopelessly deep in mud or dust according to the season. A few wood and brick houses, many of them quite rude, were scattered in the clearings between the half-finished Capitol and the other government buildings. Chase and his Supreme Court colleagues vied with senators and congressmen for accommodations in overcrowded boardinghouses. No provision had been made for housing the Court itself, and for eight years it sat in a small committee room in the Capitol.[1]

Beginning their session on February 4, the judges introduced themselves to a new chief justice recently appointed to lead the high court through what was for Federalists a political as well as a physical wilderness. President Adams's nomination of John Marshall to succeed Oliver Ellsworth, who had resigned because of ill health, was not popular among Federalists, nor did Marshall's installation attract the attention which in retrospect it deserved.

Marshall's appointment was the first of several actions the Federalists took in the interval between the election of 1800 and Jefferson's inauguration in March 1801 to strengthen their party's hold on the judicial branch. Having lost control of the presidency and of Congress, Federalists viewed the judiciary as their most promising instrument to maintain influence in the federal government and minimize the damage they feared the Republicans would do.

Accordingly, in February the lame-duck Federalist Congress adopted the Judiciary Act of 1801, which combined partisan objectives with salutary reform. The reform was the long-sought termination of the Supreme Court justices' circuit-court responsibilities, a great boon to Chase in his declining health. The number of federal district courts was increased. Six new federal circuit courts with expanded original jurisdiction were created. The number of Supreme Court justices was to be reduced from six to five upon the next vacancy, depriving the the incoming president of his first opportunity to make an appointment to the Court. President Adams in his last days in office appointed loyal Federalists, the so-called ''midnight judges,'' to all of the new judgeships created by the Judiciary Act of 1801, as well as to forty-five justiceships of the peace for the District of Columbia established by another act.[2]

The Judiciary Act outraged the Republicans. It extended the jurisdiction of the federal judiciary at the expense of the state courts, which was contrary to Republican philosophy. More immediately, the passage of the bill and the appointment of the new judges by the outgoing administration seemed to them a blatantly unfair circumvention of the people's mandate. Jefferson concluded that the act should be repealed, though he hesitated because he realized that the elimination of the just-created judgeships and the consequent removal of the judges would appear to be a threat to judicial independence.

Several instances of political self-assertiveness on the part of Federalist judges soon removed any qualms Jefferson may have felt. The most important of these events was the commencement of the case of *Marbury v. Madison*. William Marbury and his three co-plaintiffs had been among the justices of the peace for the District of Columbia appointed by Adams. Somehow Secretary of State John Marshall had neglected to deliver the commissions of these ''midnight judges'' before Adams's term expired, and the new secretary of state, James Madison, refused on Jefferson's order to do so. In December 1801 Marbury and the others filed suit in the Supreme Court requesting a writ of *mandamus* ordering Madison to deliver their commissions. With characteristic impetuousness Justice Chase expressed his readiness to decide the case immediately, but his colleagues were not prepared to proceed so quickly. The Court granted the plaintiffs' motion that Madison be required to show cause why the writ should not be issued and scheduled a hearing in the case early in the next term.

Republicans viewed the Court's apparent challenge to the executive branch as a provocation, an abuse of judicial power, and an attack on the president. The Federalists, Jefferson wrote, "have retired into the Judiciary as a stronghold . . . and from that battery all the works of Republicanism are to be beaten down and erased." The president took the lead in calling for repeal of the Judiciary Act of 1801. Many Republicans in Congress were even more eager to strike at the judiciary than he.[3]

From January through March 1802 Congress debated the repeal bill. Federalists saw it as an unconstitutional attack on the independence of the judiciary. Federal judges held office during good behavior. If judges could be arbitrarily removed by abolishing their offices, Federalists urged, the judicial branch could not function as an independent check on the popularly elected branches of the government. Republicans replied that Congress's right to create inferior federal courts implied the right to abolish them and claimed that the work load of the judiciary did not warrant the recent increase in its size. The repeal measure passed, restoring the judicial arrangements of the late 1790s with one major modification. There would now be six circuits, with one Supreme Court justice permanently assigned to each. To eliminate the possibility that the Supreme Court might declare the repeal act unconstitutional before it could take effect, the Republicans soon adopted another act eliminating the Court's August term. As a result the Supreme Court did not meet between December 1801 and February 1803.[4]

The Supreme Court justices now had to decide how they would respond to the repeal act. Should they tacitly accept its validity by holding the circuit courts assigned to them, or should they refuse to ride circuit on the grounds that abolition of the circuit courts created in 1801 was unconstitutional? A caucus of Federalist congressmen urged the latter course, and Marshall and Chase transmitted the proposal to their colleagues. "I believe a Day of severe trial is fast approaching for the friends of the Constitution," Chase told Justice Paterson, "and we I fear must be principal actors, and maybe suffrers therein."[5]

Of all the justices, only Samuel Chase was strongly inclined to defy Congress and the president by refusing to hold the circuit courts. "It is a *great* doubt with me whether the Circuit Courts, established by the Law, can be *abolished*," Chase wrote to Marshall; "but I have *no doubt*, that the Circuit Judges cannot *directly*, or *indirectly*, be deprived of their *offices*, or commissions, or salaries, during their lives; unless only on impeachment for, and conviction of, high crimes and misdemeanours, as prescribed in the Constitution. . . . The distinction of taking the *Office* from the *Judge*, and not the *Judge* from the *Office*, I consider as puerile, and nonsensical." Chase believed that Congress could abolish a judgeship upon the death of the incumbent, but not before. The abolition of the circuit courts being unconstitutional, Chase concluded, the judges appointed under the Judiciary Act of 1801 still legally held office. In recognition of their authority, the Supreme Court justices (if they agreed with Chase) could not constitutionally hold circuit court sessions under the repeal act. If they did so, Chase commented, the high court judges would become "the Instruments to destroy the independance of the Judiciary." An independent judiciary, Chase believed, could not survive if Congress might at any time remove a judge by abolishing his office. Chase added that he now doubted whether Supreme Court justices could constitutionally be assigned to circuit court duty in any event, a question he said he had not previously considered in accepting circuit court assignment in the 1790s.

Despite the positiveness of his argument, Chase expressed to Marshall his eagerness to learn the views of his colleagues on the court. He indicated that their ideas might change his mind. He urged that the justices meet in Washington, determine their position, and "lay the result before the President." Admitting that he needed his judicial salary to support his family, Chase added that he could not "hesitate one moment between a performance of my duty, and the loss of Office. . . . I feel every desire to yield my opinion to my Brethren; but my conscience must be satisfied, although my ruin should be the certain consequence."[6]

Ruin might indeed have been the consequence of Chase's position. Had the Supreme Court defied the repeal act, the conflict between the branches of government might have escalated into a constitutional crisis. Radical Republicans in Congress would have gained greater support for an all-out assault on the judiciary, and the consequences for the judiciary's long-range role in the American political system might have been serious. Whatever the merits of Chase's constitutional argument, it was perhaps fortunate from a practical standpoint that his colleagues did not agree with him. Marshall, though he basically agreed with Chase that Supreme Court justices should not constitutionally perform circuit duty, believed that their acquiescence in the practice in the 1790s had settled the issue. He was inclined to accept the repeal act, dreading serious consequences if the Court refused, and the other justices agreed with his position. Satisfied by his colleagues' reasoning or unwilling to defy the repeal act alone, Chase too bowed to the law in the end. At least the Maryland-Delaware circuit assigned to him was convenient. In 1803 the Supreme Court upheld the constitutionality of the repeal act in the case of *Stuart v. Laird*.[7]

The February 1803 session of the Court also brought to a close the politically charged case of *Marbury v. Madison*. The Court had been generally expected to order Madison to deliver the commissions of Marbury and his fellow plaintiffs, and Madison had been expected to defy the order. Instead the Court's opinion, announced by Chief Justice Marshall, threaded its way through the political pitfalls of the case with an argument more distinguished as practical politics than as constitutional law. The Court held that Marbury was entitled to his commission, but that it lacked jurisdiction to order Madison to deliver it because the section of the Judiciary Act of 1789 authorizing the Supreme Court to issue writs of *mandamus* was an unconstitutional extension of the Court's precisely defined original jurisdiction. Some Republicans were unhappy that the Court had presumed to infringe upon the executive power by lecturing Madison on his responsibilities, but since he had not been ordered to act confrontation was again avoided.[8]

The decision was precedent setting as the first formal declaration of the Supreme Court that it possessed the power to strike down unconstitutional acts of Congress. But that principle had earlier been asserted by many, and by none more vigorously than Samuel Chase. There is reason to believe that Chase had considerable influence on Marshall's opinion in *Marbury v. Madison*. Marshall's argument for the Court's power to pass upon the constitutionality of federal laws was similar to Chase's reasoning in his opinion on that point in the Callender case. Marshall had been in the courtroom when Chase delivered that opinion, and Chase reasserted some of the same points in his 1802 letter to Marshall concerning the repeal of the Judiciary Act of 1801. Chase must have reiterated his reasoning in the *Marbury* case deliberations. In one respect, though, Marshall stopped short of embracing Chase's conclusions. The *Marbury* decision did not assert that the Supreme Court had the sole or final power to determine questions of constitutionality, as Chase had earlier done.[9]

Chase's health took a turn for the worse during this session of the Court. Early in March 1803 he wrote to John Francis Mercer that he had "received a Shock which would probably have terminated fatally, but for copious Bleedings," and he had not fully recovered. Chase's physical ills were compounded by low spirits as he contemplated the nation's prospects under its Republican leadership. Jefferson's first two years in office had only strengthened Chase's fear of the opposition party and its measures. "There is but one Event (which will probably never happen) in which I will interfere with politics," Chase told Mercer; "I mean the establishment of a *new* Government. I believe nothing can save the *present* one from dissolution. Some Events, as a War with France, may delay it for a few years. The Seeds are sown, they ripen daily. Men without *Sense* and without *property* are to be our *Rulers*, there can be no Union between the Heads of the two Parties. Confidence is destroyed."[10]

The grim outlook reflected in this letter resulted from developments in Maryland as well as at the national level. In its 1802 session the Maryland legislature had completed passage of an amendment to the state constitution establishing universal white male suffrage.[11] Chase had always supported property qualifications for voting, and their elimination appeared to him to undermine the very foundations of good government. Equally alarming to him was a proposed constitutional amendment that would abolish Maryland's General Court. An independent judiciary, it seemed, was under assault at both state and national levels.

Chase found an opportunity to speak out against these dangers when the federal circuit court met at Baltimore on May 2, 1803. Carefully reading from a prepared text, Chase delivered the most controversial grand jury charge of his career. He explained in some detail his view that liberty consisted not in equal participation in politics but in equal rights under law and equal justice, which only an independent judiciary could assure. Again he denounced what he saw as the extravagant and fanciful notions of natural rights then current in the nation. Chase continued:

> You know, Gentlemen, that our State, and national Institutions were framed to secure to every member of the Society *equal Liberty*, and equal rights; but the late alteration of the federal Judiciary, by the abolition of the office of the sixteen Circuit Judges, and the *recent* change in our State Constitution, by the establishing *universal suffrage;* and the *further* alteration that is contemplated in our State Judiciary, (if adopted) will, in my Judgement, *take away all security for property*, and personal Liberty. The independance of the National Judiciary is already shaken to its foundation; and the virtue of the people alone can restore it. The independance of the Judges of this State will be entirely destroyed, if the Bill for the abolishing the two Supreme Courts, should be ratified by the next General Assembly. The change of the State Constitution, by allowing *universal* suffrage, will, in my opinion, certainly, and *rapidly* destroy all protection to property, and all security to personal Liberty; and our Republican Constitution will sink into a *Mobocracy,* the worst of all possible Governments.

Universal suffrage, Chase said, destroyed "the *main pillar*" of the state constitution. Undermining the independence of state judges would complete its ruin, "and there will be nothing left in *it* worthy the Care, or support of freemen." Chase recalled "the great and patriotic characters" who framed the Maryland constitution and lamented "that the Sons of some of these Characters have united to pull down the beautiful fabric of wisdom, and republicanism, that their fathers erected."[12]

Chase's outburst provoked a sustained assault on him in the Republican press throughout the spring and summer of 1803. Late in May, for example, the Philadelphia *Aurora* inveighed, "This monster in politics, is the last man who ought to mention the revolution, or his participation in it, because it must call to the public mind the illicit commerce which he carried on with the enemy, and his breach of confidence as a member of Congress.... His holding a seat on the bench, is the most convincing argument that could be produced of the error of that principle which now constitutes the tenure of the Judiciary office."[13] The flour scandal of 1778 haunted Chase for the rest of his life.

In Maryland the Republican outcry was led by John Montgomery, a state legislator who had drafted and sponsored the amendments Chase denounced and who had been in the courtroom at the time of the grand jury charge. On June 13 Montgomery published in the *Baltimore American* his memory of what Chase had said. Montgomery considered Chase's charge "a violent and malevolent attack upon the present administration, the Congress of the United States and the legislature of Maryland." According to Montgomery, Chase had said that the Jefferson administration "was weak, relaxed, and inadequate to [its] duties. . . ; and that its acts proceeded not from a view to promote the general happiness, but from a desire for the continuance of unfairly-acquired power." This statement, if accurate, would have constituted a much more direct assault on the administration than anything contained in Chase's prepared text of the charge. Montgomery next pointed out the impropriety of "electioneering speeches" from the bench and advocated Chase's impeachment for "misbehavior in office." He concluded, "It must rest with the next congress to wipe off this defilement from our courts, by removing from the bench the obnoxious rubbish which has occasioned it."[14]

Montgomery did not know that Jefferson had already taken action to set the impeachment mechanism in motion. On May 13 the president wrote to Maryland's influential Republican congressman, Joseph H. Nicholson, "You must have heard of the extraordinary charge of Chace to the Grand Jury at Baltimore. Ought this seditious and official attack on the principles of our Constitution, and on the proceedings of a State, to go unpunished? and to whom so pointedly as yourself will the public look for the necessary measures? I ask these questions for your consideration, for myself it is better that I should not interfere."[15]

Impeachment was by that time an established part of the Republicans' arsenal in their fight with the Federalist judiciary. In January 1803 the Pennsylvania legislature had completed the impeachment, conviction, and removal of state district judge Alexander Addison. Addison had also made political addresses to grand juries and in defiance of a state supreme court opinion had refused to let his Republican colleague on the bench do likewise. Addison's conviction encouraged some Pennsylvania Republicans to initiate action against other Federalist judges. Three justices of the state supreme court were impeached in March 1804, but they were not convicted.[16]

At the federal level, Jefferson in February 1803 had instigated the House of Representatives to impeach District Judge John Pickering of New Hampshire. Once an impressive figure, Pickering in his old age had become an insane alcoholic, but he refused to resign his post. His outrageous courtroom conduct led the Republicans to turn to impeachment as the only remedy. Pickering would be convicted and removed from office in March 1804.

Despite these precedents, for almost eight months nothing came of Jefferson's suggestion that Chase be impeached. Part of the delay can be attributed to Nicholson, who did not leap at the chance to introduce the proposal in the House. Instead he asked House speaker Nathaniel Macon for advice. Though he was a Republican, Macon questioned whether Chase's conduct merited impeachment. The expression of political opinion from the bench, after all, was not unusual; suppose a judge should speak with equal vehemence on the Republican side? Furthermore, Macon advised, Nicholson might not wish to take the lead in assailing Chase since Nicholson would be a likely appointee to Chase's seat on the Court if the prosecution succeeded. Nicholson should not appear to be destroying Chase for his own gain. Nicholson took Macon's advice and did nothing. Busy with the Pickering impeachment and the Louisiana Purchase, Congress took no action against Chase during 1803.[17]

Eventually John Randolph of Roanoke took the initiative for Chase's impeachment. Talented but eccentric and erratic, Randolph was a leader of the "Old Republicans" who followed a states' rights agrarian philosophy and desired much more than Jefferson to reduce the power of the central government and bring the Federalist judiciary to heel. On January 5, 1804, Randolph moved in the House of Representatives for a committee of inquiry to investigate Chase's conduct on the bench and determine if he should be impeached. In the lengthy debate that followed, opponents of the proposal protested that a general inquisition into Chase's conduct was improper. Specific allegations and evidence should be presented before the House took action, they said. Randolph's supporters replied that gathering facts and evidence was the whole point of the investigation. On January 7 Randolph's motion passed by a vote of eighty-one to forty. Randolph himself was appointed to head the committee of inquiry.

The investigation took only two months. Early in March the committee recommended to the House that Chase be impeached. On the same day that Judge Pickering was convicted in the Senate, the House agreed to impeach Chase by a vote of seventy-three to thirty-two and appointed a committee, again headed by Randolph, to draw up formal articles of impeachment. Seven articles were reported to the House on March 26. They charged Chase with impeachable conduct in the Fries and Callender trials, the Newcastle grand jury incident, and the Baltimore grand jury charge.[18] The session ended the next day, and no further action could be taken until Congress convened again in November.

It has been suggested that Randolph deliberately timed the introduction of the articles for the end of the session in order to get the maximum publicity and political mileage from the charges before the House had a chance to approve or reject them. At any rate, Chase saw immediately that that was the likely consequence of the House's proceedings. He had drawn up a memorial to the House protesting its inquiry as not based on specific accusations and probable cause, and requesting that the House remain in session until articles of impeachment were adopted so that he could know the specific charges against him and begin to prepare his defense. The memorial was not presented, but Chase later published it as an appeal to the country "against the injuries and illegality of the proceedings in this case, and as a solemn protest against the principles on which they are founded." Chase angrily predicted that the committee's proposed articles of impeachment, containing "the most aggravated and inflamed construction, which it was possible for passion and party spirit to put on the ex parte evidence," would "become a very powerful engine in the hands of calumniators and party zealots."

The unpresented memorial clearly reveals Chase's view of the motives behind the impeachment proceedings. How, he asked, could republican government survive

> should the time ever arrive, which God avert! when a majority of congress, inflamed by party spirit, and seeking the destruction of its

opponents, shall desire to criminate a judge, in order to heap odium on the party with which he is connected; when a president at the head of this majority...shall desire, from motives of private resentment, the ruin of any judge; when the schemes of the dominant party, or of its leader, may require the removal of all firm, upright and independent judges, and the substitution of others more complying or more timid.[19]

Chase knew that his protests would not stop the proceedings against him. He took it for granted that the House would vote to impeach him. As soon as he learned of the impeachment move, he began to organize his defense. He first approached Robert Goodloe Harper, former Federalist congressman, son-in-law of Charles Carroll of Carrollton, and rising star of the Maryland bar. Harper immediately agreed to act as defense counsel, even though he realized that there would be no fee. Chase also wanted James Bayard of Delaware and Alexander Hamilton to help lead the defense team. Apparently Chase had never learned that Hamilton was responsible for publicizing the flour scandal charge in 1778. Harper offered to sound out Bayard and Hamilton. "This is a great public cause, in which the honour of the federal party, the independence of the Judiciary, and even the personal safety of the Judges, are involved," urged Harper.[20]

Bayard declined. He pleaded personal difficulties but at bottom seemed most concerned that all prominent Federalists maintain a safe distance from Chase, whose cause he considered lost. Chase should defend himself, Bayard advised. "If he appears singly against the host of [impeachment] managers his condition becomes at once distinguished and interesting. The great[est] effect would be produced by seeing an Individual struggling against the efforts of the House of Representatives." As lone underdog, Chase would gain sympathy whether convicted or not—and the impeachment controversy would be more likely to focus on him personally, minimizing the damage to the Federalist party.[21] Hamilton's response is not known, but in July 1804 he was killed in a duel with Vice-President Aaron Burr.

Fortunately for Chase, other lawyers of distinction rallied to his support. Faithful friend Luther Martin would of course help. Joseph Hopkinson, a brilliant young Philadelphia attorney whose courtroom performance had impressed Chase, was delighted to lend a hand. "I consider your acceptance of my small services as the brightest honour of my life," Hopkinson told Chase. "Before a tribunal disposed to do justice," he added, Chase would surely be acquitted. "But God knows! what the mad fury of these people may drive them to."[22] Maryland's Philip Barton Key and former U.S. attorney general Charles Lee of Virginia eventually rounded out the defense team.

Chase and his counsel immediately began to collect evidence and identify witnesses for the defense. Even though the House had not adopted articles of impeachment, Randolph's committee draft gave them a good idea of what the charges would be. Expressions of sympathy and encouragement reached Chase from his colleague, Justice Bushrod Washington, from old friend Luke Wheeler, and from others. One disconcertingly weak note was struck by John Marshall, whom Chase had asked for his recollection of the Callender trial. Marshall found some of the grounds advanced for Chase's impeachment "very extraordinary" and lamented the new Republican doctrine "that a Judge giving a legal opinion contrary to the opinion of the legislature is liable to impeachment." Rather than see the judges subjected to that sort of impeachment, Marshall added, he would prefer to have "an appellate jurisdiction [lodged] in the legislature."[23]

Marshall's apparent willingness so thoroughly to compromise the position of the judiciary reflected an alarm only slightly greater than that of other Federalists. Most Federalists were convinced that the attack on Chase was only "the entering wedge to the compleat anihilation of our wise and independant Judiciary." Jefferson, they believed, planned to follow Chase's removal by impeaching other justices. Robert Goodloe Harper thought that Justice Paterson would be "the next victim." Federalists expected that the administration would not rest until Marshall himself was removed.[24]

Jefferson's ultimate aims are in fact unknown, but he has left no record of any intention to assail the judiciary beyond the Chase impeachment. Probably, as one recent historian has remarked, the assault on the judiciary was a process of step-by-step improvisation on Jefferson's part.[25] Other Republicans, like Randolph and William Branch Giles, were always willing to go further than the president.

The Chase impeachment, however, clearly began as an administration measure. After his initial letter to Nicholson, Jefferson played no direct role, as he had indicated he would not. But he continued to take an interest in the case. He told Federalist senator William Plumer of New Hampshire that he supposed the Fries, Cooper, and Callender trials would be proper objects of the House's attention. "This business of removing Judges by impeachment is a *bungling way*," Jefferson complained. He would have preferred a constitutional amendment allowing the removal of judges by the president "on application of Congress." On another occasion in 1804 Jefferson burst out before British diplomats "into abuse of Judge Chase . . . whom he called an insolent and overbearing man." The president advised British minister Anthony Merry "to avoid making his acquaintance."[26]

Events were taking place during 1804, however, that probably dampened Jefferson's enthusiasm for an impeachment which would increase Randolph's prestige. Randolph was disappointed that the administration had not moved more strongly to repudiate the Federalist policies of the 1790s and adopt an agrarian states' rights philosophy. Jefferson did not rely on Randolph as a floor leader in Congress, and Randolph probably did not consult the president in planning Chase's impeachment. An open break between the two began to emerge in 1804 over the Yazoo lands issue. Through bribery of the Georgia legislature, speculators had obtained title to a large tract of southwestern land. A great public outcry had ensued, and a subsequent legislature had repudiated the grant. In the meantime, third parties had purchased some of the land from the speculators, and they now stood to lose. Georgia later ceded the land to the United States. The Jefferson administration proposed to satisfy the third-party purchasers by a grant of federal land for the sake of harmony. Randolph opposed the measure, crying corruption, and many southern Republicans agreed with him. The issue remained unsettled through 1804, and Republican unity was badly shaken. Vice-President Burr was another problem for the party. Dropped from the Republican ticket for the 1804 election following his duel with Hamilton, Burr was in political disgrace after intriguing with the Federalists in an unsuccessful bid for the governorship of New York.[27]

Chase took these emerging divisions into account in planning his defense. He hoped that, given enough time, ripening Republican dissension might disrupt what he viewed as a party vendetta against him. When Congress reconvened in November 1804, Chase confidentially wrote to Congressman Roger Griswold of Connecticut, one of his most active supporters, "It is my desire to have the Business so conducted, that I shall not be hastened into a trial; and that, when I am ready, it may be in my Power to expedite it. I gain everything by Delay, and can lose only by Haste."[28]

Delay was not on Randolph's agenda. On November 6, the day after Congress convened, he had the proposed articles of impeachment referred to a select committee under his chairmanship. Randolph reported a revised version to the House on November 30. There were now eight articles instead of seven, two new ones having been added and two of the old ones having been combined into one. But the charges against Chase remained the same except for the two new articles.

Article I charged that Chase had acted "in a manner highly arbitrary, oppressive and unjust" in the treason trial of John Fries. His written opinion on the law of treason, his preventing Fries's counsel from citing certain English and American authorities, and his barring defense counsel from addressing the jury on questions of law as well as fact were specifically alleged. The result, the article charged, was to deny Fries his constitutional right to counsel.

The next five articles dealt with the Callender trial. Article II complained of Chase's refusal to excuse juror John Basset even though Basset had already made up his mind about the seditious nature of Callender's pamphlet. Article III charged that Chase had improperly barred John Taylor from testifying, "with intent to oppress and procure the conviction of the prisoner." The fourth article charged Chase with having behaved throughout the trial with "manifest injustice, partiality, and intemperance" by compelling Callender's counsel to put their proposed questions to Taylor in writing; by refusing on proper application to continue the trial to the next term; by using "unusual, rude and contemptuous expressions" to Callender's counsel and repeatedly interrupting them; and by showing "an indecent solicitude . . . for the conviction of the accused."

Articles V and VI were the new additions. They charged Chase with technical violations of Virginia procedure, which the Judiciary Act of 1789 made binding on federal courts in Virginia. Article V complained that Chase had issued a *capias* rather than a summons against Callender when the latter was presented by the grand jury.

Article VI said that Chase had acted ''contrary to law'' in trying Callender at the same term during which he was indicted.

Article VII declared that Chase had ''descend[ed] from the dignity of a judge, and stoop[ed] to the level of an informer, by refusing to discharge the [Newcastle] grand jury'' in 1800 and by urging the investigation of a seditious newspaper there.

The final article charged that Chase did prostrate his ''high judicial character'' and ''pervert his official right and duty to address the grand jury'' in Baltimore in 1803 by ''delivering... an intemperate and inflammatory political harangue, with intent to excite the fears and resentment of the said grand jury, and of the good people of Maryland, against their State government and constitution.''[29] There was considerable irony in this turnabout: the Republicans virtually accused Samuel Chase of seditious libel.

After a rather desultory debate the House of Representatives approved the articles. Article IV drew the most support. It was adopted eighty-four to thirty-four, while the first three articles got comparable endorsements. The new articles, V and VI, were the weakest from the start. They were passed by votes of seventy to forty-five and seventy-three to forty-two. The House then elected managers to prosecute Chase before the Senate. Besides Randolph, they were Joseph H. Nicholson (who throughout had displayed a willingness to assist in the impeachment as long as he was not the leader), Caesar Rodney of Delaware, Peter Early of Virginia, John Boyle of Kentucky, Roger Nelson of Maryland (later replaced by Christopher Clark of Virginia), and George Washington Campbell of Tennessee.

The articles of impeachment were presented to the Senate on December 7. It was now up to that body to arrange for Chase's trial. Randolph's close ally, William Branch Giles of Virginia, led the impeachment forces in the Senate. Losing no time, the Senate issued a summons ordering Chase to appear before it on January 2, 1805.[30]

That gave the defense little time to complete its preparations. Legal and political considerations made it important for Chase to continue his strategy of delay. Appearing before the Senate on January 2, Chase asked that the trial be postponed until the next session of Congress. He said that he needed time to study the legal issues, find witnesses, and prepare the formal answer to the charges on which the defense must, by the rules of law, base its entire case.

He added that his deteriorating health, which "affords me, at this season of the year, especially, but short and uncertain intervals of fitness for mental or bodily exertion," had severely hampered his preparations. In fact Chase's health had become poor enough to give rise to exaggerated rumors "that he might not live" to stand trial.[31]

The Senate rejected Chase's plea by a vote of eighteen to twelve and decided that the trial should begin on February 4. Only a month remained for the defense to perfect its case. Hopkinson was almost beside himself with worry at what he considered the injustice of rushing the trial. "Sure I am that *it is not possible* you can be ready either in your evidence or counsel at the time now appointed," he wrote to Chase.[32] In fact, though, Chase had known most of the charges for the better part of a year and had done considerable preparation.

While Chase and his lawyers frantically pulled their case together, the Republicans made their preparations as well. Not long before, Randolph, Giles, and the administration had suddenly begun to cultivate the disgraced Aaron Burr, who as president of the Senate would preside over the trial. Jefferson invited Burr to dinner several times; Madison and Treasury Secretary Albert Gallatin called upon him. The president appointed Burr's stepson to a judgeship in the Louisiana Territory and made Burr's brother-in-law territorial secretary. Jefferson accepted Burr's recommendation that General James Wilkinson be named governor of Louisiana. In Congress, Senator Giles circulated an address asking the governor of New Jersey to drop a murder indictment against Burr for his duel with Hamilton. Most Republican senators signed the address. A Federalist newspaper remarked that "formerly. . .it was the practice in Courts of Justice to arraign the *murderer* before the *Judge*, but now we behold the *Judge* arraigned before the *murderer*."[33]

A more favorable development for Chase occurred at the end of January, when the Yazoo land question again came before the House of Representatives. John Randolph went beyond his previous opposition to the administration's land settlement plan to castigate the administration itself over the issue. Several Republican congressmen replied by denouncing Randolph. The latter's motion to repudiate the administration bill was narrowly defeated. Republican unity was openly disrupted; increasingly Jefferson and Randolph stood at odds with each other. Chase could only benefit from the widening split in Republican ranks.[34] But as the trial opened most Federalists remained wrapped in gloom, convinced that the majority party would do anything to destroy their hated adversary Samuel Chase.

Chase himself shared that conviction. Shortly before he left for Washington, he wrote to William Tilghman that he expected before long to "have a good deal of idle time." Chase asked if Tilghman would support his application for a vacant directorship of the Office of Discount and Deposit in Baltimore, which would afford him some income after his removal from the Supreme Court. Chase lamented that he was not ready to submit his "imperfect" answer to the charges, "and altogether unprepared to proceed to trial. But *power* will forget *right*, and I do not expect any further time will be allowed me. You may be assured the Independency of the Judiciary shall not Suffer in my hands, if I can prevent it."[35]

Seventeen

THE TRIAL

HYSICAL arrangements for the trial had been left in the hands of Aaron Burr. His model for the setting was the celebrated British impeachment trial of Warren Hastings. Under Burr's direction the Senate chamber was transformed. As in the Hastings trial members of the House of Lords were ranged on each side of the Lord Chancellor, so for the Chase trial the thirty-four senators occupied benches and desks covered with red cloth on either side of the president of the Senate. The secretary of the Senate and the sergeants at arms of both houses sat in front of the president. At the opposite end of the room were three tiers of benches, covered in green, for the members of the House of Representatives, and a box for the president's cabinet. In the center were two boxes, each containing two rows of seats covered in blue. One box was for the impeachment managers, the other for Chase and his counsel. To supplement the permanent visitors' gallery, a semicircular temporary gallery, decked in green, was constructed above the benches provided for the House. This gallery was intended particularly for the ladies. Both galleries were packed as the public turned out in large numbers for a trial that promised to be as entertaining as it was momentous.[1]

Far more was at stake than the fate of Samuel Chase. John Randolph's prestige was squarely on the line. Randolph "had boasted with great exultation that this was *his* impeachment—that every article was drawn by *his* hand, and that *he* was to have the whole merit of it."[2] The outcome of the trial would do much to determine the future influence of Randolph and his "Old Republican" faction in the Republican party and the government. That in turn might determine whether or not the Republican assault on the judiciary went any further. The implications of the trial for the independence of the federal judiciary were important. Finally, the Chase trial was the first real test of the meaning of impeachment under the United States Constitution.

The Constitution gave to the House of Representatives the sole power to impeach, i.e., to bring charges against a civil officer of the United States. Impeachments were to be tried by the Senate, where a two-thirds majority was necessary to convict. Conviction resulted only in removal from office and disqualification from future office, but the offending official could later be tried in a court of law and subjected to criminal punishment. The Constitution defined impeachable offenses as "Treason, Bribery, or other high Crimes and Misdemeanors." But what precisely was the meaning of "high Crimes and Misdemeanors?" Could an officer be impeached only for an indictable criminal offense, as suggested by the constitutional provision that "the Trial of all Crimes, except in Cases of Impeachment, shall be by Jury" and by the offender's liability to subsequent criminal prosecution? Or was the term "misdemeanor" synonymous with misconduct or malfeasance in office, whether indictable or not? In the case of the judiciary, the constitutional provision that judges were to hold office "during good Behaviour" could be read to imply that judges were removable for bad behavior, however Congress chose to define that term. An extreme interpretation was William Branch Giles's comment that "impeachment is nothing more than an enquiry, by the two Houses of Congress, whether the office of any public man might not be better filled by another.... And a removal by impeachment was nothing more than a declaration by Congress to this effect: You hold dangerous opinions, and if you are suffered to carry them into effect you will work the destruction of the nation. *We want your offices,* for the purpose of giving them to men who will fill them better."[3]

Neither American or English precedent offered a clear answer to the problem of definition. In England impeachment was a criminal prosecution in form, but in fact a political proceeding based upon a high and dangerous, though not necessarily an indictable, offense. American colonial precedents reinforced the view of impeachment as a political weapon, a check by the elected lower houses of assembly upon the actions of royal or proprietary officers. The tendency since independence had been to narrow the scope of impeachment, but the two previous impeachments under the Constitution offered little guidance for the Chase trial. Senator William Blount of Tennessee was impeached in 1797 "for allegedly conspiring to aid the English to secure Louisiana and Florida from Spain," but proceedings were dropped because Blount's expulsion from the Senate made him no longer an officeholder. The other case, that of Judge Pickering, was a poor precedent because of Pickering's insanity.[4] Chase's fate rested as much upon the Senate's judgment of what constituted an impeachable offense as upon the evidence produced at the trial.

Observers at the trial noted that Chase's hair "was thick and white with the snows of his sixty-four winters." His countenance, "rendered venerable by age," "was placid and serene without any marks either of trepidation or of contempt." Infirmity made the trial a physical strain on Chase and evoked considerable sympathy for him.

The first day of the trial, February 4, was occupied with the reading of Chase's answer to the articles of impeachment. Chase himself began to read this lengthy document, but soon turned over the task to Robert Goodloe Harper and then Joseph Hopkinson. Chase read the conclusion, nearly four hours after he had begun.[5]

The answer had been prepared by Harper from a thorough brief of the case that Chase furnished him. A full month in the writing,[6] it was a very skillfully drawn document that belied the defense's anxiety over their supposed unreadiness. The answer confronted each accusation directly and in detail. It denied the truth of several of the charges. Where the facts were admitted, Chase erected a formidable defense in depth. First, he endeavored to show that his actions had been legally correct or, in the case of the Newcastle and Baltimore grand juries, at least proper and justified. Second, he argued that if in fact he had erred in any instance, it had been an honest mistake. There had been no criminal or malicious intent on Chase's part, and he could not be impeached for an honest error. Third, the defense contended, an officer could be impeached only for an indictable criminal offense, not simply for improprieties. If Chase's conduct was found to be improper, he had still done nothing criminal. Finally, the answer called attention to the fact that the district judges who had sat with Chase in the Fries, Callender, and Newcastle grand jury cases, and who had concurred in his decisions, had not been impeached. Though the answer limited itself to matters of law and fact and avoided questioning the motives of Chase's accusers, the implication was clear. Chase concluded by entrusting his cause to God and the court of impeachment "with an humble trust in Providence, and a consciousness that he has discharged all his *official* duties with justice and impartiality, to the best of his knowledge and abilities."

When Chase had finished, Randolph asked for time for the House to compose a reply. That document, presented three days later, was a brief statement that Chase had "endeavored to cover the crimes and misdemeanors laid to his charge, by evasive insinuations, and misrepresentations of facts." Only on February 9 was Randolph prepared to proceed further.[7]

Each side having established its position, it was now time for the presentation of evidence. Randolph made an opening statement for the prosecution and then examined his witnesses, beginning with those whose testimony supported the first article of impeachment and proceeding through the articles in order. The prosecution rested on February 15. After a brief opening statement by Harper, he and Hopkinson examined the defense witnesses, again presenting testimony on the articles in order. Testimony concluded on February 20, after more than fifty witnesses had been called. By that time the defense had virtually demolished some of the articles and cast considerable doubt on the others. It was also evident that Randolph, who had some legal training but had never practiced law, was no match for the expertise of Chase's counsel.

The disparity began to appear with Randolph's opening statement. He commenced on an apologetic note. He would do his best given his own illness and the short time he had had to consider Chase's answer. Randolph was reasonably cogent in supporting the first article, but his arguments became progressively shorter and less persuasive until he passed over the seventh article almost entirely, explaining that he was "nearly exhausted" and simply asserting that Chase had admitted the essence of the charge. He did not try to refute the careful arguments on points of law contained in Chase's answer. Federalist senator William Plumer reflected that Randolph had managed in one speech to traduce Chase, vilify several other judges, insult Senator John Quincy Adams "by unnecessarily abusing his father," and make Burr uneasy by digressing into "a dissertation on *murder*." Plumer thought that the speech was "the most feeble—the most incorrect" he had ever heard Randolph make.[8]

The impeachment managers could draw little comfort from the testimony of their own witnesses on the first article, the Fries trial. Fries's attorneys, William Lewis and Alexander J. Dallas, District Attorney William Rawle, and the other prosecution witnesses gave an account of the trial that basically substantiated Chase's version of it in his answer. Rawle did not remember that Chase had prevented counsel from citing American statutes or precedent, and Lewis could only say that he thought Chase had probably done so. That admission undermined part of one specific charge against Chase. Another count contained in the first article fell when Rawle and another prosecution witness, Henry Tilghman, could not recall that Chase had prevented defense counsel from addressing the jury on matters of law as well as fact. Rawle said he thought Lewis had misunderstood Chase on that point. Lewis admitted on cross-examination that he and Dallas had withdrawn and advised Fries to be tried without counsel in order to lay the groundwork for a pardon, which cast great doubt on the charge that Chase had deprived Fries of his right to counsel. In regard to Chase's early delivery of his written opinion on the law of treason, the prosecution witnesses left the impression that Chase had blundered through impetuousness and a desire to save time, but had then tried to correct his error and offered to allow the defense considerable latitude. Chase's defense witnesses could only confirm and strengthen the impressions left by the prosecution's evidence. They added nothing new.[9]

The testimony on the Callender trial (articles II through VI) produced a greater clash between the witnesses on either side. Two of Callender's attorneys, George Hay and Philip Norborne Nicholas, gave accounts of the trial that substantiated the facts alleged in the articles of impeachment. Nicholas spoke dispassionately, but it was obvious that Hay still felt hurt by Chase's conduct toward him at the trial. Hay's apparent "anxiety to represent Judge Chase in the most disagreeable and criminal point of view" detracted from the impact of his testimony. John Taylor, the witness for Callender whose testimony Chase had barred, agreed that Chase's interruptions of Hay and Wirt had been "extremely well calculated to abash and disconcert counsel," but otherwise contributed nothing of importance.

Three other witnesses effectively established a strong presumption of bias on Chase's part before the Callender trial. John Thomson Mason and James Triplett recalled Chase's comments, in Annapolis and on the stage to Richmond, that indicated his determination to see Callender convicted. Even more damaging to Chase was the testimony of John Heath. Heath said that he had been present at a meeting between Chase and U.S. marshal David Randolph after Callender's indictment. Randolph brought with him a list of the panel of jurors he intended to summon for the trial. According to Heath, Chase asked, "Have you any of those creatures called Democrats on the panel?...Look it over, sir, and if there are any of that description, strike them off."[10] Heath's assertion that Chase had tried to pack the jury climaxed prosecution testimony that made a strong case against Chase's fairness in the Callender trial.

When the defense's turn came, though, Chase's witnesses presented a very different picture. Marshal Randolph strongly denied that Chase had ever tried to influence his selection of the jury. William Marshall, clerk of the circuit court, who had gone with Randolph to see Chase, also refuted Heath's testimony. In fact, Marshall said, Chase had commented privately to him that he would have preferred to try Callender before a jury of Democratic-Republicans if it had been proper for him to influence jury selection. The testimony of Mason and Triplett was not challenged beyond one witness's statement that Chase's remarks had been jocular, which Mason himself admitted. But the emphatic testimony of Randolph and Marshall destroyed the most dangerous single allegation against Chase arising from the Callender trial.

William Marshall, brother of the chief justice, was the most effective witness for the defense. He gave a precise and detailed account of the Callender trial that put Chase in a good light. Marshall's version supported Chase's fairness throughout the trial and tended to highlight, instead, the failings of Callender's counsel. According to Marshall, Chase's verbal sallies against the defense counsel were good-humored and not at all abusive or insulting. Two other defense witnesses put the confrontations between court and counsel in the same light. Juror John Basset agreed that Chase had tried to give Callender a fair trial and testified that he himself had never asked to be excused from the jury. He had simply informed Chase of his opinion of the excerpts he had seen from *The Prospect before Us* in order to satisfy his own conscience about serving, Basset said. The defense concluded this section of its evidence by establishing through the testimony of several experienced lawyers that Virginia practice on the procedural points that comprised articles V and VI of the impeachment charges was not uniform. At least a few Virginia precedents existed for Chase's procedure in those respects at the Callender trial. Moreover, as John Randolph was compelled to concede, Chase's issuance of a *capias* for Callender and the latter's trial at the same session as his indictment followed the established practice of the Maryland courts with which Chase was familiar. That, argued Luther Martin, showed that Chase had no malicious intent if he did err in following the same procedures in Virginia.[11]

Chase's witnesses virtually destroyed the fifth and sixth articles of impeachment and presented a version of the Callender trial at least as cogent as that of the prosecution witnesses. The only major disappointment among the defense witnesses on these articles was Chief Justice John Marshall, who had attended part of the Callender trial. Marshall seemed uneasy and fearful. Senator Plumer thought that he was disposed "to accommodate the [impeachment] managers." His testimony was often evasive, and his memory proved poor. The burden of what Marshall had to say was that Chase's rulings and procedures in the Callender trial were unusual, but Marshall avoided labeling them improper.[12] Chase certainly received no aid or comfort from his chief, but Marshall's testimony did him little harm either.

In regard to the seventh article, the Newcastle grand jury incident, both sides offered relatively brief testimony. The prosecution relied upon District Attorney George Read, who gave a straight, factual account of what had occurred. Two other prosecution witnesses added little. The principal defense witness was District Judge Gunning Bedford, who had sat on the bench with Chase at Newcastle. His account, supported by several other witnesses, differed from Read's only in some details of just what Chase had said about the existence of sedition in Delaware. The defense testimony was that Chase's words were somewhat less inflammatory than Read recalled. The defense witnesses emphasized that Chase said he was only doing his duty and that his request that the grand jury look into reports of a seditious newspaper was made in "his usual manner, which is always warm and earnest," but in good humor and without apparent vindictiveness.[13] That assertion reflected favorably on Chase's motives. In the end, though, the evidence on the seventh article was not nearly as important as the Senate's construction of what Chase had done.

Much the same could be said in regard to the final article, the Baltimore grand jury charge of 1803, except that the testimony made a substantial difference on one important point. The principal witness for the prosecution, John Montgomery, gave his account of what Chase had said, including Chase's supposed direct attack on the Jefferson administration. Other prosecution witnesses added nothing of substance. Harper, introducing the defense testimony on this article, stated that the defense would prove that Montgomery "in his strong anxiety to get Judge Chase impeached, has remembered things which nobody else remembers, and has heard things which nobody else heard." A parade of defense witnesses testified that Chase had read the entire charge from a prepared text and had not directly attacked Jefferson. The text from which Chase had read was then offered in evidence. Chase's son Thomas, who had transcribed the paper from his father's notes, was introduced to authenticate it. What Chase had actually said in the charge was anathema to Republicans, of course, but the single most provocative statement attributed to him had been thoroughly refuted. The defense admitted that the grand jury charge had been indiscreet, but Harper introduced evidence of political charges by other judges to prove that such indiscretions were far from unusual. With that the defense rested.[14]

The evidence as a whole favored Chase. While the facts established by the testimony revealed some instances of indiscretion and impropriety on Chase's part, there was no showing that he had done anything criminal. Even if a judge could be impeached for misconduct that fell short of an indictable offense, the defense had raised considerable doubt that any of Chase's indiscretions were serious enough to merit removal from office. The fifth, sixth, and part of the first articles of impeachment were largely discredited. John Randolph had utterly failed to prove evil or oppressive intent on Chase's part, unless his pretrial comments in the Callender case were so construed. Even so gloomy a Federalist as Timothy Pickering began to believe that Chase might be acquitted.[15]

Samuel Chase did not testify, nor did he take an active part in his own defense at the trial. He was suffering from "a severe attack of the gout," and it was all he could do to sit through the sessions day after day. Immediately upon the conclusion of the testimony he asked to be excused from further attendance because of his ill health. The request was granted and Chase withdrew, confident that he could safely leave the rest of the trial in the competent hands of his counsel.[16]

Only the closing arguments on each side remained, but these consumed seven days. The managers opened, the defense replied, and the managers were given a final opportunity for rebuttal. Peter Early opened for the managers. The salient point of the first article, he maintained, was that Chase had prejudged the Fries case and nullified the jury's right to decide it with his prematurely given opinion on the law of treason. Likewise, in the Callender trial, Chase had not only tried his best to convict Callender but had heaped "shame and odium" on counsel "because they would not tamely yield to his unwarrantable invasion of long established rights." That a learned judge could act in such a manner established his corrupt intent, Early asserted. He dwelt upon the first four articles and passed more quickly over the final four. Early's speech was largely an elaboration of the charges contained in the articles. He made little reference to the testimony or to points of law. "Much declamation and little argument," commented Plumer, and other hearers agreed.[17]

George Washington Campbell followed Early. A poor speaker, Campbell seemed confused in sorting through his own copious notes. He drank nine glasses of water during the first half hour of his speech, rocked constantly on his feet as he spoke, became ill, and had to ask the court to adjourn until the next morning. The spectators considered his performance so dull that many of them left the galleries. Unfortunately for the managers, Campbell's poor delivery almost totally obscured the merits of his substantive argument, which was in fact the most cogent and thorough case anyone made against Chase.[18]

Unlike Early, Campbell directly confronted the issues of law and evidence raised at the trial. Impeachment, he argued, was a check upon "abuses of power." Impeachment...may fairly be considered a kind of inquest into the conduct of an officer, merely as it regards his office; the manner in which he performs the duties thereof; and the effects that his conduct therein may have on society. It is more in the nature of a civil investigation, than a criminal prosecution." The managers did not have to show that Chase had done anything criminal, but only "that the accused has transgressed the line of his official duty...and that this conduct can only be accounted for on the ground of impure and corrupt motives."

Campbell contended that Chase's whole conduct showed "a corrupt partiality and predetermination unjustly to oppress" those he disliked, thus "turning the judicial power...into an engine of political oppression." Carefully Campbell reviewed the Fries and Callender trials, supporting his central contention by citations of law, precedent, and the testimony of the prosecution witnesses. He skipped over the fifth and sixth articles of impeachment, remarking that he would leave them to those of his colleagues who were better acquainted with Virginia procedure. His treatment of the final two articles was brief, but Campbell cleverly linked the Newcastle and Baltimore grand jury incidents to his major theme by arguing that Chase's conduct in those instances constituted further proof of the "spirit of oppression, partiality, and political intolerance" manifest in the Fries and Callender cases. Christopher Clark followed Campbell with a brief and unimpressive speech on the fifth and sixth articles, and then it was the turn of the defense.[19]

In contrast to the managers, Chase's counsel had divided the articles of impeachment among them for the closing arguments. This strategy was well conceived. It would allow counsel to prepare more thoroughly and be more persuasive than if each of them had tried to deal with all the articles. Nor would they bore the Senate with repetitious arguments on the same points.

Joseph Hopkinson spoke first, covering the first article only. His speech of three and a half hours combined eloquent oratory, emotional appeal, and solid arguments on the law and the evidence. "We appear," he began, "for an ancient and infirm man, whose better days have been worn out in the service of that country which now degrades him; and who has nothing to promise you for an honorable acquittal but the approbation of your own consciences." Repeating the defense's contention that only an indictable offense

{ 235 }

was impeachable, Hopkinson went on to construe the constitutional wording "high Crimes and Misdemeanors" to mean "high Crimes and high Misdemeanors." Impeachment, he said, did not extend to "paltry errors and indiscretions, too insignificant to have a name in the penal code." The charges against Chase amounted only to "a petty catalogue of frivolous occurrences. . . . Is the Senate. . . solemnly convened and held together in the presence of the nation to fix a standard of politeness in a judge, and mark the precincts of judicial decorum?"

Chase's answer at the beginning of the trial had avoided any reflection on the motives of his accusers, but growing confidence in the relative strength of their case had made the defense counsel more bold. Hopkinson noted that few judges had ever been impeached in England, but there had been seven in the last two years in the United States—"a melancholy proof either of extreme and unequalled corruption in our Judiciary, or of strange and persecuting times among us." Chase, he insisted, had been impeached simply for offending the House of Representatives. The House seemed to be claiming the power "to make anything criminal at their pleasure, at any period after its occurrence." Why, Hopkinson asked, had it taken them five years to prosecute Chase for offenses so heinous as the House alleged against him?

Finally Hopkinson turned to the substance of the first article. Reviewing the charges against Chase and the evidence in detail, Hopkinson made Chase's conduct of the Fries trial sound almost like an exceptionally praiseworthy model of judicial fairness. His listeners considered Hopkinson's performance something of a *tour de force*. Plumer called the speech "one of the most able arguments I ever heard delivered on any occasion," and a spectator wrote that "the gallery would have acquitted the Judge at the close of this argument of every crime."[20]

On the next morning Philip Barton Key rose to defend Chase's conduct of the Callender trial, articles II through IV. Almost anything would have been an anticlimax after Hopkinson, and the spectators believed Key fell short of his young colleague's brilliance. Still, though he was not feeling well, Key favorably impressed his hearers with a sound and logical speech of three and a half hours. He argued convincingly that all of Chase's controversial rulings at the Callender trial were legally correct. The worst Chase could justly be charged with was indecorous language toward Callender's counsel, which was hardly an impeachable offense. Charles Lee followed with a two-hour refutation of the breaches of Virginia procedure alleged against Chase in articles V and VI. Lee was not a good speaker, but his argument was soundly based in law and precedent.[21]

Next came the turn of the redoubtable Luther Martin, who had thus far taken little part in the trial despite his great reputation. To the surprise of his colleagues, Martin departed from the defense's plan by reviewing all of the first six articles. Martin's anxiety to do all he could to help his close friend Chase probably accounted for his conduct. Harper and Hopkinson were irritated, and they feared that Martin's repetition of points previously covered might be counterproductive.[22] They need not have worried, however, for Martin was as effective as usual.

Martin spoke for five and a half hours one day and finished the next morning. It was a classic Martin performance—a long-winded, "diffuse desultory argument" delivered ungrammatically and without grace, "uninteresting for the greater part of the time," yet displaying great legal knowledge and studded with flashes of logical brilliance, "keen satire and poignant wit," which made the whole memorable and persuasive.[23] Though Martin was speaking on issues previously covered, he was able to strengthen the defense's justification of Chase with new arguments and additional legal authorities.

Unwilling even to concede imprudence or indecorum on Chase's part, Martin maintained that his friend was thoroughly justified in every instance. His most damaging satirical sallies were reserved for the defense counsel in the Fries and Callender trials. Martin argued that their improper conduct was entirely responsible for the pyrotechnics at those trials. If Lewis and Dallas's behavior was typical of the Pennsylvania bar, Martin quipped, he now understood the great popular hostility to lawyers in that state. As for Callender's counsel, Chase's only mistake at the trial had been his failure to jail them for contempt of court. Martin clearly believed the articles of impeachment were silly, and his contempt for them was apparent in the ridicule that laced his substantive argument. Before Martin was through, one of the managers, Peter Early, remarked to a friend that he was tired of the proceedings and sorry that Chase's impeachment had ever been attempted.[24]

Robert Goodloe Harper concluded the defense arguments. He reviewed all eight articles in a very able speech of some seven hours. He made few new points of substance on the first six articles. On the last two, he reminded the Senate that the weight of the testimony showed Chase had not made the most inflammatory of the statements charged against him at Newcastle and Baltimore, nor had he done anything unprecedented or unjustified in either case. Harper made a very convincing case for the defense's contention that only indictable offenses were impeachable under the Constitution. He was confident, he said, that the Senate would rise above partisanship, judge justly, and not depart from the Constitution "to commit ourselves to the storms of party rage, personal animosity, and popular caprice." Strongly suggesting that the impeachment was political, Harper like Hopkinson portrayed Chase as an object of sympathy: "An aged patriot and statesman, bearing on his head the frost of seventy [sic] winters, and broken by the infirmities brought upon him by the labors and exertions of half a century, is arraigned as an offender, and compelled to employ, in defending himself...the few and short intervals of ease allowed to him by sickness."

Senator Plumer noted that Chase's counsel had "made a rare exhibition—a splended display of talents and oratory. Very large and numerous audiences have listened with great attention. The impression...is unequivocally in favor of the Judge."[25] The impeachment managers had one final chance to reverse that impression before the Senate pronounced judgment.

Joseph H. Nicholson followed Harper and immediately introduced a new note of confusion into the managers' case. Directly contradicting Campbell's earlier statement, Nicholson denied that the managers considered impeachment "a mere inquest of office. ...We do contend that this is a criminal prosecution, for offences committed in the discharge of high official duties." But, since judges served during good behavior, "misbehavior in office" was a criminal offense for purposes of impeachment whether indictable or not. Caesar Rodney, who followed Nicholson, agreed with this position but asserted that Chase had committed indictable offenses, notably by denying Fries his constitutional rights to counsel and to trial by an impartial jury. Neither Nicholson nor Rodney made much reference to the testimony at the impeachment trial.

Both, but Rodney more clearly, complained that "party feelings" and "political bigotry" had made the judiciary an instrument of faction rather than a defender of impartial justice. Here was the clearest exposition of the real Republican complaint behind the impeachment. Rodney stated that he favored the independence of the judiciary but not the "inviolability of judges. . . . Give any human being judicial power for life, and annex to the exercise of it the kingly maxim 'that he can do no wrong,' . . . you transform him into a despot, regardless of all law, but his own sovereign will and pleasure." To most Republicans, impeachment represented the only existing constitutional mechanism whereby judges might be made to answer for misbehavior in office, however that term might be defined.

John Randolph concluded the arguments for the prosecution. It was another poor effort on his part. By way of explanation, Randolph apologized for his illness during the trial and lamented that he had lost his notes. He added little beyond impassioned rhetoric delivered with "much distortion of face, and contortion of body, tears, groans, and sobs." Randolph concluded, "We adjure you, on behalf of the House of Representatives, and of all the people of the United States, to exorcise from our courts the baleful spirit of party, to give an awful memento to our judges."[26]

Following Randolph's speech the Senate decided that it would pass judgment in the case two days later, on Friday, March 1, at noon. While any senators who were still undecided made up their minds, public speculation assessed the probable verdict. The reports that Charles Carroll of Carrollton heard predicted that Chase would "be acquitted by a majority."[27] Carroll's strong bias against the integrity of Republicans made him disbelieve the report, and undoubtedly numbers of other Federalists still shared his gloom. Chase's nervous anxiety can be imagined.

"Anxious spectators" crowded the galleries when the court of impeachment assembled half an hour late on March 1. The crowd was impressed when Federalist senator Uriah Tracy of Connecticut entered and was helped to his seat. Tracy had been very sick with pneumonia, and his unexpected presence emphasized the importance of the occasion.[28] Since there were only nine Federalists in the Senate to twenty-five Republicans, Tracy knew that the defense would need every vote it could get.

The Senate had decided after much debate that, as each article was considered in turn, each senator should be asked whether Chase was guilty or not guilty of high crimes and misdemeanors as charged in that article. The solemn business of voting took two hours. When the process was completed, Aaron Burr announced the vote:

Article	Guilty	Not Guilty
I	16	18
II	10	24
III	18	16
IV	18	16
V	0	34
VI	4	30
VII	10	24
VIII	19	15

Burr then concluded the proceedings by officially stating the result: there not being a constitutional two-thirds vote for conviction on any article, Samuel Chase stood acquitted. "The Gallery was perfectly silent," Plumer noticed, "though from their countenances they appeared not only *satisfied* but highly *gratified.*"[29]

Chase's acquittal resulted from the fact that the Federalist senators supported him as a bloc, while most Republicans in the end voted their honest convictions of justice, whichever side they took. Six Republicans joined the nine Federalists in voting not guilty on every article. Every Republican voted not guilty at least once. Even William Branch Giles voted guilty only four times.

The verdict, surely, was decided at the trial and not before. The defense case grew in strength day by day, while the prosecution never progressed far beyond the foundation laid in the articles of impeachment. Chase owed much to the excellent work of his counsel, who outshone the managers at every turn and were ingenious at presenting his conduct in the best possible light. Randolph, by any standard, handled the prosecution badly, beginning with his preparation of the articles. His last-minute inclusion of the weak articles V and VI detracted from the impact of the rest, and flaws in other articles were exposed in the course of the trial. In the end, from the evidence and arguments presented at the trial it was apparent that Chase's conduct could plausibly be considered impeachable only under a very broad definition of an impeachable offense. Chase's impeachment was political, not criminal, in nature. The Senate, of course, gave no explicit ruling on the question of what offenses were impeachable, but Chase's acquittal did much to limit the future use of the impeachment mechanism. By demonstrating that that device was likely to be unworkable except in a clear case of criminal or totally outrageous conduct, the Chase trial "virtually eliminated impeachment. . . as a means of controlling the Court."[30] The independence of the judiciary was strengthened. Nevertheless, after the trial federal judges were more careful to mind their manners and stay out of public politics. That, at least, Randolph had achieved.

If some Republican senators believed Chase guilty of no serious offense and others hesitated to undermine judicial independence, the open split in the Republican party early in 1805 made it easier for them to vote their personal convictions. The breach between Jefferson and Randolph over the Yazoo issue so weakened party unity that Randolph could not muster a party-line vote against Chase—and perhaps he could not have in any event. Indeed, hostility to Randolph among many Republicans helped Chase.[31]

On the afternoon of Chase's acquittal, an angry and frustrated Randolph arose in the House to assail Chase as an *"acquitted felon"* and to propose a constitutional amendment. He wanted to enable the president to remove federal judges upon the joint request of both houses of Congress. After an impassioned debate the House postponed the proposal until the next session, when it quietly died. This episode gave Chase the opportunity for a parting shot at his prosecutor in a letter to Hopkinson. "I have always said that my enemies are as great *fools* as *knaves*," Chase remarked.[32]

Eighteen

TWILIGHT

MMEDIATELY after his acquittal Samuel Chase left Washington for Baltimore. His gout was still bothering him greatly; apparently he was not even present in the Senate to hear the verdict. Now that his ordeal was over, Chase was eager to quit his capital boardinghouse for the comforts of home, where he could share his triumph with his family and no doubt recover more rapidly. Chase left Washington so quickly that he did not get the chance to thank all of his lawyers personally, an omission that he promptly made up by letter.[1]

The family was jubilant. Chase's half sister Elizabeth wrote that her brother "will be more Honoured by his Country and friends than if he had never been Accused[.] He has indeed passed Seven Times thro the Furnace and like pure gold remains unhurt and shines with undiminished Lustre." William Plumer, who called shortly after the trial to congratulate Chase, wrote, "I never saw a family more happy—his daughters were much gratified at my visit—they are very charming girls. I was much pleased to witness the strong affection love and tenderness that mutually subsists between him and them."[2]

In addition to visitors like Senator Plumer, Chase received congratulations by mail from friends and Federalist partisans. He noted with pleasure that even the Republicans in Baltimore professed satisfaction with the verdict. Replying to a letter from Rufus King, Chase generously acknowledged his debt to his counsel. "The whole labor rested on them, as I was unable, from indisposition to take any Part; and to the Justice of my Case, and their abilities I impute my acquittal.'' He was especially grateful to Robert Goodloe Harper, who had prepared his answer and generally directed the defense. As word of Chase's acquittal spread across the Atlantic, Chase even received congratulations from an almost forgotten companion of his boisterous youth, the Reverend Bennet Allen. Allen, it developed, really wanted to enlist Chase's help in recovering a prerevolutionary debt.[3]

Chase's preoccupation with the impeachment had not entirely prevented him from participating in the work of the Supreme Court, though he did not take part in many of the cases decided in 1804 and 1805. A number of cases during this period involved ship seizures arising from the Napoleonic wars in Europe. Chase's most prominent contribution to the Court's consideration of those cases was his insistence that presidential instructions governing seizures and construing American nonintercourse laws should not be considered by the Court. In one 1804 case Chase ''said he was always against reading the instructions of the executive; because, if they go no further than the law, they are unnecessary; if they exceed it, they are not warranted.'' Executive power had to be restrained to its legal limits. Marshall overruled Chase in that case and allowed the instructions to be read, but in a subsequent case the chief justice appeared to reverse himself and accept Chase's point of view.[4]

After his acquittal Chase's conduct on the bench was relatively subdued. There were no more political charges to grand juries. In May 1805 a newspaper reported that ''Judge Chase delivered a short and pertinent charge to the grand jury—his remarks were pointed, modest and well applied.'' Chase intended to stay out of politics. ''My age, Infirmities, and the wicked Persecution I have suffered, have determined Me never to take any Part in any public Measure whatsoever,'' he wrote. His ill health forced him to miss the entire Supreme Court terms of 1806 and 1810, and the Court did not meet in 1811. When he could attend, his infirmity impaired his performance. Justice William Johnson recalled later that Chase in his last years ''could not be got to think or write.'' That was an exaggeration; Joseph Story's comment in 1807 that Chase ''yet possesses considerable vigor and vivacity; but the flashes are irregular and sometimes ill-directed'' is more accurate.[5] In the 1807 and 1808 terms Chase exhibited considerable independence of thought and figured prominently in the Supreme Court's deliberations.

The most sensational cases of 1807 arose from the Burr conspiracy. Burr's intentions are still a matter of debate; perhaps he intended a filibustering expedition against Spanish Mexico, perhaps an attempt to separate the west from the United States, perhaps both. After Burr's co-conspirator, General James Wilkinson, turned against him and denounced the plot, President Jefferson became convinced that Burr's intentions were treasonable. Wilkinson arrested several of the conspirators and sent them to Washington, where they arrived early in 1807.

The matter first came before the Supreme Court on February 5, when one of the conspirators, New Orleans attorney James Alexander, applied to the high court for a writ of *habeas corpus*. Chase urged that the Court postpone consideration of the motion until the next day, explaining that "he doubted the jurisdiction of the court to issue a *habeas corpus* in any case." Chase believed that an individual justice could issue the writ in his circuit, but the precedent of *Marbury v. Madison* made him unwilling to act on Alexander's motion without further reflection on the Court's jurisdiction. Justice William Johnson agreed with Chase, and the issue was postponed until the next day. In the meantime, a circuit-court judge ordered Alexander's release, which ended the matter.[6]

A few days later, however, two other conspirators, Erick Bollman and Samuel Swartwout, who had been jailed on a charge of treason by the circuit court for the District of Columbia, also applied to the Supreme Court for writs of *habeas corpus*. Chase meanwhile had become ill, and did not participate in the Court's three-to-one decision to affirm its jurisdiction and grant the writ. When the marshal responded that Bollman and Swartwout were being held on the order of the circuit court, the defense attorneys moved for their clients' release. By then Chase had recovered sufficiently to participate in the case, though he did not take part in some of the Court's deliberations on collateral issues raised at the hearings. The Supreme Court ordered Bollman and Swartwout released from custody. Three of the four justices participating in the decision believed that the evidence did not establish probable cause of treason against the prisoners, and all four agreed that the circuit court lacked jurisdiction, no part of the alleged crime having taken place in the District of Columbia.

The significance of the decision arose from the construction of treason contained in John Marshall's opinion. The Court held that a conspiracy to commit treason did not constitute treason unless an overt act took place—the use of force, or at least the assembly of men, to carry out the conspiracy. Marshall added in an *obiter dictum* that, if such an overt act did occur, "all those who perform any part, however minute, or however remote from the scene of action, and who are actually leagued in the general conspiracy, are to be considered as traitors." Marshall believed at the time that the four justices who participated in the decision all agreed with this interpretation. Chase, however, had been absent during the discussion of this peripheral issue, and he later told Marshall that he did not concur. In the Fries trial Chase had held that some force must actually be employed to constitute the crime of treason. Perhaps he believed that even an assembly of men with treasonable intent was insufficient in the absence of a forcible act, and conceivably he had other objections as well. Chase's unregistered dissent was important; four justices would have constituted a majority of the full Court, but if the absent judges agreed with Chase, Marshall's *dictum* would be deprived of clear majority support and hence lose much of its force.

The *dictum* caused Marshall some embarrassment later in 1807 when he presided over the treason trial of Aaron Burr in the circuit court for Virginia. The case turned largely upon the definition of treason. The prosecution relied upon the construction of treason laid down by Marshall himself in the Bollman and Swartwout case. But Burr's attorneys, particularly Luther Martin and John Wickham, contended that his *obiter dictum* was neither binding nor correct. Marshall, now unsure of his ground, secretly wrote to Justice William Cushing (and perhaps other justices as well) asking for advice on the issue. It is conceivable that he learned of Chase's disagreement as a result of this inquiry. In the end Marshall "explained" his opinion in the Bollman and Swartwout case in a way that further restricted the definition of treason he had then given. His lengthy new opinion on the law of treason was instrumental in Burr's acquittal.[7]

In the 1808 term of the Supreme Court, Chase made his presence felt in several issues involving ship seizures. In one case the question was whether or not a French prize court on the West Indian island of Guadeloupe had jurisdiction to condemn an American vessel seized by a French privateer and taken to a port in neutral Spanish Cuba. The Court ruled that it did, but Chase and Justice Henry Livingston dissented on the ground that the ship should have been taken to a French port in order to give French courts jurisdiction. In another case, a technical issue involving the effect of bottomry bonds, Chase gave the opinion of the Court. A third case, *Croudson and Others v. Leonard,* raised the important issue of whether or not ''the American Courts should follow the British doctrine as to conclusiveness of the decision of foreign prize courts.'' Was a British prize court's condemnation of an American vessel conclusive evidence of the latter's attempt to violate the British blockade of French Martinique, an intention that would bar the American ship's owners from collecting insurance on their seized vessel? The Court ruled that the English doctrine of conclusiveness should be adopted, but again Chase and Livingston dissented. The case was controversial, for the Jefferson administration did not accept the validity of many British and French restrictions on American neutral rights. The Court's decision operated to England's advantage and ran counter to the thrust of American diplomacy.[8]

At the same term Chase had the satisfaction of seeing his son Samuel make his first appearance as an attorney before the Supreme Court. The family remained close, united in love for their husband and father, but the rift between Hannah Kitty and her stepchildren continued to be a source of tension not far beneath the surface. Chase's domestic tranquility was also shaken in September 1808, when his youngest daughter Mary eloped with William Barney. They were married in Princeton, New Jersey. Barney, the son of a naval hero and prominent social figure in Baltimore, was a good catch. So for that matter was Mary Chase. She was a ''celebrated'' belle of Baltimore, ''her eye sparkling with intelligence, and her conversation full of wit and sense, envied by her own sex, and feared and admired by the other.''[9] The Chases accepted the match and delighted in the new flock of grandchildren who soon began to appear.

Chase's son Thomas had become an enduring source of anxiety to the family. He had contracted a mysterious malady that left him with constant stomach trouble, headaches, an eye very sensitive to light, and a cheek very sensitive to cold and threatened with paralysis. Unable to take the Maryland winter, Thomas Chase became a ceaseless traveler in the southern United States, Florida, and the West Indies, always in search of relief from his affliction but never finding it.[10] There is no indication that Thomas had a regular income of his own, and he probably relied on his father for support.

That placed a considerable burden on the family's always strained finances. Chase continued constantly to borrow money, but there are no signs of real distress during his last years. The settlement of the English bank stock case in 1804 brought Chase a large commission, but he had to sue the state in 1807 to get an additional sum he thought he deserved. Only in December 1810 was that matter settled. The proceeds not only strengthened family finances but also allowed Chase to make a promising commercial investment. Around 1806–1807 he constructed a wharf on land he owned at the point where Jones Falls empties into the Baltimore Harbor basin. It was an excellent location for unloading cargo in Baltimore proper, saving the long haul from the older docks on Fell's Point. The wharf also contained a lumberyard that made barrel staves as its major product.[11]

When he was physically able, Chase remained the gregarious, entertaining man he had always been. Henry M. Brackenridge, son of an old friend who came to Baltimore to study law in 1808, recalled that Chase particularly enjoyed the company "of young men, and talked to them with great familiarity, and sometimes very bluntly." Once when Chase invited Brackenridge to dinner, the latter forgot to come. "Some evenings after this sin of omission," Brackenridge wrote, "I dropped in before tea, and had scarcely taken my seat, when he inquired in a stentorian voice, why I had not come to dinner. In my simplicity I told him the truth. 'What, sir, forget an invitation to dine with me; I admire your candour, sir, but d—n your politeness.' " Brackenridge added that Chase "was no doubt more amused than offended."[12]

Another visitor to Baltimore, Judge Joseph Story, wrote in 1807 that Chase struck him as "a rough, but very sensible man . . . . I suspect he is the American Thurlow—bold, impetuous, overbearing, and decisive." Upon further acquaintance, Story reflected,

I am satisfied that the elements of his mind are of the very first excellence; age and infirmity have in some degree impaired them. His manners are coarse, and in appearance harsh; but in reality he abounds with good humor. He loves to croak and grumble, and in the very same breath he amuses you extremely by his anecdotes and pleasantry. His first approach is formidable, but all difficulty vanishes when you once understand him. In person, in manners, in unwieldy strength, in severity of reproof, in real tenderness of heart, and above all in intellect, he is the living, I had almost said the exact, image of Samuel Johnson. To use a provincial expression, I like him hugely.[13]

Some of Chase's grumbling was no doubt reserved for politics. He remained gloomy about the future as the nation drifted toward the War of 1812. "We have fallen on *Evil Times,*" Chase wrote to Timothy Pickering early in 1811, "but I hope your firmness and Perseverance will never forsake you; the Compatriot of Washington should never despair. I see little Room for Hope, and trust only in providence. I almost believe, that War, the Scourge of Nations, would relieve Us from our present Rulers; and I fear Nothing else will."[14] Chase's revolution had been completed a generation before. He never reconciled himself to the changes that time and Republican rule made in the political order he had helped to create.

By 1811 only a dwindling band of "compatriots of Washington" remained on the scene. Soon there would be one fewer. Chase's health continued gradually but steadily to deteriorate. In the spring of 1811 he was no longer able to go horseback riding, heretofore his favorite exercise. He continued to enjoy daily carriage rides around the city or the nearby countryside, but his growing debility made him aware that his days were numbered. He sent for his pastor at St. Paul's, Reverend Joseph G. J. Bend, and received the sacraments of his church. On June 19, 1811, a hot and sultry day, he "returned much exhausted" from his daily ride. "After the physicians were summoned to attend him, he spoke of his domestic concerns, gave several directions concerning his household, and was perfectly calm and resigned." He told his family not to grieve and refused a dose of medicine, saying, "God gives life." Around eleven that evening, "he expired so gently, that those around him scarcely knew when he had ceased to breathe." The cause of death was given as "ossification of the heart."[15] After a simple funeral he was buried in the St. Paul's Church cemetery.

It was surprising for a lawyer but consistent with his carelessness about his personal affairs that Samuel Chase left no valid will. There was indeed a purported will in Chase's handwriting, but it was not signed in the presence of witnesses as required by Maryland law. In Luther Martin's opinion, the document was good in regard to Chase's personal property but could not legally convey his real estate. The personal property of the estate fell short of meeting Chase's debts by more than $1,700 current money. Fortunately Chase had had the foresight to convey "at least 15 lots in Baltimore City to his sons...shortly before his death." With the Chase home already in trust for Hannah Kitty and her daughters, much of the real property seemed secure for the family. The lack of an incontestable will, plus Mrs. Chase's assertion of her claim to dower rights and disputes over the trust, resulted in a tangled situation for a family that began to fall apart as soon as death removed its great unifying force. Off and on for the next fourteen years Hannah Kitty Chase, her children, and her stepchildren were involved in quarrels and law suits over the estate.[16]

IN 1820 John Sanderson visited John Quincy Adams to discuss his projected book on the signers of the Declaration of Independence. The conversation turned to Samuel Chase. "I told him," Adams recorded in his diary,

> I considered Mr. Chase as one of the men whose life, conduct, and opinions had been of the most extensive influence upon the Constitution of this country. He not only signed the Declaration of Independence, but was an active and distinguished member of the Congress during the early and most critical period of the Revolution. He was a man of ardent passions, of strong mind, of domineering temper. His life was consequently turbulent and boisterous. He had for some years almost uncontrolled dominion over the politics of the State of Maryland; at other times was unpopular in the extreme, and was more than once impeached.[17]

Yet, for all his prominence, this "strange inconsistent man," as Alexander Contee Hanson called him, has remained something of a mystery. Inconsistencies there were in Chase's career, reflecting tendencies built into his character from his boyhood. Yet there was at the level of fundamental belief a core of consistency in Samuel Chase that was not always readily apparent.

Samuel Chase was nominally born a gentleman, but without most of the attributes of gentility. His father gave him the equivalent of a gentleman's education, but he lacked landed wealth, social status, and polish. Chase aspired eagerly to wealth and status, and he pursued those goals impatiently until late middle age. He never completely succeeded, despite his growing prominence, political and legal achievements, and acceptance in the company of the governing elite. In those circles Chase was ever the parvenu. His manners were always crude. Temperamentally a plunger, Chase engaged in speculation, mixed business and politics, damaged his reputation, and at times antagonized many of the gentlemen whose acceptance he sought. He never built a secure landed estate, and around 1788 that dream died in financial collapse. Chase was compelled to accept defeat in one of his deepest personal aspirations.

While Chase pursued gentility, there was much in his personality, tastes, and family background that gave him an affinity to the "middling sort" of small property owners. He had a natural sympathy for the interests and problems of small farmers, shopkeepers, artisans, and mechanics. Chase soon found that he had an exceptional talent for appealing to the "middling sort" as legal defender of debtors, orator, agitator, and political spokesman. He brought this constituency actively into the political arena to a degree previously unknown in Maryland. His championing of their interests was at times a further source of conflict between Chase and many of the gentry.

Chase's affinities for both the gentry and the "middling sort," arising from his personality and the ambiguities of his origins, were reflected also in his political philosophy. Chase's political thought drew most heavily upon the traditional and the concrete—the common law, judicial and legislative precedent, the rights of Englishmen. He was well acquainted with the law of nature and of nations, but these strains played a lesser role in his thinking. In later life, at least, he found the doctrines of some natural rights philosophers extravagant, fanciful, and altogether dangerous.

The clearest extant statement of Chase's political philosophy is contained in his grand jury charges of 1799–1803. One must exercise caution before concluding that Chase's statements at one time accurately reflect his views at other periods of his life, but the central ideas contained in the charges do seem to express his consistent life-long beliefs.

The key to Chase's political thought was his commitment to a particular definition of freedom and equality: the rule of law, equality before the law, and equal protection for personal and property rights—these and nothing more. A society that met these criteria was a free society in Chase's view, whatever its form of government. Some forms were more conducive to liberty than others, of course. Chase believed freedom required that the people have a share in the legislative process, and after 1776 he was committed to republicanism. But in his mind the extension of political participation to all citizens had nothing to do with either freedom or equal rights. Throughout his career Chase supported property qualifications for voting and maintained that allowing the propertyless to vote was destructive of freedom.

To Chase, ordered liberty required that each social class—the gentry, small property holders, the propertyless—be protected in and restricted to its proper role. He favored elite leadership in politics. The ideal ruling elite in his view was a natural aristocracy of wisdom and talent, which to be sure generally went hand in hand with wealth and social status. This elite should be fluid, open ended, accessible to talent; an elite of artificial privilege Chase despised. Above all, the gentlemen who governed must maintain equal liberty and equal justice. They would command the deference of lesser men, and so would have considerable scope to exercise their own judgment on political issues and to persuade the voters of the soundness of their views. But they must in the end be responsible to their constituents. Chase consistently upheld the binding force of instructions upon a representative. He changed his mind only in regard to the applicability of that doctrine to the Maryland Senate. The "middling sort" who made up the great mass of the electorate therefore possessed ultimate sovereignty, however much they might (and should) defer to the leadership of their social superiors on most issues. The propertyless, while playing no political role, must nevertheless be protected in their enjoyment of freedom and equal justice. Religion and morality provided the underpinnings for Chase's vision of a free society.

Chase's political career reflected the tensions inherent in his affinities for both the gentry and the "middling sort," but his basic philosophy provided a thread of consistency. In 1764–1766 he burst upon the political stage as the radical agitator, mobilizer of the "middling sort" against the Annapolis city government, the proprietary officers, and the Stamp Act. His attacks on the proprietary government in 1764–1766 and 1772–1773 reflected his hostility to an elite of artificial privilege, resting on patronage rather than merit, that he believed was acting irresponsibly. In those battles personal resentment of men whose connections had allowed them easily to achieve the status Chase sought reinforced his political philosophy. Few contemporaries matched Chase's skillful use of the press in these and later campaigns. Simultaneously, from 1765 to 1776 he upheld equal rights and equal justice for Britain's American subjects in a conflict with a British government that sought to relegate its colonists to an inferior status. Convinced in 1775 that a corrupt Britain falling to tyranny would not concede American rights, he worked for independence.

Independence provided an opportunity to establish equal rights and equal justice in a new republican framework. Chase's revolution had no place for the social upheaval that some Marylanders feared, and he sought to contain the revolutionary forces unleashed in 1776 within the bounds of ordered liberty as he understood it. His political philosophy guided him as he helped establish the Maryland constitution. It was not exactly what he would have liked, but it did embody his basic ideals.

Chase's political battles of the war years revolved around his fierce insistence on a vigorous prosecution of the struggle upon which American liberty depended. The strong actions that he believed necessary for a successful war effort met resistance from those who considered them ill advised or too drastic. Chase's combination of speculation with politics complicated the issue in several of these political battles.

After the war Chase turned his energies to restoring Maryland's finances and laying the foundations of long-term prosperity. But by 1785 depression was causing widespread distress, including Chase's own imminent bankruptcy. Moved by personal interest as well as sympathy for the plight of debt-ridden small property owners, Chase believed that paper money and debt relief were needed to alleviate distress and restore prosperity. The Senate disagreed, and Chase reverted to his political role of the 1760s to wage what he saw as another battle against a selfish and irresponsible faction of the wealthy and powerful. The rhetoric of the paper money struggle carried over into Chase's fight against the Constitution, which ini-

tially appeared to him to emasculate the states, concentrate dangerous power at the center, and place the nation in the hands of an un-
checked aristocracy.

Chase gradually became reconciled to the Constitution, and in
the 1790s he saw equal rights and equal justice endangered again, as
in 1776, from below. The contagion of the French Revolution
seemed in his eyes to threaten all the horrors of democracy, social
upheaval, and irreligion. From 1794 on, Chase sought to defend *his*
American Revolution from Democratic-Republicans who sought to
change the political arrangements Chase had helped to create, and
to change them in ways he considered destructive to freedom.

There was thus a fundamental consistency to Chase's actions. In
all of his major political battles he was guided by a particular view of
freedom, equal rights, and equal justice, to be achieved in a socially
mobile but still socially ordered country. Chase found the best hope
for freedom in this view of a balance between order and liberty. If
his position appeared to oscillate from radical to conservative, it was
largely because the threats to his vision of freedom and good
government appeared alternately from different directions.

Chase's stands, of course, were not determined entirely by political philosophy, nor was his consistency in action complete. Personal
self-interest and other immediate considerations entered strongly
into his motivation. Fiery and impulsive, Chase often seemed to
speak or act without reflection. But he rarely if ever adopted his fundamental stand on a major issue on the spur of the moment. His impulsiveness was reflected rather in tactics, in a desire for quick and
decisive action once his mind was made up, and in the vehemence
with which he expressed himself. Any stand that Chase took was
likely to be announced in the strongest terms. In the heat of political combat, he often made extreme, imprudent, or inflammatory
statements, some of which he later regretted. This impulsive ex-
tremism of expression frequently made Chase appear more radical
than he actually was. His fiery rhetoric helped conceal his philosophical consistency and added to his reputation for swinging from
radical to conservative. Throughout, Chase faced his political
battles with great personal courage and an obstinate dedication to
doing his duty as he saw it.

Behind the fiery political warrior was a rough but likable personality. Chase was a devoted husband and father, though he tended

to be careless of personal finances and often lived beyond his means. Good humored, sociable, warm hearted, and sympathetic to those in distress behind a sometimes forbidding exterior, Chase did not let his political battles give rise to enduring personal enmities. His world revolved around family, church, politics, and the law, and he loved all four. Not always on the popular side and at least occasionally in the wrong, Chase was guided politically by devotion to duty and to freedom as well as by self-interest. Often a "strange inconsistent man" in the eyes of others, Samuel Chase tried to be consistently true to himself.

Notes

1. Alexander Contee Hanson to ?, July 25, 1790, Chase Papers, MS 1235, Maryland Historical Society, Baltimore (hereafter MHS).
2. Samuel Chase, statement of family property in London, n.d., Chase Papers, MS 1235, MHS; draft article, n.d., copy, Samuel Chase Letters, MS 1234, MHS. See also Rosamond Randall Beirne, "The Reverend Thomas Chase: Pugnacious Parson," *Maryland Historical Magazine*, LIX (1964), 1–14, from which a few sentences are reproduced here.
3. John and J. A. Venn, comps., *Alumni Cantabrigienses* (Cambridge, Eng., 1922), pt. I, vol. I, 326; copy of sketch from *National Portraits*, Samuel Chase Letters, MS 1234, MHS; Ethan Allen, "History of St. Paul's Parish" (1855), copy, 85, MS 13, MHS; Francis F. Beirne, *St. Paul's Parish, Baltimore* (Baltimore, 1967), 18; Nelson Waite Rightmyer, *Maryland's Established Church* (Baltimore, 1956), 169.
4. Clayton Torrence, *Old Somerset on the Eastern Shore of Maryland* (Richmond, Va., 1935), 139, 288, 393, 395, 424, 513–514. The Walker house has been restored.
5. Somerset County Wills, liber EB no. 9, 252; Accounts, 22, 80–82; Deeds, liber O26, 118, Maryland Hall of Records, Annapolis (hereafter MHR). The bequest, presumably with accumulated interest, eventually totaled £125.
6. Council Proceedings, Mar. 17, 1742, July 1, 1743, in William H. Browne *et al.*, eds., *Archives of Maryland* (Baltimore, 1883–), XXVIII, 293–294, 305 (hereafter *Archives*); Proceedings of the Upper House of Assembly, Oct. 26, 1742, and Edmund Jenings to Lord Baltimore, July 8, 1744, *Archives*, XLII, 295, 668–669; John T. Scharf, *History of Maryland* (Hatboro, Pa., 1967 repr. of 1879 ed.), I, 424–425.
7. Proceedings of the Lower House of Assembly, June 5, 1747, *Archives*, XLIV, 527–530; Rightmyer, *Maryland's Church*, 169.
8. Allen, "History of St. Paul's," 86, MS 13, MHS; Neil Strawser, "The Early Life of Samuel Chase" (M.A. thesis, George Washington University, 1958), 20. The latter is an excellent study and indispensable source.
9. Provincial Court Judgments, vol. 36, liber EI no. 13, 288–295, MHR.
10. Council Proc., Dec. 3, 1746, *Archives*, XXVIII, 370–376.
11. Provincial Court Judgments, vol. 36, liber EI no. 13, 340–343, MHR.
12. *Ibid.*, 291–295; Chancery Court Records, vol. 8, liber IR no. 5, 584, 638, 971–975, MHR.

13. Proc. Lower House, Oct. 29, 1753, Apr. 28, May 2, 1757, *Archives*, L, 198–205; LV, 79–80, 86–87; Council Proc., May 11, 1757, *Archives*, XXXI, 208–210; Horatio Sharpe to Lord Baltimore, Dec. 16, 1758, *Archives*, IX, 316–317.

14. Prerogative Court, Testamentary Proceedings, vol. 37, 22, 94, 130, 236–237; Provincial Court Judgments, vol. 52, liber DD no. 8, 19–28; Chancery Court Records, vol. 11, liber DD no. 2, 447–458, and vol. 13, 130–168, all MHR.

15. Chase Notebooks, MS 229, MHS.

16. Journal of Francis Asbury, Dec. 14, 1773, Mar. 23, 1774, Jan. 18, 1777, in Elmer T. Clark, ed., *The Journal and Letters of Francis Asbury*, I (Nashville, 1958), 99, 111, 114, 228.

17. This theme is an elaboration upon the interpretation offered by Strawser, "Early Life," 5–13.

Chapter Two

1. See especially Edward C. Papenfuse, *In Pursuit of Profit: The Annapolis Merchants in the Era of the American Revolution, 1763-1805* (Baltimore, 1975), 5–34.

2. *Ibid.*, 80–81n.; Charles Warren, *A History of the American Bar* (Boston, 1911), 166.

3. Strawser, "Early Life," 39.

4. *Ibid.*, 29–34, 59–62; Warren, *American Bar*, 166–167; Samuel Chase Law Notes, ca. 1760, Gift Collection G457, MHR.

5. Annapolis City Corporation Records, 2:173, 178, 182, 197, 204–205, MHR; Chase, *To the Publick*, July 18, 1766, broadside, in Yale University Microfilm of Annapolis *Maryland Gazette*, after issue of June 25, 1767; Strawser, "Early Life," 51–54.

6. For Paca, see Gregory A. Stiverson and Phebe R. Jacobsen, *William Paca: A Biography* (Baltimore, 1976).

7. *Ibid.*, 38–39; Strawser, "Early Life," 40–43; Forensic Club Minutes, typescript, MHR.

8. Jonathan Boucher, *Reminiscences of an American Loyalist, 1783-1789*, ed. Jonathan Bouchier (Port Washington, N.Y., 1967), 66–67; Chase to President and Members of Homony Club, Jan. 2, 1772, Gilmor Papers, MS 387.1, MHS; Independent Club, Sioussat Papers, MS 1497, MHS; Ann. *Md. Gaz.*, Dec. 12, 19, 1771.

9. Chase Family Bible Records, copy, Gift Collection D603(3), MHR; Samuel Chase folder, Filing Case A, Genealogy Section, MHS; Prerogative Court, Testamentary Papers, box 65, folder 10, MHR; Annapolis City Corp. Records, 2:247, MHR; Strawser, "Early Life," 48–49.

10. Statement of Thomas Chase, n.d., Chase Home Book, MS 969, MHS (originals of papers in this collection are held by the Maryland Diocesan Archives of the Protestant Episcopal Church, on deposit at MHS); Allen, "History of St. Paul's," 98, 107, MS 13, MHS.

11. Strawser, "Early Life," 59–64, 134.

12. *Ibid.*, 66–73, 84.

13. *Ibid.*, 83–93.

14. *Ibid.*, 108, 112; Neil Strawser, "Samuel Chase and the Annapolis Paper War," *Md. Hist. Mag.*, LVII (1962), 182; Annapolis City Corp. Records, 2:230, MHR.

15. Strawser, "Chase and Paper War," *Md. Hist. Mag.*, LVII (1962), 180–181.

16. *Ibid.*, 183; Annapolis City Corp. Records, 2:241, MHR.

17. Autobiography of Charles Willson Peale, in Horace Wells Sellers, "Charles Willson Peale, Artist-Soldier," *Pennsylvania Magazine of History and Biography*, XXXVIII (1914), 261–262; Chase, *To the Publick*, July 18, 1766; Strawser, "Chase and Paper War," *Md. Hist. Mag.*, LVII (1962), 183–184.

Chapter Three

1. For accounts of the Stamp Act crisis in Maryland, see Ronald Hoffman, *A Spirit of Dissension: Economics, Politics, and the Revolution in Maryland* (Baltimore, 1973), 28–55, and James A. Haw, "Politics in Revolutionary Maryland, 1753–1788" (Ph.D. diss., University of Virginia, 1972), 81–115. The discussion of the Stamp and Townshend Acts crises here is based on the latter source unless otherwise noted.

2. Chase, *To the Publick*, July 18, 1766; Ann. *Md. Gaz.*, Aug. 29, Sept. 5, 1765.

3. Horatio Sharpe to Cecilius Calvert, Oct. 2, 1765, and to Lord Baltimore, Oct. 3, 1765, *Archives*, XIV, 230, 231–232.

4. Proc. Lower House, Sept. 23–28, 1765, *ibid.*, LIX, 18–36.

5. Chase, *To the Publick*, July 18, 1766; Strawser, "Early Life," 165.

6. Isaac Q. Leake, *Memoir of the Life and Times of General John Lamb* (Albany, 1850), 3–4; Charles Carroll of Carrollton to Daniel Barrington, Mar. 17, 1766, in Thomas Meagher Field, ed., *Unpublished Letters of Charles Carroll of Carrollton, and of His Father, Charles Carroll of Doughoregan* (New York, 1902), 112–113.

7. Carroll of Carrollton to Barrington, Mar. 17, 1766, Field, ed., *Unpublished Letters of Carroll*, 112–113.

8. *Ibid.*; Chase, *To the Publick*, July 18, 1766; Ann. *Md. Gaz.*, Mar. 6, Apr. 3, 1766.

9. Chase, *To the Publick*, July 18, 1766; Strawser, "Early Life," 131, 145–148.

10. Ann. *Md. Gaz.*, Mar. 13, 20, 27, May 1, 8, June 19, 1766.

11. Chase, *To the Publick*, July 18, 1766.

12. Chase to George Washington, Sept. 3, 1789, Samuel Chase Letters, MS 1234, MHS.

13. Strawser, "Chase and Paper War," *Md. Hist. Mag.*, LVII (1962), 192–194; Ann. *Md. Gaz.*, Oct. 14, 1773.

14. Strawser, "Early Life," 151; Proc. Lower House, 1765–1771, *Archives*, LIX, LXI, LXII, LXIII.

15. Nathaniel Ramsey to Otho Holland Williams, Sept. 24, 1788, Otho Holland Williams Papers, MS 908, MHS.

16. Proc. Lower House, Nov. 15, 1765, May 10, Nov. 29, 1766, *Archives,* LIX, 157; LXI, 21, 195; Haw, "Politics in Revolutionary Maryland," 117–119; Scharf, *History of Maryland,* II, 106.

17. James Haw, "The Patronage Follies: Bennet Allen, John Morton Jordan, and the Fall of Horatio Sharpe," *Md. Hist. Mag.,* LXXI (1976), 134–150.

18. Proc. Lower House, June 16, 1768, Oct. 25, 1770, *Archives,* LXI, 383; LXII, 284; Strawser, "Early Life," 212; Ann. *Md. Gaz.,* Aug. 9, 1770.

19. Strawser, "Early Life," 217–218; Ann. *Md. Gaz.,* Mar. 4, 1773.

20. Proc. Lower House, June 21, 1768, *Archives,* LXI, 405.

21. Ann. *Md. Gaz.,* Aug. 2, 9, 16, 1770.

22. Anne Arundel County Court Judgments, MHR; Strawser, "Early Life," 209, 214–215.

23. Hoffman, *Spirit of Dissension,* 88.

24. Strawser, "Early Life," 49–50; Chase Family Bible Records, copy, Gift Collection D603(3), MHR.

25. Thomas Chase to Ann Chase, Apr. 14, 1804, copy, Chase Home Book, MS 969, MHS.

26. Provincial Court Deeds, liber DD no. 4, 502–504, MHR; Council Proc., Sept. 16, 1769, *Archives,* XXXII, 314.

27. Anne Arundel County Deeds, liber IB and JB no. 1, 374–375, MHR.

28. Strawser, "Early Life," 216, 231–232; Provincial Court Deeds, liber DD no. 5, 259–261, MHR; Carroll of Carrollton to Charles Carroll, Barrister, Aug. 9, 1771, in J. G. D. Paul, ed., "A Lost Copy-Book of Charles Carroll of Carrollton," *Md. Hist. Mag.,* XXXII (1937), 201.

29. William Faris Account Book, MS 1104, MHS; Charles Coleman Sellers, *Portraits and Miniatures by Charles Willson Peale* (Philadelphia, 1952), 52–53. The portraits are now at MHS.

30. Testimony of Robert Smith, Dec. 1, 1788, and Thomas Eden, Feb. 22, 1787, on memorial of Thomas Eden on behalf of Robert Eden, Loyalist Transcripts from New York Public Library, microfilm, MHS.

Chapter Four

1. James Haw, "Maryland Politics on the Eve of Revolution: The Provincial Controversy, 1770–1773," *Md. Hist. Mag.,* LXV (1970), 104–107.

2. Jean H. Vivian, "The Poll Tax Controversy in Maryland, 1770–76: A Case of Taxation *with* Representation," *ibid.,* LXXI (1976), 152; Ann. *Md. Gaz.,* Mar. 28, 1771.

3. Ann. *Md. Gaz.,* Dec. 13, 1770; Proc. Lower House, Sept. 28, Nov. 5, 10, 13, 21, 1770, Oct. 10, 18, 31, 1771, *Archives,* LXII, 213–214, 374, 391, 399, 430; LXIII, 98, 114–115.

4. Vivian, "Poll Tax Controversy," *Md. Hist. Mag.,* LXXI (1976), 154–160.

5. Though thirty-two pounds of tobacco seems at first glance an increase in clergy salaries over the thirty pounds set by the inspection act, the 1770 compromise's extension to all taxpayers of an option to pay in currency at the rate of 12/6

per hundred pounds of tobacco would actually have reduced clergy salaries. Tobacco at the time sold for 20 to 25s. per hundred pounds. *Ibid.*, 161–164.

6. Ann. *Md. Gaz.*, Jan. 3, 1771.

7. *Ibid.*, Aug. 6, Sept. 3, 1772.

8. *Ibid.*, July 30, Aug. 6, 13, 20, 1772; Vivian, "Poll Tax Controversy," *Md. Hist. Mag.*, LXXI (1976), 164.

9. Ann. *Md. Gaz.*, Aug. 6, Sept. 3, 1772.

10. Vivian, "Poll Tax Controversy," *Md. Hist. Mag.*, LXXI (1976), 165–166n., 175.

11. *Ibid.*, 167–169; Ann. *Md. Gaz.*, Mar. 4, 11, 1773.

12. *The Maryland Gazette, or the Baltimore General Advertiser*, Sept. 22, 1788.

13. Chase and Paca's joint letters are in Ann. *Md. Gaz.*, Jan. 14, Mar. 18, 1773; other letters in issues of Dec. 31, 1772, Feb. 11, Mar. 11, 18, 25, Apr. 1, 8, 15, 29, May 27, 1773.

14. Charles Albro Barker, *The Background of the Revolution in Maryland* (n.p., 1967 repr. of 1940 ed.), 162–164, 364–365; Anne Y. Zimmer, "The 'Paper War' in Maryland, 1772–73: The Paca-Chase Political Philosophy Tested," *Md. Hist. Mag.*, LXXI (1976), 177–193.

15. Ann. *Md. Gaz.*, Jan. 14, Mar. 18, 1773.

16. *Ibid.*, Feb. 4, 1773; Zimmer, " 'Paper War,' " *Md. Hist. Mag.*, LXXI (1976), 188, 191–192.

17. Boucher, *Reminiscences,* 71.

18. Hoffman, *Spirit of Dissension,* 104–105.

19. Haw, "Maryland Politics on the Eve," *Md. Hist. Mag.*, LXV (1970), 103–129. Carroll's and Dulany's articles are in Ann. *Md. Gaz.*, Jan. 7, Feb. 4, 18, Mar. 11, Apr. 8, May 6, June 3, July 1, 1773.

20. Charles Carroll of Annapolis to Charles Carroll of Carrollton, Mar. 17, 1773, Carroll Papers, MS 206, MHS.

21. Ann. *Md. Gaz.*, Sept. 9, 1773.

22. Carroll of Annapolis to Carroll of Carrollton, Mar. 17, May 15, 1773, Carroll Papers, MS 206, MHS.

23. Ann. *Md. Gaz.*, May 20, 27, 1773; Thomas Jenings to Horatio Sharpe, Apr. 28, 1774, in Bernard C. Steiner, "New Light on Maryland History from the British Archives," *Md. Hist. Mag.*, IV (1909), 256.

24. Ann. *Md. Gaz.*, May 20, 27, June 10, 24, 1776; Chase to Captain Charles Ridgely, May 26, 1773, Ridgely Papers, MS 692.1, MHS.

25. Hoffman, *Spirit of Dissension,* 113–116.

26. Vivian, "Poll Tax Controversy," *Md. Hist. Mag.*, LXXI (1976), 172; Proc. Lower House, Dec. 14, 16, 1773; *Archives*, LXIV, 132, 139.

27. Proc. Lower House, Mar. 31, Apr. 1, 15, 1774, *Archives*, LXIV, 315, 316, 347; Carroll of Annapolis to Carroll of Carrollton, Apr. 15, 1774, Carroll Papers, MS 206, MHS.

28. Jenings to Sharpe, Apr. 28, 1774, Steiner, "New Light," *Md. Hist. Mag.*, IV (1909), 256.

Chapter Five

1. Proc. Lower House, Oct. 13, 1773, *Archives,* LXIV, 18.

2. Ann. *Md. Gaz.,* May 26, 1774.

3. Committee of Annapolis to Gentlemen of Virginia, May 25, 1774, Purviance Papers, MS 1394, MHS; Haw, "Politics in Revolutionary Maryland," 214–219.

4. Ann. *Md. Gaz.,* June 30, 1774.

5. Edmund Cody Burnett, *The Continental Congress* (New York, 1964 repr. of 1941 ed.), 30, 45; John Adams to Mrs. Adams, Sept. 29, 1774, and diary of Adams, Oct. 11, 13, 1774, in Edmund C. Burnett, ed., *Letters of Members of the Continental Congress* (Washington, D.C., 1921–1936), I, 60–61, 71, 74 (hereafter *LMCC*).

6. Notes of Daniel Webster and Mr. and Mrs. Ticknor on a conversation with Thomas Jefferson in 1824, in George Ticknor Curtis, *Life of Daniel Webster* (New York, 1889), I, 588.

7. Sept. 7, 1774, in Worthington Chauncey Ford, ed., *Journals of the Continental Congress, 1774–1789* (Washington, D.C., 1904–1937), I, 29.

8. Diary of Adams, Sept. 26–27, 1774, in Lyman H. Butterfield, ed., *The Adams Papers,* ser. I: *Diaries: Diary and Autobiography of John Adams* (Cambridge, Mass., 1961), II, 138.

9. *Ibid.,* 148.

10. James Duane to Chase, Dec. 29, 1774, and Chase to Duane, Feb. 5, 1775, *LMCC,* I, 88, 305–306.

11. Haw, "Politics in Revolutionary Maryland," 220–224. There is an old account, relied upon by Hoffman, *Spirit of Dissension,* 135–136, which states that Chase was in Annapolis and tried to prevent the burning of the *Peggy Stewart.* But contemporary accounts do not mention Chase, and I believe this version to be inaccurate. Burnett gives Chase's attendance at Congress as September 5 through October 26, *LMCC,* I, xlv. Though daily attendance is not recorded in the journal, it seems unlikely that Chase left Philadelphia while Congress was in session.

12. Haw, "Politics in Revolutionary Maryland," 224–226.

13. Ann. *Md. Gaz.,* Dec. 29, 1774, Jan. 19, 1775.

14. William Fitzhugh to James Russell, Jan. 25, 1775, Russell Papers, microfilm, Virginia Colonial Records Project, University of Virginia Library, Charlottesville (originals in possession of Messrs. Coutts & Co., Bankers, London).

15. Ann. *Md. Gaz.,* Jan. 19, 1775; *To the Citizens of Annapolis,* Jan. 11, 1775, broadside, MHS; extract of a letter from a merchant at Annapolis to his friend in Philadelphia, Jan. 28, 1775, in Peter Force, ed., *American Archives* (New York, 1972 repr. of 1837–1853 ed.), 4th ser., I, 1194.

16. Boucher, *Reminiscences,* 105–108.

17. Benjamin Galloway to [Thomas Ringgold?], May 7, 1775, Galloway-Maxcy-Markoe Papers, Library of Congress, Washington, D.C.

18. Merchant at Annapolis to his friend in Philadelphia, Jan. 28, 1775, Force, ed., *American Archives,* 4th ser., I, 1194; *To the Citizens of Annapolis,* Jan. 11, 1775.

19. Chase to Duane, Feb. 5, 1775, *LMCC,* I, 304–306.

20. Chase to John Dickinson, Apr. ?, 1775, in *The Decisive Blow Is Struck*, introd. by Edward C. Papenfuse and Gregory A. Stiverson (Annapolis, 1977), [i]; Ann. *Md. Gaz.*, May 4, 1775.

21. Proc. of Convention, July 27–Aug. 14, 1775, *Archives*, XI, 5, 15–31.

22. Fredericktown Committee to John Hancock, Jan. 10, 1776, and enclosures; George Washington to President of Congress, Jan. 30, 1776; excerpt from J. F. D. Smith's Tour, all Force, ed., *American Archives*, 4th ser., IV, 615–618, 891–892.

23. Diary of Adams, Sept. 18, 1775, Butterfield, ed., *Adams Papers: Diaries*, II, 176; George Read to Mrs. Read, May 18, 1775, *LMCC*, I, 92.

24. Oct. 9, 1775, Feb. 9, 14, 1776, Ford, ed., *Journals of Cong.*, III, 285; IV, 123, 147.

25. Diary of Adams, Oct. 6–7, 1775, Butterfield, ed., *Adams Papers: Diaries*, II, 194, 198; H. James Henderson, *Party Politics in the Continental Congress* (New York, 1974), 58–60.

26. Henderson, *Party Politics*, 59: Dec. 14, 1775, Ford, ed., *Journals of Cong.*, III, 427; Joseph Hewes to Samuel Purviance, Jan. 29, 1776, Purviance Papers, MS 1394, MHS.

27. Diary of Adams, Oct. 4, 20, 21, 1775, Butterfield, ed., *Adams Papers: Diaries*, II, 190–191, 212–213, 215–217.

28. Oct. 12, 1775, *ibid.*, 207; diary of Richard Smith, Sept. 14, 1775, *LMCC*, I, 194.

29. Diary of Adams, Oct. 4, 20, 21, 1775, Butterfield, ed., *Adams Papers: Diaries*, II, 190–191, 212–213, 215–216.

30. Samuel Ward to Henry Ward, Nov. 2, 1775, in Paul H. Smith, ed., *Letters of Delegates to Congress, 1774–1789* (Washington, D.C., 1976–), II, 291.

31. John Sanderson, *Biography of the Signers to the Declaration of Independence*, IV (Philadelphia, 1828), 82; Scharf, *History of Maryland*, II, 218n.

32. Diary of Adams, Sept. 15, 18, 1775, and autobiography of Adams, Butterfield, ed., *Adams Papers: Diaries*, II, 172, 176; III, 311; autobiography of Adams, *LMCC*, I, 351–352n.

33. Burnett, *Continental Congress*, 122–123; Nov. 3, 1775, Ford, ed., *Journals of Cong.*, III, 319; autobiography of Adams, *LMCC*, I, 248n.

34. Chase to Adams, Nov. 25, Dec. 8, 1775, Smith, ed., *Letters of Delegates*, II, 453, 453n.; Adams to Chase, July 9, 1776, *LMCC*, II, 8.

35. Diary of Smith, Feb. 13, Mar. 22, 1776, *LMCC*, I, 348, 404; Burnett, *Continental Congress*, 139–140.

36. Diary of Smith, Feb. 21, 16, 1776, *LMCC*, I, 359, 351–352.

37. Haw, "Politics in Revolutionary Maryland," 254.

Chapter Six

1. Gunning Bedford to [Philip Schuyler?], Mar. 20, 1776, in J. C. Wylie, ed., "Letters of Some Members of the Old Congress," *Pa. Mag. Hist. Biog.*, XXIX (1905), 192.

2. Burnett, *Continental Congress*, 68, 108–112; Allen French, *The First Year of the American Revolution* (New York, 1968 repr. of 1934 ed.), 68–69, 143–159,

376–442, 595–620; Thomas Fleming, *1776: Year of Illusions* (New York, 1975), 1–22.

3. Chase to John Adams, Jan. 12, 1776, Smith, ed., *Letters of Delegates*, III, 276n.

4. *Ibid.;* Feb. 14–15, 1776, Ford, ed., *Journals of Cong.*, IV, 148–152; Adams to James Warren, Feb. 18, 1776, *LMCC*, I, 354; Burnett, *Continental Congress*, 113–114.

5. Diary of Richard Smith, Mar. 12, 1776, *LMCC*, I, 385–386.

6. Instructions of Congress to Benjamin Franklin, Chase, and Charles Carroll of Carrollton, Mar. 20, 1776, Force, ed., *American Archives*, 4th ser., V, 411–413.

7. Carroll of Carrollton to Charles Carroll of Annapolis, Mar. 4, 8, 1776, Carroll Papers, MS 206, MHS.

8. Carroll of Carrollton to Carroll of Annapolis, Mar. 25, 1776, Carroll Papers, MS 206, MHS; Charles Carroll, *Journal of Charles Carroll of Carrollton During His Visit to Canada in 1776...* (Baltimore, 1845), 37–39.

9. Carroll, *Journal*, 42–46; Carroll of Carrollton to Molly Carroll, Apr. 8, 1776, Carroll Papers, MS 206, MHS; Franklin to Josiah Quincy, Apr. 15, 13, 1776, Force, ed., *American Archives*, 4th ser., V, 947, 927–928.

10. Carroll, *Journal*, 52–74; Chase to Adams, Apr. 18, 1776, Smith, ed., *Letters of Delegates*, III, 556; French, *First Year of Revolution*, 693; Franklin, Chase, and Carroll of Carrollton to John Hancock, May 1, 1776, and John Carroll to ?, May 1, 1776, Force, ed., *American Archives*, 4th ser., V, 1166–1168.

11. Franklin, Chase, and Carroll of Carrollton to Hancock, May 1, 8, 1776. Force, ed., *American Archives*, 4th ser., V, 1166, 1237.

12. Fleming, *1776*, 220–222; French, *First Year of Revolution*, 694–697.

13. Carroll of Carrollton to Carroll of Annapolis, May 10, 17, 1776, Carroll Papers, MS 206, MHS; Carroll, *Journal*, 75; Franklin to Commissioners in Canada, May 27, 1776, in Albert Henry Smith, ed., *The Writings of Benjamin Franklin* (New York, 1906), VI, 448–449; Commissioners in Canada to President of Congress, May 17, 1776, Force, ed., *American Archives*, 4th ser., VI, 587–588.

14. Carroll of Carrollton to Carroll of Annapolis, May 17, 1776, Carroll Papers, MS 206, MHS; Commissioners to Schuyler, May 17, 1776, and to President of Congress, May 27, 1776, Force, ed., *American Archives*, 4th ser., VI, 586–587, 589–592; Chase to Richard Henry Lee, May 17, 1776, Lee Family Papers, U. Va.

15. Carroll of Carrollton to Carroll of Annapolis, May 27, 1776, Carroll Papers, MS 206, MHS; Fleming, *1776*, 223–224: Carroll, *Journal*, 81–84.

16. Chase to Adams, Apr. 28, 1776, Smith, ed., *Letters of Delegates*, III, 597.

17. Haw, "Politics in Revolutionary Maryland," 233–272.

18. Burnett, *Continental Congress*, 171–173; Matthew Tilghman, Thomas Stone, and John Rogers to Council of Safety, June 11, 1776, *Archives*, XI, 478–479.

19. June 11, 1776, Ford, ed., *Journals of Cong.*, V, 431; Chase to Horatio Gates, June 13, 1776, and Adams to Chase, June 14, 1776, *LMCC*, I, 486–487, 490–492.

20. Chase to Adams, June 21, 1776, in Charles Francis Adams, ed., *Works of John Adams...*, IX (Boston, 1854), 412.

21. Chase to Adams, June 28, 1776, and to Lee, June 29 , 1776, Samuel Chase Letters, MS 1234, MHS.

22. Carroll of Carrollton to Carroll of Annapolis, July 5, 1776, Carroll Papers, MS 206, MHS; Chase to Gates, July 18, 1776, Force, ed., *American Archives,* 5th ser., I, 410–411; Chase to Adams, July 5, 1776, and Adams to Chase, July 9, 1776, *LMCC,* II, 8, 8n.

23. Burnett, *Continental Congress,* 191.

24. Chase to Adams, June 28, 1776, Samuel Chase Letters, MS 1234, MHS.

Chapter Seven

1. Haw, "Politics in Revolutionary Maryland," 275–286. For a general discussion of conditions in Maryland around 1776, see Hoffman, *Spirit of Dissension,* 144–151, 184–205.

2. Chase to Richard Henry Lee, June 29, 1776, Samuel Chase Letters, MS 1234, MHS; July 3, 1776, *Proceedings of the Conventions of the Province of Maryland . . .* (Baltimore, 1836), 184–186.

3. Ann. *Md. Gaz.,* July 18, 1776.

4. Haw, "Politics in Revolutionary Maryland," 289–293: *Dunlap's Maryland Gazette* (Baltimore), Aug. 13, 1776.

5. Aug. 14, 15, 1776, *Proceedings of Conventions,* 210–216.

6. Charles Carroll of Carrollton to Charles Carroll of Annapolis, Aug. 20, 23, Oct. 10, 1776, Carroll Papers, MS 206, MHS.

7. Aug. 17, 1776, *Proceedings of Conventions,* 220–222.

8. Ann. *Md. Gaz.,* Aug. 22, 1776.

9. *Ibid.,* Dec. 11, 1777.

10. *Ibid.,* Aug. 22, 1776.

11. Aug. 27, Sept. 10, 1776, *Proceedings of Conventions,* 228–229, 251; Balt. *Md. Gaz.,* Sept. 12, 1788.

12. Sept. 11, 17, 1776, *Proceedings of Conventions,* 251–252, 258–259; Carroll of Carrollton to Carroll of Annapolis, Sept. 13, 1776, Carroll Papers, MS 206, MHS; Chase to John Dickinson, Sept. 29, Oct. 4, 19, 1776, Smith, ed., *Letters of Delegates,* V, 261–262.

13. Nov. 1–2, 1776, *Proceedings of Conventions,* 305, 307.

14. Oct. 31, Nov. 2, 4, 1776, *ibid.,* 303, 309, 333.

15. Carroll of Carrollton to Carroll of Annapolis, Sept. 13, 1776, Carroll Papers, MS 206, MHS.

16. *The Constitution and Form of Government proposed for the Consideration of the Delegates of Maryland* [Annapolis, 1776].

17. "An Elk Ridger," *Maryland Journal and Baltimore Advertiser,* May 1, 1787; Nov. 4, 1776, *Proceedings of Conventions,* 331.

18. Nov. 4, 1776, *Proceedings of Conventions,* 329–330.

19. Nov. 5, 8, 1776, *ibid.,* 335–339, 348–349.

20. Chase to Philip Schuyler, Aug. 9, 1776, *LMCC,* II, 44, and to Lee, July 30, 1776, Force, ed., *American Archives,* 5th ser., I, 672.

21. Thomas Jefferson, notes of proceedings in Congress, in Julian Boyd, ed., *The Papers of Thomas Jefferson* (Princeton, N.J., 1950–), I, 320; diary of John Adams, July 30, 1776, Butterfield, ed., *Adams Papers: Diaries,* II, 245.

22. William Williams to Oliver Wolcott, Aug. 12, 1776, *LMCC,* II, 48; Merrill Jensen, *The Articles of Confederation* (Madison, Wis., 1940), 147–150.

23. Oct. 7, 1777, Ford, ed., *Journals of Cong.,* IX, 780–781; Jefferson, notes, Boyd, ed., *Papers of Jefferson,* I, 323–324; Jensen, *Articles of Confederation,* 140–145.

24. Diary of Adams, July 25, 1776, Butterfield, ed., *Adams Papers: Diaries,* II, 241; Jensen, *Articles of Confederation,* 152–155, 158–159; Oct. 15, 1777, Ford, ed., *Journals of Cong.,* IX, 806–807.

25. Chase to Adams, Apr. 28, 1776, Smith, ed., *Letters of Delegates,* III, 597; Thomas Perkins Abernethy, *Western Lands and the American Revolution* (New York, 1959), 116–118, 122, 148, 202, 234–235, 238–239; Jensen, *Articles of Confederation,* 120–124, 211.

26. *Votes and Proceedings of the House of Delegates of the State of Maryland* (Annapolis, published after each session), Dec. 12, 14, 1778 (hereafter *VPHD*).

27. Abernethy, *Western Lands,* 171; Jensen, *Articles of Confederation,* 155–158; Chase to Council of Safety, Nov. 21, 1776, *Archives,* XII, 470–471; Nov. 23, 1776, Ford, ed., *Journals of Cong.,* VI, 978; Charles Thomson, notes of debates in Congress, July 25, 1777, *LMCC,* II, 422.

28. Jensen, *Articles of Confederation,* 195–197; *VPHD,* June 18, 1778; Nathaniel Scudder to Speaker of New Jersey Assembly, July 13, 1778, *LMCC,* III, 327; Chase, Ann. *Md. Gaz.,* Oct. 11, 1781.

29. Abernethy, *Western Lands,* 244–245, 272–273; Jensen, *Articles of Confederation,* 225–238; *VPHD,* June 27, 1781; Chase to James McHenry, Dec. 10, 1797, in Bernard C. Steiner, *The Life and Correspondence of James McHenry* (Cleveland, 1907), 273–274.

Chapter Eight

1. Chase to John Sullivan, Dec. 24, 1776, Force, ed., *American Archives,* 5th ser., III, 1395; William Hooper to Joseph Hewes, Nov. 30, 1776, Smith, ed., *Letters of Delegates,* V, 558.

2. Diary of Benjamin Rush, [Feb. 20, 1777], *LMCC,* II, 263–264.

3. Balt. *Md. Jour.,* Feb. 25, 1777.

4. The Whig Club's leaders included James Nicholson as president, David Stewart as secretary, Nathaniel Ramsey, Benjamin Nicholson, David Plunkett, Robert Purviance, and Nathaniel Smith. Ward L. Miner, *William Goddard, Newspaperman* (Durham, N.C., 1962), 150–162; Lawrence C. Wroth, *A History of Printing in Colonial Maryland* (Baltimore, 1922), 136–140; deposition of William Goddard, Mar. 8, 1777, Scharf Papers, MS 1999, MHS; Goddard to Thomas Johnson, Apr. 14, 1777, Red Books, III, MHR; *VPHD,* Feb. 22, Mar. 10, Apr. 2, 11, 1777; Ann. *Md. Gaz.,* Apr. 17, 1777; W. Bird Terwilliger, "William God-

dard's Victory for the Freedom of the Press," *Md. Hist. Mag.*, XXXVI (1941), 139–149.

5. Burnett, *Continental Congress,* 322–325; Chase to Johnson, Apr. 20, 1778, *Archives,* XXI, 43–44.

6. Chase to Johnson, Apr. 21, 1778, *LMCC,* III, 178n.

7. Chase to Johnson, May 3, 1778, *ibid.,* 218; Burnett, *Continental Congress,* 330–332.

8. See in general the correspondence in *Archives,* XI, XII, XVI, and Samuel Chase Letters, MS 1234, MHS.

9. Chase to Sullivan, Dec. 24, 1776, John Sullivan Letters, I, Massachusetts Historical Society, Boston; Burnett, *Continental Congress,* 311–315; Apr. 25–26, 1778, Ford, ed., *Journals of Cong.,* X, 392–395.

10. Chase to Benedict Arnold, Aug. 7, 1776, Force, ed., *American Archives,* 5th ser., I, 810–811, and to Sullivan, Oct. 23, Dec. 24, 1776, John Sullivan Letters, I, Mass. Hist. Soc.

11. Commissioners in Canada to President of Congress, May 27, 1776, Force, ed., *American Archives,* 4th ser., VI, 589; Jonathan Gregory Rossie, *The Politics of Command in the American Revolution* (Syracuse, N.Y., 1975), 49–55, 100–101, 122–123; Benjamin Rush, memorial, *LMCC,* II, 46n.

12. Chase to Horatio Gates, June 13, 1776, *LMCC,* I, 486–487; Rossie, *Politics of Command,* 104–111; Chase to Arnold, Aug. 7, 1776, and to Gates, Aug. 9, 1776, Force, ed., *American Archives,* 5th ser., I, 810–811, 864 (Gates's letter to Samuel Adams is quoted in the latter letter); Chase to Gates, Sept. 21, 1776, copy, Samuel Chase Letters, MS 1234, MHS.

13. Rossie, *Politics of Command,* 114–164; Charles Thomson, notes, July 26, 1777, *LMCC,* II, 424.

14. James Lovell to William Whipple, Sept. 17, 1777, *LMCC,* II, 495–496; Sept. 16, 1777, Ford, ed., *Journals of Cong.,* VIII, 749–750; Rossie, *Politics of Command,* 177–178, 181–184.

15. Rossie, *Politics of Command,* 180–202; Apr. 28, 1778, Ford, ed., *Journals of Cong.,* X, 399.

16. Feb. 5, 11, 1777, Ford, ed., *Journals of Cong.,* VII, 94, 107; diary of Benjamin Rush, Feb. 14, 1777, *LMCC,* II, 251; Burnett, *Continental Congress,* 234–235.

17. Feb. 27, 1777, Ford, ed., *Journals of Cong.,* VII, 164n. Thomas Burke's abstract of the debates, *LMCC,* II, 285, states that Chase wanted to open Congress's sessions to the public, except where secrecy was required, and does not mention publication of the journal.

18. Henry Laurens to President of South Carolina, Aug. 11, 1778, *LMCC,* III, 372–373.

19. *VPHD,* Feb. 15, 1777; William Eddis to Robert Eden, July 23, 1777, Eden Correspondence, Fisher Transcripts, MS 360, MHS.

20. Council of Safety to Maryland Delegates in Congress, Nov. 29, 1776, *Archives,* XII, 491.

21. Scharf, *History of Maryland,* II, 285n.

22. Eddis to Eden, July 23, 1777, Eden Correspondence, Fisher Transcripts, MS 360, MHS.

23. Daniel of St. Thomas Jenifer to Charles Carroll of Annapolis, June 18, 1777, Carroll Papers, MS 206, MHS.

24. Jan. 14, 1777, Ford, ed., *Journals of Cong.*, VII, 35–36; Ann. *Md. Gaz.*, Oct. 11, 1781.

25. *VPHD*, Mar. 8, 1777; *Votes and Proceedings of the Senate of the State of Maryland* (Annapolis, published after each session), Apr. 9, 1777 (hereafter *VPS*); *Laws of Maryland*...(Annapolis, published after each session), Feb. sess. 1777, chap. IX.

26. Charles Carroll of Carrollton to Carroll of Annapolis, Mar. 28, Apr. 4, Nov. 2, 1777, and Jenifer to Carroll of Annapolis, June 10, 1778, Carroll Papers, MS 206, MHS; Hoffman, *Spirit of Dissension*, 222.

27. Carroll of Carrollton to Carroll of Annapolis, Mar. 15, Apr. 4, 15, 1777, Carroll Papers, MS 206, MHS; Ann. *Md. Gaz.*, Aug. 23, 1781.

28. Carroll of Annapolis to Carroll of Carrollton, Mar. 13, Apr. 1, 1777, Carroll Papers, MS 206, MHS.

29. Carroll of Annapolis to Chase, June 5, 1777, Carroll Papers, MS 206, MHS.

30. Chase to Carroll of Annapolis, June 6, 1777; Carroll of Carrollton to Carroll of Annapolis, June 16, 26, Nov. 2, 8, 13, 1777; Carroll of Annapolis to Chase, June 9, Nov. 1, 1777; Carroll of Annapolis to Carroll of Carrollton, Nov. 7, 10, 1777, all Carroll Papers, MS 206, MHS.

31. Carroll of Annapolis to Chase, June 5, 1777, Carroll Papers, MS 206, MHS; Ann. *Md. Gaz.*, Aug. 23, Oct. 11, 1781.

32. *VPHD*, Mar. 4, Apr. 10, 1777; *VPS*, Apr. 16, 17, 18, 1777; *Laws of Maryland*, Feb. sess. 1777, chap. XX; Carroll of Carrollton to Carroll of Annapolis, Apr. 11, 1777, Carroll Papers, MS 206, MHS.

33. *VPHD*, June 21, 26, 1777; *VPS*, June 26, 1777; Ann. *Md. Gaz.*, July 10, 1777.

34. Ann. *Md. Gaz.*, July 17, 1777; Chase to Carroll of Carrollton, Jan. 28, 1782, Carroll Papers, MS 206, MHS.

35. *VPHD*, Nov. 14, 1777; *Laws of Maryland*, Oct. sess. 1777, chap. XX.

36. Carroll of Carrollton to Carroll of Annapolis, Nov. 15, 1777, Carroll Papers, MS 206, MHS.

37. Carroll of Carrollton to Chase, Aug. 1777, quoted in Chase to Carroll of Carrollton, Jan. 28, 1782, and Carroll of Annapolis to Carroll of Carrollton, Nov. 18, 1777, Carroll Papers, MS 206, MHS; Chase to Johnson, Apr. 21, 1778, *Archives*, XII, 51; "Pacificus," Balt. *Md. Jour.*, June 16, 1778.

38. Ann. *Md. Gaz.*, Aug. 23, 1781; Chase to Carroll of Carrollton, Jan. 28, 1782, Carroll Papers, MS 206, MHS.

39. *VPHD*, Nov. 4, 18, 22, 1777; John Hall to ?, June 11, 1778, William Henry Hall Papers, Duke University Library, Durham, N.C.; Jenifer to Carroll of Annapolis, Nov. 27, 1777, Carroll Papers, MS 206, MHS.

40. Ann. *Md. Gaz.*, Dec. 11, 1777; Carroll of Carrollton to Carroll of Annapolis, Nov. 25, 1777, Carroll Papers, MS 206, MHS; *VPHD*, Nov. 26, 1777.

41. Chase to Stephen West, Oct. 16, 1778, Bamberger Autograph Collection, New Jersey Historical Society, Newark.

Chapter Nine

1. Allen, "History of St. Paul's," 107, MS 13, MHS; Thomas Chase to his brother, Apr. 24, 1774, copy, Chase Home Book, MS 969, MHS.

2. R. R. Beirne, "Reverend Thomas Chase," *Md. Hist. Mag.*, LIX (1964), 13; John Adams to Abigail Adams, Feb. 3, 1777, in Charles Francis Adams, ed., *Familiar Letters of John Adams and His Wife Abigail Adams, During the American Revolution* (Boston, 1875), 239; Oaths of Fidelity (Baltimore County, 1778), box 3, folder 15, MHR.

3. Allen, "History of St. Paul's," 106–107, MS 13, MHS; will of Thomas Chase, Baltimore County Wills, box 16, folder 42, MHR.

4. Anne Arundel County Tax List, 1782, Scharf Papers, MS 1999, MHS (currently on deposit at MHR).

5. Michael Edward Ranneberger, "Samuel Chase: The Evolution of a Federalist" (M.A. thesis, University of Virginia, 1973), 45; Anne Arundel County Index to Land Records; Washington County Index to Land Records, liber A, folio 91, liber B, folio 491; Frederick County Index to Land Records, all MHR; Ann. *Md. Gaz.*, Oct. 11, 1781.

6. *William Whetcroft v. Allen Quynn and Samuel Chase*, Feb. term 1793, Chancery Court Records, vol. 26, liber RCC no. H, 211–226, MHR.

7. *Ibid.*, 219; Ann. *Md. Gaz.*, Sept. 27, 1781; Council Journal, Mar. 25, 1778, *Archives*, XVI, 551.

8. Council Proc., 1779–1781, *Archives*, XLIII, 35, 62, 79, 90, 92, 104, 119, 226, 302, 330, 340, 380; XLV, 207, 214, 244, 247–248, 263–264, 303, 330, 367, 402, 409, 429, 435, 509, 511, 551; XLVII, 94, 386.

9. *Ibid.*, XXI, 456, 461, 462, 468, 477, 485, 541; XLIII, 43, 47, 109, 111; XLVIII, 83; Charles Henry Lincoln, ed., *Naval Records of the American Revolution, 1775–1788* (Washington, D.C., 1906), 239, 250, 296, 299, 300, 321, 346, 366, 369, 401, 424, 469, 481; Benjamin Franklin to Chase, Jan. 6, 1784, Smith, ed., *Writings of Franklin*, IX, 152–154.

10. *Whetcroft v. Quynn and Chase*, Feb. term 1793, Chancery Court Records, vol. 26, liber RCC no. H, 220, MHR; Council Proc., Oct. 10, Nov. 8, 1782, Jan. 21, Mar. 12, May 16, 1783, *Archives*, XLVIII, 281, 300, 347–348, 379, 415; agreement of John and Thomas Dorsey, Oct. 4, 1784, General Court Deeds, liber TBH no. 1. 242–247, MHR.

11. Ann. *Md. Gaz.*, June 21, Aug. 23, Sept. 27, 1781; Balt. *Md. Jour.*, Sept. 24, 1782; John Cadwalader to Charles Carroll of Carrollton, Feb. 6, 1782, Carroll Papers, MS 206, MHS; "Publius" to James McHenry, Feb. 26, 1782, Vertical File, MHS; "Publius" letters, in Harold Syrett, ed., *The Papers of Alexander Hamilton*, I (New York, 1961), 562–563, 567–570, 580–582.

12. *VPHD*, Nov. 6, 12, 18, 24, 1778; *VPS*, Nov. 28, 1778; *Laws of Maryland*, Oct. sess. 1778, chap. VIII.

13. Chase to Carroll of Carrollton, Jan. 28, 1782, Carroll Papers, MS 206, MHS; Chase, letter to the printer and July 1779 speech, referred to in Ann. *Md. Gaz.*, Sept. 27, 1781; Daniel of St. Thomas Jenifer to ?, May 26, 1779, Gilmor Papers, III, 76, MS 387.1, MHS; Edward Giles to Otho Holland Williams, Jan. 19, 1782, Otho Holland Williams Papers, MS 908, MHS.

14. Ann. *Md. Gaz.*, Sept. 27, 1781.

15. Carroll of Carrollton to William Carmichael, May 31, 1779, *LMCC*, IV, 239; deleted Senate instruction, in Hoffman, *Spirit of Dissension*, 246, and Balt. *Md. Jour.*, Sept. 24, 1782; Balt. *Md. Gaz.*, Sept. 30, 1788; *VPS*, July 20, 21, 23, 1779; *VPHD*, July 27, 1779; *Laws of Maryland*, July sess. 1779, chap. II.

16. Ann. *Md. Gaz.*, June 21, Aug. 23, 1781; Chase to Carroll of Carrollton, Jan. 28, 1782, and Carroll of Carrollton to Chase, Feb. 3, 1782, Carroll Papers, MS 206, MHS.

17. *VPS*, Mar. 17–18, July 29, Aug. 3, 1779; Jenifer to Charles Carroll of Annapolis, May 26, Aug. 2, 12, 1779, Carroll Papers, MS 206, MHS.

18. Ann. *Md. Gaz.*, June 21, 1781.

19. *Ibid.*, Aug. 23, 1781.

20. *VPHD*, Nov. 24, 26, Dec. 15, 20, 21, 30, 1779; *VPS*, Dec. 20, 23, 1779.

21. Ann. *Md. Gaz.*, Feb. 11, 18, 25, Mar. 3, 10, 1780; Balt. *Md. Jour.*, Feb. 29, Mar. 21, 28, 1780; Chase to Carroll of Carrollton, Jan. 28, 1782, Carroll Papers, MS 206, MHS.

22. *VPHD*, Apr. 3, 4, 12, May 5, 1780; *VPS*, Apr. 3, 14, May 14, 1780.

23. *VPHD*, Apr. 24, May 4, 5, 16, 1780; *VPS*, May 6, 10, 16, 1780; John Cadwalader to Carroll of Carrollton, July 23, 1780, Cadwalader Collection, Historical Society of Pennsylvania, Philadelphia; Carroll of Carrollton to Carroll of Annapolis, May 6, 11, 1780, Carroll Papers, MS 206, MHS.

24. Ann. *Md. Gaz.*, Feb. 14, 1782, Oct. 11, 1781.

25. *Laws of Maryland*, Oct. sess. 1780, chap. V; Ann. *Md. Gaz.*, May 24, 1781.

26. Morris L. Radoff, *Calendar of Maryland State Papers, No. 2: The Bank Stock Papers* (Annapolis, 1947), xiv–xlvii; *VPS*, Jan. 29–31, 1781; *VPHD*, Jan. 30–31, 1781; *Laws of Maryland*, June sess. 1780, chap. XXIV; Oct. sess. 1780, chap. XLV.

27. Mordecai Gist to George Washington, Nov. 24, 1780, Gist Papers, MS 390, MHS; *VPHD*, Nov. 11, 15, 16, 29, 1780.

28. Ann. *Md. Gaz.*, Sept. 27, 1781.

29. *Ibid.*, May 24, 31, June 7, 21, 1781.

30. *Ibid.*, Aug. 23, 30, Sept. 27, Oct. 4, 11, 1781; Carroll of Carrollton to Carroll of Annapolis, June 14, 22, 1781, Carroll Papers, MS 206, MHS.

31. Cadwalader to Carroll of Carrollton, July 23, 1780, Cadwalader Collection, Hist. Soc. Pa.

32. Ann. *Md. Gaz.*, Jan. 3, 1782; *VPHD*, Jan. 11, 12, 1782.

33. *VPHD*, Jan. 15–17, 1782; Ann. *Md. Gaz.*, Jan. 24, 1782. For an abstract of the testimony, see Cadwalader to Carroll of Carrollton, Feb. 6, 1782, Carroll Papers, MS 206, MHS.

34. Ann. *Md. Gaz.*, Jan. 10, 17, 1782.

35. *Ibid.*, Feb. 14, 1782; Cadwalader, *To the Public*...(n.p., 1782), MHS; Balt. *Md. Jour.*, Sept. 24, 1782.

36. Carroll of Carrollton to Chase, Jan. 25, Feb. 3, 1782, and Chase to Carroll of Carrollton, Jan. 28, Feb. 11, 1782, Carroll Papers, MS 206, MHS.

37. Ann. *Md. Gaz.*, Aug. 24, 1786; *VPHD*, Jan. 17, 21, 1782; *Laws of Maryland*, Nov. sess. 1781, chap. XXVII; Jenifer to Robert Morris, Feb. 9, 1782, Intendant's Letterbook No. 10, MHR.

38. Commissioners Ledger and Journal of Confiscated British Property and Sale Books of Confiscated British Property, MHR. The partners in the two companies were Captain Charles Ridgely, Samuel Chase, William Goodwin, Darby Lux, John Sterrett, Benjamin Nicholson, John Dorsey, and Elam Bailey, most of whom were Baltimore merchants.

39. Philip A. Crowl, *Maryland During and After the Revolution* (Baltimore, 1943), 45, 59–60; Chase to Capt. Charles Ridgely, Sept. 23, 1782, Ridgely Papers, MS 692.1, MHS.

40. Haw, "Politics in Revolutionary Maryland," 378–380; *VPHD*, Dec. 4, 1781, Jan. 21, 1782, May 31, Dec. 24, 26, 1783; *VPS*, Dec. 4, 1781, May 31, June 1, Dec. 26, 1783.

41. John Ridout to Horatio Sharpe, June 22, 1783, Ridout Papers, MHR.

42. Council Proc., Jan, 21, 28, Mar. 15, 19, 1783, *Archives*, XLVIII, 347–348, 351, 381, 385–386; Balt. *Md. Gaz.*, June 27, 1783, Sept. 25, 1787; Ann. *Md. Gaz.*, Sept. 28, 1786.

43. McHenry to Washington, June 14, 1795, in Charles Warren, *The Supreme Court in United States History*, I (Boston, 1923), 126. McHenry added that his criticism of Chase's opponents in this letter did not apply to Carroll of Carrollton.

Chapter Ten

1. Sanderson, *Biography of Signers*, IV, 83–84; Scharf, *History of Maryland*, II, 619; Claude M. Newlin, "Hugh Henry Brackenridge," in Allen Johnson and Dumas Malone, eds., *Dictionary of American Biography* (New York, 1928–1936), II, 545 (hereafter *DAB*); Curtis M. Garrison, "Kensey Johns," *DAB*, X, 76–77.

2. "A Course of Law and Literary Study, prepared by the late Judge Samuel Chase, of Maryland," Vertical File, MHS; Chase to Timothy Pickering, Oct. 9, 1796, Pickering Papers, Mass. Hist. Soc. See also Chase to Nancy, Sammy, and Tommy Chase, July 8, 1784, copy, Samuel Chase Letters, MS 1234, MHS.

3. *Laws of Maryland*, Apr. sess. 1783, chap. XXXV. The best accounts of the bank stock case, on which this chapter is based unless otherwise noted, are Radoff, *Calendar, No. 2*, and Jacob M. Price, "The Maryland Bank Stock Case: British-American Financial and Political Relations before and after the American Revolution," in Aubrey C. Land, Lois Green Carr, and Edward C. Papenfuse, eds., *Law, Society, and Politics in Early Maryland* (Baltimore, 1977), 3–40.

4. Chase to Benjamin Franklin, Oct. 25, 1781, typescript, Samuel Chase Letters, MS 1234, MHS.

5. Dorothy Mackay Quynn and William Rogers Quynn, "Letters of a Maryland Medical Student in Philadelphia and Edinburgh," *Md. Hist. Mag.*, XXXI (1936), 181-183, 190-191; Chase to William Paca, Feb. 23, 1784, Blue Books, III, MHR; Chase to Jeremiah Townley Chase, Oct. 13, 1783, copy, Chase Home Book, MS 969, MHS.

6. Chase to his child, Nov. 12, 1783, copy, Chase Home Book, MS 969, MHS; deed in trust, Chase to William Cooke, Sept. 7, 1789, Anne Arundel County Deeds, liber NH no. 5, 64-65, MHR.

7. Horatio Sharpe to John Ridout, n.d., in Lady Edgar [Matilda Ridout], *A Colonial Governor in Maryland: Horatio Sharpe and His Times, 1753-1773* (New York, 1912), 278; Walter Dulany to [Mary] Fitzhugh, Aug. 8, 1784, in Elizabeth H. Murray, *One Hundred Years Ago: The Life and Times of the Rev. Walter Dulany Addison* (Philadelphia, 1895), 70.

8. Henry Addison to Daniel Dulany Addison, [1787], copybook, Addison Papers, MS 3, MHS.

9. Ridout to Sharpe, June 22, 1783, Jan. 28, 1786, Ridout Papers, MHR.

10. Chase to J. T. Chase, Oct. 13, 1783, copy, Chase Home Book, MS 969, MHS.

11. Sanderson, *Biography of Signers,* IV, 86-88; William Vans Murray to Chase, Jan. 7, 1785, Vertical File, MHS; card from Lord Buchan, copy, Chase Home Book, MS 969, MHS; H. Addison to D. D. Addison, [1787], Addison Papers, MS 3, MHS.

12. Chase to J. T. Chase, Oct. 13, 1783, and to his child, Nov. 12, 1783, copies, Chase Home Book, MS 969, MHS.

13. Chase to his child, Nov. 12, 1783, and bill of lading, Dec. 10, 1783, copies, Chase Home Book, MS 969, MHS.

14. Chase to N., Sammy, and T. Chase, July 8, 1784, copy, Samuel Chase Letters, MS 1234, MHS.

15. Sanderson, *Biography of Signers,* IV, 88; Samuel Chase folder, Filing Case A, Genealogy Section, MHS.

16. Chase to Paca, Mar. 31-Apr. 1, 1784, Blue Books, III, MHR.

17. Chase to Paca, May 20, 1784, Blue Books, III, MHR.

18. Chase to Paca, June 9, July 17, 22, 1784, Blue Books, III, MHR; Price, "Maryland Bank Stock Case," Land *et al.,* eds., *Law, Society, and Politics,* 14, 18.

Chapter Eleven

1. Scharf, *History of Maryland,* II, 519-522; James Thomas Flexner, *George Washington and the New Nation* (Boston, 1969), 74-82; *VPHD,* Dec. 27, 1784; George Washington to Chase, Dec. 3, 1785, George Washington Papers, ser. 2, Library of Congress; Normal K. Risjord, *Chesapeake Politics, 1781-1800* (New York, 1978), 243-244.

2. Scharf, *History of Maryland,* II, 529-533; diary of George Washington, Mar. 20-28, 1785, in John C. Fitzpatrick, ed., *The Diaries of George Washington,* II (Boston, 1925), 352-354; James Madison to Thomas Jefferson, Apr. 27, 1785,

Boyd, ed., *Papers of Jefferson,* VIII, 113. For the agreement, see Robert A. Rutland, ed., *The Papers of George Mason,* II (Chapel Hill, N.C., 1970), 814–821.

3. *VPHD,* Nov. 18, 20, 1785; Risjord, *Chesapeake Politics,* 257–266.

4. *VPHD,* Nov. 30, Dec. 3, 29, 30, 1784; *Laws of Maryland,* Nov. sess. 1784, chaps. VII, XXXVII; William Pinkney, *The Life of William Pinkney* (New York, 1853), 14–15.

5. Horace Wemyss Smith, *Life and Correspondence of the Rev. William Smith, D.D.* (New York, 1972 repr. of 1880 ed.), II, 36–38, 41, 90–96; *VPHD,* May 6, 1783, Dec. 31, 1784; Ann. *Md. Gaz.,* Jan. 20, 1785; Henry Addison to Jonathan Boucher, Sept. ?, 1785, copybook, Addison Papers, MS 3, MHS.

6. *VPHD,* Jan. 8, 14, Nov. 19, 1785; *Pennsylvania Journal and the Weekly Advertiser* (Philadelphia), Feb. 5, 1785.

7. *VPHD,* Dec. 15, 1783; [Alexander Contee Hanson], *Political Schemes and Calculations, Addressed to the Citizens of Maryland* (Annapolis, 1784).

8. *VPHD,* Dec. 7, 15, 20, 29, 1784; *Laws of Maryland,* Nov. sess. 1784, chap. LV.

9. [Hanson], *To the Members of The General Assembly of Maryland,* Dec. 17, 1784, broadside, MHS; *VPS,* Jan. 13, 1785.

10. Haw, "Politics in Revolutionary Maryland," 364–368, 370, 384.

11. *Ibid.,* 393–396; Louis Maganzin, "Economic Depression in Maryland and Virginia, 1783–1787" (Ph.D. diss., Georgetown University, 1967).

12. Edward C. Papenfuse, Alan F. Day, David W. Jordan, and Gregory A. Stiverson, eds., *A Biographical Dictionary of the Maryland Legislature, 1635–1789,* I (Baltimore, 1979), 216; agreement of John and Thomas Dorsey, Oct. 4, 1784, General Court Deeds, liber TBH no. 1, 242–247, MHR.

13. *VPS,* Dec. 14, 1784; *Laws of Maryland,* Nov. sess. 1784, chap. LXXVI.

14. *VPHD,* Dec. 15, 21, 1784, Jan. 15, 17, 1785; *VPS,* Jan. 14, 16, 17, 20, 1785; Chase to William Paca, Dec. 21, 1784, Blue Books, III, MHR.

15. Paca to Daniel of St. Thomas Jenifer, and Jenifer to Paca, both Apr. 22, 1785, Intendant's Letterbook No. 12, MHR; *VPS,* Nov. 19, 1785, Mar. 12, 1786; *VPHD,* Nov. 21, Dec. 23, 24, 26, 1785, Feb. 18, Mar. 1, 11, 1786.

16. Jenifer to Chase and Thomas Stone, Feb. 16, 1785, Intendant's Letterbook No. 12, MHR; T. Stone and Chase to Jenifer, Feb. 18, 1785, Intendant's Papers, 1782–1785, MHR.

17. Chase to Charles Ridgely, Mar. 5, Apr. 19, 1785, and Daniel Dulany to Benjamin Nicholson, Jan. 5, 1785, Ridgely Papers, MS 692, MHS; Jenifer to Gabriel Duvall, Sept. ?, 1785, Executive Papers, box 46, MHR.

18. Agreement of Jenifer with John Churchman and Chase, Aug. 2, 1785, Intendant's Papers, 1782–1785, MHR.

19. John Ridout to Horatio Sharpe, Jan. 28, 1786, Ridout Papers, MHR; *VPHD,* Dec. 29, 1785, Jan. 10, 11, 14, Feb. 9, 1786; *VPS,* Mar. 2, 1786; Ann. *Md. Gaz.,* Oct. 26, 1786, Feb. 8, 1787; T. Stone to Walter Stone, Jan. 15, 1786, Dec. 21, 1785, Walter Stone Papers, Library of Congress.

20. Balt. *Md. Jour.,* July 8, Aug. 12, Nov. 22, Dec. 2, 1785; Balt. *Md. Gaz.,* Sept. 5, 26, Nov. 7, 28, 1786; Ann. *Md. Gaz.,* Jan. 25, 1787.

21. Balt. *Md. Gaz.*, Sept. 19, Nov. 28, 1786; Ann. *Md. Gaz.*, Aug. 31, 1786; Balt. *Md. Jour.*, Jan. 16, 1787.

22. *VPHD*, Dec. 1, 2, 13, 22, 1785.

23. Haw, "Politics in Revolutionary Maryland," 416–418.

24. *VPHD*, Dec. 3, 6, 8, 1785, Jan. 6, 1786; *VPS*, Dec. 12, 19, 1785; Ridout to Sharpe, Jan. 28, 1786, Ridout Papers, MHR.

25. *Laws of Maryland*, Oct. sess. 1780, chap. V; Crowl, *Maryland*, 67; A List of Monies deposited in the Treasury on Account of British Creditors..., Red Books, XXVI, MHR.

26. Ridout to Sharpe, June 22, 1783, Ridout Papers, MHR; Balt. *Md. Jour.*, Dec. 24, 1784; Ann. *Md. Gaz.*, Aug. 24, 1786.

27. Council Journal, July 1786, *Archives*, LXXI, 120; H. Addison to Daniel Dulany Addison, Aug. 14, 1784 [1787], and to Chase, n.d., copybook, Addison Papers, MS 3, MHS; *VPHD*, Jan. 15–16, 1785; Crowl, *Maryland*, 80.

28. Ann. *Md. Gaz.*, Aug. 17, 31, Sept. 28, 1786.

29. *Ibid.*, Aug. 24, Sept. 14, 1786.

30. *Ibid.*, Sept. 15, 21, Oct. 19, Nov. 9, 23, 1786.

31. *To the Voters of Ann-Arundel County*, Sept. 23, 1786, broadside, MHS.

32. The election returns showed Richard Harwood receiving 725 votes, Nicholas Worthington 566, Chase 545, Brice Worthington 512, James Carroll 485, Dennis Griffiths 432, and Benjamin Harrison 313. *The Maryland Chronicle, or the Universal Advertiser* (Frederick-Town), Oct. 18, 1786; Balt. *Md. Jour.*, Nov. 21, 1786.

33. *VPHD*, Dec. 2, 20, 22, 1786, Jan. 1, 4, 1787; Ann. *Md. Gaz.*, Jan. 11, 1787; Fred. *Md. Chron.*, Mar. 7, 1787. Paper money could, of course, be used to purchase state certificates that were received at par in payment for confiscated property, offering indirect relief to speculators.

34. Dulany to George Fitzhugh, Jan. 27, 1787, Vertical File, MHS.

35. *VPHD*, Dec. 12, 15, 1786, Jan. 1, 4, 1787; Balt. *Md. Gaz.*, Jan. 9, 16, Feb. 6, 1787; *VPS*, Dec. 30, 1786, Jan. 5, 17, 1787.

36. *VPHD*, Jan. 5, 9, 11, 16, 1787.

37. Ann. *Md. Gaz.*, Feb. 22, 1787.

38. *Ibid.*, Apr. 19, June 14, Aug. 2, 1787.

39. Balt. *Md. Jour.*, Mar. 2, 9, 1787.

40. Balt. *Md. Gaz.*, Feb. 27, Apr. 24, 1787; Haw, "Politics in Revolutionary Maryland," 438–441.

41. *VPHD*, Apr. 19, 23, May, 11, 12, 15, 16, 22, 26, 1787; *VPS*, Apr. 20, 24, May, 12, 24, 1787; *Laws of Maryland*, Apr. sess. 1787, chap. XXXIV.

Chapter Twelve

1. Papenfuse, *Pursuit of Profit*, 129, 133–134, 167–168; John Ridout to Horatio Sharpe, Jan. 28, 1786, Ridout Papers, MHR; Papenfuse *et al.*, eds., *Biog. Dict. Md. Leg.*, I, 216.

2. Sanderson, *Biography of Signers*, IV, 89; statement of John Eager Howard, July 22, 1811, Chase Papers, MS 1235, MHS; Ann. *Md. Gaz.*, Jan. 19, Aug. 31, Nov. 23, 1786; Ranneberger, "Samuel Chase," 90–91.

3. *VPHD*, Apr. 20, 21, 23, 26, May 3, 7, 10, 22, 24, 1787; John B. Cutting to Thomas Jefferson, July 11, 1788, in *Documentary History of the Constitution of the United States,* IV (Washington, D.C., 1905), 772–773.

4. Chase did not want Congress to have the power to appoint the tax collectors, however. *VPHD,* June 4, 7, 1782.

5. Until 1787 the term "federal" referred to a league of sovereign states like the Confederation.

6. Objections of Samuel Chase to the Federal Government, n.d., copy, Bancroft Transcripts, New York Public Library, New York; Chase to John Lamb, June 13, 1788, Leake, *Memoir of Lamb,* 310–311.

7. Cutting to Jefferson, July 11, 1788, *Documentary Hist. of Const.,* IV, 772; Paul S. Clarkson and R. Samuel Jett, *Luther Martin of Maryland* (Baltimore, 1970), 72–150; Luther Martin, *The Genuine Information . . . ,* in Max Farrand, ed., *The Records of the Federal Convention of 1787,* III (New Haven, Conn., 1937), 172–232.

8. Balt. *Md. Jour.,* Sept. 25, 28, 14, 1787.

9. *Ibid.,* Oct. 5, 9, 1787.

10. *Ibid.,* Oct. 12, 1787.

11. James Madison to Jefferson, Oct. 24, 1787, Boyd, ed., *Jefferson Papers,* XII, 281; Daniel Carroll to Madison, Oct. 28, 1787, *Documentary Hist. of Const.,* IV, 352.

12. Balt. *Md. Jour.,* Apr. 1, 4, 1788; Ann. *Md. Gaz.,* Jan. 31, 1788; Balt. *Md. Gaz.,* Feb. 29, 1788.

13. *Pennsylvania Gazette,* Apr. 30, 1788, in L. Marx Renzulli, Jr., *Maryland: The Federalist Years* (Rutherford, N.J., 1972), 68; [Alexander Contee Hanson], *Remarks on the Proposed Plan of a Federal Government . . .* (Annapolis, 1788), 28, 35–36; Balt. *Md. Gaz.,* Sept. 28, 1787, Feb. 1, 1788; Balt. *Md. Jour.,* Feb. 1, 1788.

14. *VPHD,* Nov. 26, 29–30, 1787; *VPS,* Nov. 26, Dec. 1, 1787; Balt. *Md. Gaz.,* Oct. 3, 1788.

15. Cyrus Griffin to Thomas FitzSimons, Feb. 18, 1788, and Abraham Baldwin to [Joseph Clay?], Mar. 31, 1788, *LMCC,* VIII, 700, 712.

16. Balt. *Md. Jour.,* Apr. 18, 1788; D. Carroll to Madison, May, 28, 1788, *Documentary Hist. of Const.,* IV, 636–642.

17. Balt. *Md. Jour.,* Mar. 25, Apr. 4, 15, 1788; Balt. *Md. Gaz.,* Apr. 11, 15, 1788.

18. Chase to Lamb, June 13, 1788, Leake, *Memoir of Lamb,* 310–311.

19. D. Carroll to Madison, Feb. 10, 1788, and James McHenry to George Washington, Apr. 20, May 18, 1788, *Documentary Hist. of Const.,* IV, 497–498, 580–581, 618; Crowl, *Maryland,* 145–149; Ann. *Md. Gaz.,* May 15, 1788.

20. Hanson, "To the People of Maryland," MS address, *Documentary Hist. of Const.,* IV, 647–664; William Paca *et al., To the People of Maryland* (n.p., 1788). The account of the convention is based on these sources unless otherwise noted.

21. Gordon S. Wood, *The Creation of the American Republic, 1776–1787* (Chapel Hill, N.C., 1969), 475–518, argues that the Federalists' aim was precisely to ensure that "only established social leaders would . . . be elected by a broad con-

stituency," though of course with the intention of saving rather than undermining republicanism. Chase, like some other Antifederalist leaders, saw very clearly what sort of men would be likely to hold office under the Constitution.

22. Objections of Chase, Bancroft Transcripts, N.Y. Pub. Lib.

23. William Smith to Otho Holland Williams, Apr. 28, 1788, Otho Holland Williams Papers, MS 908, MHS.

24. Paca *et al.*, *To the People*.

25. Chase to Lamb, June 13, 1788, Leake, *Memoir of Lamb*, 310–311.

26. Ann. *Md. Gaz.*, Oct. 16, 1788; Robert Lemmon to Robert Carter, Sept. 16, 1788, Carter Papers, MS 1228, MHS. Detailed accounts of the Baltimore election are given by Lee Lovely Verstandig, "The Emergence of the Two-Party System in Maryland, 1787–1796" (Ph.D. diss., Brown University, 1970), 53–73, and Renzulli, *Maryland*, 106–113.

27. Balt. *Md. Jour.*, Aug. 10, Sept. 19, 23, 26, 1788; Balt. *Md. Gaz.*, July 29, Sept. 22, 26, Oct. 7, 1788.

28. Chase and David McMechen, *To the Voters of Baltimore-Town*, Oct. 3, 1788, broadside, MHS.

29. Ann. *Md. Gaz.*, Oct. 16, 30, 1788; *VPHD*, Nov. 4–11, Dec. 4, 1788.

Chapter Thirteen

1. Chase to Richard Henry Lee, May 16, 1789, Lee Family Papers, U. Va.; Matthew Ridley to John Jay, Sept. 22, 1789, Ridley Papers, Mass. Hist. Soc.; Risjord, *Chesapeake Politics*, 351.

2. Ann. *Md. Gaz.*, Aug. 31, 1786; Robin D. Coblentz, "The Judicial Career of Samuel Chase, 1796–1811" (M.A. thesis, Columbia University, 1966), 42; Edward S. Corwin, "Samuel Chase," *DAB*, IV, 37; Warren, *Supreme Court*, I, 465; Strawser, "Early Life," 7; Balt. *Md. Jour.*, Feb. 14, 1792.

3. *VPHD*, Nov. 11, 14, 19, 20, 1789; *VPS*, Dec. 1, 1789; *Laws of Maryland*, Nov. sess. 1789, chap. X; Chase and Thomas Dorsey, statement of case, Nov. 19, 1789, Samuel Chase Papers, Duke U.

4. Ranneberger, "Samuel Chase," 129–131, 103; Anne Arundel County Deeds, liber NH no. 5, 64–65, and Baltimore County Land Records, liber WG no. DD, 406–410, and liber WG no. EE, 419–421, MHR; Chase and Dorsey, statement, Nov. 19, 1789, Samuel Chase Papers, Duke U.

5. Ranneberger, "Samuel Chase," 130–131; Risjord, *Chesapeake Politics*, 397; Baltimore County Land Records, liber WG no. FF, 314–315, MHR.

6. Chase Family Bible Records, Gift Collection D603(3), MHR; extracts from newspaper and letter of Capt. William Buchanan, Nov. 7, 1791, copies, Chase Home Book, MS 969, MHS; Balt. *Md. Jour.*, Dec. 13, 1791; John E. Semmes, *John H. B. Latrobe and His Times, 1803–1891* (Baltimore, 1917), 112–113.

7. Samuel Chase folder, Filing Case A, Genealogy Section, MHS; Chase Family Bible Records, Gift Collection D603(3), MHR; statement of John Eager Howard, July 22, 1811, Chase Papers, MS 1235, MHS; *Barney v. Chase et al.*, Chancery Court Records, liber 128, p. 193, MHR.

8. See Hannah Kitty Chase to Bishop James Kemp, Nov. 10, 1817, Vertical File, Maryland Diocesan Archives of the Protestant Episcopal Church (on deposit at MHS).

9. Thomas Chase to Ann Chase, Apr. 14, 1804, and to Samuel Chase, Jr., Aug. 25, 1811, copies, Chase Home Book, MS 969, MHS.

10. Allen, "History of St. Paul's," 108, MS 13, MHS; Rev. William Smith to Rev. William West, Dec. 11, 1788; Rev. John Bissett to Rev. James Kemp, Apr. 28, 1796; Bishop Thomas Claggett to Maryland Parishes, Oct. 11, 1796; Rev. Joseph G. J. Bend to Kemp, Jan. 23, Dec. 20, 1797, and to Claggett, Nov. 13, 1797; Claggett to Kemp, Dec. 9, 1797, all Vertical File, Md. Diocesan Archives, MHS.

11. Clarkson and Jett, *Luther Martin*, 164–165; Balt. *Md. Jour.*, Dec. 15, 1789, Dec. 17, 1790, Feb. 10, 14, 1792; Dwight Lowell Dumond, *Antislavery: The Crusade for Freedom in America* (Ann Arbor, Mich., 1961), 47–48, 52.

12. *Butler v. Craig*, 2 Harris and McHenry 214, 232–233 (1791). See also *Butler v. Boarman*, 1 Harris and McHenry 371 (1770).

13. Council Journal, June 16, 1790, Feb. 5, Nov. 1, 1791, Nov. 20, 1792, *Archives*, LXXII, 108, 173, 231, 302; *VPHD*, Nov. 21, 1794; *VPS*, Dec. 12, 1794.

14. Council Journal, June 12, 1788, *Archives*, LXXI, 268; Balt. *Md. Jour.*, July 22, 1788; Chase to William Smallwood, July 5, 1788, copy, Samuel Chase Letters, MS 1234, MHS.

15. Ranneberger, "Samuel Chase," 127–128; *Federal Intelligencer, and Baltimore Daily Gazette*, Nov. 12, 1794; Chase to Howard, Feb. 2, 1790, Vertical File, MHS; Council Journal, Mar. 6, 1790, *Archives*, LXXII, 89; Richard Buel, Jr., *Securing the Revolution: Ideology in American Politics, 1789-1815* (Ithaca, N.Y., 1972), 244.

16. Proceedings of Commissioners of Baltimore Town, in Wilbur F. Coyle, ed., *First Records of Baltimore Town and Jones' Town, 1729-1797* (Baltimore, 1905), 68–108.

17. William Smith to Otho Holland Williams, Oct. 8, 1792, Otho Holland Williams Papers, MS 908, MHS; Verstandig, "Emergence of Party System," 143–144. The word "Federalist" can refer either to supporters of the Constitution in 1787–1788 or to the Federalist party that emerged in the 1790s. We do not assume that the two groups were identical. Usage of the word in this chapter can be determined from the context.

18. Chase to R. H. Lee, July 2, 16, 1789, Lee Family Papers, U. Va.

19. Chase to George Washington, Sept. 3, 1789, copy, Samuel Chase Letters, MS 1234, MHS, and to R. H. Lee, May 16, 1789, Lee Family Papers, U. Va.

20. Chase to R. H. Lee, July 2, 1789, Lee Family Papers, U. Va.

21. Chase to Washington, Sept. 3, 1789, and Ridley to Jay, Sept. 7, 1789, Samuel Chase Letters, MS 1234, MHS; Ridley to Jay, Sept. 22, 1789, Ridley Papers, Mass. Hist. Soc.

22. Jay to Ridley, Oct. 8, 1789, copy, Ridley Papers, Mass. Hist. Soc.

23. Renzulli, *Maryland*, 146–154; Verstandig, "Emergence of Party System," 110–121; Risjord, *Chesapeake Politics*, 396–399, 409; Ranneberger, "Samuel Chase," 133–136.

24. Balt. *Md. Jour.*, Sept. 2, 9, 23, Nov. 18, 1791; Council Journal, Aug. 30, Oct. 7, 1791, *Archives,* LXXII, 218, 233; Chase to [Howard], Sept. 9, 1791, Etting Papers, Hist. Soc. Pa.; Luther Martin to ?, Sept. 10, 1791, Emmet Collection, N.Y. Pub. Lib.

25. Carroll T. Bond, *The Court of Appeals of Maryland: A History* (Baltimore, 1928), 92; Balt. *Md. Jour.*, Oct. 28, Nov. 29, Dec. 6, 13, 16, 23, 1791; *Laws of Maryland,* Nov. sess. 1791, chap. L; Council Journal, Dec. 31, 1791, *Archives,* LXXII, 245; *French v. O'Neale,* 2 Harris and McHenry 401 (1793); Ranneberger, "Samuel Chase," 138.

26. Bond, *Court of Appeals,* 59–60, 88, 93; Ranneberger, "Samuel Chase," 131; Council Journal, Oct. 7, 1791, *Archives,* LXXII, 223.

27. *Egan v. Charles County Court,* 3 Harris and McHenry 169 (1793). See, in general, 3 Harris and McHenry and General Court, Arguments of Cases, 1781–1792, 1793–1798, MHR.

28. Balt. *Md. Jour.*, May 31, June 18, 1793.

29. Balt. *Md. Jour.*, Apr. 23, May 5, 21, 1794; *The Baltimore Daily Intelligencer,* May 27, July 16, 1794, and in general these papers for the first half of 1794.

30. Ranneberger, "Samuel Chase," 139–140; Chase to James McHenry, Dec. 4, 1796, McHenry Papers, Library of Congress. In this letter Chase condemns a later French ambassador, Pierre Adet, but he comments that Adet was as bad as Genêt. Sanderson, *Biography of Signers,* IV, 94, quotes Chase as having written that he hoped for a French victory over England (no date given). If so, his support for France was brief. This quotation is inconsistent with all other available evidence.

31. Ranneberger, "Samuel Chase," 145–147; Balt. *Md. Jour.*, Aug. 15, 1794; F. F. Beirne, *St. Paul's Parish,* 48–57; Thomas Jefferson to James Monroe, May 26, 1800, in Paul Leicester Ford, ed., *The Works of Thomas Jefferson,* IX (New York, 1905), 136.

32. *Balt. Daily Intelligencer,* Mar. 20, 1794; Balt. *Md. Jour.*, Mar. 21, 1794.

33. Scharf's statement, *History of Maryland,* II, 590, that the riot occurred after the embargo ended is erroneous. See Balt. *Md. Jour.*, Apr. 21, 1794; *Balt. Daily Intelligencer,* May 16, 1794.

34. Scharf, *History of Maryland,* II, 590–591; Chase, *To the Citizens of Baltimore-Town,* May 4, 1794, broadside, MHS; Chase to Thomas Sim Lee, May 6, 1794, Personal Miscellany, N.Y. Pub. Lib.; Balt. *Md. Jour.*, May 7, 1794; Sanderson, *Biography of Signers,* IV, 95–97; Ranneberger, "Samuel Chase," 142–145.

35. Chase to T. S. Lee, May 6, 1794, Personal Miscellany, N.Y. Pub. Lib.

36. Balt. *Md. Jour.*, June 9, Dec. 12, 1794; Philip S. Foner, ed., *The Democratic-Republican Societies, 1790–1800* (Westport, Conn., 1976), 335–343; Eugene Perry Link, *Democratic-Republican Societies, 1790–1800* (New York, 1942).

37. This was John Steele. Balt. *Md. Jour.*, July 7, 23, 1794; Chase to T. S. Lee, May 6, 1794, Personal Miscellany, N.Y. Pub. Lib.; Ranneberger, "Samuel Chase," 149.

38. Balt. *Md. Jour.*, June 9, Oct. 13, 1794; Ranneberger, "Samuel Chase," 149; John Thomas Scharf, *History of Baltimore City and County . . .* (Philadelphia,

1881), 83; Chase to James McHenry, Nov. 2, 1794, Steiner, *Life of McHenry*, 154, and Dec. 10, 1796, McHenry Papers, Library of Congress; Balt. *Federal Intelligencer*, Nov. 18, 1794.

39. "Samuel Chase and the Grand Jury of Baltimore County," *Md. Hist. Mag.*, VI (1911), 131–137; *Balt. Daily Intelligencer*, Aug. 26, 1794; Chase, draft article, Aug. 27, 1794, Chase Papers, MS 1235, MHS.

40. *VPHD*, Nov. 10, Dec. 2, 1794; Balt. *Md. Jour.*, Dec. 5, 1794.

41. Ranneberger, "Samuel Chase," 155.

42. Chase to Tench Coxe, Apr. 2, 1793, Tench Coxe Papers, Hist. Soc. Pa., and to Washington, July 19, 1794, George Washington Papers, ser. 7, Library of Congress.

43. Chase to McHenry, Nov. 2, 1794, Steiner, *Life of McHenry*, 153–154.

44. McHenry to Washington, June 14, 1795, Warren, *Supreme Court*, I, 125–126; Steiner, *Life of McHenry*, 159, 160n.

45. Washington to Alexander Hamilton, Oct. 29, 1795, in John C. Fitzpatrick, ed., *The Writings of George Washington*, XXXIV (Washington, D.C., 1940), 349.

46. Washington to McHenry, Jan. 20, 28, 1796, *ibid.*, 423–424, 428–429; McHenry to Washington, Jan. 24, 1796, Steiner, *Life of McHenry*, 164; William Plumer, Oliver Wolcott, and James Iredell, quoted in Warren, *Supreme Court*, I, 143–144.

Chapter Fourteen

1. Corwin, "Samuel Chase," *DAB*, IV, 36.

2. Warren, *Supreme Court*, I, 11, 89; Edward S. Corwin, *John Marshall and the Constitution* (New Haven, Conn., 1919), 16.

3. Warren, *Supreme Court*, I, 85–88; Charles Grove Haines, *The Role of the Supreme Court in American Government and Politics, 1789-1835* (New York, 1960 repr. of 1944 ed.), 148.

4. R. Kent Newmyer, *The Supreme Court under Marshall and Taney* (New York, 1968), 26; Haines, *Role of Supreme Court*, 121–123, 146, 183.

5. George Washington to James McHenry, Jan. 20, 28, 1796, Fitzpatrick, ed., *Writings of Washington*, XXXIV, 424, 428–429; Chase to William Cushing, Mar. 10, 1796, copy, Samuel Chase Letters, MS 1234, MHS.

6. William Sullivan, *The Public Men of the Revolution*...(Philadelphia, 1847), 224n.

7. Julius Goebel, Jr., *Antecedents and Beginnings to 1801*, in Paul A. Freund, ed., *The Oliver Wendell Holmes Devise History of the Supreme Court of the United States* (New York, 1971), 751; *Ware v. Hylton*, 3 Dallas 199 (1796); Warren, *Supreme Court*, I, 144, 146.

8. *Ware v. Hilton*, 3 Dallas 199, 221 (1796); Goebel, *Antecedents*, 751, 753.

9. *Ware v. Hylton*, 3 Dallas 199, 222–245 (1796).

10. James Iredell, quoted in Irving Dilliard, "Samuel Chase," in Leon Friedman and Fred L. Israel, eds., *The Justices of the United States Supreme Court, 1789-1969: Their Lives and Major Opinions*, I (New York, 1969), 190.

11. *Hylton v. United States,* 3 Dallas 171, 173–175 (1796); Warren, *Supreme Court,* I, 147–148; Coblentz, "Judicial Career," 39.

12. *Hunter v. Fairfax's Devisee,* 3 Dallas 305 (1796); Warren, *Supreme Court,* I, 151–152.

13. Chase to Iredell, Mar. 7, 1797, Simon Gratz Collection, Hist. Soc. Pa., and Mar. 15, 1797, James Iredell Sr. and Jr. Papers, Duke U.

14. Henri Joseph Stier to ?, Nov. 23, 1797, in William D. Hoyt, ed., "The Calvert-Stier Correspondence: Letters from America to the Low Countries, 1797–1828," *Md. Hist. Mag.,* XXXVIII (1943), 126–127.

15. Chase to William Paterson, Mar. 17, 1799, Samuel Chase Miscellaneous Manuscripts, New-York Historical Society, New York, and to Iredell, Mar. 17, Apr. 28, 1799, James Iredell Sr. and Jr. Papers, Duke U.

16. Goebel, *Antecedents,* 575, 580.

17. *Brown v. Van Braam,* 3 Dallas 344, 356, 346 (1796).

18. *United States v. Worrall,* 2 Dallas 384, 393, 395 (1798); Francis Wharton, *State Trials of the United States during the Administrations of Washington and Adams...* (New York, 1970 repr. of 1849 ed.), 199, 49n.; Haines, *Role of Supreme Court,* 159, 175, 240.

19. Dilliard, "Samuel Chase," Friedman and Israel, eds., *Justices of Court,* I, 193; *Calder v. Bull,* 3 Dallas 386, 390, 388 (1798); Corwin, *John Marshall,* 149–150; Coblentz, "Judicial Career," 45–47; Corwin, "Samuel Chase," *DAB,* IV, 36.

20. Chase, charges to grand jury, 1803, 14–16, Vertical File, MHS.

21. *Ware v. Hylton,* 3 Dallas 199, 236, 222–223 (1796).

22. *Calder v. Bull,* 3 Dallas 386, 388 (1798).

23. Chase, charges to grand jury, 1803, and no. 2 (ca. 1799), Vertical File, MHS.

24. *Cooper v. Telfair,* 4 Dallas 14, 19 (1800); Chase, charges to grand jury, no. 1 (ca. 1799–1800), 12, Vertical File, MHS; Wharton, *State Trials,* 638, 716.

25. Wharton, *State Trials,* 714–716; Chase, charges to grand jury, no. 1, 10–11, 15, Vertical File, MHS.

26. *United States v. Worrall,* 2 Dallas 393–394 (1798); *Calder v. Bull,* 3 Dallas 387 (1798). In each case Chase was speaking specifically of the federal judicial power, but he made no distinction among branches.

Chapter Fifteen

1. Haines, *Role of Supreme Court,* 175–176; Warren, *Supreme Court,* I, 165–167.

2. Chase to James McHenry, Dec. 4, 10, 1796, Steiner, *Life of McHenry,* 203–204, 205–206.

3. Chase, charges to grand juries, no. 2 (ca. 1799), Vertical File, MHS; Chase to McHenry, Jan. 19, 1799, copy, Samuel Chase Letters, MS 1234, MHS.

4. *The Eliza (Bas v. Tingy),* 4 Dallas 37, 45 (1800).

5. Chase, charges to grand juries, no. 2 (ca. 1799), Vertical File, MHS; James Morton Smith, *Freedom's Fetters: The Alien and Sedition Laws and American Civil Liberties* (Ithaca, N.Y., 1956), 94–95, 155, 185, (and the text of Sedition Act) 441–442; Haines, *Role of Supreme Court*, 159–160; John C. Miller, *Crisis in Freedom: The Alien and Sedition Acts* (Boston, 1952), 79.

6. Smith, *Freedom's Fetters*, 144–145; Miller, *Crisis in Freedom*, 80–83.

7. Smith, *Freedom's Fetters*, 183, 185–186, 270–271; Haines, *Role of Supreme Court*, 161.

8. Smith, *Freedom's Fetters*, 257–268; Miller, *Crisis in Freedom*, 114–120.

9. Chase to [his wife], Jan. 4, 1800, Dreer Collection, Hist. Soc. Pa.

10. Dumas Malone, *The Public Life of Thomas Cooper, 1783-1839* (New Haven, Conn., 1926), 4–120; Smith, *Freedom's Fetters*, 307–316, 319.

11. Malone, *Public Life of Cooper*, 121–122; Smith, *Freedom's Fetters*, 317–318; Thomas Cooper, *An Account of the Trial of Thomas Cooper...* (Philadelphia, 1800), 8–14, 22–31; Wharton, *State Trials*, 662–670.

12. Wharton, *State Trials*, 670–677; Smith, *Freedom's Fetters*, 324–327.

13. Wharton, *State Trials*, 677–679.

14. Malone, *Public Life of Cooper*, 129–130; Smith, *Freedom's Fetters*, 328; Wharton, *State Trials*, 679; Mary Jane Shaffer Elsmere, "The Impeachment Trial of Justice Samuel Chase" (Ph.D. diss., Indiana University, 1962), 37.

15. Chase, charges to grand jury, no. 1 (ca. 1799–1800), Vertical File, MHS; Wharton, *State Trials*, 638.

16. *Report of the Trial of the Hon. Samuel Chase... Taken in Short hand by Charles Evans* (Baltimore, 1805), app., 41; Wharton, *State Trials*, 616.

17. Wharton, *State Trials*, 613–618.

18. *The Debates and Proceedings in the Congress of the United States... 1789-1824* (Washington, D.C., 1834–1856), 8th Cong., 2d sess., 166–167, 185–186, 191 (hereafter *Annals of Congress*); Strawser, "Early Life," 10.

19. *Annals of Congress*, 8:2, 167–168, 172; Wharton, *State Trials*, 622, 624.

20. Wharton, *State Trials*, 629–633, 637.

21. Scharf, *History of Maryland*, II, 43–44.

22. *Annals of Congress*, 8:2, 245–246; Wharton, *State Trials*, 688–690.

23. *Annals of Congress*, 8:2, 120, 216–218, 246–247.

24. *Ibid.*, 202, 209; Smith, *Freedom's Fetters*, 344–346; Wharton, *State Trials*, 692.

25. Wharton, *State Trials*, 690–695; *Annals of Congress*, 8:2, 129–134, 204, 209, 249–250, 267, 269, 472.

26. Wharton, *State Trials*, 691–697, 700–704; *Annals of Congress*, 8:2, 221, 224.

27. Wharton, *State Trials*, 706–709; *Annals of Congress*, 8:2, 211; Goebel, *Antecedents*, 644–645, 649.

28. Wharton, *State Trials*, 709–710, 713–717; *Report of Trial of Chase*, app., 65–67. See also above, chap. fourteen.

29. Wharton, *State Trials*, 710–712; *Annals of Congress*, 8:2, 135.

30. Wharton, *State Trials*, 712, 718; *Annals of Congress*, 8:2, 203, 207, 213, 255.

31. Smith, *Freedom's Fetters*, 356; Leonard Chester to Ephraim Kirby, Sept. 26, 1800, Ephraim Kirby Papers, Duke U.; James Thompson Callender to St. George Tucker, Nov. 4, 1800, mentioned in Elsmere, "Impeachment Trial," 46, 60.

32. *Annals of Congress*, 8:2, 143-144, 227-231, 284-285, 290; Smith, *Freedom's Fetters*, 184.

33. John Adams to John Marshall, July 30, Aug. 7, 13, 1800, C. F. Adams, ed., *Works of John Adams*, IX, 66, 71-72, 76-77. For a different interpretation, see Elsmere, "Impeachment Trial," 48-49.

34. Renzulli, *Maryland*, 211-217; Edward G. Roddy, "Maryland and the Presidential Election of 1800," *Md. Hist. Mag.*, LVI (1961) 244-268; Steiner, *Life of McHenry*, 463n., 465, 468-469; McHenry to Oliver Wolcott, Sept. 23, 1800, in George Gibbs, *Memoirs of the Administrations of Washington and John Adams*...(New York, 1846), II, 419-420.

35. Roddy, "Maryland and Election of 1800," *Md. Hist. Mag.*, LVI (1961), 256-257; Philadelphia *Aurora*, Aug. 4, 8, 1800; Thomas Jefferson to James Monroe, May 26, 1800, Ford, ed., *Works of Jefferson*, IX, 136.

36. Phila. *Aurora*, Aug. 9, 1800.

37. Smith, *Freedom's Fetters*, 335.

Chapter Sixteen

1. Albert J. Beveridge, *The Life of John Marshall*, III (Boston, 1919), 1-7; Warren, *Supreme Court*, I, 170-171.

2. Haines, *Role of Supreme Court*, 180-181; Richard E. Ellis, *The Jeffersonian Crisis: Courts and Politics in the Young Republic* (New York, 1971), 14-15.

3. Ellis, *Jeffersonian Crisis*, 19-30, 36-45; Merrill D. Peterson, *Thomas Jefferson and the New Nation* (New York, 1970), 693-696: Dumas Malone, *Jefferson the President: First Term, 1801-1805* (Boston, 1970), 113-119; Warren, *Supreme Court*, I, 193, 195-205.

4. Ellis, *Jeffersonian Crisis*, 45-51, 59; Haines, *Role of Supreme Court*, 227-235.

5. Ellis, *Jeffersonian Crisis*, 60-61; Chase to William Paterson, Apr. 6, 1802, Samuel Chase Miscellaneous Manuscripts, N.-Y. Hist. Soc.

6. Chase to John Marshall, Apr. 24, 1802, Robert Treat Paine Papers, Mass. Hist. Soc., and to Paterson, Apr. 6, 1802, Samuel Chase Miscellaneous Manuscripts, N.-Y. Hist. Soc.; Chase to ?, n.d., copy, Samuel Chase Letters, MS 1234, MHS.

7. Ellis, *Jeffersonian Crisis*, 61-65; Warren, *Supreme Court*, I, 269-272.

8. Warren, *Supreme Court*, I, 232-243; Haines, *Role of Supreme Court*, 247-253.

9. Goebel, *Antecedents*, 650-651; Ellis, *Jeffersonian Crisis*, 66; Peterson, *Jefferson*, 699.

10. Chase to John Francis Mercer, Mar. 6, 1803, Wylie, ed., "Letters of Members of Congress," *Pa. Mag. Hist. Biog.*, XXIX (1905), 205-206.

11. Renzulli, *Maryland*, 228–229.

12. Chase, charges to grand jury, May 2, 1803, Vertical File, MHS.

13. Ellis, *Jeffersonian Crisis*, 81; Phila. *Aurora*, May 27, 1803, in Coblentz, "Judicial Career," 98–99.

14. Beveridge, *Life of Marshall*, III, 170; *Annals of Congress*, 8:2, 231; *Baltimore American*, June 13, 1803; William Plumer, *Memorandum of Proceedings in the United States Senate, 1803-1807*, ed. Everett Somerville Brown (New York, 1923), 288.

15. Thomas Jefferson to Joseph H. Nicholson, May 13, 1803, in Albert Ellery Bergh, ed., *The Writings of Thomas Jefferson*, X (Washington, D.C., 1907), 390.

16. Ellis, *Jeffersonian Crisis*, 164–170; Elsmere, "Impeachment Trial," 108–111.

17. Ellis, *Jeffersonian Crisis*, 69–75, 80–81; Malone, *Jefferson: First Term*, 468.

18. *Annals of Congress*, 8:1, 805–840, 856–860, 873–876, 1093, 1171–1182, 1237–1240.

19. Elsmere, "Impeachment Trial," 73; Coblentz, "Judicial Career," 111; Chase, unpresented memorial, in letter to *Federal Gazette*, Mar. 29, 1804, in *Report of Trial of Chase*, 5–7.

20. Robert G. Harper to James Bayard and Alexander Hamilton, Jan. 22, 1804, Etting Papers, Hist. Soc. Pa.

21. Bayard to Harper, Jan. 30, 1804, Etting Papers, Hist. Soc. Pa.

22. Joseph Hopkinson to Chase, Jan. 20, 1804, Etting Papers, Hist. Soc. Pa.; Elsmere, "Impeachment Trial," 160; Plumer, *Memorandum of Proceedings*, 297.

23. Chase to Richard Peters, Jan. 22, 1804, copy, Samuel Chase Letters, MS 1234, MHS; Luke Wheeler to Chase, Jan. 24, 1804, and James Winchester to Chase, Jan. 26, 1804, Chase Papers, MS 1235, MHS; Hopkinson to Chase, Mar. 14, 1804, Edmund Lee to Chase, Nov. 15, 1804, Bushrod Washington to Chase, Jan. 24, 1804, Marshall to Chase, Jan. 23, 1804, all Etting Papers, Hist. Soc. Pa.

24. J. Stephenson to Moses Rawlings, Jan. 6, 1804, Rawlings Papers, MS 1399, MHS; Plumer, *Memorandum of Proceedings*, 101–102; Harper to Bayard and Hamilton, Jan. 22, 1804, Etting Papers, Hist. Soc. Pa.; Malone, *Jefferson: First Term*, 469.

25. The observation is Peterson's, *Jefferson*, 796–797; see also Malone, *Jefferson: First Term*, 467–468.

26. Plumer, *Memorandum of Proceedings*, 100–102; Richard Beale Davis, ed., *Jeffersonian America: Notes on the United States . . . by Sir Augustus John Foster, Bart.* (San Marino, Cal., 1954), 10.

27. Ellis, *Jeffersonian Crisis*, 83–90; Malone, *Jefferson: First Term*, 448–451.

28. Ellis, *Jeffersonian Crisis*, 92–93; Chase to Roger Griswold, Nov. 8, 1804, W. G. Lane Memorial Collection, Yale University Library, New Haven, Conn.

29. *Annals of Congress*, 8:2, 680, 726, 728–731.

30. *Ibid.*, 731–763, 88, 776, 791; Malone, *Jefferson: First Term*, 472.

31. *Annals of Congress*, 8:2, 92–98; Elsmere, "Impeachment Trial," 121.

32. *Annals of Congress*, 8:2, 99–100; Hopkinson to Chase, Jan. 14, 17, 1805, Etting Papers, Hist. Soc. Pa.

33. Beveridge, *Life of Marshall*, III, 182; *Trenton Federalist*, reprinted in *New York Herald*, Feb. 9, 1805, in Coblentz, "Judicial Career," 119; Ellis, *Jeffersonian Crisis*, 92.

34. Ellis, *Jeffersonian Crisis*, 93–94.

35. Chase to William Tilghman, Jan. 28, 1805, in Elsmere, "Impeachment Trial," 132.

Chapter Seventeen

1. *Report of Trial of Chase*, 13; Beveridge, *Life of Marshall*, III, 179–180; Elsmere, "Impeachment Trial," 134–135.

2. Diary of John Quincy Adams, Mar. 1, 1805, in, Allan Nevins, ed., *The Diary of John Quincy Adams, 1794–1845* (New York, 1928), 33.

3. Diary of J. Q. Adams, Dec. 20–21, 1804, in Charles Francis Adams, ed., *Memoirs of John Quincy Adams, Comprising Portions of His Diary from 1795 to 1848*, I (Philadelphia, 1874), 321–322.

4. Elsmere, "Impeachment Trial," 85–116; Raoul Berger, *Impeachment: The Constitutional Problems* (Cambridge, Mass., 1973), 53–102: Peter C. Hoffer and N. E. H. Hull, "Power and Precedent in the Creation of an American Impeachment Tradition: The Eighteenth-Century Colonial Record," *William and Mary Quarterly*, 3d ser., XXXVI (1979), 51–77; Richard B. Lillich, "The Chase Impeachment," *American Journal of Legal History*, IV (1960), 54–57.

5. Beveridge, *Life of Marshall*, III, 184; Samuel Taggart to Rev. John Taylor, Feb. 6, 1805, in Elsmere, "Impeachment Trial," 144–145; William Sullivan, *Familiar Letters on Public Characters* (Boston, 1834), 202.

6. Years later, when Harper publicly claimed credit for the answer, Chase's son denied it. But Chase himself acknowledged Harper's authorship shortly after the trial. Robert G. Harper to Robert Walsh, May 29, 1824, Harper-Pennington Papers, MS 431, MHS; Samuel Chase, Jr. to Eliza Chase, n.d., Chase Papers, MS 1235, MHS; Chase to Rufus King, Mar. 13, 1805, King Papers, N.-Y. Hist. Soc.

7. *Annals of Congress*, 8:2, 101–153.

8. *Ibid.*, 153–164; Plumer, *Memorandum of Proceedings*, 280.

9. *Annals of Congress*, 8:2, 165–192, 241–245.

10. *Ibid.*, 193–219; Plumer, *Memorandum of Proceedings*, 283.

11. *Annals of Congress*, 8:2, 221–225, 245–262, 267–283.

12. *Ibid.*, 262–266; Plumer, *Memorandum of Proceedings*, 291; Elsmere, "Impeachment Trial," 165.

13. *Annals of Congress*, 8:2, 227–231, 284–290.

14. *Ibid.*, 231–236, 291–305.

15. Timothy Pickering to King, Feb. 15, 1805, in Ellis, *Jeffersonian Crisis*, 100. Berger, *Impeachment*, 224–251, argues that Chase should have been convicted for his conduct of the Callender trial.

16. *Annals of Congress*, 8:2, 310; Plumer, *Memorandum of Proceedings*, 294; Chase to King, Mar. 13, 1805, King Papers, N.-Y. Hist. Soc.

17. *Annals of Congress,* 8:2, 313–329; Plumer, *Memorandum of Proceedings,* 295; John Davenport, Jr. to John C. Smith, Feb. 25, 1805, John Cotton Smith Letters, Library of Congress.

18. Plumer, *Memorandum of Proceedings,* 295–297; Davenport to Smith, Feb. 25, 1805, John Cotton Smith Letters, Library of Congress; Elsmere, "Impeachment Trial," 171–172.

19. *Annals of Congress,* 8:2, 329–354.

20. *Ibid.,* 354–394; Plumer, *Memorandum of Proceedings,* 297; Davenport to Smith, Feb. 25, 1805, John Cotton Smith Letters, Library of Congress.

21. *Annals of Congress,* 8:2, 394–425; Plumer, *Memorandum of Proceedings,* 298; Davenport to Smith, Feb. 25, 1805, John Cotton Smith Letters, Library of Congress.

22. Diary of J. Q. Adams, Feb. 24, 1805, in Elsmere, "Impeachment Trial," 179.

23. Davenport to Smith, Feb. 25, 1805, John Cotton Smith Letters, Library of Congress; Plumer, *Memorandum of Proceedings,* 300.

24. *Annals of Congress,* 8:2, 429–502; Plumer, *Memorandum of Proceedings,* 300.

25. William Plumer to Daniel Plumer, Feb. 25, 1805, William Plumer Papers, Library of Congress; *Annals of Congress,* 8:2, 502–559.

26. *Annals of Congress,* 8:2, 559–662; Coblentz, "Judicial Career," 158–159.

27. Charles Carroll of Carrollton to Harper, Feb. 28, 1805, Harper-Pennington Papers, MS 431, MHS.

28. Plumer, *Memorandum of Proceedings,* 308; Davenport to Smith, Feb. 25, 1805, John Cotton Smith Letters, Library of Congress.

29. *Annals of Congress,* 8:2, 664–669; Plumer, *Memorandum of Proceedings,* 308–310.

30. Newmyer, *Supreme Court,* 32–33.

31. Lillich, "Chase Impeachment," *Am. Jour. Legal Hist.,* IV (1960), 71–72; Ellis, *Jeffersonian Crisis,* 101–105; Elsmere, "Impeachment Trial," 185–189.

32. Plumer, *Memorandum of Proceedings,* 331; Elsmere, "Impeachment Trial," 196–197; Chase to Joseph Hopkinson, Mar. 10, 1805, copy, Samuel Chase Letters, MS 1234, MHS.

Chapter Eighteen

1. Chase to Joseph Hopkinson, Mar. 10, 1805, Samuel Chase Letters, MS 1234, MHS.

2. Eliza Chase to Ann Chase, Mar. 10, 1805, copy, Chase Home Book, MS 969, MHS; Plumer, *Memorandum of Proceedings,* 316.

3. Chase to Hopkinson, Mar. 10, 1805, and Rufus King to Chase, Mar. 6, 1805, copies, Samuel Chase Letters, MS 1234, MHS; Chase to King, Mar. 13, 1805, King Papers, N.-Y. Hist. Soc.; Bennet Allen to Chase, Mar. 2, 1807, Chase Papers, MS 1235, MHS.

4. *Talbot v. Sieman*, 1 Cranch 10 (1801); *Murray v. Schooner Charming Betsy*, 2 Cranch 64, 78 (1804); *Little et al. v. Barreme et al.*, 2 Cranch 170, 179 (1804); Warren, *Supreme Court*, I, 283–284.

5. *National Intelligencer* (Washington), May, 5, 1805, in Elsmere, "Impeachment Trial," 194–195; Chase to King, Mar. 13, 1805, King Papers, N.-Y. Hist. Soc.; Joseph Story to Samuel P. P. Fay, [1807], in Strawser, "Early Life," 10.

6. 4 Cranch 75n. (1807).

7. *Ex parte Bollman* and *Ex Parte Swartwout*, 4 Cranch 75, 126, 128 (1807), and app., 474–475; Leonard Baker, *John Marshall: A Life in Law* (New York, 1974), 495, 502–514.

8. *Hudson and Others v. Guestner, and LaFont v. Bigelow*, 4 Cranch 293, 298 (1808); *Blaine v. The Ship Charles Carter, and Donald and Burton, and Others*, 4 Cranch 328 (1808); *Croudson and Others v. Leonard*, 4 Cranch 434 (1808); Warren, *Supreme Court*, I, 319–320.

9. Warren, *Supreme Court*, I, 320; Chase Family Bible Records, Gift Collection D603(3), MHR; Henry M. Brackenridge, *Recollections of Persons and Places in the West* (Philadelphia, 1834), 156–157.

10. Letters of Thomas Chase to his family, Chase Home Book, MS 969, MHS.

11. Samuel Chase Checkbook, MS 275, MHS; Chase to Thoroughgood Smith, Mar. 9, 1807, Vertical File, MHS; Chase and Thomas Mulderry to Smith, Mar. 17, 1807, Miscellaneous Papers, General Manuscripts, Princeton University Library, Princeton, N.J.; Papenfuse *et al.*, eds., *Biog. Dict. Md. Leg.*, I, 215. For the bank stock case, see above, chap. ten.

12. Brackenridge, *Recollections*, 154–155.

13. Story, quoted in Strawser, "Early Life," 10, and Warren, *Supreme Court*, I, 465.

14. Chase to Timothy Pickering, Jan. 5, 1811, Pickering Papers, Mass. Hist. Soc.

15. Sanderson, *Biography of Signers*, IV, 105–106; Scharf, *History of Baltimore*, 709; Chase Family Bible Records, Gift Collection D603(3), MHR. Sanderson apparently talked to the family around 1820. Papenfuse *et al.*, eds., *Biog. Dict. Md. Leg.*, I, 216, gives the place of death as Washington, D.C.

16. Luther Martin, opinion of July 24, 1811, Chase Papers, MS 1235, MHS; T. Chase to Samuel Chase, Jr., Aug. 25, 1811, July 20, 27, 1812, and decree in chancery, Sept. term 1816, Chase Home Book, MS 969, MHS; Hannah K. Chase to Bishop James Kemp, Nov. 10, 1817, Vertical File, Md. Diocesan Arch., MHS; Chancery Court Records, Mar. term 1821, liber 117, 353, and Dec. term 1825, liber 128, 193, MHR; Papenfuse *et al.*, eds., *Biog. Dict. Md. Leg.*, I, 216.

17. Adams apparently referred to the Maryland legislature's hearing on the flour scandal and/or the attempt to remove Chase as chief judge of the General Court in 1794 as other "impeachments." Diary of John Quincy Adams, Dec. 18, 1820, Nevins, ed., *Diary of Adams*, 247.

Sources Cited

I. Manuscripts

Duke University Library, Durham, N.C.
 Samuel Chase Papers
 William Henry Hall Papers
 James Iredell Sr. and Jr. Papers
 Ephraim Kirby Papers
Historical Society of Pennsylvania, Philadelphia, Pa.
 Cadwalader Collection
 Tench Coxe Papers
 Dreer Collection
 Etting Papers
 Simon Gratz Collection
Library of Congress, Washington, D.C.
 Galloway-Maxcy-Markoe Papers
 McHenry Papers
 William Plumer Papers
 John Cotton Smith Letters
 Walter Stone Papers
 George Washington Papers
Maryland Diocesan Archives of the Protestant Episcopal
Church (on deposit at Maryland Historical Society)
 Vertical File
Maryland Hall of Records, Annapolis, Md.
 Annapolis City Corporation Records
 Anne Arundel County Court Judgments
 Anne Arundel County Deeds
 Anne Arundel County Land Records
 Baltimore County Land Records
 Baltimore County Wills
 Blue Books
 Chancery Court Records
 Chase Family Bible Records
 Samuel Chase Law Notes

Commissioners Ledger and Journal of Confiscated
  British Property
Executive Papers
Forensic Club Minutes
Frederick County Land Records
General Court, Arguments of Cases
General Court Deeds
Intendant's Letterbooks No. 10 and No. 12
Intendant's Papers, 1782–1785
Oaths of Fidelity
Prerogative Court, Testamentary Papers
Prerogative Court, Testamentary Proceedings
Provincial Court Deeds
Provincial Court Judgments
Red Books
Ridout Papers
Sale Books of Confiscated British Property
Somerset County Accounts
Somerset County Deeds
Somerset County Wills
Thomas Papers
Washington County Land Records
Maryland Historical Society, Baltimore, Md.
  Addison Papers, MS 3
  Ethan Allen, "History of St. Paul's Parish," MS 13
  Carroll Papers, MS 206
  Carter Papers, MS 1228
  Chase Home Book, MS 969
    (the originals of the papers in this collection are held
    by the Maryland Diocesan Archives of the Protestant
    Episcopal Church)
  Chase Notebooks, MS 229
  Chase Papers, MS 1235
  Samuel Chase Checkbook, MS 275
  Samuel Chase Letters, MS 1234
  William Faris Account Book, MS 1104
  Fisher Transcripts, MS 360
  Genealogy Section
  Gilmor Papers, MS 387.1
  Gist Papers, MS 390
  Harper-Pennington Papers, MS 431
  Loyalist Transcripts from New York Public Library
  Purviance Papers, MS 1394
  Rawlings Papers, MS 1399
  Ridgely Papers, MS 692 and 692.1
  Scharf Papers, MS 1999

Sioussat Papers, MS 1497
Vertical File
Otho Holland Williams Papers, MS 908
Massachusetts Historical Society, Boston, Mass.
Robert Treat Paine Papers
Pickering Papers
Ridley Papers
John Sullivan Letters
New Jersey Historical Society, Newark, N.J.
Bamberger Autograph Collection
New-York Historical Society, New York, N.Y.
Samuel Chase Miscellaneous Manuscripts
King Papers
New York Public Library, New York, N.Y.
Bancroft Transcripts
Emmet Collection
Personal Miscellany
Princeton University Library, Princeton, N.J.
General Manuscripts
University of Virginia Library, Charlottesville, Va.
Lee Family Papers
Russell Papers, Virginia Colonial Records Project
Yale University Library, New Haven, Conn.
W. G. Lane Memorial Collection

II. Newspapers

Aurora (Philadelphia)
Baltimore American
The Baltimore Daily Intelligencer
Federal Intelligencer, and Baltimore Daily Gazette
The Maryland Chronicle, or the Universal Advertiser (Frederick-Town)
Maryland Gazette (Annapolis)
The Maryland Gazette, or the Baltimore General Advertiser (originally pub-
lished as *Dunlap's Maryland Gazette*)
Maryland Journal and Baltimore Advertiser
Pennsylvania Journal, and the Weekly Advertiser (Philadelphia)

III. Broadsides and Pamphlets

Cadwalader, John. *To the Public.* . . . N.p., 1782. Maryland Historical Society.
Chase, Samuel. *To the Citizens of Baltimore-Town,* May 4, 1794. Broadside,
Maryland Historical Society.
_____. *To the Publick,* July 18, 1766. Broadside, Yale University Microfilm of
Annapolis *Maryland Gazette,* after issue of June 25, 1767.

_____, and David McMechen. *To the Voters of Baltimore-Town,* Oct. 3, 1788. Broadside, Maryland Historical Society.

The Constitution and Form of Government proposed for the Consideration of the Delegates of Maryland. [Annapolis, 1776].

Cooper, Thomas. *An Account of the Trial of Thomas Cooper....* Philadelphia, 1800.

[Hanson, Alexander Contee]. *Political Schemes and Calculations, Addressed to the Citizens of Maryland.* Annapolis, 1784.

[_____]. *Remarks on the Proposed Plan of a Federal Government....* Annapolis, 1788.

[_____]. *To the Members of The General Assembly of Maryland,* Dec. 17, 1784. Broadside, Maryland Historical Society.

Paca, William, *et al. To the People of Maryland.* N.p., 1788. Thomas Papers, Maryland Hall of Records.

To the Citizens of Annapolis, Jan. 11, 1775. Broadside, Maryland Historical Society.

To the Voters of Ann-Arundel County, Sept. 23, 1786. Broadside, Maryland Historical Society.

IV.   Court Reports

2–4 Dallas (U.S.)
1–2, 4 Cranch (U.S.)
1–3 Harris and McHenry (Md.)

V.   Other Published Primary Sources

Adams, Charles Francis, ed. *Familiar Letters of John Adams and His Wife Abigail Adams, During the American Revolution.* Boston: Houghton-Mifflin, 1875.

_____, ed. *Memoirs of John Quincy Adams, Comprising Portions of His Diary from 1795 to 1848,* I. Philadelphia: J.B. Lippincott, 1874.

_____, ed. *Works of John Adams...,* IX. Boston: Little, Brown, 1854.

Bergh, Albert Ellery, ed. *The Writings of Thomas Jefferson,* X. Washington, D.C.: Thomas Jefferson Memorial Association, 1907.

Boucher, Jonathan. *Reminiscences of an American Loyalist, 1783–1789,* ed. Jonathan Bouchier. Port Washington, N.Y.: Kennikat, 1967.

Boyd, Julian, ed. *The Papers of Thomas Jefferson,* 19 vols. to date. Princeton, N.J.: Princeton University Press, 1950– .

Brackenridge, Henry M. *Recollections of Persons and Places in the West.* Philadelphia: James Kay, 1834.

Browne, William H., *et al.,* eds. *Archives of Maryland,* 72 vols. to date. Baltimore: Maryland Historical Society, 1883– .

Burnett, Edmund C., ed. *Letters of Members of the Continental Congress,* 10 vols. Washington, D.C.: Carnegie Institution, 1921–1936.

Butterfield, Lyman H., ed. *The Adams Papers,* ser. I: *Diaries: Diary and Autobiography of John Adams,* 4 vols. Cambridge, Mass.: Belknap Press, 1961.

Carroll, Charles. *Journal of Charles Carroll of Carrollton During His Visit to Canada in 1776....* Baltimore: Maryland Historical Society, 1845.

Clark, Elmer T., ed. *The Journal and Letters of Francis Asbury,* I. Nashville: Abingdon Press, 1958.

Coyle, Wilbur F., ed. *First Records of Baltimore Town and Jones' Town, 1729-1797.* Baltimore: Mayor and City Council of Baltimore, 1905.

Davis, Richard Beale, ed. *Jeffersonian America: Notes on the United States... by Sir Augustus John Foster, Bart.* San Marino, Cal.: Huntington Library, 1954.

The Debates and Proceedings in the Congress of the United States...1789-1824, 42 vols. Washington, D.C.: Gales and Seaton, 1834-1856 *(Annals of Congress).*

The Decisive Blow Is Struck, introd. by Edward C. Papenfuse and Gregory A. Stiverson. Annapolis: Hall of Records Commission, 1977.

Documentary History of the Constitution of the United States, IV. Washington, D.C.: Department of State, 1905.

Farrand, Max, ed. *The Records of the Federal Convention of 1787,* III. New Haven, Conn.: Yale University Press, 1937.

Field, Thomas Meagher, ed. *Unpublished Letters of Charles Carroll of Carrollton, and of His Father, Charles Carroll of Doughoregan.* New York: U.S. Catholic Historical Society, 1902.

Fitzpatrick, John C., ed. *The Diaries of George Washington,* II. Boston: Houghton-Mifflin, 1925.

_____, ed. *The Writings of George Washington,* 39 vols. Washington, D.C.: Government Printing Office, 1939-1944.

Foner, Philip S., ed. *The Democratic-Republican Societies, 1790-1800.* Westport, Conn.: Greenwood Press, 1976.

Force, Peter, ed. *American Archives,* 9 vols. New York: Johnson Reprint Corporation, 1972 repr. of 1837-1853 ed.

Ford, Paul Leicester, ed. *The Works of Thomas Jefferson,* IX. New York: G. P. Putnam's Sons, 1905.

Ford, Worthington Chauncey, ed. *Journals of the Continental Congress, 1774-1789,* 34 vols. Washington, D.C.: Government Printing Office, 1904-1937.

Gibbs, George. *Memoirs of the Administrations of Washington and John Adams...,* II. New York: William Van Norden, 1846.

Hoyt, William D., ed. "The Calvert-Stier Correspondence: Letters from America to the Low Countries, 1797-1828," *Maryland Historical Magazine,* XXXVIII (1943), 123-140.

Laws of Maryland.... Annapolis: Frederick Green, published after each session.

Lincoln, Charles Henry, ed. *Naval Records of the American Revolution, 1775-1788.* Washington, D.C.: Government Printing Office, 1906.

Nevins, Allan, ed. *The Diary of John Quincy Adams, 1794-1845.* New York: Longmans, Green & Co., 1928.

{ 289 }

Paul, J. G. D., ed. "A Lost Copy-Book of Charles Carroll of Carrollton," *Maryland Historical Magazine*, XXXII (1937), 193–224.

Plumer, William. *Memorandum of Proceedings in the United States Senate, 1803-1807*, ed. Everett Somerville Brown. New York: Macmillan, 1923.

Proceedings of the Conventions of the Province of Maryland. . . . Baltimore: J. Lucas and E. K. Deaver, 1836.

Quynn, Dorothy Mackay, and William Rogers Quynn. "Letters of a Maryland Medical Student in Philadelphia and Edinburgh," *Maryland Historical Magazine*, XXXI (1936), 181–215.

Report of the Trial of the Hon. Samuel Chase. . . Taken in Short hand by Charles Evans. Baltimore: Samuel Butler and George Keatinge, 1805.

Rutland, Robert A., ed. *The Papers of George Mason*, II. Chapel Hill, N.C.: University of North Carolina Press, 1970.

"Samuel Chase and the Grand Jury of Baltimore County," *Maryland Historical Magazine*, VI (1911), 131–137.

Smith, Albert Henry, ed. *The Writings of Benjamin Franklin*, 10 vols. New York: Macmillan, 1906.

Smith, Paul H., ed. *Letters of Delegates to Congress, 1774-1789*, 5 vols. to date. Washington, D.C.: Library of Congress, 1976– .

Steiner, Bernard C. "New Light on Maryland History from the British Archives," *Maryland Historical Magazine*, IV (1909), 251–262.

Syrett, Harold, ed. *The Papers of Alexander Hamilton*, I. New York: Columbia University Press, 1961.

Votes and Proceedings of the House of Delegates of the State of Maryland. Annapolis: Frederick Green, published after each session.

Votes and Proceedings of the Senate of the State of Maryland. Annapolis: Frederick Green, published after each session.

Wharton, Francis. *State Trials of the United States during the Administrations of Washington and Adams.* . . . New York: Burt Franklin, 1970 repr. of 1849 ed.

Wylie, J. C., ed. "Letters of Some Members of the Old Congress," *Pennsylvania Magazine of History and Biography*, XXIX (1905), 191–206.

VI.   *Theses and Dissertations*

Coblentz, Robin D. "The Judicial Career of Samuel Chase, 1796–1811." M.A. thesis, Columbia University, 1966.

Elsmere, Mary Jane Shaffer. "The Impeachment Trial of Justice Samuel Chase." Ph.D. diss., Indiana University, 1962.

Haw, James A. "Politics in Revolutionary Maryland, 1753–1788." Ph.D. diss., University of Virginia, 1972.

Maganzin, Louis. "Economic Depression in Maryland and Virginia, 1783–1787." Ph.D. diss., Georgetown University, 1967.

Ranneberger, Michael Edward. "Samuel Chase: The Evolution of a Federalist." M.A. thesis, University of Virginia, 1973.

Strawser, Neil. "The Early Life of Samuel Chase." M.A. thesis, George Washington University, 1958.

Verstandig, Lee Lovely. "The Emergence of the Two-Party System in Maryland, 1787-1796." Ph.D. diss., Brown University, 1970.

VII.   Published Secondary Sources

Abernethy, Thomas Perkins. *Western Lands and the American Revolution.* New York: Russell & Russell, 1959.

Baker, Leonard. *John Marshall: A Life in Law.* New York: Macmillan, 1974.

Barker, Charles Albro. *The Background of the Revolution in Maryland.* N.p.: Archon Books, 1967 repr. of 1940 ed.

Beirne, Francis F. *St. Paul's Parish, Baltimore.* Baltimore: Horn-Shafer, 1967.

Beirne, Rosamond Randall. "The Reverend Thomas Chase: Pugnacious Parson," *Maryland Historical Magazine,* LIX (1964), 1-14.

Berger, Raoul. *Impeachment: The Constitutional Problems.* Cambridge, Mass.: Harvard University Press, 1973.

Beveridge, Albert J. *The Life of John Marshall,* III. Boston: Houghton Mifflin, 1919.

Bond, Carroll T. *The Court of Appeals of Maryland: A History.* Baltimore: Barton-Gillet, 1928.

Buel, Richard, Jr. *Securing the Revolution: Ideology in American Politics, 1789-1815.* Ithaca, N.Y.: Cornell University Press, 1972.

Burnett, Edmund Cody. *The Continental Congress.* New York: Norton, 1964 repr. of 1941 ed.

Clarkson, Paul S., and R. Samuel Jett. *Luther Martin of Maryland.* Baltimore: Johns Hopkins University Press, 1970.

Corwin, Edward S. *John Marshall and the Constitution.* New Haven, Conn.: Yale University Press, 1919.

Crowl, Philip A. *Maryland During and After the Revolution.* Baltimore: Johns Hopkins University Press, 1943.

Curtis, George Ticknor. *Life of Daniel Webster,* I. New York: D. Appleton & Co., 1889.

Dilliard, Irving. "Samuel Chase," in Leon Friedman and Fred L. Israel, eds., *The Justices of the United States Supreme Court, 1789-1969: Their Lives and Major Opinions,* I, 185-197. New York: Chelsea House, 1969.

Dumond, Dwight Lowell. *Antislavery: The Crusade for Freedom in America.* Ann Arbor, Mich.: University of Michigan Press, 1961.

Edgar, Lady [Matilda Ridout]. *A Colonial Governor in Maryland: Horatio Sharpe and His Times, 1753-1773.* New York: Longmans, Green & Co., 1912.

Ellis, Richard E. *The Jeffersonian Crisis: Courts and Politics in the Young Republic.* New York: Oxford University Press, 1971.

Fleming, Thomas. *1776: Year of Illusions.* New York: Norton, 1975.

Flexner, James Thomas. *George Washington and the New Nation.* Boston: Little, Brown, 1969.

French, Allen. *The First Year of the American Revolution.* New York: Octagon, 1968 repr. of 1934 ed.

Goebel, Julius, Jr. *Antecedents and Beginnings to 1801,* in Paul A. Freund, ed., *The Oliver Wendell Holmes Devise History of the Supreme Court of the United States,* I of 11 vols. projected. New York: Macmillan, 1971.

Haines, Charles Grove. *The Role of the Supreme Court in American Government and Politics, 1789–1835.* New York: Russell & Russell, 1960 repr. of 1944 ed.

Haw, James. "Maryland Politics on the Eve of Revolution: The Provincial Controversy, 1770–1773," *Maryland Historical Magazine,* LXV (1970), 103–129.

_____. "The Patronage Follies: Bennet Allen, John Morton Jordan, and the Fall of Horatio Sharpe," *Maryland Historical Magazine,* LXXI (1976), 134–150.

Henderson, H. James. *Party Politics in the Continental Congress.* New York: McGraw-Hill, 1974.

Hoffer, Peter C., and N. E. H. Hull. "Power and Precedent in the Creation of an American Impeachment Tradition: The Eighteenth-Century Colonial Record." *William and Mary Quarterly,* 3d ser., XXXVI (1979), 51–77.

Hoffman, Ronald. *A Spirit of Dissension: Economics, Politics, and the Revolution in Maryland.* Baltimore: Johns Hopkins University Press, 1973.

Jensen, Merrill. *The Articles of Confederation.* Madison: University of Wisconsin Press, 1940.

Johnson, Allen, and Dumas Malone, eds. *Dictionary of American Biography,* 20 vols. New York: Charles Scribner's Sons, 1928–1936.

Leake, Isaac Q. *Memoir of the Life and Times of General John Lamb.* Albany: Joel Munsell, 1850.

Lillich, Richard B. "The Chase Impeachment," *American Journal of Legal History,* IV (1960), 49–72.

Link, Eugene Perry. *Democratic-Republican Societies, 1790–1800.* New York: Columbia University Press, 1942.

Malone, Dumas. *Jefferson the President: First Term, 1801–1805.* Boston: Little, Brown, 1970.

_____. *The Public Life of Thomas Cooper, 1783–1839.* New Haven, Conn.: Yale University Press, 1926.

Miller, John C. *Crisis in Freedom: The Alien and Sedition Acts.* Boston: Little, Brown, 1952.

Miner, Ward L. *William Goddard, Newspaperman.* Durham, N.C.: University of North Carolina Press, 1962.

Murray, Elizabeth H. *One Hundred Years Ago: The Life and Times of the Rev. Walter Dulany Addison.* Philadelphia: G. W. Jacobs, 1895.

Newmyer, R. Kent. *The Supreme Court under Marshall and Taney.* New York: Crowell, 1968.

Papenfuse, Edward C. *In Pursuit of Profit: The Annapolis Merchants in the Era of the American Revolution, 1763–1805.* Baltimore: Johns Hopkins University Press, 1975.

_____, Alan F. Day, David W. Jordan, and Gregory A. Stiverson, eds. *A Biographical Dictionary of the Maryland Legislature, 1635-1789*, I. Baltimore: Johns Hopkins University Press, 1979.

Peterson, Merrill D. *Thomas Jefferson and the New Nation*. New York: Oxford University Press, 1970.

Pinkney, William. *The Life of William Pinkney*. New York: D. Appleton & Co., 1853.

Price, Jacob M. "The Maryland Bank Stock Case: British-American Financial and Political Relations before and after the American Revolution," in Aubrey C. Land, Lois Green Carr, and Edward C. Papenfuse, eds., *Law, Society, and Politics in Early Maryland*, 3-40. Baltimore: Johns Hopkins University Press, 1977.

Radoff, Morris L. *Calendar of Maryland State Papers, No. 2: The Bank Stock Papers*. Annapolis: Hall of Records Commission, 1947.

Renzulli, L. Marx, Jr. *Maryland: The Federalist Years*. Rutherford, N.J.: Fairleigh Dickinson University Press, 1972.

Rightmyer, Nelson Waite. *Maryland's Established Church*. Baltimore: Church Historical Society for the Diocese of Maryland, 1956.

Risjord, Norman K. *Chesapeake Politics, 1781-1800*. New York: Columbia University Press, 1978.

Roddy, Edward G. "Maryland and the Presidential Election of 1800," *Maryland Historical Magazine*, LVI (1961), 244-268.

Rossie, Jonathan Gregory. *The Politics of Command in the American Revolution*. Syracuse, N.Y.: Syracuse University Press, 1975.

Sanderson, John. *Biography of the Signers to the Declaration of Independence*, IV. Philadelphia: W. Brown and C. Peters, 1828.

Scharf, John Thomas. *History of Baltimore City and County*.... Philadelphia: L. H. Everts, 1881.

_____. *History of Maryland*. Hatboro, Pa.: Tradition Press, 1967 repr. of 1879 ed.

Sellers, Charles Coleman. *Portraits and Miniatures by Charles Willson Peale*. Philadelphia: American Philosophical Society, 1952.

Sellers, Horace Wells. "Charles Willson Peale, Artist-Soldier," *Pennsylvania Magazine of History and Biography*, XXXVIII (1914), 257-286.

Semmes, John E. *John H. B. Latrobe and His Times, 1803-1891*. Baltimore: Norman, Remington Co., 1917.

Smith, Horace Wemyss. *Life and Correspondence of the Rev. William Smith, D.D.* New York: Arno Press, 1972 repr. of 1880 ed.

Smith, James Morton. *Freedom's Fetters: The Alien and Sedition Laws and American Civil Liberties*. Ithaca, N.Y.: Cornell University Press, 1956.

Steiner, Bernard C. *The Life and Correspondence of James McHenry*. Cleveland: Burrows Brothers, 1907.

Stiverson, Gregory A., and Phebe R. Jacobsen. *William Paca: A Biography*. Baltimore: Maryland Historical Society, 1976.

Strawser, Neil. "Samuel Chase and the Annapolis Paper War," *Maryland Historical Magazine*, LVII (1962), 177-194.

Sullivan, William. *Familiar Letters on Public Characters*. Boston: Russell, Odiorne & Metcalf, 1834.

———. *The Public Men of the Revolution*. . . . Philadelphia: Carey & Hart, 1847.

Terwilliger, W. Bird. "William Goddard's Victory for the Freedom of the Press," *Maryland Historical Magazine*, XXXVI (1941), 139–149.

Torrence, Clayton. *Old Somerset on the Eastern Shore of Maryland*. Richmond, Va.: Whittet & Shepperson, 1935.

Venn, John, and J. A. Venn, comps. *Alumni Cantabrigienses*, pt. I, vol. I. Cambridge, England: Cambridge University Press, 1922.

Vivian, Jean H. "The Poll Tax Controversy in Maryland, 1770–76: A Case of Taxation *with* Representation," *Maryland Historical Magazine*, LXXI (1976), 151–176.

Warren, Charles. *A History of the American Bar*. Boston: Little, Brown, 1911.

———. *The Supreme Court in United States History*, I. Boston: Little, Brown, 1923.

Wood, Gordon S. *The Creation of the American Republic, 1776–1787*. Chapel Hill, N.C.: University of North Carolina Press, 1969.

Wroth, Lawrence C. *A History of Printing in Colonial Maryland*. Baltimore: Typothetae of Baltimore, 1922.

Zimmer, Anne Y. "The 'Paper War' in Maryland, 1772–73: The Paca-Chase Political Philosophy Tested," *Maryland Historical Magazine*, LXXI (1976), 177–193.

Index

New Hampshire—*continued*
217, 221
New Jersey, 67, 80, 82, 83, 179, 195,
224, 246
New Orleans, 244
New York, 18, 20, 49, 51, 52, 58, 60,
62, 65, 67, 83, 89, 90, 104, 114,
119, 151, 178, 221
New York Journal, 107
Newark, New Jersey, 195
Newcastle, Delaware, 206, 218, 223,
228, 229, 232, 235, 238
Newport, 119
Nicholas, Philip Norborne, 203–205,
230
Nicholson, Joseph H., 216, 217, 220,
223, 238
North America, 53
North Carolina, 90, 179, 182
Northwest Territory, 83, 159
Nottingham Iron Works, 117, 123,
127, 158

O'Donnell, John, 164
Office of Discount and Deposit, 225
Ogle, Samuel, Governor, 3
Ohio River, 80, 83
Ohio Valley, 130
"Old Bacon Face," nickname for
Samuel Chase, 30
Paca, William, 10, 11, 20, 24, 28,
34–41, 43, 44, 48, 49, 71, 73–75,
80, 93, 99, 122, 132, 135, 140,
141, 145, 148, 150, 151, 153,
154, 159, 160, 167
Pacific Ocean, 80
Paine, Thomas, 55, 170
Parliament, 17, 42, 44–46, 49, 50,
55, 56, 85, 87, 95
Patapsco River, 196
Paterson, William, 179, 200, 212, 220
Patuxent, 21
Payne, William, 5
Peale, Charles Willson, 16, 30
Peggy Stewart, 46–49
Pennsylvania, 3, 44, 55, 67, 73,

79–81, 106, 115, 120, 131, 172,
179, 184, 199, 216, 217, 237
Peru, 92
Peters, Richard, 184, 185, 197,
199–201
Philadelphia, 43, 51, 60, 61, 65, 67,
68, 73, 90–92, 104, 108, 121,
145, 146, 149, 159, 176–178,
197, 202, 209, 215, 219
Philadelphia *Aurora,* 215
Pickering, John, 217, 218, 228
Pickering, Timothy, 234, 248
Pinkney, Charles Cotesworth, 207,
208
Pinkney, Ninian, 175
Pinkney, William, 120, 128, 150,
166, 175
Pitt, William, 125
Pittsburgh, 51
Plan of Union, 44–46
Plater, George, 71
Plumer, William, 176, 221, 229, 230,
232, 234, 236, 238, 240, 242
Pocomoke River, 131
Political Essays, 197
Potomac Company, 131
"Potomac" party, 166
Potomac River, 51, 130, 131, 151, 166
Potomac Valley, 131
Prince George's County, 13
Princeton, 246
The Prospect before Us, 202–204, 232
Protestants, 6, 61
Provincial Court of Maryland, 12, 19,
23, 34, 40
The Prowess of the Whig Club, 86
Punicks, 7
Purviance, Samuel, 52

Quakers, 74, 77, 161
Quebec, 56, 58, 59, 61, 63, 64
Queen Anne, 14, 15
Queen Elizabeth I, 92
Quynn, Allen, 15, 104
Quynn, William, 122

Stevenson, John, Dr., 6
Stewart, Anthony, 39
Stewart, David, 52
Stodder, David, Captain, 171, 172
Stoddert, Benjamin, 159, 207
Stone, Thomas, 50, 131, 135
Story, Joseph, 243, 247
Stuart Preterder
  see "Bonnie Prince Charlie"
Stuart v. Laird, 213
Suffolk Resolves, 44
Sugar Act of 1764, 17
Sullivan, John, General, 84, 88–91
Supreme Court of the United States,
  2, 166, 175–186, 189, 191, 193,
  208–214, 217, 225, 243–246
Supreme Court
  Eastern circuit, 178, 182, 183
  Maryland-Delaware circuit, 213
  Middle circuit, 178, 197
  Southern circuit, 178, 182
Sunbury and Northumberland
  Gazette, 197
Susquehanna River, 4
Swartwout, Samuel, 244, 245

Talbot County, 29, 33, 113
Tasker, Benjamin, 13
Taylor, John, 204, 205, 222, 230
Tea Act, 42
Tennessee, 223, 228
Thomas, John, General, 61–63
Tilghman, Edward, 19
Tilghman, Henry, 230
Tilghman, Matthew, 40, 43, 49, 71,
  93, 97, 109, 110
Tilghman, William, 225
Tobacco inspection act, 31
Tories, 47–49, 61, 69, 86, 92, 93,
  96, 98, 99, 109, 110, 113, 114,
  116, 124, 156
Townsend, Robert, 172
Townshend Acts, 27, 30
Tracy, Uriah, 239
Treaty of Paris of 1783, 179, 180
Triplett, James, 231
Tucker, St. George, 206

United States, 78, 80–82, 87, 88, 121,
  128, 152, 155, 161, 178, 181,
  184, 186, 187, 189, 190,
  192–194, 197, 199, 203, 205,
  216, 220, 221, 227, 231, 236,
  239, 244, 247
United States v. Worrall, 184, 190,
  194
University of Maryland, 132

Vincennes, 80
Virginia, 44, 51, 52, 56, 66, 80, 81,
  83, 106, 130, 131, 151, 154, 176,
  179–182, 189, 202, 203, 209,
  220, 222, 223, 232, 235, 237,
  245
Virginia and Kentucky Resolutions,
  195

Wabash Land Company, 80, 81
Wadsworth, Jeremiah, 106, 107
Walker plantation, 3
Walker, Matilda
  see Chase, Matilda Walker
Walker, Thomas, Captain, 3
Walker, Thomas, Jr., 3
War of 1812, 248
Ward, Samuel, 54
Ware v. Hylton, 179, 180
Warwick, England, 12
Washington, Bushrod, 220
Washington College, 132
Washington County, 150
Washington, D.C., 209, 212, 225,
  242, 244
Washington, George, 2, 51, 64, 73,
  88–91, 130, 131, 165–167, 169,
  174–176, 178, 206, 248
Weiser, Conrad, 4
West Florida, 82
West Indies, 3, 104, 169, 247
  French, 169, 246
Western Shore, 168
Wheeler, Luke, 105, 134, 158, 221
Whetcroft, William, 104
Whig Club, 76, 87
Whigs, 75, 87, 102